Paradox® 4
QuickStart

Jeffry Byrne

Paradox 4 QuickStart.
Copyright © 1992 by Que® Corporation.

All rights reserved. Printed in the United States of America. No part of this book may be used or reproduced in any form or by any means, or stored in a database or retrieval system, without prior written permission of the publisher except in the case of brief quotations embodied in critical articles and reviews. Making copies of any part of this book for any purpose other than your own personal use is a violation of United States copyright laws. For information, address Que Corporation, 11711 N. College Ave., Carmel, IN 46032.

Library of Congress Catalog No.: 92-60570

ISBN: 0-88022-982-9

This book is sold *as is*, without warranty of any kind, either express or implied, respecting the contents of this book, including but not limited to implied warranties for the book's quality, performance, merchantability, or fitness for any particular purpose. Neither Que Corporation nor its dealers or distributors shall be liable to the purchaser or any other person or entity with respect to any liability, loss, or damage caused or alleged to have been caused directly or indirectly by this book.

94 93 92   6 5 4 3 2 1

Interpretation of the printing code: the rightmost double-digit number is the year of the book's printing; the rightmost single-digit number, the number of the book's printing. For example, a printing code of 92-1 shows that the first printing of the book occurred in 1992.

Paradox 4 QuickStart is based on Version 4.0 of Paradox.

Screen reproductions in this book were created using Collage Plus from Inner Media, Inc., Hollis, NH.

Publisher: Lloyd J. Short

Associate Publisher: Rick Ranucci

Product Development Manager: Thomas H. Bennett

Book Designer: Scott Cook

Production Team: Claudia Bell, Mark Enochs, Bob LaRoche, Juli Pavey, John Sleeva, Angie Trzepacz, Johnna VanHoose, Lisa Wilson

Acquisitions Editor
Tim Ryan

Product Director
Kathie-Jo Arnoff

Production Editor
Pamela Wampler

Editors
Barbara K. Koenig
J. Christopher Nelson
Heather Northrup

*Composed in ITC Garamond and
MCPdigital by Que Corporation.*

About the Author

Jeffry Byrne lives in Portland, Oregon, with his wife, Marisa. He is the author of several instructional books on popular spreadsheets and database applications. He has been involved with computers and computer applications since 1979 in both the accounting and personnel fields.

Acknowledgments

Thanks to the following individuals for their help and expertise in bringing this book together:

Rick Ranucci for help and assistance in bringing this project to fruition.

Nan Borreson, Borland's Publishing Relations Manager, for providing copies of Paradox and needed technical assistance.

Kathie-Jo Arnoff, Pamela Wampler, and the other members of Que's outstanding editing staff.

Finally, to my wife Marisa for her help, encouragement and fortitude during this project.

Trademark Acknowledgments

Que Corporation has made every effort to supply trademark information about company names, products, and services mentioned in this book. Trademarks indicated below were derived from various sources. Que Corporation cannot attest to the accuracy of this information.

3Com is a registered trademark of 3Com Corporation.

AT&T is a registered trademark of American Telephone & Telegraph Company.

IBM is a registered trademark of International Business Machines.

Microsoft and MS-DOS are registered trademarks and Windows is a trademark of Microsoft Corporation.

Novell and NetWare are registered trademarks of Novell, Inc.

Paradox is a registered trademark of Borland International, Inc.

PostScript is a registered trademark of Adobe Systems, Inc.

Contents at a Glance

	Introduction	1
1	An Overview of Paradox 4	5
2	Getting Started	19
3	Creating a Table	59
4	Adding, Editing, and Viewing Data with a Table	83
5	Using the Standard Form	133
6	Sorting a Table	153
7	Querying the Database	167
8	Constructing a Report	199
9	Restructuring a Table	235
10	Creating Free-Form and Multi-Table Forms	273
11	Using Advanced Queries	305
12	Creating Tabular, Free-Form, and Multi-Table Reports	335
13	Representing Data with Graphs	375
14	Using Paradox Scripts	409
A	Installing Paradox 4.0	425
B	Shortcut Keys	429
	Index	439

Contents

Introduction 1

1 An Overview of Paradox 4 5

What Is a Database? 6
    The Flat-File Database 6
    The Relational Database 7
Understanding Paradox Objects 8
    The Paradox Family 9
        Tables 9
        Forms 10
        Reports 11
        Other Paradox Family Objects 11
        Scripts 12
    Other Paradox Objects 12
        Graphs 12
        Scripts 12
A Tour of Program Features 13
What Is New in Paradox 4.0? 14
    Mouse Support 15
    Other New Features 15
What Do You Need To Run Paradox 4.0? 16
Summary 17

2 Getting Started 19

Starting Paradox 20
Understanding the Opening Display 23
    The Menu Bar 23
        The System Menu (≡) 24
        Other Menu Items 24
    The Status Bar 24
Understanding the Paradox Desktop 25
    The Menu and Desktop Window Structure 25
    Paradox Menus 25
    The Mode Indicator 27
    The Message Window 29

	The Mouse 30
	Paradox Object Windows 31
	Resizing Windows 32
	Moving Windows 34
	Maximizing and Restoring Windows 34
	Using the Scroll Bars 36
	Using the Next and Window Commands 38
	Closing Windows 40
Using Paradox 40
	Creating Small vs. Large Tables 41
	Using View vs. Modify 41
	Canceling a Function 42
	Accessing the Paradox Help Screens 42
Designing the Customer Database 45
	Creating the Database Structure 46
	Adding Customer Information 48
	Asking Questions about Your Data 52
	Sorting the Information 54
	Printing a Report 56
Quitting Paradox 57
Summary 57

3 Creating a Table 59

| Creating a New Database .... 60 |
| | Planning the Table Structure .... 61 |
| | Naming the Table .... 62 |
| Designing the Table .... 63 |
	Entering Field Names 64
	Specifying Field Type and Size 65
	Designating Key Fields 70
	Borrowing an Existing Table Structure 71
	Editing the Field Types 73
	Editing Field Names 74
	Inserting Fields 75
	Deleting Fields 77
	Using the FileFormat Command 77
Saving a New Table Structure 78
Viewing a Table 78
Deleting a Table 79
Summary 81

4 Adding, Editing, and Viewing Data with a Table 83

Working With Tables in Edit Mode 84
    Using Edit Mode 85
    Adding Records 86
    Using Field View 90
    Using Undo 91
    Deleting a Record 94
    Using the Ditto Function 94
    Searching for Records 95
    Using Zoom with Wild Cards 97
    Inserting New Records 98
    Using Keys and Key Violations in Edit 99
    Saving or Canceling Changes 99
Working With Tables in DataEntry Mode 99
    Using DataEntry Mode 100
    Adding Records 100
    Using Undo 104
    Using the Ditto Function 105
    Searching for Records 106
    Inserting New Records 111
    Deleting a Record 112
    Saving or Canceling Changes 113
    Working With Keys and Key Violations in DataEntry 113
Using CoEdit Mode 115
    Adding and Editing Records 116
    Using Undo 118
    Deleting a Record 120
    Inserting New Records 120
    Using the Ditto Function 120
    Searching for Records 120
    Treating Keys and Key Violations in DataEntry 122
    Saving Changes 123
Using Paradox Table Images 123
    Changing the Table's Size 124
    Changing the Column Width 124
    Choosing a Display Format 126
    Moving Columns 127
        Using the Move Command 128
        Using the Rotate Command 128
    Saving the New Image Settings 129
Summary 130

5 Using the Standard Form 133
Parent Versus Child Windows 134
Displaying the Standard Form 134
The Form Window 135
Form Menus 137
Using the Standard Form 139
Moving among Fields 139
Moving among Records 140
Working with the Standard Form 141
Adding Records 141
Changing Field Data 143
Editing a Field 143
Using Field View 144
Searching for a Record 144
Closing a Form 150
Summary 151

6 Sorting a Table 153
Using the Standard Sort Order 154
Using the Sorted Table Options 155
Selecting the Sort To Table 155
Using the Sort Menu 156
Sorting By One Field 157
Sorting By Many Fields 159
Defining the Sort Order 162
Ascending Order 163
Descending Order 163
Summary 164

7 Querying the Database 167
Asking the Question 168
Forming a Query 168
Using Query By Example 169
Querying a Table 169
Selecting a Table 170
Choosing Fields 171
Displaying Duplicates 176
Matching Exact Values 177
Finding Similar Values 177

    Working with Special Operators 180
        Using AS 181
        Using LIKE 182
        Using NOT 183
        Using BLANK 184
        Using Multiple Conditions 186
    Using Comparison Operators 191
    Using the Answer Table 193
        Sorting the Answer Table 193
        Editing the Answer Table 194
        Saving the Answer Table 194
    Saving the Query Form 195
    Summary 196

8 Constructing a Report 199

    Creating an Instant Report 200
    Creating Other Types of Paradox Reports 201
    Understanding the Report Designer
        and Previewer 202
        The Report Designer 202
        The Report Previewer 203
        An Overview of the Report Menu Options 203
    Using the Report Designer 204
        Working with the Tabular Report 205
        Planning the Report Layout 205
        Understanding Report Bands 205
        Designing a Report Specification 207
            Removing Page Widths 211
            Removing Columns 213
            Adding Columns 214
            Using Literals 215
        Adding Fields 216
        Reformatting and Editing Fields 218
        Using Groups 220
        Adjusting the Table Bands 221
        Previewing the Report 223
        Changing Settings 225
        Saving the Report Specification 226

    Specifying the Output 226
        Printing a Report 227
        Previewing a Report 228
        Saving a Report as a Text File 230
    Summary 231

9   Restructuring a Table 235

    Rules Regarding Restructuring 236
    Changing a Table's Structure 238
        Adding and Moving Fields 239
        Erasing Fields 242
        Changing Existing Fields 243
        Modifying Key and Non-Key Fields 245
    Using the Key Violations Table 249
    Using the Problems Table 254
    Using Validity Checks 255
        Using LowValue and HighValue Checks 256
        Using Default Values 259
        Using Picture Fields 260
        Entering Required Fields 263
        Using TableLookup Fields 264
        Creating Auto Fields 268
    Summary 271

10   Creating Free-Form and Multi-Table Forms 273

    An Overview of the Paradox Form 274
        The Paradox Form 274
        The Paradox Form Designer 275
    Designing a Free-Form Form 275
    Working with the Form Design Features 276
        Opening the Form Designer Window 277
        Using Field Labels and Prompts 279
        Placing Fields 281
        Using Calculated Fields 285
        Resizing a Field 287
    Designing a Multi-Record Form 288

Designing a Multi-Table Form 290
    Understanding Table Relationships 291
        Referential Integrity 291
        Understanding Multi-Table Forms 292
    Creating the Master Form 292
    Using Linked Tables 294
    Using Unlinked Tables 295
Strengthening Your Form Design 296
    Drawing Lines or Boxes 296
    Working with Multiple Line Fields 298
    Using Color 299
    Using On-Screen Prompts 300
    Editing Screen Characteristics 300
Editing an Existing Form 301
Summary 302

11 Using Advanced Queries 305

Querying Multiple Tables 306
    Choosing Tables for the Multi-Table Query Statement 306
    Selecting Fields for the Multi-Table Query 307
    Creating Table Links with Examples 309
    Refining the Query Statement 311
Using Calculations 313
    CALC with Arithmetic Values 313
    CALC with Alphanumeric Values 316
Executing Table Operations 318
    INSERT Queries 318
    DELETE Queries 322
    CHANGETO Queries 324
    FIND Queries 325
Using Groups 325
    Creating Query Groups 326
    Using CALC on Groups 327
Creating Inclusive Link Queries 329
    Single Inclusive Links 329
    Multiple Inclusive Links 331
Summary 332

xv

12 Creating Tabular, Free-Form, and Multi-Table Reports 335

An Overview of the Paradox Report 336
Using the Tabular Report 336
Creating Reports with Linked Tables 337
    Choosing the Master Table 337
    Choosing the Lookup Tables 337
    Establishing the Link 339
    Unlinking Tables 341
    Relinking Tables 342
    Customizing the Report Specification 342
Using Groups 345
    Using the Group Bands 346
        Adjusting the Group Band 347
        Placing Fields in the Group Band 347
    Working with Calculated Fields 350
    Using the Summary Operations 352
        Using Group Summary Calculations 352
        Using Overall Summary Calculations 355
    Augmenting the Report 357
        Using the Report Previewer 357
        Adjusting the Report Specification 358
Printing the Report 362
    Selecting a Printer 362
    Using Setup Strings 364
    Temporary Printer Overrides 366
Creating Free-Form Reports 366
    Designing a Free-Form Report 366
    Grouping Records 368
    Designing a Mailing Label 370
Summary 372

13 Representing Data with Graphs 375

An Overview of Paradox Graphs 376
    Elements of a Graph 376
    Paradox Graph Types 378
Designing Graphs 383
    Working with Transformations 383
    Using the Default Graph 384
    Creating a Crosstab 386

Modifying the Graph 388
   Selecting the Graph Type 388
   Using the Overall Settings 392
      Adding Titles 392
      Altering the Graph Colors 394
      Customizing the Graph Axes 395
      Changing Grids and Frames 396
   Altering the Series Settings 398
   Selecting Pie Graph Settings 400
   Choosing the Output and Saving 402
   Setting the Page Layout and Printing 403
   Saving the Graph as a File 405
   Saving the Graph Specification 405
   Retrieving the Graph Specification 406
Summary 406

14 Using Paradox Scripts 409

An Overview of the Paradox Script 409
Creating an Instant Script 411
Creating a New Script 412
   Recording the Script 413
   Ending the Recording of the New Script 414
Playing a Script 414
   Using Play for a Script 415
   Using ShowPlay for a Script 415
   Using RepeatPlay for a Script 416
Editing a Script 417
Working with Special Script Codes 419
Recording a Query Script 422
Using an Automatic Script 423
Summary 424

A Installing Paradox 4.0 425

Starting the Installation 425
Completing the Signature Screen 426
Editing the Configuration File 427
Completing the Installation Screen 427
Completing the Installation 427

B Shortcut Keys	**429**
The Function Keys and Other Main Keyboard Keys	429
Menu Keys	431
Table View Keys	432
Form View Keys	432
Field View Keys	433
Edit and CoEdit Mode Keys	434
Form Designer Keys	434
Report Designer Keys	435
Report Previewer Keys	436
Other Special Key Combinations	437
Index	**439**

Introduction

If you are new to Paradox, or to database programs in general, this book will give you a flying start. You can use this book as a self-teaching guide. *Paradox 4 QuickStart* will help you with all the basics of using Paradox 4.0. If you need information about a specific subject and you are familiar with Paradox, jump ahead.

Paradox 4 QuickStart uses an easy-to-grasp tutorial style that leads you through the essential parts of the program. You will quickly grasp the concepts of tables, forms, reports, and graphs. The text supplies the fundamental information and is completely illustrated throughout the book.

While Paradox 4.0 is a powerful, full-featured database program, *Paradox 4 QuickStart* will get you through the learning curve quickly by enabling you to master the basic concepts. Even if you already have used an earlier version of Paradox or another database program, you will find that *Paradox 4 QuickStart* provides you with a solid background in the new Paradox 4.0.

Introduction

What Does This Book Contain?

The chapters in *Paradox 4 QuickStart* are arranged so that you learn the basic tasks and proceed to the more complex. The book contains the following chapters:

Chapter 1, "An Overview of Paradox 4," introduces the subject of database programs and the Paradox Family of Objects. You quickly tour the program features, find out what you need to run the program, and learn what is new to Paradox.

Chapter 2, "Getting Started," begins with a quick lesson on Paradox's features and capabilities. The chapter discusses the various features on the Paradox desktop, and then shows you how to use key combinations and Paradox's on-line Help.

Chapter 3, "Creating a Table," shows you how to create a table structure, and shows you how to use field types.

Chapter 4, "Adding, Editing, and Viewing Data with a Table," explains how to add records to a table, and then how to edit the data. You also learn the differences between Paradox's various editing modes, and the uses for keyed tables.

Chapter 5, "Using the Standard Form," shows you how to use the Paradox Standard Form for adding, editing, and viewing records.

Chapter 6, "Sorting a Table," teaches you how to sort your data by one or several fields.

Chapter 7, "Querying the Database," focuses on extracting information from your database. You learn how to construct a query statement and then how to use the resulting Answer table.

Chapter 8, "Constructing a Report," describes how to create a report specification to print a report from a table.

Chapter 9, "Restructuring a Table," shows you why you may need to restructure your tables and how to use key fields to link several tables together.

Chapter 10, "Creating Free-Form and Multi-Table Forms," teaches you how to use a form to link several tables together through the use of a single form, and then how to create a free-form form.

Chapter 11, "Using Advanced Queries," shows you how to link several tables to create complex query statements, and how to calculate fields in queries.

Chapter 12, "Creating Tabular, Free-Form, and Multi-Table Reports," covers the more advanced aspects of reports. You learn how to link several tables to a single report, group records, and use calculated fields and summaries.

Chapter 13, "Representing Data with Graphs," teaches you how to present your data using several graph styles.

Chapter 14, "Using Paradox Scripts," explains Paradox scripts and how you can use them to create shortcuts and simplify many tasks.

This book concludes with two appendixes. The first shows you how to install Paradox 4.0. The second is a group of tables listing the various Paradox shortcut keys.

Who Should Use This Book?

Paradox 4 QuickStart is designed as an introductory book for new Paradox 4.0 users. Even if you are just beginning to learn the program, or are upgrading from an earlier version of Paradox or another database program, *Paradox 4 QuickStart* can provide all the information you need to get started by showing you the concepts and illustrating their uses.

Learning More about Paradox 4.0

After you have learned the basics of using Paradox 4.0 presented in this book, you may want to learn the more advanced applications of Paradox 4.0. Que Corporation offers these books on Paradox 4.0:

Using Paradox 4, is an in-depth reference book that provides comprehensive coverage of all aspects of using Paradox 4.0.

Paradox 4 Quick Reference is an affordable, compact reference guide containing the most commonly used Paradox commands and functions. This book is an invaluable aid you will want to keep next to your computer.

Conventions Used in This Book

Paradox 4 QuickStart uses a number of conventions to help you learn the program quickly. This section shows you examples of these conventions.

Introduction

Keystrokes refer to the keyboard of an IBM Personal Computer and most compatibles. The function keys, F1 through F12, perform specific commands in Paradox.

Exact quotations of words that appear on-screen are spelled as they appear on-screen and are printed in a `special typeface`. Information you are asked to type is printed in **boldface and blue**.

Menu letters you type to activate a command after you have accessed the menu by pressing the F10 key, appear in boldface and blue, such as **V**iew. Keys you press appear as blue keyboard icons, such as [↵Enter].

When two keys are shown together separated by a – (hyphen), such as [Alt]-[F7], you press and hold the first key as you press the second key. When two keys appear together without the hyphen between them, such as [F4] [F5], the first key is pressed and released before the second key is pressed.

Blue lines highlight the most important parts of illustrations.

An Overview of Paradox 4

The name of this program, Paradox, is a very apt description of the power and ease of use it brings to you. The authors of the program selected the name because the program itself was a contradiction when compared to other database programs—a powerful, full-featured database that is simple to learn and use.

As you read through *Paradox 4 QuickStart* and follow the examples and illustrations, you will quickly begin to create your own set of database tools and grasp the concepts behind them.

This book has been written for users of Paradox 4.0, which is the most current version of Paradox. If you have not yet upgraded, the illustrations and many of the command options are not the same as those to which you are accustomed.

What is a database?

Understanding Paradox objects

A tour of program features

What is new in Paradox 4.0?

What do you need to run Paradox 4.0?

An Overview of Paradox 4

1

> **Key Terms in This Chapter**
>
> *Relational database* — A group of tables, containing records and fields, that are or can be linked together by a common field or fields.
>
> *Objects* — Any of a large variety of files and settings that are part of the components of a database, including tables, reports, forms, and scripts.
>
> *Family* — A group of objects that are related directly to a specific table. Any object that is part of a table's family shares the same file name with the table, but has a different file extension.

What Is a Database?

A database is any collection of information that is organized in some logical way. You are probably familiar with some common examples of databases. An encyclopedia is a database of information; a dictionary is a database of words; and your telephone book is a database of names, addresses, and phone numbers. The files maintained in your office are another type of database.

The database can be kept on paper, as all of the above examples generally are, or a database can be maintained in a computer, using a database program such as Paradox 4.0. Computer databases come in two flavors: flat-file and relational. Paradox is one of the most powerful relational databases and is the easiest one to use.

The Flat-File Database

The flat-file database is the simplest type of database. Most simple card-file and telephone number databases are flat-file systems.

The term *flat-file* means that the program creates a single file for each group of records. You can create as many files as you want with most programs, but each of the database files is a separate entity. For example, a flat-file database contains two files: one that lists customer names, addresses, and phone numbers and one that lists invoices and items purchased. Generally, a flat-file database cannot combine data from two or more files into a single report or form.

The Relational Database

The relational database consists of a group of tables. Each table is made up of rows and columns, called *records* and *fields*. Each record you enter uses a row in the table. Each piece of the record takes up one field. The relational part comes in when you connect two separate tables with a common or key field. Tables that are connected with a common field can each contribute data in a report or form.

If you create the same database with the customer and invoice files, you can link the files together using a key field. A relation exists between the two files if a key field in one file exists in the other file. For example, the fields from the customer and invoice files are listed below:

Customer File	*Invoice*
Customer ID (key field)	Invoice #
Customer Name	Invoice Date
Street	**Customer ID**
City	Item Code
State	Quantity
Zip Code	Cost
Phone Number	

The two files are linked by the key field in the customer file, Customer ID. This field is common to both files, enabling Paradox to use it as a link between them.

The capacity for connecting different tables enables you to keep smaller, simpler tables, each containing a particular data type. This makes updating and changing different parts of your database simpler and quicker.

1 Understanding Paradox Objects

The major components of the Paradox database are referred to as *objects*. Each Paradox object is stored as a file on your disk. Paradox can distinguish between the various objects without your having to intervene. Because Paradox does most of the work, your job of maintaining the database becomes much simpler. Table 1.1 lists the most common Paradox objects and the file extension for each.

Table 1.1
Paradox Objects

Table	File Extension
Tables	DB
Forms	F or F*nn*
Reports	R or R*nn*
Memos	MB
Script	SC or SC2
Image Settings	SET
Graph Settings	G
Validity Checks	VAL
Primary Index	PX
Secondary Index	X*nn* or Y*nn*

The *nn* is a number Paradox adds to the file extension. If you have more than one report for a table, Paradox lists the Standard Report with the extension R, and the remaining reports are R1, R2, and so forth.

The script is the only case where Paradox creates a copy of the original script for its own use. Any script with the file extension of SC2 is a copy Paradox has made and then optimized so that it can run faster. You can edit the original SC script file, but not the SC2 file.

Understanding Paradox Objects

The Paradox Family

Some of the Paradox objects belong to a specific table. These objects are members of the table's *family*. The file names of the family members are the same as the table name, but their file extensions distinguish them. The Paradox table family includes the following files:

Table.DB

Form.F*nn*

Report.R*nn*

Memo.MB

Primary Index.PX

Validity Check.VAL

Image Settings.SET

Secondary Index.X*nn* or .Y*nn*

Table.DB is the primary object, and all family members belong to the table. If you delete the table, then all the associated family objects also are deleted.

Tables

The Paradox table is the primary object. Without the table, and the data associated with it, the other objects have no purpose. The table provides the functional framework on which the family member objects are based. The form and report objects both must draw their information and basic structure from the table to which they belong. The other family members—such as primary and secondary indexes, validity checks, and image settings—serve no purpose other than to assist the table.

9

An Overview of Paradox 4

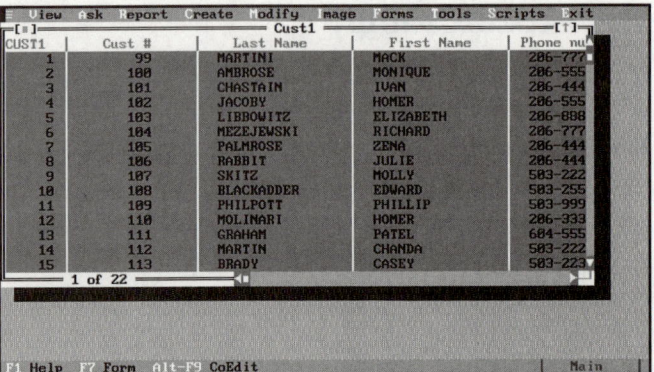

Here, you see the table Cust1.

The table is similar in many ways to a spreadsheet format. A complete piece of data is kept as a record. A record can be a customer's name, address, and phone number, or a single inventory item, with item number, description, cost, price, and quantity on hand. Paradox maintains the record in a single row of the table.

The table record is then divided into columns, or fields. Each field contains a part of the record. For example, the customer's first name is field 1, last name is field 2, street address is field 3, and so on. The division of a record into separate fields is the secret behind the relational database.

You can link separate tables by including a common field between the tables. For example, using a Customer Number field as the first field in the customer list table, and then including the Customer Number field in a table about orders placed by customers, enables you to link the tables together. This saves you from having to include all of the customer information with each individual order.

Forms

A Paradox form can represent on-screen a paper form you already use. You can make the form as simple as a single record from the table, or as complex as a multiple table form that displays and updates information from several tables.

Understanding Paradox Objects

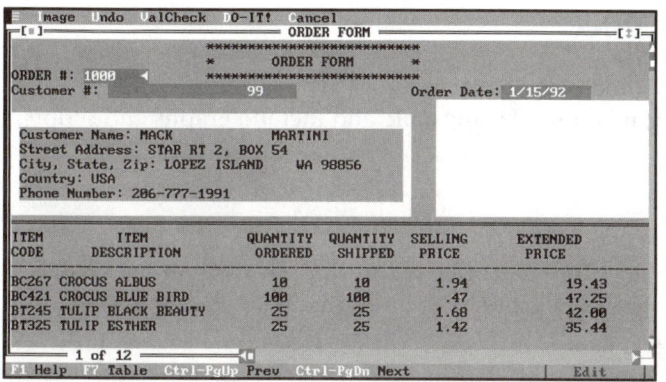

Here, you see a multiple table form displaying data from several tables, using drawn boxes and on-screen instructions.

Reports

You use a Paradox report to create a printed document. A report can be anything from a printout of the table data to an invoice or form letter. Reports also can use a single table or multiple tables.

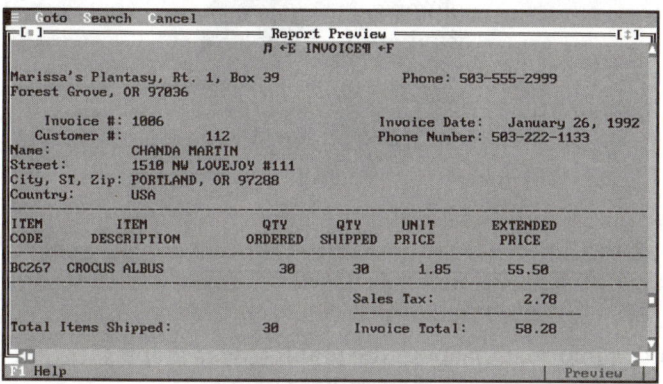

Here, you see a multiple table report: an invoice as it appears on-screen.

Other Paradox Family Objects

The other members of a table's family of objects are settings, or parts, of tables. You do not interact directly with them. However, you do add objects, such as validity checks, as settings and aids.

11

An Overview of Paradox 4

Other Paradox Objects

Paradox also includes some objects that are not part of a specific table's family. These objects can be used by any table and include graphs and scripts.

Graphs

The Paradox graph object is not a specific graph you can view on-screen or print out. The graph object is a group of settings that tell Paradox how you want to display a graph.

This is a graph displaying the most often ordered items.

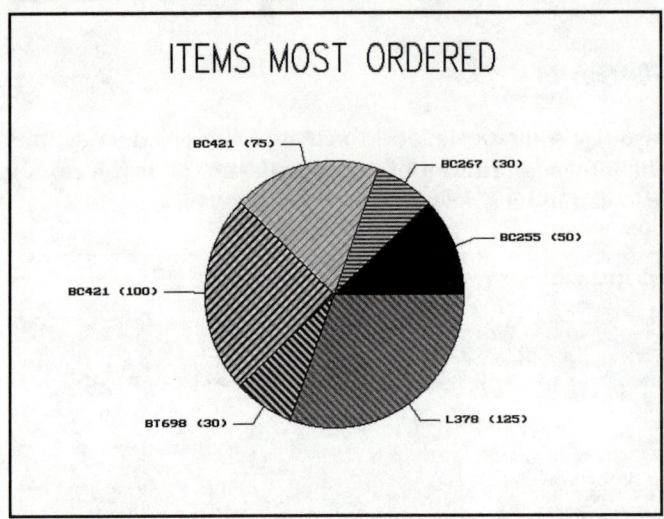

The graph object includes information about the graph type, a graph title, colors or fill patterns, and where to print the resulting graph.

Scripts

A script is a recorded set of keystrokes and operations you can play back later. Scripts can be as simple or complex as you want to make them.

A Tour of Program Features

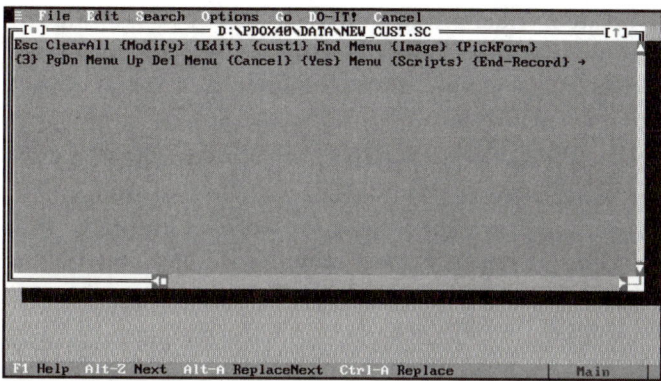

Here, you see a script displayed in the Editor window.

You can create a simple script that just opens a table, finds the next blank record, and then stops, allowing you to start adding new records. Or, you can create and link scripts that can query a table and find, for example, all of your customers in one state who have bought a certain amount of a product and then print out a letter to each of these customers about your next special promotion.

Scripts can save you much time and effort.

A Tour of Program Features

Create and restructure the tables as needed. Linking tables into a powerful relational database is as simple as including a linking field in each table and then telling Paradox to create the link.

Adding or editing data can be done in several modes. In the Edit mode, you can change any field of any record, whereas you can only add new records in the DataEntry mode. The CoEdit mode enables several users to work in the same database together.

The essence of Paradox remains Query By Example (QBE). This is the Paradox method of assisting you in finding information about or from your database. You provide Paradox with an example of what you need to know, and Paradox finds and displays the information.

Creating new reports with the Paradox Reports Designer is a highly interactive process, which enables you to view a report with real data before you finish and save the report. With the Paradox Forms Designer, you can quickly create a form for a specialized purpose. Linking forms and reports to several tables is a quick and simple process.

An Overview of Paradox 4

Paradox enables you to create a visual product through the use of fully functional graphing tools. Use the Paradox Graph to create bar, stacked bar, pie, and many other graphs. You can customize them completely to your specific needs.

Paradox 4.0 can use tables and objects created by an earlier version of Paradox. Generally, however, objects created with Paradox 4.0 are not compatible with Paradox 3.5 and earlier versions. You do have the option of using a *compatible* format when creating tables. Tables created with the compatible file format can be used by earlier versions of Paradox. You cannot use the new field type of memo with compatible files.

What Is New in Paradox 4.0?

Paradox 4.0 has updated much of its on-screen interface. For those of you who have used earlier versions of Paradox, or other DOS-based databases, you will now see a database that uses a Graphical User Interface (GUI). Paradox creates a blank *desktop* on which you place tables, forms, and other objects with which you work.

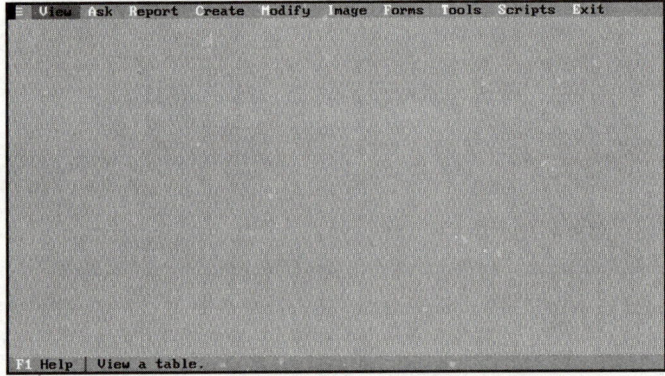

When Paradox finishes loading, you see the Paradox desktop.

Tables and forms are now displayed in resizeable and moveable windows. You can open and use several windows in the same Paradox session.

What Is New in Paradox 4.0?

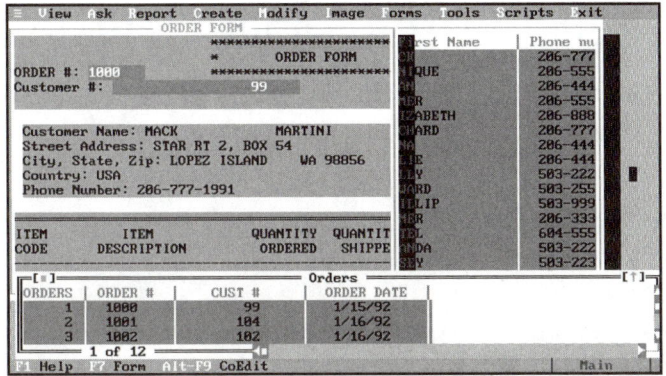

As you can see, here Paradox displays two tables and a form on the desktop.

Paradox 4.0 now offers a System menu option that is available from all menu bars throughout the program. Many of the options are available for use at any point in the program.

Mouse Support

Paradox 4.0 is now a "mouseable" program. If you have a Microsoft compatible mouse, you can use it with Paradox.

A mouse pointer in the shape of a large rectangle is displayed when you load the program. You can use the mouse to select menu items, display lists of tables, use the scroll bars, and choose a window to activate by moving the mouse pointer to the window and clicking the mouse key.

Other New Features

Paradox 4.0 is now fully compliant with the DOS Protected Mode Interface (DPMI), which enables Paradox to utilize all of your computer's memory.

Paradox 4.0 supports the use of PostScript compatible printers.

Paradox 4.0 now supports a new field type, the memo field. This field is a variable length field with a maximum capacity of 64M.

1 What Do You Need To Run Paradox 4.0?

To run Paradox 4.0 in a single-user environment, you must have, at a minimum, all of the following:

- 286K or higher processor capable of running in protected-mode
- 2M of Random-Access Memory (RAM)
- A hard disk with a minimum of 4M free
- One floppy drive
- Monitor capable of supporting MDA, MCGA, CGA, EGA, VGA, and an appropriate adapter
- DOS 3.0 or higher
- A CONFIG.SYS file with the following minimum parameters:
    FILES=40
    BUFFERS=40

The FILES setting can vary between 40 and 90 depending on the number of file-handles you need.

To run Paradox 4.0 on a network station, you must have a minimum of all of the above and DOS 3.1 or higher.

To run Paradox 4.0 on a network server, you must use one of the following network operating systems:

- 3Com 3+, version 1.5.1 or higher
- Microsoft LANMAN, version 2.0 or higher
- Novell Advanced NetWare, version 2.0A or higher
- IBM Token Ring or PC Network with IBM PC LAN program, version 1.12 or higher
- Banyan VINES, version 2.10 or higher
- AT&T StarGROUP DOS software, version 3.1 or higher
- DEC Pathworks, version 1.0 or higher
- Other networks that are 100% compatible with DOS 3.1 and one of the networks listed above

Optional equipment and software include the following:

- Mouse or other pointing device that is 100% compatible with a Microsoft Bus or Serial mouse, Logitech Bus or Serial mouse, or IBM PS/2 mouse

- Microsoft Windows, version 3.0 or higher
- 80X87 Math coprocessor
- Printer capable of printing ASCII files
- PostScript-compatible printer

Summary

In this overview chapter, you were introduced to Paradox 4.0 and some of the special capabilities of the program. You learned about Paradox's new graphical interface. You also learned what a database is and some of the functions Paradox can perform for you.

Specifically, you learned the following key points about Paradox 4.0:

- Paradox is a fully relational database, able to link many tables together.
- Paradox builds a family of objects around each table. Paradox is able to perform most file maintenance functions.
- You can now use a mouse, or similar pointing device, to move or size windows, select menu options, and move the cursor to new locations.
- Paradox 4.0 can read and use any file that has been created in an earlier version of Paradox, but a Paradox 4.0 file must be created using a compatible file mode if you need to use the table with an earlier version of Paradox.
- Paradox is fully compliant with the DOS Protected Mode Interface (DPMI), which allows Paradox to utilize all of your computer's available memory.

Now that you are familiar with Paradox 4.0, you are ready to begin learning about specific commands and features of the program. In the next chapter, you will learn how to use the Paradox menus and to navigate through windows, using the mouse, scroll bars, and menu commands.

2

Getting Started

This chapter explains how Paradox 4 displays the desktop and your data. Included in this chapter is a complete explanation of the new graphical elements in the Paradox 4 interface. This chapter also introduces you to using the mouse, the special keyboard keys, and the Paradox 4 on-line Help available at any time within the program.

For those of you who have used Paradox 3.5 and are ready to get started with Paradox 4, take a few moments to scan the sections on menu and desktop structure and on using Paradox 4. These sections introduce many of the new features and how they operate.

This chapter assumes you have successfully loaded the Paradox 4 program onto your computer. If you have not yet done so, see Appendix A for help.

Starting Paradox

Understanding the opening display

Understanding the Paradox desktop

Using Paradox

Designing the customer database

Quitting Paradox

Getting Started

Key Terms in This Chapter

Desktop	The area of the screen below the menu that contains the images, tables, and forms with which you are working.
Window	A Paradox window is a rectangular area on the desktop. Each Paradox object, such as a form or table, is contained within a window. Each window can be resized, moved on the desktop, and arranged one on top of the other.
Menu bar	The bar at the top of your screen that contains the menu items. Each of the menu items activates a pull-down menu or dialog box.
Pull-down menu	A list of menu items or commands activated from the menu bar. Some menu items activate additional menus.
Dialog box	A box displayed in answer to certain menu selections. Usually a response is required, like filling in a table name.
Scroll bar	Vertical and horizontal bars located at the bottom and right side of the table or form window. Each bar has an arrow at each end and a single box. You can use the scroll bars to display other parts of the table or form.
Title bar	The top part of the window that contains the path and file name of the table.
Mouse pointer	A rectangular block that indicates the position of the mouse cursor on your screen.

Starting Paradox

Paradox 4 is intended to be installed onto your computer's hard drive. To start Paradox 4 from the hard drive, the following assumptions are made:

- You have installed Paradox 4 in the default installation directory named PDOX40

Starting Paradox

- You have allowed Paradox 4 to add itself to the Path statement in your AUTOEXEC.BAT file

If you have a different setup than this, you need to make the appropriate changes by following these steps:

1. First, create a directory to hold the tables and files you will make in Paradox 4. From the DOS prompt (probably C:\>), type **md\pdox40\data** and press ⏎Enter. This creates a subdirectory in your Paradox 4 directory.
2. Now, to start Paradox, type **paradox** and press ⏎Enter.

Your screen should go blank for a moment. Then the Introduction screen appears, containing the signature information you provided during installation.

When Paradox has finished loading itself into memory, you then see the Paradox desktop screen.

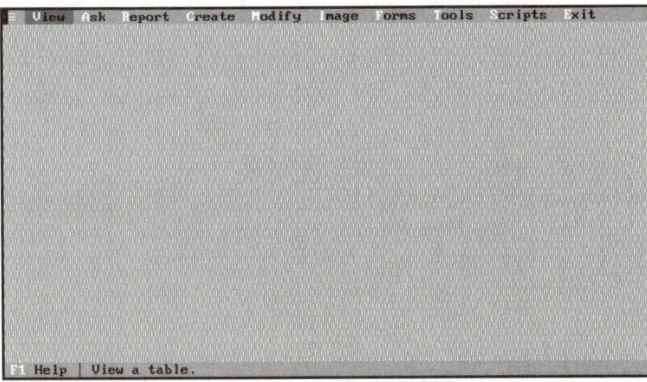

Here, you see the Paradox 4 desktop screen.

Now change the working directory of Paradox from C:\PDOX40 to the directory you just created: C:\PDOX40\DATA. This ensures that your new table will be saved in that directory. To change your working directory, do the following:

1. Select **T**ools from the menu bar by pressing T, or by moving the mouse pointer to the **T**ools option and clicking it, or by using the arrow keys to highlight **T**ools and then pressing ⏎Enter.
2. Select the **M**ore option by pressing M, or by choosing the option with the mouse and clicking once.

21

Getting Started

Here, you see the submenu of the **T**ools **M**ore option.

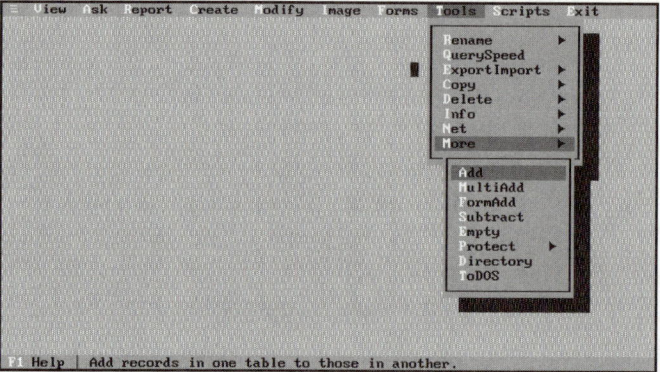

3. Select the **D**irectory option.

   The current working directory is C:\PDOX40 and is displayed in the dialog box. To change the working directory, type the name of the new directory. This erases the current directory.

4. Type **C:\pdox40\data**.

This is the **T**ools **M**ore **D**irectory dialog box, ready to change the working directory.

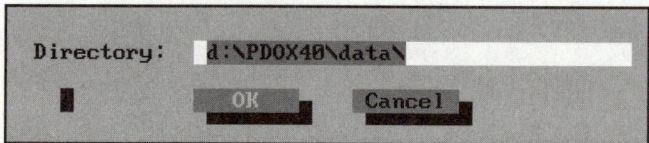

5. Press ⏎Enter. You now see two messages displayed in the message box:

   Clearing desktop...

   Working directory is now c:\PDOX40\data\

You can use a shortcut method. If you will be using a subdirectory of the current working directory (like you are doing here), you can press the Insert key (Ins), add the subdirectory name **\data**, and press ⏎Enter. You save a few keystrokes by not typing the entire path name.

22

Understanding the Opening Display

Now that you have installed and started the Paradox program, take a few moments to familiarize yourself with the various parts of the Paradox display. After Paradox is loaded, the display opens with a blank desktop, the menu bar, and the status bar.

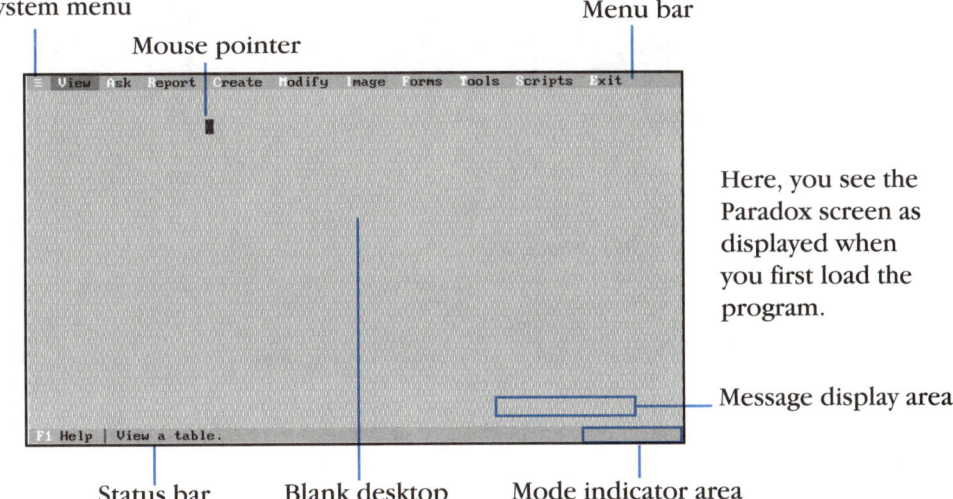

As you make selections and open tables, your available options change on the screen. The menu items change depending on your current mode. The status bar contains additional **F**-key options you can use. Paradox modes and the **F**-key functions are discussed in the next section of this chapter.

The Menu Bar

The Paradox menu bar is the top line on your screen. The menu bar consists of two primary items: the System menu and other menu items.

23

Getting Started

The System Menu (≡)

The System menu appears in the upper left-hand corner of the screen. It is indicated by the symbol ≡. You can select the box by clicking it once with the mouse, or by moving the menu selector highlight to it with the arrow keys and pressing `Enter`, which displays the pull-down System menu. This option is available from any of the menus.

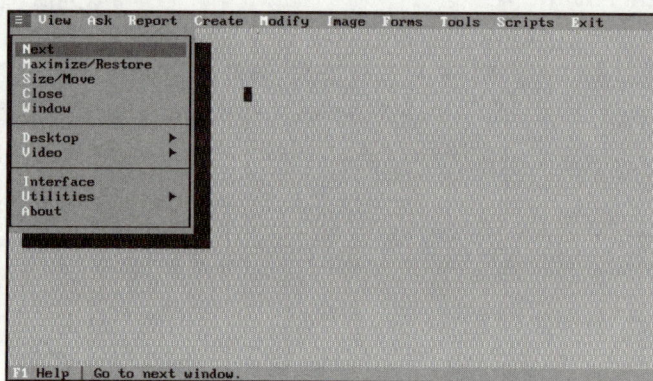

Here, the System menu is displayed.

Other Menu Items

The other menu items on the menu bar vary, depending on your current mode. Each item can be selected by using one of the following methods:

- Click the required menu item with the mouse.
- Select the menu item by moving the highlight with the arrow keys and pressing `Enter`.
- Press the first letter of the required menu item.
- If the menu bar is not active, you can activate it by pressing `F10`. The menu bar is active when you can see the highlight displayed.
- For those items that display a pull-down menu box, you can activate the pull-down menu by pressing `↓`.

The Status Bar

The last line of your screen contains an information area called the status bar. The Paradox status bar is composed of three parts:

- The first part always contains `F1 Help`. When you display a table or form in the desktop, additional valid **F**-function key alternatives also are displayed. When you make a selection from or activate the menu bar, all of the additional **F**-key selections are replaced by the menu bar description. They reappear when your menu selection has been made.
- The second part of this box contains a short description of the currently selected menu item.
- The third part of the box contains the mode indicator. The mode indicator message varies depending on your current actions and selections.

Understanding the Paradox Desktop

The Paradox desktop is the blank area between the menu bar and the status bar. All of the Paradox objects you work with are contained on the desktop. The desktop can contain several tables and forms, each enclosed within its own window.

The Menu and Desktop Window Structure

The Paradox menu and desktop are the action areas. You use the Paradox menus to access tables, forms, reports, and other Paradox objects. Again, the Paradox desktop is the workspace that contains the Paradox objects with which you work.

In many ways, you can think of the Paradox desktop as your own desk. The Paradox objects are contained within their own windows on the desktop, just like papers on your desk. You can move the windows on the desktop, stack them on top of each other, enter data into one, copy information to another, then file them away, removing them from the desktop.

Paradox Menus

When you open Paradox, you see the Main menu bar displayed at the top of your screen. The menu bar options change as you move to lower-level modes, with the exception of the System menu (≡) option.

25

Getting Started

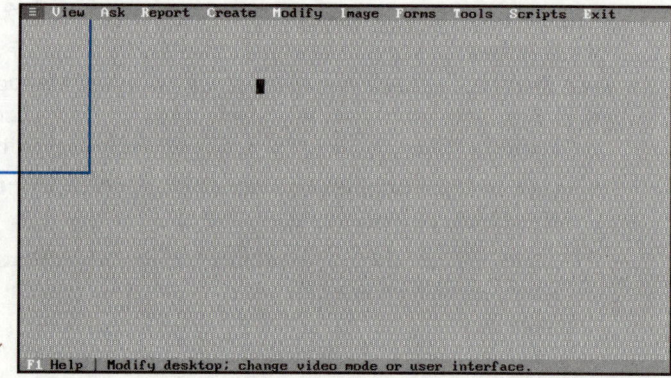

This is the Main menu bar in Main mode.

Each mode has its own menu bar options. In Main mode, the menu bar contains the following options:

Table 2.1
Main Menu Bar Options

Option	Description
View	Selecting View displays a dialog box. The View option enables you to view or look at a table. You cannot edit or enter data when using View. The dialog box displays a text box into which you enter the name of the table you want to view. If you do not know the table name, you can press 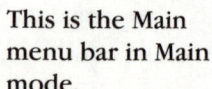, or click the Table list box to display a list of available tables.
Ask	Selecting Ask also displays the dialog box. Use Ask to create a Query form for the selected table.
Report	Selecting Report displays a pull-down menu of available options. Use the Report menu to select, design, and print a report. The Report menu options are Output, Design, Change, RangeOutput, and SetPrinter.
Create	Selecting Create displays a dialog box. Use this option to create a new table.
Modify	Selecting Modify displays a pull-down menu of available options. Use these menu options to sort, add, or change data, and to make changes to a table's structure. The Modify menu options are Sort, Edit, CoEdit, DataEntry, MultiEntry, Restructure, and Index.

Understanding the Paradox Desktop

Option	Description
Image	Selecting **I**mage displays its pull-down menu. With the options on this menu, you can make temporary or permanent changes to the current table's image. The Paradox Graph functions also are on this menu. You can also select a form in which to display records. The **I**mage menu options are **T**ableSize, **C**olumnSize, **F**ormat, **Z**oom, **M**ove, **P**ickForm, **K**eepSet, **O**rderTable, and **G**raph.
Forms	Selecting **F**orms displays its pull-down menu. Use this menu to **D**esign or **C**hange a form for the selected table.
Tools	Selecting **T**ools displays a pull-down menu. This menu contains a variety of tools that help you maintain your Paradox files. The first pull-down menu contains these options: **R**ename, **Q**uerySpeed, **E**xportImport, **C**opy, **D**elete, **I**nfo, **N**et, and **M**ore. The **M**ore option displays a cascading menu with the options **A**dd, **M**ultiAdd, **F**ormAdd, **S**ubtract, **E**mpty, **P**rotect, **D**irectory, and **T**oDOS.
Scripts	Selecting **S**cripts displays a pull-down menu that enables you to write, edit, and use scripts. The **S**cripts menu options are **P**lay, **B**eginRecord, **Q**uerySave, **S**howPlay, **R**epeatPlay, and **E**ditor.
Exit	Selecting the **E**xit option displays a pull-down menu. Use this option to exit or leave the Paradox program.

The Mode Indicator

The Mode indicator block on the Paradox screen is in the lower right-hand corner. The Paradox mode varies depending on your current actions. When viewing a table, for example, you are in Main mode. When editing a table, you are generally in Edit mode. Table 2.2 lists the various Paradox modes and the commands that lead to them.

Getting Started

2 Here, you can see the mode indicator, in the lower right-hand corner, displaying Main.

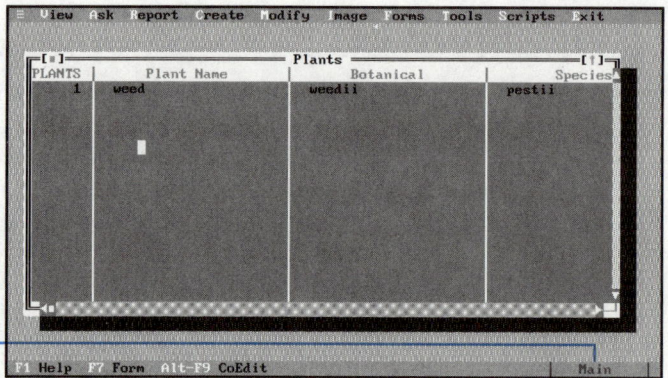

Table 2.2
Modes in Paradox 4

Mode	To Access Mode
Main	Open a table. Save or cancel work done at a lower-level menu such as Edit or Report.
Create	Choose Create and enter a new table name into the dialog box.
CoEdit	Select Modify CoEdit, then enter the table name into the dialog box.
DataEntry	Select Modify DataEntry, then enter the table name into the dialog box. Choose Modify MultiEntry Entry, enter the source table name into the dialog box, and then enter the map table name into the next dialog box.
Edit	Pick Modify Edit and enter the table to be edited into the dialog box.
Form	Select Forms Design or Forms Change and enter the table name and then the form name.
Graph	Select Image Graph Modify.
Index	Choose Modify Index and select the table name in which to create a secondary index.
Password	Pick Tools More Protect Password and enter the table to which to add a password.

Understanding the Paradox Desktop

Mode	To Access Mode
Preview	Select **R**eport **O**utput and the table and report names **S**creen. Select **R**eport **R**angeOutput and the table and report names **S**creen. From the **R**eport **D**esigner menu, select **O**utput **S**creen. When the **S**creen option is selected, Paradox enters the Preview mode.
Report	Select **R**eport **D**esign and enter into the dialog box the table name on which to base the report. Select **R**eport **C**hange and enter table and report name to be changed.
Restructure	Choose **M**odify **R**estructure and enter the table name into the dialog box.
Sort	Choose **M**odify **S**ort and enter into the dialog box the name of the table you want to sort. If you are sorting a keyed table, enter a name for the newly sorted table into the dialog box. If you are sorting an unkeyed table, you can place the sorted data into the **S**ame table or into a **N**ew table. Selecting the **N**ew option requires that you enter a name into the Table Name dialog box.

The mode indicators serve to remind you what you currently are doing on the screen. As you can see from table 2.2, Paradox uses many different mode indicators. Each reminds you of the actions that you are or can be performing on the data.

The Message Window

The message window is the area of the desktop above the mode indicator. Paradox displays error messages or information messages in this area. If you have a color monitor, messages are displayed in a bright color. The default color is red with bright white text. With a monochrome monitor, the message window is displayed in reverse video.

Getting Started

Here, you can see a message displayed in the message window.

Message window

The Mouse

Paradox now supports the use of a mouse for many of its operations. You can use the mouse to select any of the menu commands or any of the **F**-key options listed on the status bar, and to resize and move windows.

To select a menu bar item, position the mouse pointer on the item and click either mouse button. This displays the menu or dialog box for the selected menu item. Many of the dialog boxes require that you enter the name of the relevant table. Instead of entering the name, you also can move the mouse pointer into the Table list box and click once. This displays a list of all available tables. Select the required table by double-clicking the name, or by choosing the table with the mouse or the arrow keys and pressing ⏎Enter.

Here, you see the View dialog box displayed. The mouse pointer is positioned within the Table list box and has been clicked once. The available tables are listed in the box.

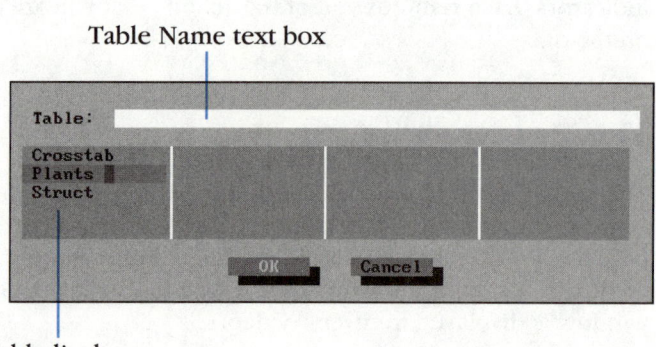

Table Name text box

Table list box

Understanding the Paradox Desktop

When working within a table, you can use the mouse to move from field to field. By moving the mouse pointer to the required field and clicking either mouse key, the selected field becomes the active field.

Paradox Object Windows

Paradox contains all of the objects you use within their own windows. Each type of window has several things in common with other types, regardless of whether it is a table window, a form window, or a report window.

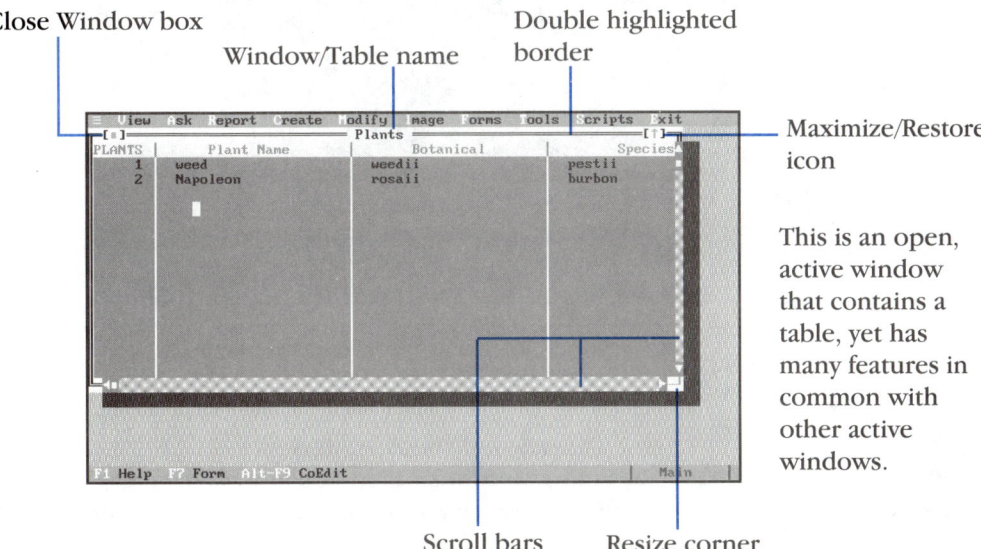

Close Window box
Window/Table name
Double highlighted border
Maximize/Restore icon

This is an open, active window that contains a table, yet has many features in common with other active windows.

Scroll bars   Resize corner

When you have several windows open at one time, only one of the windows is the active window. The active window always has the following distinct features:

- A double, highlighted line border around the window
- A visible text cursor

  The only exception to this is in the Report Preview window. This window displays what a report will look like when printed. Because the cursor does not print on your report, it is not displayed.

- The appearance of mouse window features like the Resize corner, the Maximize or Restore icon, Scroll bars on the right and bottom of the window, and the Close Window box

31

Getting Started

Inactive windows, on the other hand, have the following features:

- A single, unhighlighted line border
- No text cursor
- No mouse window features
- May be partially hidden behind or underneath the active window

When you tile the windows, the inactive ones are not hidden.

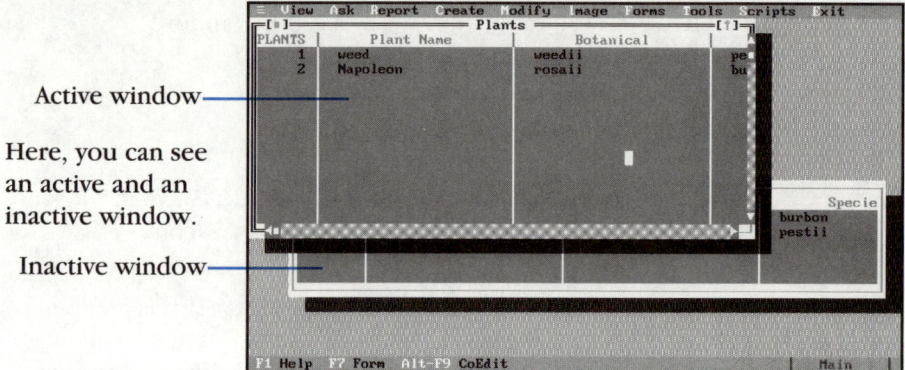

Active window

Here, you can see an active and an inactive window.

Inactive window

Resizing Windows

You can resize an active window as needed. If you need to view more of another table, you can make the active window smaller. You also can change its shape from square to rectangular. To resize a window with a mouse, do the following steps:

1. Position the mouse pointer on the Resize corner, the bottom right-hand corner of the active window. The Resize corner is designated by the symbol of a corner, ⌋.

2. Press and hold either mouse button. Move the mouse, still holding the button down. As you drag the mouse, you see the window resize. When you have resized the window to the size and shape you require, release the mouse button. The window will now stay in the shape you have selected.

If you do not have a mouse, you can still resize a window by using the menu bar and the arrow keys. To resize the active window without a mouse, perform the following steps:

1. Press F10. This activates the menu bar.

Understanding the Paradox Desktop

2. Use ← to move the menu bar highlight to the System menu (≡). Press ↵Enter or ↓ to select the System menu.

3. Choose **S**ize/Move from the menu by pressing S, or by moving the highlight with ↓ and pressing ↵Enter. The status bar now displays a new prompt. The active window still displays its mouse features, but now has only a single-line border which indicates you can move or resize it.

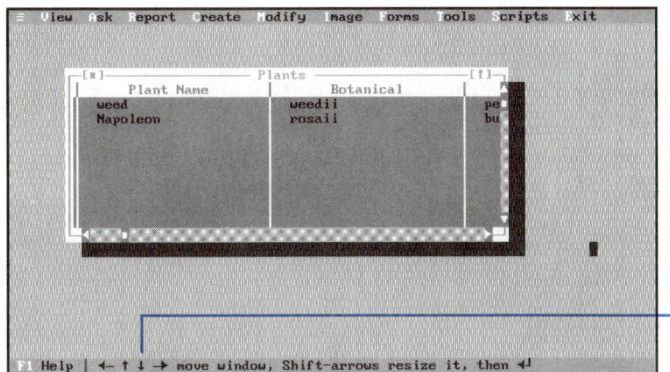

Here, you see the status bar prompt, displaying the arrow symbols for resizing or moving a window.

4. To resize the window, press and hold ⇧Shift and then press the appropriate arrow key to resize the window as required.

   When using the ⇧Shift-**arrow key** combination, it is easiest to experiment a little to see what the effects will be. Different combinations produce the following changes in the window:

⇧Shift-←	Moves the right side of the window towards the left side of the screen and makes the window smaller.
⇧Shift-→	Moves the right side of the window towards the right side of the screen and makes the window larger.
⇧Shift-↑	Moves the bottom side of the window up towards the top of the screen and makes the window smaller.
⇧Shift-↓	Moves the bottom side of the window down towards the bottom of the screen and makes the window larger.

5. Press ↵Enter to end resizing and return to the window.

33

Getting Started

You also can use a short-cut method. Press `Ctrl`-`F5`. Then use the `Shift`-**arrow key** combination to resize the window.

Moving Windows

Paradox enables you to move the active window to another position on the desktop. You then can view another window that is positioned partially underneath the active window. Again, you have the option of using a mouse or the menus and arrow keys to perform this function. To move the active window using a mouse, do the following:

1. Position the mouse pointer on the Name or Title bar.
2. Click and hold either mouse button. Move the mouse to the new position. As you drag the mouse, the window also moves. Release the mouse button when you are at the required position.

Even without a mouse you can move a window. The System menu enables you to move a window by doing the following:

1. Press `F10`. This step activates the menu bar.
2. Use `←` to move the menu bar highlight to the System menu (≡). Press `Enter` to select the System menu.
3. Choose **S**ize/Move from the menu by pressing `S`, or by moving the highlight with `↓` and pressing `Enter`. The status bar now displays the Size/Move arrow prompts.
4. Use the arrow keys to move the window. Each arrow key will move the window in the direction indicated on the key. Press `Enter` when the window is in the required position.

Again, you can use the shortcut method here. Press `Ctrl`-`F5`. Then use the arrow keys to move the window as required.

Maximizing and Restoring Windows

When working with a single table or form, you may want to display the window so that it fills the entire Paradox desktop. Using a single click of the mouse or a single command from the System menu, you can expand the current window to fill the desktop. Alternatively, if you later want to return the window to its previous size and position on the desktop, you also can do this with a single mouse click or simple command. To use the mouse to expand and then contract the current window, do the following:

1. Move the mouse pointer to the Maximize icon, ↑.

Understanding the Paradox Desktop

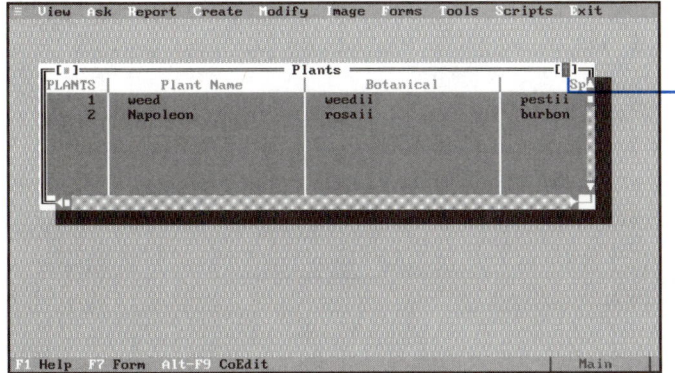

Here, you see the current window with the Maximize icon. The mouse pointer is positioned on the icon.

2. Click either mouse button. The window fills the entire desktop workspace.

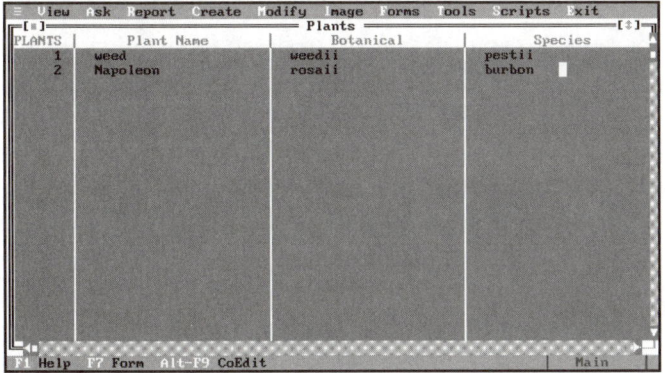

You now see the same table has been maximized to fill the entire desktop.

3. Notice that the Maximize icon has changed. It is now displaying the Restore icon ↕.

   Move the mouse pointer to the Restore icon and click either mouse button. This restores the window to its original size and position on the desktop.

You also can use the Maximize and Restore options by using a simple set of System menu commands. To use the System menu, do the following:

1. Press F10. This activates the menu bar.
2. Use ← to move the menu bar highlight to the System menu (≡). Press ↵Enter to select the System menu.

35

Getting Started

3. Choose **M**aximize/Restore from the menu by pressing [M], or by using [↓] to highlight the **M**aximize/Restore command and then pressing [⏎Enter].

You now see the window has been expanded to its maximum size. To restore the window to its original size and location, again follow steps 1 through 3 above. The **M**aximize/Restore command is a simple toggle switch from one size to the other.

You can also use the shortcut combination of [⇧Shift]-[F5]. This toggles the display from maximized to restored.

Using the Scroll Bars

Two scroll bars are on the active window in Paradox. One is on the right-hand side of the active screen, and the other is at the bottom. Each scroll bar has an arrow button at each end and a position box. With a mouse, you can use the scroll bars to move or scroll through the active window.

The right-hand scroll bar enables you to scroll up or down the window, so you can see additional records in a table. Using the bottom scroll bar, you can scroll left or right through the window and see additional fields in a table.

You have several methods of using a scroll bar. The following steps involve using the bottom scroll bar, but they are applicable to either scroll bar. To use the scroll bar, do the following:

1. Place the mouse pointer on the right-arrow button located at the right-hand side of the bottom scroll bar.

Here, you can see the mouse pointer positioned on the right-hand arrow of the bottom scroll bar.

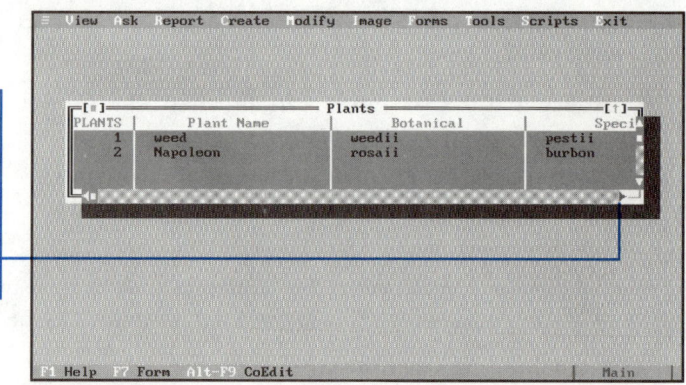

2. Click either mouse button once.

Understanding the Paradox Desktop

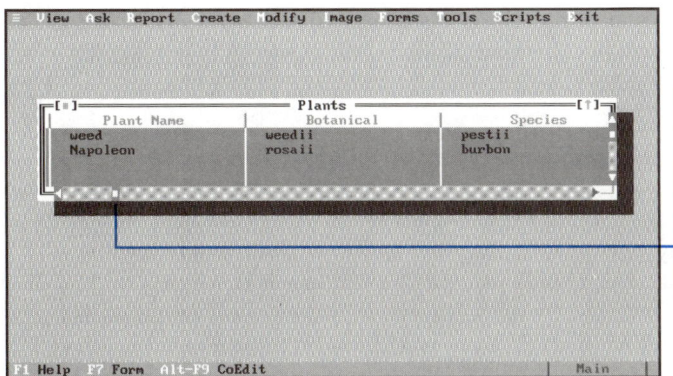

You now see that the table has moved or scrolled one field to the right. Notice that the position box also has moved.

3. To scroll through several fields, or to the last field in the table, position the mouse pointer on the right-arrow button again. Now press and hold the mouse button.

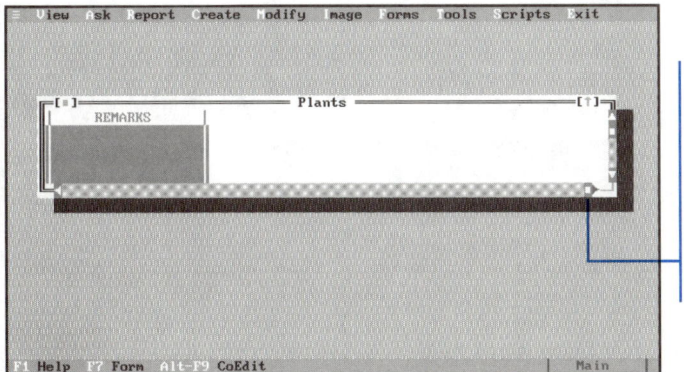

Now you see the last field, Remarks, displayed. Notice that the position box is now located beside the right-arrow button.

4. Now, place the mouse pointer on the position box.
5. Press the mouse button and drag the position box left, along the scroll bar.

   You see that the table fields scroll through the window as you drag the box along the scroll bar. You also can use the left-arrow button in the same manner as you used the right-arrow button. Each time that you click the mouse pointer on the left-arrow button, the window will scroll or move towards the left side of the table.

Getting Started

As mentioned above, each of these actions used with the bottom scroll bar applies to the right scroll bar. Instead of the window scrolling from side to side, it scrolls up or down.

Using the Next and Window Commands

Paradox enables you to display several windows on the desktop. When you have more than a single window open, one is the current or active window and the others are inactive. Usually, the active window is displayed on top of or over the inactive windows. By using the **N**ext and **W**indow commands on the System menu, you can move from one window to another. As with the previous window commands, you have several options for activating and moving to other windows.

You now see that three windows are open on the desktop. The top, or active, window contains the mouse pointer.

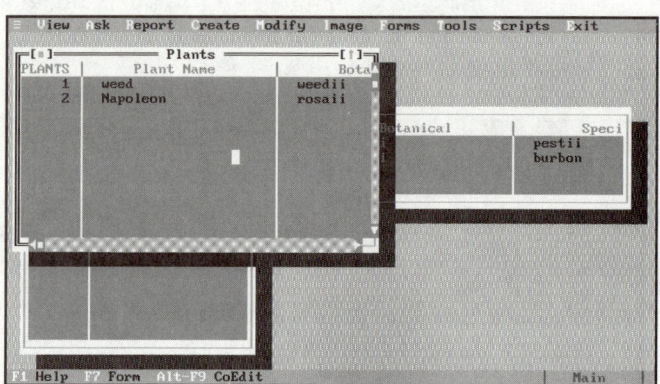

To use the mouse to move from window to window, do the following:

1. Move the mouse pointer to the window to which you want to move.
2. Click the mouse in the new window.

Understanding the Paradox Desktop

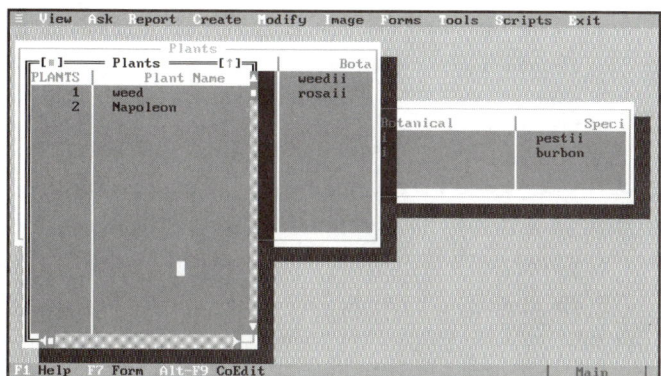

Here, the new window has moved to the forefront and is now the active window.

The System menu has two options to use for moving between windows. They perform similar functions, but in different ways:

Next This command moves the window from the bottom of the stack to the top. For example, if you have three windows (1, 2, and 3) open, 1 is the top, active window, and 3 is the bottom window. Selecting the **N**ext command moves window 3 to the top position, with 1 just below it and 2 at the bottom.

Window When the **W**indow command is selected, a dialog box is displayed listing the windows that are open on the desktop. You can select a window by choosing it from the list and pressing ⏎Enter. The selected window moves to the top and becomes the active window. The current active window is always the first in the **W**indow command dialog box list.

To use the **N**ext option, do the following:

1. Press F10 to activate the menu bar.
2. Choose the System menu.
3. Select the **N**ext option by pressing N, or highlight the **N**ext command with the arrow keys and press ⏎Enter.

   The bottom window becomes the active window.

You also can use the shortcut combination of Ctrl-F4. This moves the bottom window to the top and activates it.

39

Getting Started

To use the **W**indow command, do the following:

1. Press `F10` to activate the menu bar.
2. Choose the System menu.
3. Select the **W**indow option by pressing `W`, or highlight the **W**indow command with the arrow keys and press `Enter`.
4. Choose the required window from the list contained in the dialog box and press `Enter`. The selected window becomes the active window.

If you are currently in a window that is specific to a particular mode, like using a form to edit data, you cannot activate another window. If you attempt to move to another window, Paradox beeps at you. You must first finish the actions for the mode-specific window by canceling the operation, or by completing it and selecting `F2` **D**o-It!.

Even if you cannot activate another window, you can use the **W**indow command to display the dialog box with the list of open windows. This can be a quick method of finding out what you currently have open on the desktop.

Closing Windows

When you are finished with a table, form, or graph, then it is time to close the window containing the object. Using the **C**lose command from the System menu closes the active window. The next window on the desktop then becomes the active window.

If you are in a mode-specific window, choosing **C**lose from the System menu is the same as choosing **C**ancel from the window's menu bar, which cancels all changes you have made since opening the window. The active window also has a Close box located in the upper left-hand corner of the window. Using the mouse pointer and clicking this box is the same as choosing the **C**lose command from the System menu.

You also can use the shortcut combination of `Ctrl`-`F8`. This key combination closes the active window. Again, using this combination in a mode-specific window is the same as using the **C**ancel option on the window's menu bar.

Using Paradox

Paradox 4 is a full-featured relational database program. As you work through this book and become familiar with Paradox, you will become comfortable with the program's extensive capabilities.

Paradox has the capacity to link several small tables into a single, manageable database. You can view your data or edit it, using a table or a form. Paradox uses the F-function keys on your keyboard to streamline many of the menu commands. As you become familiar with the keyboard and Paradox, you will find these shortcuts to be invaluable. In addition to the F-function keys, Paradox makes use of a number of other keys in combination with Ctrl and Alt. When necessary, canceling an operation is generally a simple one-key command, as is accessing Paradox's generous Help screens. Getting help for any command is only a keystroke away. To access Paradox's on-screen Help, press F1.

Creating Small vs. Large Tables

Paradox has a vast capacity to hold information. A single table can hold 262 million characters. If a table is nonindexed, it can hold 4,000 characters per record; if a table is indexed, it can hold 1,350 characters per record. The maximum number of fields is 255 per record with a limit of 255 characters per field. The applicable character limit per record of 4,000 or 1,350 is reached by a combination of the number of fields in a record and the number of characters in the various fields. These figures do not include Memo fields. The Memo field is a special field type discussed in the next chapter.

As you create your first database, this capacity may tempt you to include all possible pieces of information in a single table. You will find it easier to access specific information, however, if you link several smaller tables together instead of making a single large table. This is helpful when you search for specific information or sort a table. Queries and sort operations process much faster on a small table than on a large table. If you process information that spans several tables, creating a multi-form table is the best method.

Using View vs. Modify

You can look at or view your data at any time with Paradox's View option, but you cannot make any changes or additions. Look but do not touch. This option is excellent for browsing information without taking the chance of changing it accidentally.

On the other hand, the Modify option enables you to edit, sort, or restructure your tables. By using the Modify Edit command (or Modify CoEdit, or Modify DataEntry, or Modify MultiEntry) you not only can browse your data tables, but make major or minor changes to them.

Getting Started

Be aware of the differences, and if you are browsing your data, use the **V**iew option. You can easily enter an edit mode from **V**iew or the Main mode.

Canceling a Function

If you start a function and then decide you want to cancel its operation, you can do so in several different ways:

`Esc`	Use `Esc` to back out of menus and dialog boxes. This key also returns you to the active window from the menu bar.
Mouse	Using the mouse, you can click back to the active window, to a higher-level pull-down menu, or to the menu bar. If available, you can click a Close box on the active window. Clicking outside of the borders of a dialog box or pull-down menu closes the option, as does clicking **Cancel** on a dialog box.
Cancel	The **Cancel** command on any menu enables you to exit from an operation and cancel any changes you may have made.
`Ctrl`-`F8`	Using this combination from most lower-level menu bars is similar to selecting **Cancel**.
`Ctrl`-`U`	When in **E**dit mode, this key combination is the same as using the **U**ndo option from the menu bar.
`Ctrl`-`Break`	This key combination cancels an operation and returns you to the point from which you began. If you use `Ctrl`-`Break` during a query operation, it may take Paradox a few moments to stop the process. If a query has gone beyond a certain point, Paradox finishes processing the query. DO NOT turn your computer off until Paradox has backed out of the query operation completely.

Accessing the Paradox Help Screens

Paradox uses a context-sensitive Help screen system. Any time you require help on an operation or command, pressing `F1` displays information about that function.

Using Paradox

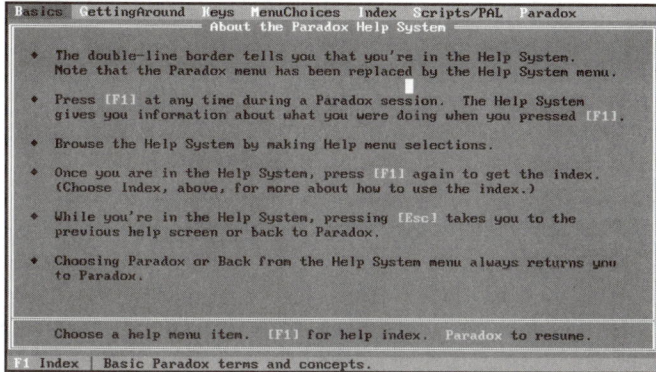

This is the About the Paradox Help System screen.

Pressing [F1] displays this Help screen. This is the beginning or introductory screen. Notice that its structure is very similar to that of the Paradox desktop display you were just viewing. The top line contains a menu bar with a series of menu choices. Again, these choices vary depending on the Help screen you are viewing. The body of the screen displays the Help messages, and the bottom line displays a short message about the menu item highlighted on the menu bar.

Paradox also contains a Help index which you can use to find information concerning a particular subject. To enter the Help index, press [F1] after you are in a Help screen.

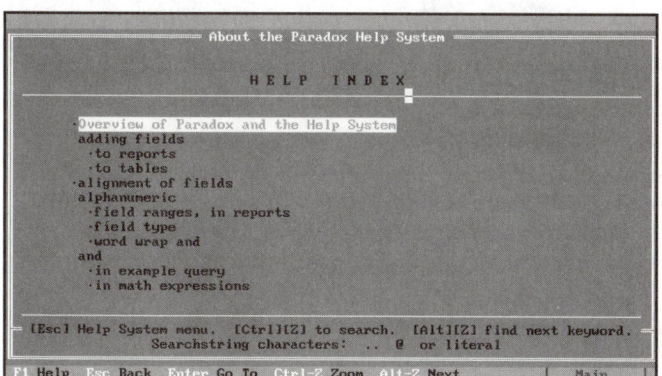

Here, you see the Help Index screen.

Getting Started

In the Help Index screen, you can use the ↑ or ↓ arrow keys to highlight an item. Press ↵Enter to move to the Help screen for that specific item. Also notice that the bottom line of the screen contains some shortcut keys and search keys. Using Ctrl-Z, the Zoom option, enables you to search for a specific item for which you need help.

Here, you see the Zoom dialog box. The item forms has been filled in.

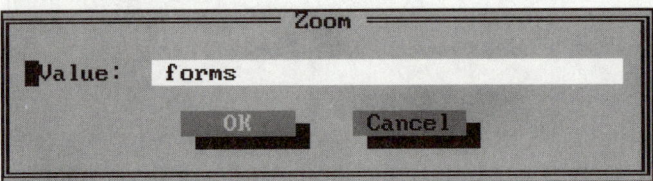

Pressing ↵Enter begins the Help search function.

You now see the Forms Help screen. This is the result of using the Zoom search function.

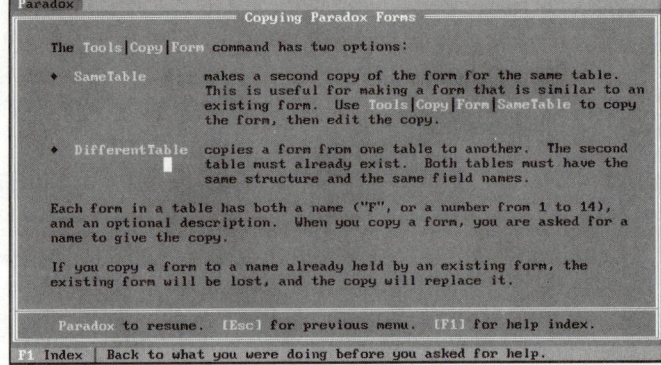

As you can see, this Help screen concerns copying a form to another table, not creating, designing, or using a form. Now, from the Main menu bar, select **F**orm and then **F1** Help .

Designing the Customer Database

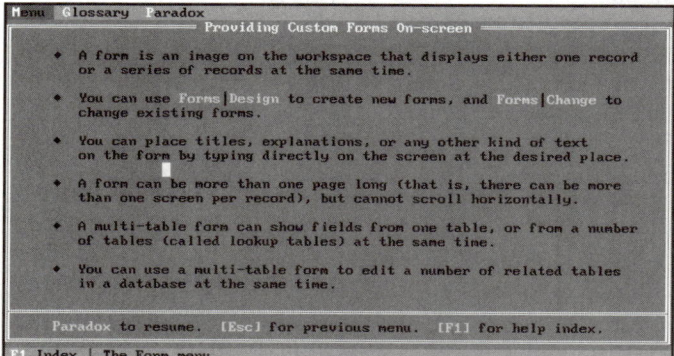

Here is the resulting Forms Help screen, displayed by using the context-sensitive Help.

As you can see, you can get different Help screens by using the different Help options. At times you may have to use both Help methods to find the piece of information for which you are looking.

Designing the Customer Database

This section is aimed at showing you how to get started quickly and easily with Paradox. You will design, step-by-step, your own Customer database. The tasks and concepts to which you will be introduced are discussed in detail in the next few chapters.

In this section, you will build a simple table structure. When you have saved the structure, you will change to the Edit mode and add a few records into the database. You also will perform a query, or ask questions of your database. Then you will sort your information and print a report.

Remember, before you can start this section, you must have properly installed and started the Paradox program. If you have not done this, please refer to Appendix A for instructions on installing the Paradox program onto your computer, and refer to the section on starting Paradox at the beginning of this chapter. Also make sure that you have the correct template for your keyboard. The template shows you at a glance what the F-keys do in various key combinations. It is usually enclosed in the box that contains your master program disks.

Getting Started

Creating the Database Structure

The basic building block of the Paradox database is the table. All of the other Paradox objects are members of a specific table's family. Without the table, the other objects, such as forms and reports, do not exist. Entering information into the table is very similar to entering data into the columns of a spreadsheet, or using a column format with a word processor.

Before you are able to enter information into the Paradox table, you must first create a structure into which Paradox can place the information. The structure of a table tells Paradox what type of data can be entered into the different fields. You will tell Paradox if a field contains alphanumeric (letters & numbers) data, numbers, short numbers, currency, dates, memos, or binary data. For some of these data types, you also need to tell Paradox how long the data field can be. This process is known as defining the table's structure.

To create the customer table, do the following:

1. Select **C**reate from the menu bar. Press [C], or use the arrow keys to highlight the **C**reate option and press [↵Enter], or select **C**reate with the mouse pointer and click once.
2. Type the table name **Customer** and press [↵Enter], or click **OK** with the mouse.

You now see the Struct table.

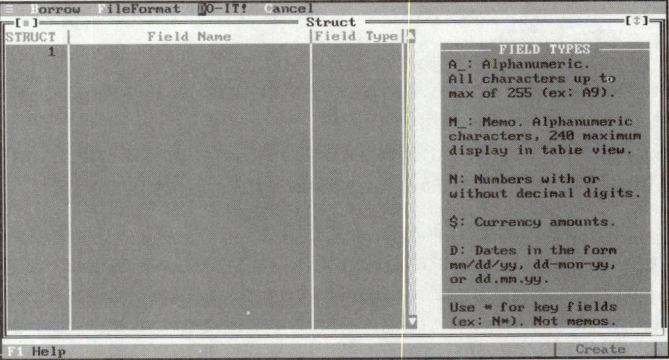

You use the Struct table to define the structure of a new table, in this case the Customer table. The Struct table contains the following features: three columns, a scroll bar, and a box labeled FIELD TYPES.

Each row of the Struct table defines a single column, or field of the Customer table. As you define the fields of the Customer table, enter

46

Designing the Customer Database

the field name and the field type in the second and third columns of the Struct table. Paradox automatically enters the row number in the first column, STRUCT.

Notice that the mode indicator has changed to Create.

3. Notice also that the blinking cursor is located in row 1, in the Field Name column. You must enter the name of each of the fields in the table. To name the first field of the Customer table, type **Last Name** and then press *Enter*. The cursor now moves to the Field Type column.

4. The choices available to you are listed in the Field Type list on the right side of your screen. Enter the field type for the Last Name field. Type **A15** and press *Enter* to create the field type, alphanumeric—length 15 characters.

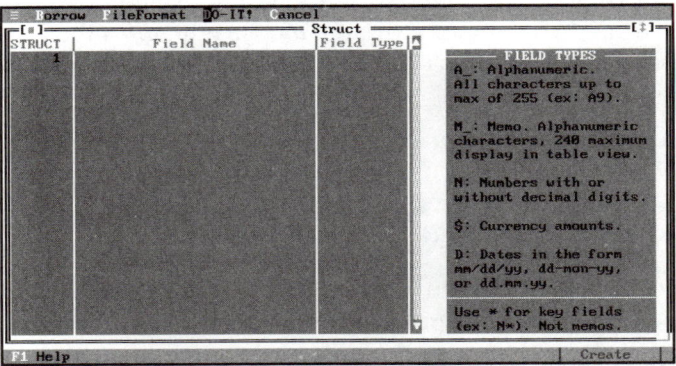

Your screen should now appear like this. You have defined the Last Name field and are ready to define the next field.

5. Now enter the remaining field definitions as shown in the next figure, repeating steps 3 and 4 for each field.

You can correct any errors you make by using *Backspace* to erase the error and then retyping the entry. To move to another field definition, you can use the mouse to move the cursor to the appropriate field. Place the mouse pointer on the field to be corrected and click. You also can use *Tab* to move to the next field, or use *Shift*-*Tab* to move back a field.

Getting Started

Your finished Customer table structure should appear like this.

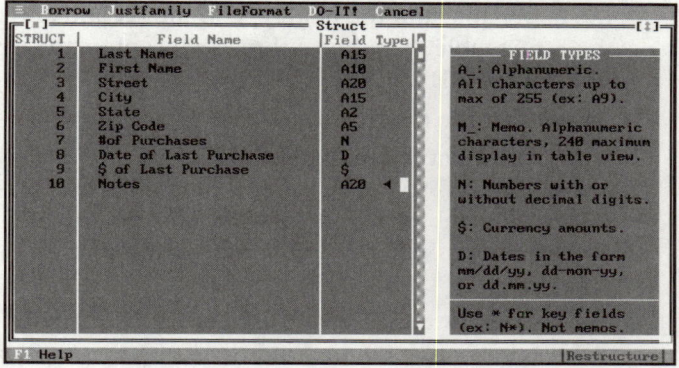

6. When you have completed the table structure, you must tell Paradox you are done by pressing [F2]; or press [F10] to activate the menu bar and select **D**O-IT! from the menu; or move the mouse pointer to the menu bar and click **D**O-IT!. Paradox then returns to the desktop.

You have now completed creating your first table. You have saved the Customer table, and it is ready for you to use.

Adding Customer Information

To enter data into the Customer table, you must retrieve the table from your hard disk. To access the Customer table, perform the following steps:

1. Select **M**odify from the menu bar. Press [M], or move the mouse pointer to the **M**odify option and click once.

2. Select **D**ataEntry from the **M**odify pull-down menu by pressing [D], or by choosing **D**ataEntry with the mouse and clicking.

3. Enter the name of the table, **Customer**, into the text box in the displayed dialog box and press [↵Enter].

   If you do not remember the table name that you require, pressing [↵Enter] or clicking the list box with the mouse displays a list of all the available tables. Choose the table and then press [↵Enter].

Designing the Customer Database

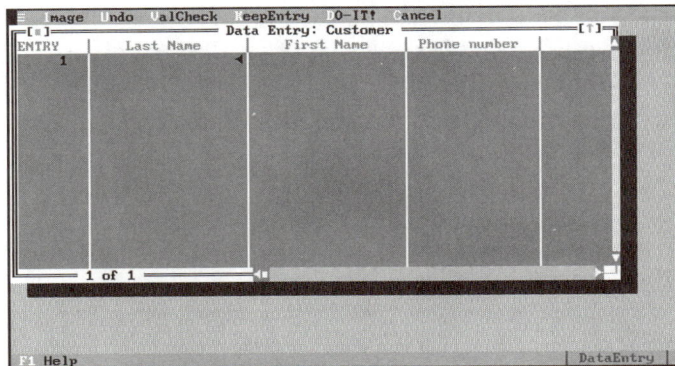

This is the DataEntry table for Customer.

Notice that the table name is displayed at the top of the table window. The name is displayed as Data Entry: Customer. This is because the **D**ataEntry option creates a temporary DataEntry table. This prevents you from accidentally altering an existing record. When you have completed entering the new records, Paradox automatically adds the new records to the Customer table.

4. Type the last name of your first customer, **MEZEJEWSKI**, and then press ⏎Enter.

   You have completed the first field, and the cursor is now in the First Name field.

5. Now type the following information into the remaining fields, pressing ⏎Enter after each entry:

First Name	**PIERRE**
Street	**3434 N. BUGSY RD**
City	**VANCOUVER**
State	**WA**
ZIP Code	**98600**
# of Purchases	**2**
Date of Last Purchase	**2/10/92**
$ of Last Purchase	**100**
Notes	**VALENTINES/PERFUME!!**

49

Getting Started

For a currency field like $ of Last Purchase, enter a whole dollar amount (like $100.00) as **100**. Paradox will supply the decimal place. Do not enter the dollar sign.

If you attempt to enter too many characters, Paradox beeps at you. Paradox also beeps if you try to enter letters into a number, currency, or date field.

When you press ↵Enter after finishing the last field, Notes, Paradox moves the cursor down one row and back to the first field.

Paradox has accepted your entry and is ready for the second record.

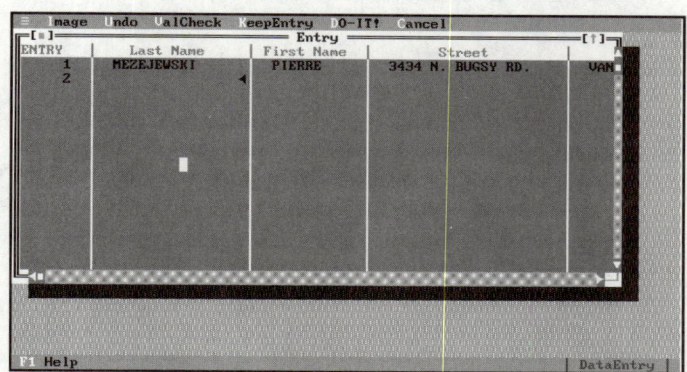

6. Now repeat steps 4 and 5, entering the data that follows:

Last	**PALMROSE**	**CHASTAIN**	**JACOBY**	**AMBROSE**
First	**ZENA**	**IVAN**	**HOMER**	**MONIQUE**
Street	**654 W. MAIN ST.**	**PO BOX 23434**	**9933 WALNUT**	**34598 SE 255TH AVE.**
City	**WASHOUGAL**	**CAMAS**	**PORTLAND**	**VANCOUVER**
State	**WA**	**WA**	**OR**	**WA**
Zip	**98666**	**98654**	**97299**	**98622**
#/Purch	**2**	**3**	**1**	**4**
Date	**12/1/91**	**12/15/91**	**2/1/92**	**1/10/92**
$/Purch	**220**	**75**	**50**	**450**
Note	**GARDENING TOOLS**	**NONE**	**PERFUME**	**GILDED PICTURE FRAME**

7. Now use the Paradox standard data-entry form by pressing the Form toggle, F7. Use the form to enter the remaining records into the table:

Designing the Customer Database

Last	**RABBIT**	**SKITZ**	**LIBBOWITZ**
First	**JULIE**	**MOLLY**	**ELIZABETH**
Street	**1312 W. RASPBERRY LN**	**312 E. SANDBOX WAY**	**459 N. SPANIEL RUN**
City	**WASHOUGAL**	**PORTLAND**	**DOGPATCH**
State	**WA**	**OR**	**WA**
ZIP	**98655**	**97211**	**98752**
#/Purch	**2**	**1**	**6**
Date	**2/14/92**	**12/15/90**	**2/29/92**
$/Purch	**150**	**225**	**85**
Note	**COAT**	**NECKLACE**	**GILDED PICTURE FRAME**

Again, press [↵Enter] after you complete each field. When you press [↵Enter] after the last field, a new blank form is displayed.

If you make an error in a field, use the arrow keys to move to the field, and then erase the entry with [←Backspace]. Enter the correct information. You can move from record to record with [PgUp] or [PgDn].

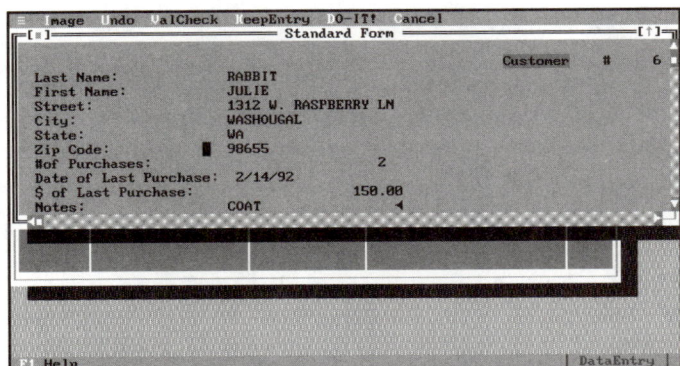

This is the completed Paradox Standard form.

8. When you are finished entering records, press [F2], or select **D**O-IT! from the menu bar.

   The records are automatically added to the Customer table. As Paradox completes this process, you see the following message:

   ```
   Adding records from Entry to Customer...
   ```

51

Getting Started

When Paradox has completed the adding process, the data will be saved on your disk. The Entry table is removed from the desktop and replaced with a view of the Customer table.

Paradox has completed adding the new records from the Entry table to the Customer table. Your screen should be similar to this.

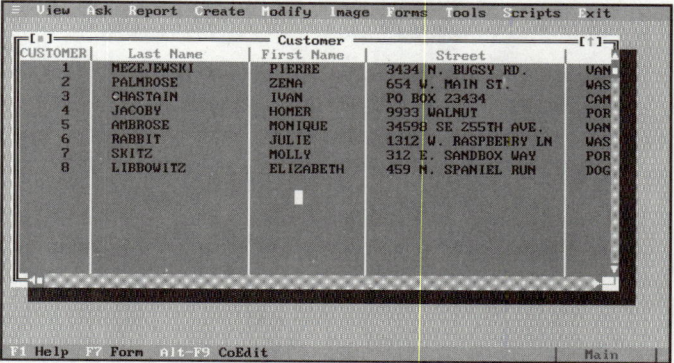

To clear the image from your screen, press F8. You now should have a blank Paradox desktop.

Asking Questions about Your Data

Paradox enables you to query your tables so you can extract specific information from them. Using the Paradox Query By Example (QBE), you can find a specific customer's record or a certain group of customers that meets criteria that you give.

For example, in the Customer table you just created, you have customers who live in two different states. If you want to extract just the customers who live in one of the states, you can use the Paradox query. To list all of your customers who live in the state of Washington, do the following:

1. Select **A**sk from the menu bar.
2. Enter **Customer** into the text box. Press ↵Enter. Paradox displays a blank Query form. The Query form displays all the fields that are contained in the Customer table.

Designing the Customer Database

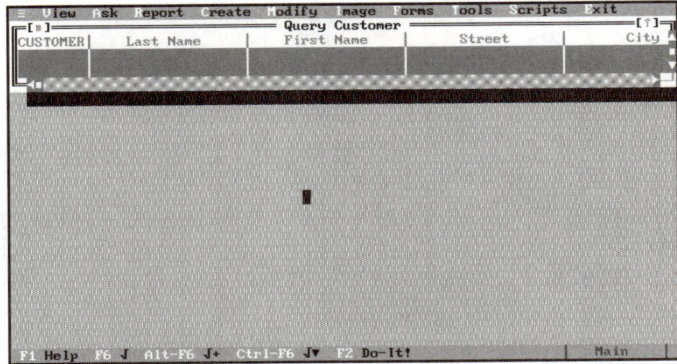

Here, you see the Query form displayed. Notice the name of the table/form is Query Customer.

See the new **F**-key choices displayed on the status bar at the bottom of the screen. These are described in table 2.3.

Table 2.3
Query Function Keys

Key	Symbol Displayed	Definition
F6	✔	Selects field to be included in the Answer table.
Alt-F6	✔+	Selects field to be included in the Answer table and includes duplicate values.
Ctrl-F6	✔▼	Selects field to be included in the Answer table and sorts the field in descending order.

3. Move the cursor to the Last Name field and press F6. Notice the check mark in the column.
4. Move the cursor to the First Name field and press F6.
5. Move the cursor to the State field and type **WA**.
6. Press F2, or use the mouse pointer and click Do-it! on the status bar.

    The message Processing query... is displayed in the message box.

53

Getting Started

2   You now see the Answer table displayed under the Query form with all of the customers who live in the state of Washington. Notice that the Answer table is sorted by the first field.

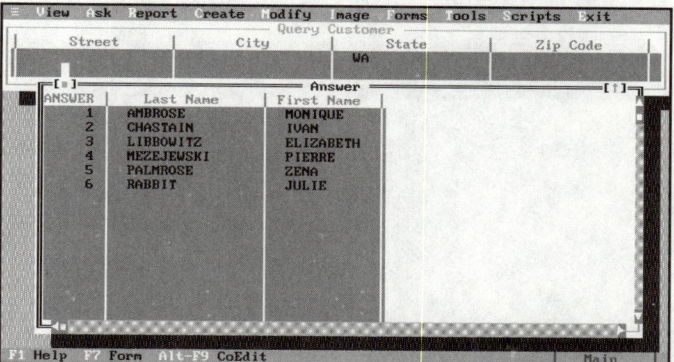

7. Press [Alt]-[F8] to clear all windows or images from the desktop.

   The table resulting from the Query process is automatically named Answer by Paradox. When the table is displayed, you can view the data using the arrow keys and the scroll bars to move the cursor to various fields.

You also can use several types of comparison operators with QBE. For example, if you want to search for all customers who have not bought from you since January 1, 1991, you can do the following:

1. Select **A**sk from the menu bar.
2. Enter **Customer** into the dialog text box. Press [↵Enter].
3. Move the cursor to the Last Name field and press [F6]. The check mark appears in the column.
4. Move the cursor to the First Name field and press [F6].
5. Move the cursor to the Date of Last Purchase field and press [F6]. Then type in **<1/1/91** and press [F2], or select Do-it! from the status bar with the mouse.

The single customer who has not bought anything since before 1/1/91 is displayed in the Answer table.

Sorting the Information

Generally, you will enter records into the table as you get new customers. Since Paradox can find a customer, or any other record, no matter what order the table is in, you do not need to order or sort a table. However, if you are

54

Designing the Customer Database

searching or browsing your data on the screen, you will want to be able to sort the records in some manner. Paradox enables you to sort a table on any field or combination of fields that you require.

Using the Customer table, follow these steps to sort by customer last name:

1. Press **Alt**-**F8** to clear any images from the desktop.
2. Now select **M**odify **S**ort from the menu bar.
3. Type **Customer** into the text box, and press **⏎Enter**.
4. Paradox gives you the option to sort to the **S**ame table or to sort to a **N**ew table. If you select **N**ew, you will have two tables after the sort function is complete. For this example select **S**ame.
5. You now see the Sort Questionnaire displayed. Type **1**, entering it next to Last Name.

   This tells Paradox that you want to sort the table by this field first, in alphabetical order.

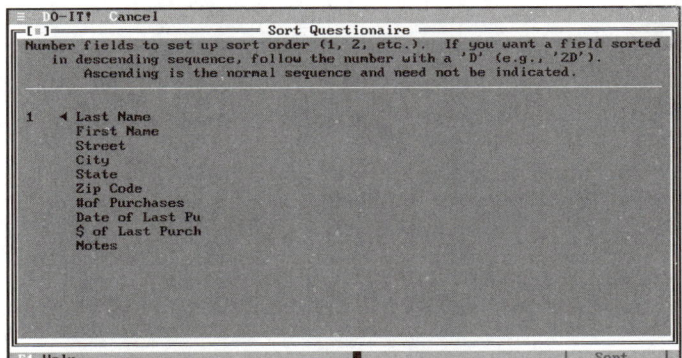

This is the completed Sort Questionnaire.

6. Press **F2**, or select **D**O-IT! from the menu bar.

   The message Sorting... is displayed in the message box while Paradox completes the sort operation.

55

Getting Started

This is the Customer table sorted by last name.

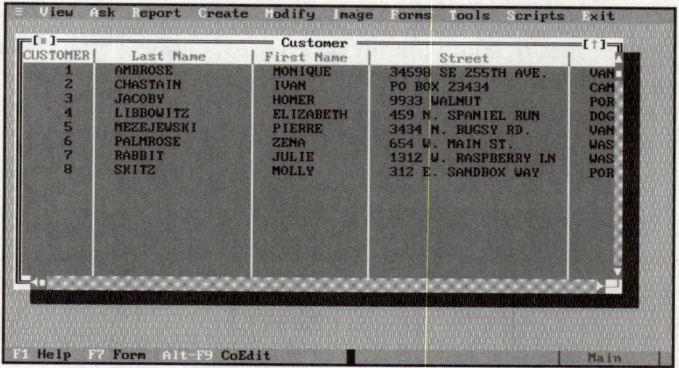

Printing a Report

Paradox has the capacity to print an Instant Report of a table you have displayed. This report is a tabular report, meaning that it prints your table, starting with the first field and going across to the last field, and includes all records. Needless to say, your Customer table will not fit on standard 8 1/2-by-11-inch paper in its current form.

To print a report that includes the customer's last name, first name, city, and state, do the following:

1. Press Alt-F8 to clear the desktop of all windows.
2. Select **A**sk from the menu bar, and then choose the Customer table.
3. Fill in the query form by placing a check mark (pressing F6) in the Last Name, First Name, City, and State fields. Then press F2 to perform the query.
4. Now, to print your report, first be sure that you have paper loaded in the printer and that the printer is turned on. When you are ready to print, press Alt-F7.

Summary

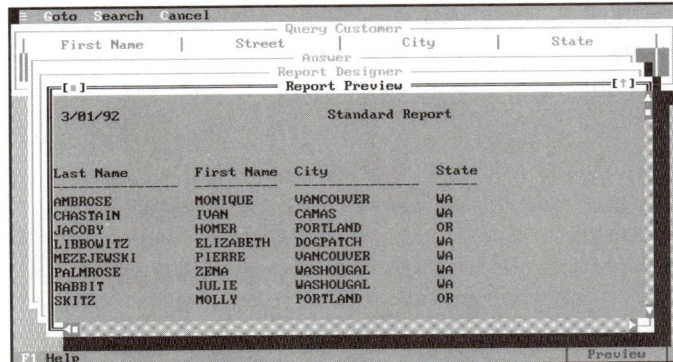

Here, you see the Customer information from the Answer table printed in alphabetical order.

Quitting Paradox

To exit Paradox, clear any windows from the desktop by pressing Alt-F8. This ensures that all necessary data is saved to the disk. Then select **E**xit from the menu bar. Choose **Y**es from the pull-down menu. You will see the message Leaving Paradox displayed in the message box, and then you will be back at the DOS prompt.

Summary

In this chapter, you learned how to start Paradox from DOS, and how to navigate through the menus. Remember, when you first start Paradox, the program opens onto a blank desktop.

Then, you learned how to use the System menu and control the size and shape of a window, and how to activate an inactive window. Those of you who have a mouse saw how easy it is to perform many functions with the mouse that otherwise can require many steps to perform. You saw how Paradox uses a wide variety of function key combinations to perform various tasks.

Finally, you created your own Customer database, creating the table structure, adding records, and then asking questions and printing a report from the data.

Getting Started

Specifically, you learned the following key points in this chapter about Paradox 4:

- To start Paradox from the DOS prompt C:\>, change to the PDOX40 directory and type **paradox**.
- To open an existing table, select **V**iew and enter the table name.
- To resize a window, place the mouse pointer on the Corner Resize icon and drag the window until it is the required size and shape. Or use the System menu and choose the **S**ize/Move command, then use the arrow keys or ⇧Shift-**arrow keys** to move or resize.
- To create a new table, select **C**reate, enter the table name, and fill in the field specifications. When you have completed that, press F2 **D**O-IT! to save and open the new table.
- To add records to a table, select **M**odify **D**ataEntry. Enter the new records into the Entry table. When completed, press F2 or choose **D**O-IT! from the menu. The records are added to the table.
- To select an individual record or a group of records, use a Query form. Select **A**sk, choose the table, and then fill in the Query form. Press F2 or select **D**O-IT!. The results are displayed in the Answer table.
- To print an Instant Report, open the table from which to print the report, and then press Alt-F7. A tabular report is sent to the printer.

In the next chapter, you will learn the details for planning and creating a table. You will create a table structure, learn relationships between tables, and borrow another table's structure and make changes to it.

3

Creating a Table

Paradox files all your data into records, and each record is stored in a table. Think of each record as a file folder, and then the folder is stored in a cabinet. As you saw in the sample customer table you created in the last chapter, Paradox can quickly find either a single record or a group of records.

In this chapter, you will learn the details of designing a table with Paradox. The table is the backbone of the Paradox database system. All other member objects of a Paradox family depend upon the table.

This chapter assumes that you have read the first two chapters and that you have worked through the sample customer database. You should know how to select menu items, using either the keyboard or the mouse.

Creating a new database

Designing the table

Saving a new table structure

Viewing a table

Deleting a table

Creating a Table

Key Terms in This Chapter

Table The table is the basic Paradox structure. All Paradox data is contained in a table and arranged in rows and columns. Most Paradox objects are based upon a table.

Record A record is contained within a table. The record is all the information about a single subject (for example, a customer) in a table. Records are arranged in rows.

Field Each field contains an item of information (for example, a customer's name) about the records. The field information is arranged in columns.

Table structure A table's definition. Includes the number of fields it contains, if any of the fields are key fields, the field types, and the order in which the fields occur.

Key field The field(s) that defines the sort order of a table and ensures that each record within a table is unique. You also can use a key field to link a table to other tables.

Borrow Process of using part or all of a table structure during the creation of a new table.

Standard Format Paradox uses by default when creating a table. Enables a table to recognize a memo field.

Compatible Format Paradox uses when creating a table to use with earlier versions of Paradox. This format does not recognize a memo field.

Creating a New Database

As you begin the design process for your Paradox database, think about all the information, or fields, you will need for each record. Paradox files your data into tables. Each table contains records, which are made up of fields. A Paradox table is similar in structure to a spreadsheet—all records are filed into rows, while fields are located in columns.

Creating a New Database

Before you create your new database, you should first plan the table. This may be a good time to sit down, get out a pad of paper, and ask yourself some questions, such as the following:

What information do I now keep, how is it used, how is it kept?

What problems am I now having with my information system?

Is it difficult to update or change records?

Am I having problems finding records?

Do I have a tough time consolidating information?

What information do I need from my data?

The answers to these questions and others you may think of will help you plan your table's structure.

Planning the Table Structure

As you plan the structure of your first table, look at the answers to the preceding questions. If you want to replace some of your paper files with your Paradox database, then you can borrow much of your table's structure from the forms you now use.

As you design your table, be thorough. Include all the necessary data, or fields, you will need. Try not to keep fields you do not use. Remember, you can always add or delete fields later if necessary.

Try to classify your data into types. For example, in the customer table you built in the last chapter, you used several types of data in the table, including name and address, information concerning purchases, and notes. You could divide this information into two tables: a name and address table, and a purchases table. With two tables, you could perform sorts faster, because Paradox would not have to sort the purchase information along with the address. You also could keep more detailed information concerning the customer's purchases, and you would not have to manually update the information.

With Paradox's linking capability, you can tie two or more tables together using a common field. You can then use a multi-table form to update all the tables at the same time. Paradox query functions can extract information from multiple tables and provide you with many different reports.

For best results, place each table or group of tables in one directory. Because Paradox cannot list tables that are not located in the working directory, you

61

Creating a Table

will find it easier to organize your database system if you locate a related group together in the same directory. You can retrieve a table from another directory by typing the complete path and name of the table's directory in the text box of the Table Name dialog box.

Naming the Table

You will find that giving your table a name that suggests its purpose will make it much easier to find and use later. For example, the table names such as Customer, Invoice, Inventory, or Salary are more descriptive than Table1 and Table2.

Paradox requires you to follow these normal DOS conventions when naming a table:

- Use a maximum of eight characters, not including the file extension. Paradox will automatically add the file extension DB for you.
- The name can include letters, numbers, and special characters like $ and _.
- Do not use spaces or the characters ? or *. These characters are reserved by DOS.
- Do not use a name you have given another table. Using the same name will cause the new table to overwrite the existing table.

Paradox creates many temporary tables as you perform different operations. Using any of these table names will cause Paradox to overwrite your own table. Do not use these temporary table names. The temporary tables are:

 ANSWER

 CHANGED

 CROSSTAB

 DELETED

 ENTRY, ENTRY1, ENTRY2...

 FAMILY

 INSERTED

 KEYVIOL, KEYVIOL1, KEYVIOL2...

 PASSWORD

 PROBLEMS

 STRUCT

Paradox also creates several internal tables that are generally hidden from you and not accessible. Using any of these table names will also cause Paradox to overwrite your table. The internal tables are:

CHANTEMP

DELTEMP

INSTEMP

KVTEMP

PASSTEMP

PROBTEMP

RESTTEMP

SORTQUES

Designing the Table

In this chapter you will redesign the customer table you created in Chapter 2. This time you will design the customer table with the intention of linking it to other tables.

The table will include a linking field and a phone number field. The table will not include the purchases information. As you answer the questions about the data you have kept on customers and how you have used it, you will come to some decisions regarding the planning of your customer database.

Suppose that you have decided to create a single table in which to keep customers' names, addresses, and phone numbers. This table will contain an identifying field, or key field, that you can later use to link this table with other tables. Assigning the Customer Number field, the key field, will help alleviate the problem of not always finding the correct customer. Later, using Paradox's linking capabilities, you will be able to easily consolidate information about customers, orders, and inventory.

To begin the process of creating a new customer table, first do the following:

1. Select **C**reate from the menu bar by pressing [C] or clicking with the mouse.

2. Enter the name you want to give the table. For this example, type **Cust1**.

Creating a Table

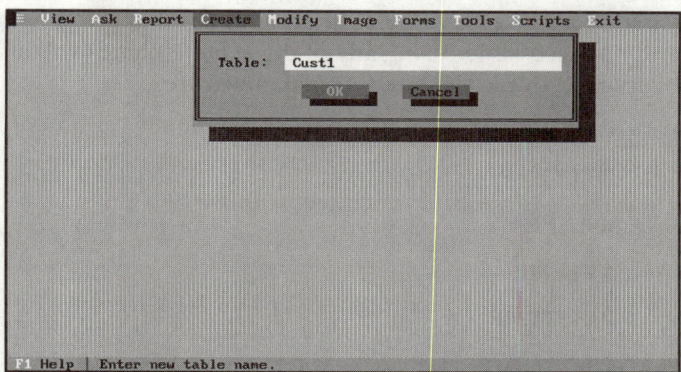

The Table Name dialog box contains the name for the new table.

3. Press ↵Enter or click **OK** with the mouse to have Paradox accept the new table name.

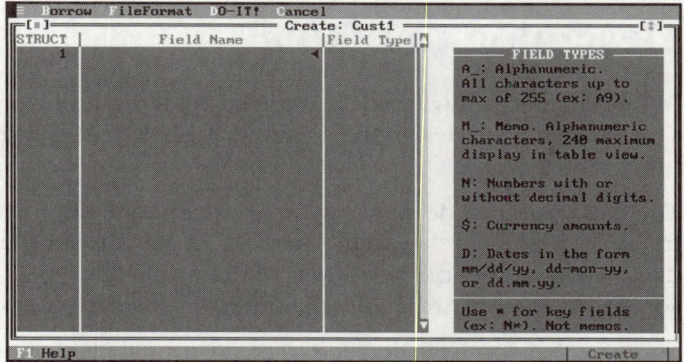

Paradox displays the Struct table Create:Cust1, which you will use to create the structure for your table.

Entering Field Names

The names you enter into the Field Name column in the Struct table will become your field names in the new table, Cust1. If you keep the following rules in mind as you create your field names, you will help simplify your database:

- Keep the name short but descriptive of the field's contents.
- A field name can be a maximum of 25 characters.
- A field name cannot start with a blank space. In other words, do not press the space bar before typing anything else.

Designing the Table

- You can use two or more words for a field name, but again—no more than 25 characters for the entire name, not each word.
- You cannot duplicate a field name within the same table—adding spaces at the end will not make the names different.
- You can use any printable character with the exception of these characters:

    double quotation marks ""

    square brackets [ ]

    braces { }

    the number sign by itself #

    parentheses ( )

    the combination of minus sign with right arrow –>

- You should not make a field name the same as a Paradox temporary table name. These temporary tables are listed in the section "Naming the Table" earlier in this chapter.

Now that you know all the Dos and Don'ts about field naming, follow these steps to name your first field for the Cust1 table:

1. Type the first field name into the Field Name block in row 1. This is the default location for the cursor when the Struct table is opened. The first field is named Cust #.
2. Press ⏎Enter to move to the next column, Field Type.

    For those of you using a mouse, you can move the mouse pointer to the Field Type column and click. The cursor moves to that field.

You are now ready to specify the field type and size.

Specifying Field Type and Size

The Paradox field type enables you to specify both the type of data a field can contain and, in some cases, the amount or length of the data.

To ensure the integrity of your data, speed up some queries, and enable you to calculate totals on some types of data, each field must have a field type. Paradox cannot distinguish on its own what type of data you have entered without the field type code. Paradox also uses the field type code to format your data. When you enter dates, for example, Paradox formats them using the default date format you selected when you installed Paradox. For example, if you type the date 1/1/92, Paradox displays the date as 1/01/92. You can

65

Creating a Table

override the default setting by choosing an alternate format with the **I**mage **F**ormat **D**ate command.

Notice the box labeled FIELD TYPES on the right-hand side of the Struct table. This box gives you a short explanation of the most common field types; it does not include the special data types of **S**hort number, **B**inary, and **U**nknown. The choices of field types are listed in table 3.1.

Table 3.1
Field Types

Field Type	Description
A*n*	Alphanumeric; 1–255 characters
M*n*	Memo; 1–240 characters
N	Number field
$	Currency field
D	Date field
S	Short number field
B	Binary field
U	Unknown data type, or not elsewhere defined

Replace the *n* in **A***n* and **M***n* with a number for the field length. Most of these field types have special uses. If you want to use a field to calculate a total, you will have to designate that field either a $ (currency) or an N (number) field. If you want to refer to a date or a date so many days in the future, you will have to use a D (date) field. Assigning field types with Paradox is easy. The following is a listing and explanation of the field type choices:

Table 3.2
Explanation of Field Types

Field Type	Explanation
Alphanumeric	To choose this field type, press [A] and type the length of the field. An alphanumeric field can measure up to 255 characters in length. Choose a field length that will fit the longest entry you will place into the field. A field type of A15 tells Paradox

66

Designing the Table

Field Type	Explanation
	that the field is alphanumeric with a maximum length of 15 characters. The alphanumeric field can contain any letters, numbers, other keyboard characters, and most ASCII characters. Some examples of valid entries in an alphanumeric field are:
	Zachary, the wonder dog
	March 24th, 1953
	#14xy9 & Z28
Memo	A memo field is similar to an alphanumeric field in all ways except these two: an alphanumeric field is fixed in length, while a memo field is not; and an alphanumeric field can be used as a key field, while a memo field cannot. When you designate a field as a memo field, press M, and then enter the number of characters you want to be displayed in the field. You can display up to 240 characters. This is not the maximum length of the field—it is the initial number of characters that is displayed when you view the table. The memo fields for a single table are limited to a maximum total size per table of 64M.
Numbers	If you want a field to contain only numbers and you want to perform calculations, use the number field type. Press N to designate a field as a number field. Paradox can display a number field of up to 15 significant digits. If a number is longer than that, Paradox will display the number using scientific notation. Paradox displays numbers in a number field without separators, or commas, and indicates a negative number with a – (minus) sign preceding it. Valid entries into a Paradox number field are:
	150000
	150.1

continues

67

Creating a Table

Table 3.2 Continued

Field Type	Explanation
	.15
	−150.1
	Note: Although it may seem natural to use the number field designation for ZIP Codes, it is not recommended. The number field will not display, nor store, leading 0 (zeros). If you use ZIP+4 codes, number fields will not allow you to enter the dash between the codes. Using the alphanumeric field type gives you greater flexibility when using ZIP Codes. With this field type, Paradox will display leading 0s. Also, you can use foreign postal codes.
Currency	A currency field is a number field with special formatting characteristics. To specify a field as a currency field, press $. When performing calculations, Paradox treats a currency field the same as a number field. A currency field is displayed with whole number separators, or commas, and with two decimal places. Negative numbers are displayed in parentheses. You need not type in the $ sign when entering numbers into a currency field. While Paradox displays only two decimal places, numbers are still stored with up to 15 significant digits. The following are valid currency entries:
	150000
	150.1
	.15
	−150.1
	150.016
	Paradox displays the last number as 150.02, but will use the actual number 150.016 in any calculations.

Designing the Table

Field Type	Explanation
Date	A date field is used for date information. To designate a field as a date field, press D. You can enter any valid date between January 1, 100, to December 31, 9999. If you use dates that do not fall within the 20th century, be sure to include the full year. Paradox uses the current version of the Gregorian calendar. Paradox also correctly handles leap years and leap centuries. If you attempt to enter an invalid date, such as February 31, 1992, Paradox will display an error message. Paradox can use the following formats to display dates in tables: 1/31/92 31-Jan-92 31.01.92 92.01.31
Short number	Short number fields are special number fields that can contain only whole numbers between –32,767 and 32,767. The primary use of a short number field is to conserve disk space. It is recommended that only advanced Paradox users use the short number field. To specify a short number field, press S.
Binary	Binary fields are also variable-length fields. These fields are used to hold special objects called Binary Large OBjects or BLOB's. If these fields are used, you cannot view them with the Paradox Editor. When a binary object is located in a field, you will see the word Blob.
Unknown	Unknown fields are fields Paradox creates when you import files Paradox does not recognize. You cannot use this field type when you design a table with the Create option.

Note: The memo, binary, and unknown fields cannot be used as key fields. The memo field will be discussed later in this chapter. If you require more

Creating a Table

information on short number, binary, and unknown fields, consult a more advanced book on Paradox, such as Que's *Using Paradox 4*.

In the preceding section, you named your field Cust #. Now you can specify the field type by following these steps:

1. Be sure that the cursor is located in the Field Type column. Press A to select the Alphanumeric field.
2. Enter the field length. For this field, enter 10.

The Struct table is shown here with the first field name and field type entered.

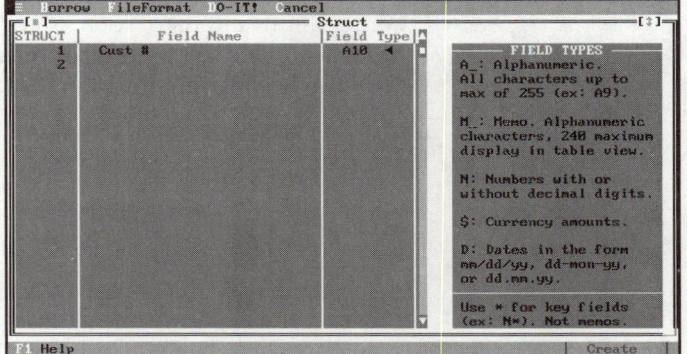

Designating Key Fields

You have seen the term *key field* several times. You may have also noticed that at the bottom of the FIELD TYPES examples in the preceding figure you can use an * (asterisk) to designate a key field.

A key field in a table is similar to the index in this book. To look up a specific subject, you can look in the index, find the subject, and then turn to the page indicated. A Paradox key is a combination of the key field or fields and the default sort order that you specified when loading Paradox. A Paradox key keeps a table sorted by the key field, alphabetically or numerically, depending upon the field type. A keyed table can also help speed up a query or search.

When you designate a single field as the key, you have created a *single key* table. As you create the structure of your table, the single key field must be the first field you create. A single key table will:

- Prevent you from entering duplicate values into the key field.
- Keep the table sorted in an ascending order based on the values in the key field. If your key field is a number field, then the table will be

Designing the Table

sorted 1, 2, 3.... If the key field is an alphanumeric field, then the table will be sorted 1, 2, 3, A, B, C, a, b, c....

The primary disadvantage of using a keyed table is the table can have a maximum record size of 1,350 bytes, while a nonkeyed table can have a maximum record size of 4,000 bytes. In a large table, you may find that some types of table editing may be slower due to Paradox sorting the table and updating the index. These disadvantages may be outweighed by the convenience of having a table sorted at all times. Multiple key tables are discussed in Chapter 9.

In your sample Cust1 table, you will designate the first field as a key field. To do this, type an * (asterisk) at the end of the field type, A10, you have entered, and then press ⏎Enter.

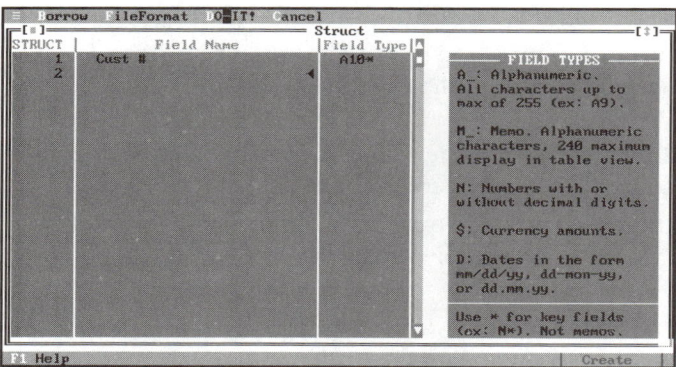

Here, you see the first field definition complete for the Cust1 table.

When you complete the definition for the field and press ⏎Enter, the cursor moves down to the next row and back over to the Field Name column.

Completing the new table definition is a simple process of entering a Field Name and Field Type for each field planned for the table. As already mentioned, be as complete as possible when planning your table; but remember, Paradox is a very forgiving program. You can always restructure your table at a later time, adding or deleting fields as needed, or changing field types. You will learn the limitations and cautions regarding restructuring a table later in Chapter 9.

Borrowing an Existing Table Structure

With Paradox, you can borrow another table's structure or field definitions when you are defining a new table. In Chapter 2, you built a table named

Creating a Table

Customer. The Customer table is similar in structure to the table you are creating now.

When you decide to borrow another table's structure, you will borrow the entire definition of the structure, but you will not borrow any of the data or records that currently belong to that table.

To borrow the structure of the Customer table from Chapter 2, do the following:

1. Place the cursor in the row where you want the borrowed fields to start.
2. Press F10 to activate the Struct menu.
3. Select **B**orrow from the menu by pressing B; or because the default when you activate the menu is **B**orrow, you can also press ↵Enter.

   For those of you using a mouse, you can use a shortcut for steps 1 and 2. Move the mouse pointer to the **B**orrow option and click either mouse button.
4. In the text box of the displayed Table Name dialog box, type the name of the table whose structure you intend to borrow.

   Remember, if you do not know the exact name of the table, press ↵Enter or click the mouse pointer on the list box to view the list of tables.

   For this example, type **Customer**.

You now see the Borrow dialog box completed.

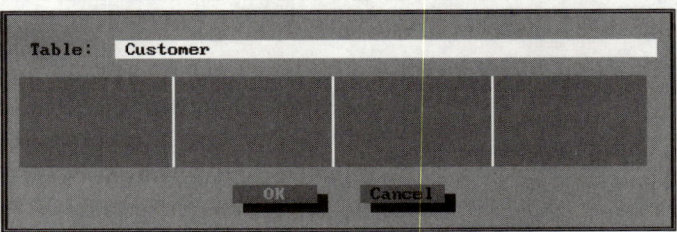

5. Press ↵Enter.

Designing the Table

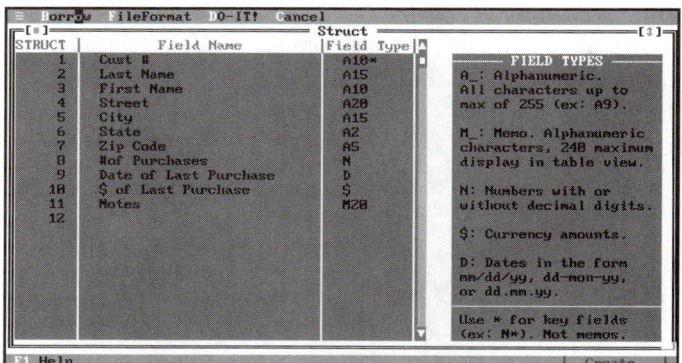

Now the borrowed field definitions are listed in the Struct table.

You will notice that the cursor appears in the first row of the Struct table. The next available empty field row is number 12, where you can place another field, if required.

Editing the Field Types

When creating a table structure—and often when borrowing another table's structure—you may decide that a field type needs to be altered, or edited. To change a field type, do the following:

1. Move the cursor to the Field Types column, and then down to the First Name row (the third row).
2. Press [+Backspace] once.

   You will notice that the cursor has moved to the left one position, and that the number 0 has been deleted.

3. Type the number **5**. The field type has now been changed from A10 to A15.
4. Move the cursor to the field type for Cust #.
5. Press [+Backspace] to delete the existing field type.
6. Type the new field type, **N**.

73

Creating a Table

First Name's field type has been changed from 10 characters to 15 characters wide, and Cust #'s type has been changed to Number.

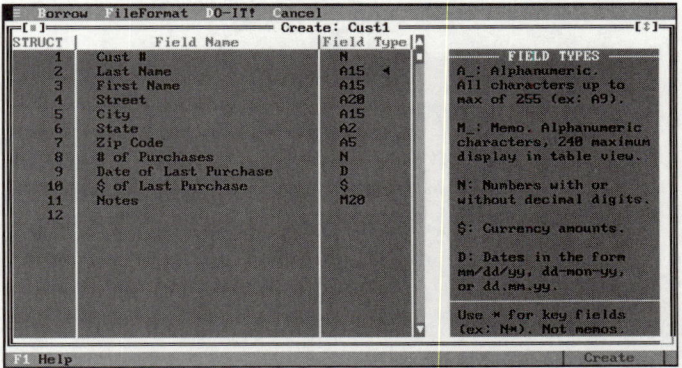

Editing Field Names

Editing a field name is very similar to editing a field type. You can simply use `Backspace` to erase the field name, and then retype the name; or you can use the Field View option.

To edit a field name, do the following:

1. Move the cursor to the Field Name column, and then down to the seventh row, Zip Code.

2. For this change, use the Field View option. To enter Field View, press `Alt`-`F5` or `Ctrl`-`F`.

You will notice that when using Field View, the cursor changes from a blinking dash to a large rectangle with a blinking dash.

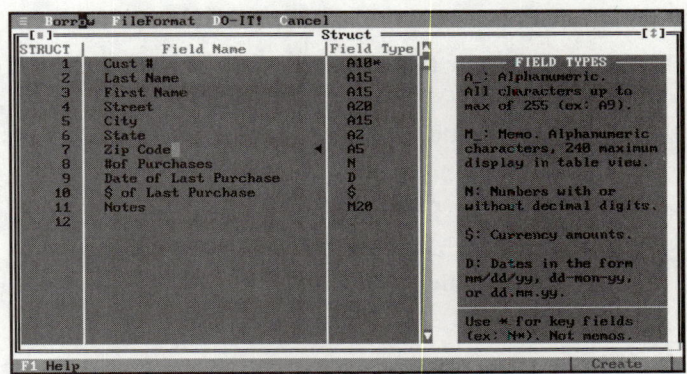

Designing the Table

3. Move the Field View cursor, using ←, so that the cursor is positioned just to the right of the letter p in Zip.
4. Type **/Postal** and press ↵Enter to exit from Field View.
5. Now move the cursor to the Field Type column. Press ←Backspace once.
6. Enter the new value, **10**, for the length. This value will enable you to enter longer ZIP+4 codes and foreign postal codes.

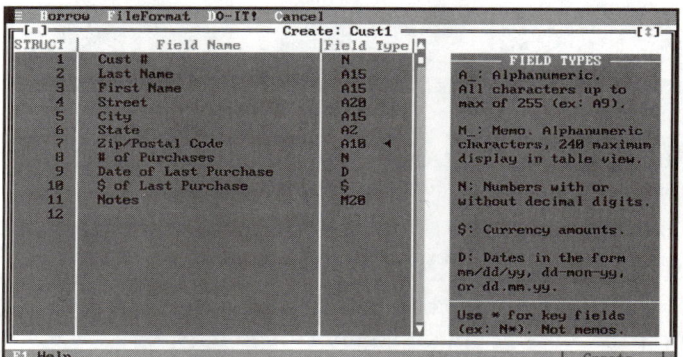

The new field name Zip/Postal Code has been entered.

Inserting Fields

As you create your field structure, you may want to move a field to a different location, or you may forget to enter a field. Using Paradox, you can insert additional fields between two existing fields.

To insert a field, do the following:

1. Move the cursor to Street (row 4) by pressing ↑.
2. Press Ins. Paradox opens a blank row above the cursor's present location.

75

Creating a Table

3

You now see the new field opened above the Street field.

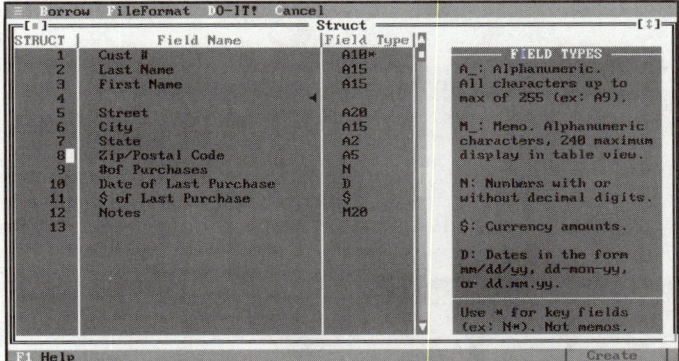

Notice that the Street field was located in row 4, and now is located in row 5. All fields from Street down have moved down one row.

3. Enter the new field definition. Type **Phone number** and press ↵Enter.
4. Enter the field type, **A12**, and press ↵Enter.

Because a phone number does not contain only numbers but also a hyphen and parentheses, a phone number field must be alphanumeric.

Here, you see the new Phone Number field complete in row 4.

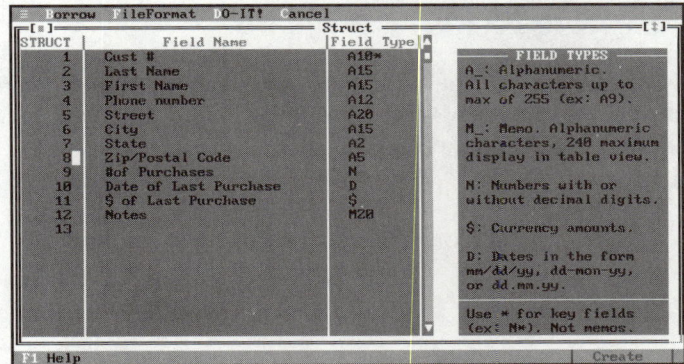

5. Now you will insert another field. Move the cursor to row 9.
6. Press Ins.
7. Type the new Field Name, **Country**, and press ↵Enter.
8. Type the Field Type, **A15**, and press ↵Enter.

76

Designing the Table

Deleting Fields

Often you will find that you may have duplicate or unneeded fields when you borrow another table's structure. Or, as you create a structure, you may decide that you do not need a field you have placed. Paradox enables you to delete a field definition from the Struct table.

To delete a field definition, do the following:

1. To delete a field, place the cursor on the field definition in any of the columns and press [Del].

    Because the cursor is currently located on row 10 in the Struct column, press [Del]. Notice that the field definition, # of purchases, has been deleted and that the three field definitions below have all moved up one row.

2. Press [Del] three more times.

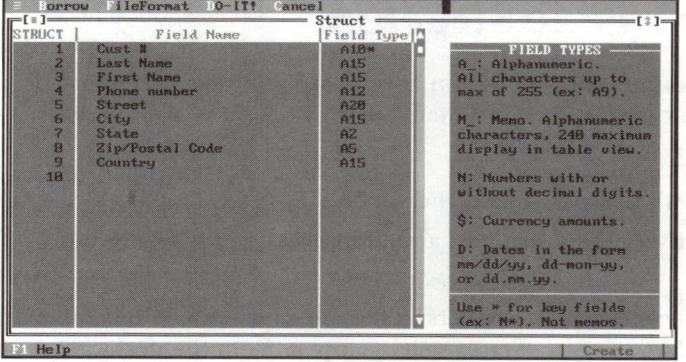

Your table definition should now look like this.

Using the FileFormat Command

Paradox can save a table structure in one of these two formats: Standard, which is the normal Paradox format, or Compatible, which can be used by earlier versions of Paradox. Paradox will automatically save the new table structure in Standard format. Paradox can read and use a Compatible table, but if you plan on using a table with an earlier version of Paradox, you must choose the Compatible format.

Earlier versions of Paradox do not understand the memo field. Therefore, if you create a table with a memo field, you must use the Standard format. Earlier versions of Paradox will not be able to read the table. If you must use a

Creating a Table

table in an earlier version of Paradox, do not use a memo field and make sure that you save the table in Compatible format.

To use the **F**ileFormat command, do the following steps:

1. Press `F10` to activate the menu bar.
2. Choose **F**ileFormat from the menu.
3. The default choice is Standard format; press `C` to choose the **C**ompatible option.

Again, if you plan on transferring the table into an earlier version of Paradox, you must use the **C**ompatible option.

If you transfer a table created in an earlier version of Paradox and want to add a memo field, then you will have to restructure the table, add the memo field, and then save the table, choosing the Standard format.

Saving a New Table Structure

As with most Paradox functions, when you have completed the table definition you must save it. You can save the Cust1 table using one of several methods:

- Press `F2`.
- Select **D**O-IT! with the mouse and click once.
- Press `F10` to activate the menu bar, and then press `D` to choose the **D**O-IT! option.

The message `Creating Cust1...` appears in the message area. When Paradox has completed the table, the Struct table will disappear from the desktop.

Viewing a Table

Now that you have completed your table, use the **V**iew command to see it. The **V**iew option enables you to browse through information or records without making any changes to them. The **V**iew command is an excellent way to show someone the records in your table, without taking the chance of saving accidental changes in the data.

To view your new Cust1 table, do the following:

1. Press `F10` to activate the menu.

Deleting a Table

2. Select the **V**iew option by either pressing <u>V</u>, or, because **V**iew is the default option, pressing <u>⏎Enter</u>.

   Remember, you can also select **V**iew with the mouse.

3. Enter the table name **Cust1** into the text box contained in the displayed dialog box.

4. Press <u>⏎Enter</u>.

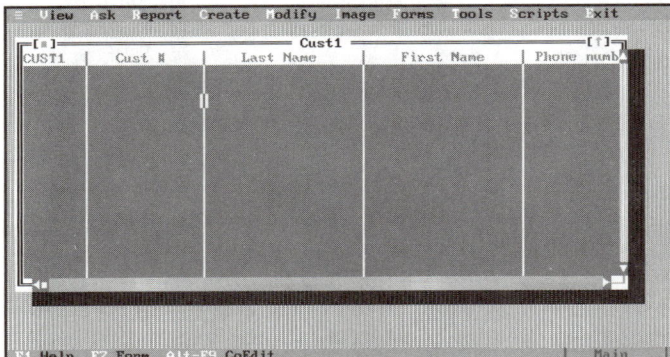

The new table Cust1 is displayed using the **V**iew option.

While you cannot edit your data, or in this case add new data to the blank table, you can use the window features discussed in Chapter 2.

You can maximize or restore the window, resize the window, and move the window. If you are viewing a table that contains data, the scroll bars will function. An empty table, like your new Cust1 table, is displayed with the cursor located in the far left field. You cannot move the cursor out of this field. Any attempt to do so results in Paradox beeping at you. After you enter records into the table, you can move the cursor within those records. Paradox does not enable you to move the cursor into a blank area.

Deleting a Table

When a table is no longer necessary, or if information is duplicated across tables, you will want to delete the table. Paradox enables you to delete tables easily. Remember that when you delete a table, you also delete its family members and the records contained in the table.

Creating a Table

To delete a table, do the following:

1. Select **T**ools from the Main menu bar.
2. Choose the **D**elete option from the cascading menu.

The Tools Delete menu appears.

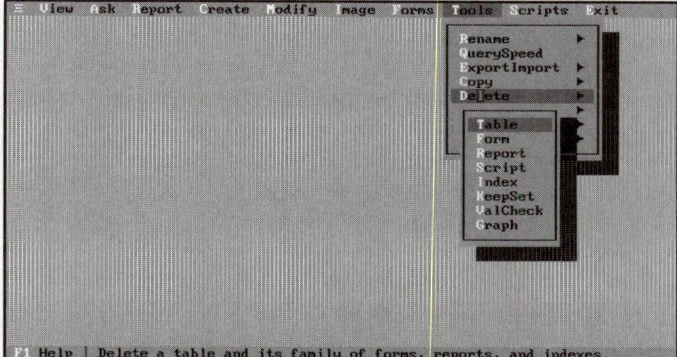

3. Select **T**able from the drop-down menu box. From this menu, you can delete most of the Paradox objects.
4. In the text box of the displayed Table Name dialog box, type the name of the table you want to delete. Type **Customer**.

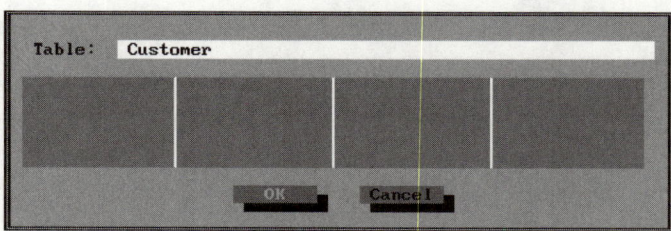

Here, you see the table name in the dialog box.

5. Press ⏎Enter.

Summary

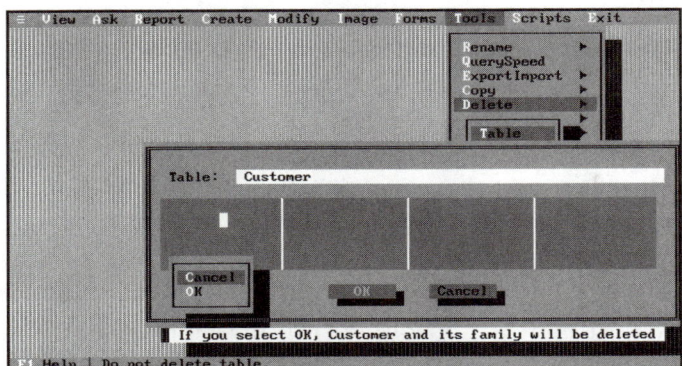

You now see the confirmation box displayed.

6. To delete the table and its associated family, select the **OK** option. To cancel the Delete command, select the **C**ancel option. Press ⓄO to delete the table.

   As Paradox deletes the table, you see the message `Deleting Customer table and its associated family...` displayed in the message box.

Deleting a table is a simple task. You should conduct such "house-cleaning" tasks on a routine basis. If you do not use certain tables, forms, graphs, and so on, you should delete them from your disk.

Summary

In this chapter, you learned how to create a new table in Paradox. You also learned about key fields, field types, and borrowing a table's structure.

Specifically, you learned the following key points about Paradox 4.0:

- ■ A table is made up of a structure of records contained in rows and fields contained in columns.
- ■ To plan a table's structure, you must know what data you need and what you want from your data.
- ■ To classify the data you want in a table, keep only a single data type, such as a name and address, in a single table.

Creating a Table

- Give a table a name that suggests its purpose, such as Customer or Vendors. You will be able to identify the table easier.
- Use field names that are descriptive of the contents of the field, such as Last Name or Address. You cannot use the same name twice in the same table.
- Use the field type specification to help classify and ensure the integrity of your data, by restricting some fields to a specific type of data.
- Use number and currency field types for fields that will be used in calculations.
- Specify key fields for use in sorting a table and provide a linking field to other tables. Use the key field to ensure that each record is unique within a table.
- Borrow the structure of an existing, similar table by using the **B**orrow option when in the Struct table.
- Edit field names and field types by using either `Backspace` and erasing the data and entering in new data, or by entering Field View by pressing `Alt`-`F5` or `Ctrl`-`F`, inserting your change, and deleting old data.
- Insert an additional field by moving the cursor to the required location and pressing `Ins` to open a blank row above the cursor.
- Delete a field by placing the cursor in any column of the field you want to remove and pressing `Del`.
- Use the **F**ileFormat command to save a table structure as a Compatible file format, enabling the table to be used by prior versions of Paradox.
- Use **D**O-IT! (or `F2`) to save the table structure.
- Use the **V**iew option on the Main menu to view, or look at, the new table.
- To delete a table or other Paradox object, use the **T**ools **D**elete option. To delete a table and its associated family, choose the **T**able option and then select the table you want to delete.

In the next chapter, you will learn to use the various Editing modes provided by Paradox, and to search for data, use the Undo feature, and resize, move, and rotate columns.

Adding, Editing, and Viewing Data with a Table

In this chapter you will begin to learn the nuts and bolts of using Paradox and your tables. Up to now, you have been preparing to enter your data.

You have learned how to make menu selections, and have toured the menus. You have created and entered data into a table, and then you learned to manipulate the table window—moving, resizing, and expanding—and use the scroll bars.

Then you created another table, each step and option explained. You are now familiar with the table, how it is displayed, and the various forms of data you can place into each field.

Working with tables in Edit mode

Working with tables in DataEntry mode

Using CoEdit mode

Using Paradox table images

Adding, Editing, and Viewing Data with a Table

In this chapter you will learn to add and edit records in each of the three modify modes available to you. You will then learn some additional ways to manipulate your table data.

Key Terms in This Chapter

Edit mode — The Paradox mode used for editing or changing records. You can also add records in Edit mode.

DataEntry mode — A specific mode that enables you to enter new records into a temporary table. The records are added to the target table when you have finished.

CoEdit mode — This mode enables you to share the table on a network system. Each user can make changes to the table, and Paradox will update each person's view of the table. When used with a keyed table, Paradox will check to ensure that a record is not duplicated before adding it to the table.

Field view — A special editing feature that enables you to edit field data using text editing features similar to a word processor.

Transaction log — A log kept by Paradox of all keystrokes performed during various editing sessions. The transaction log varies in capabilities depending upon the mode.

Working With Tables in Edit Mode

As mentioned in Chapter 3, Paradox prevents you from making accidental changes in a table by allowing you to make changes only while in Edit and CoEdit modes. The primary difference between these two modes is that Edit gives you exclusive rights to the table. In other words, no one else can use the table while you are editing it. In CoEdit mode, others can use and edit the table.

The primary purpose of Edit mode is to make an actual change to an existing record. While you can add new records using Edit mode, the process tends to be a little slower in keyed tables because Paradox tries to maintain the table index, and you run the very real risk of overwriting a record accidentally.

Working With Tables in Edit Mode

Using Edit Mode

You have two ways to enter Edit mode, depending on whether the table you want to edit is displayed upon the desktop or not. If the table is displayed, do the following:

   Press F9.

This action changes the mode from Main to Edit. The only obvious changes you will see are:

- The mode indicator window will change to Edit.
- The status bar will display a different set of options.
- The menu bar options will change.

If the table you want to edit is not currently displayed on the desktop, then do the following to display the table:

1. Press F10 to activate the menu bar.
2. Select the **M**odify option by pressing M or by moving the menu bar highlight to **M**odify and pressing Enter.

   Remember, if you are using a mouse, choose the **M**odify option with the mouse pointer and click once.

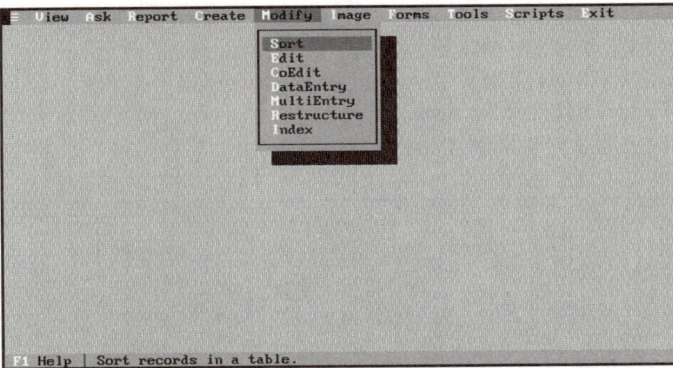

The Modify pull-down menu is displayed.

3. Choose the **E**dit option from the pull-down menu.
4. Select the table you want to edit by typing the name into the text box in the Edit dialog box, or by clicking the list box with the mouse or pressing Enter to display the list of available tables.

   For this example, type the table name **Cust1** to edit and press Enter.

85

Adding, Editing, and Viewing Data with a Table

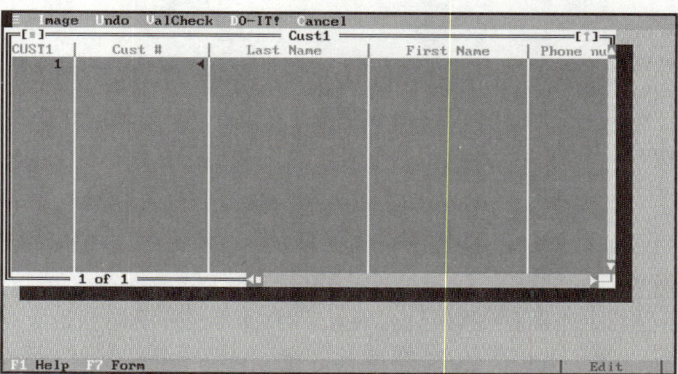

The Cust1 table is shown here in Edit mode.

The table is displayed and ready for you to add records or to edit it. In this case, because the table has just been created and, therefore, contains no records, the cursor is located in the first field, in row 1.

Adding Records

Adding records in Edit mode is a matter of entering the information into each field and pressing ⏎Enter to move from field to field.

Caution: If a table already contains a number of records, be careful when adding or editing records. It is easy to accidentally move the cursor up or down a row and edit the wrong set of records. One way around this potential problem is to press F7 and use the Standard form to enter your records. With this form, you can easily tell if you are using the correct record or not.

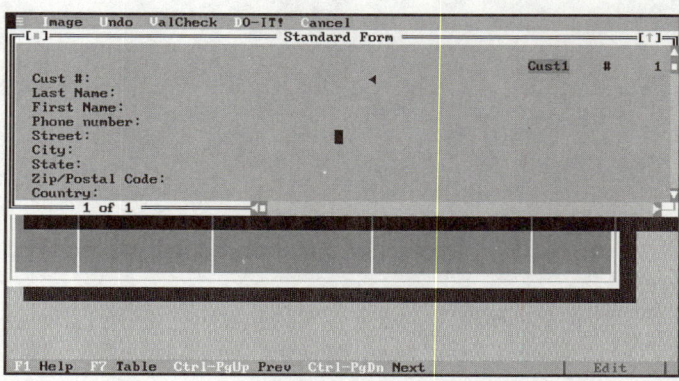

Here, you see the Standard form for table Cust1, record 1.

Working With Tables in Edit Mode

Notice that the cursor is located on the same line as the first field, Cust #. The cursor is automatically placed at the beginning, or forward, position in the first field. The left arrow indicates the end of the field. Unlike in Table View, you cannot see how large a field is unless the cursor is currently located in the field. As you move the cursor down the form, you will notice that the cursor stays in the same horizontal line, while the end marker moves, indicating the different sizes of each field.

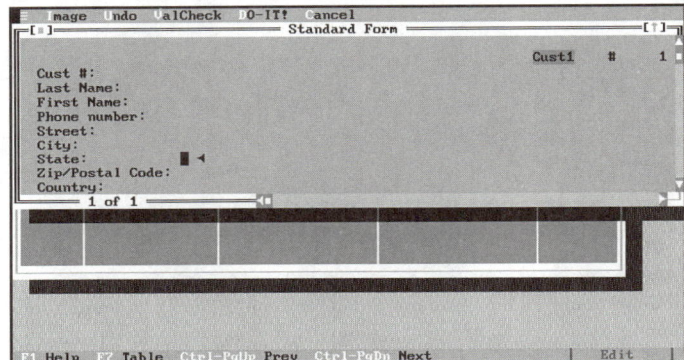

The cursor is located in the State field. Notice the difference in the location of the field end marker compared to the previous figure.

If you are using a mouse to move from field to field, remember that all the fields start at the same position horizontally and may vary in size. If you want to move to a field and you click the mouse pointer outside the field box, nothing will happen. You must place the mouse pointer within the field you want to enter before the cursor will move to that location.

For the next part of this section, you will continue to use the Standard form. To add a record to the table using the form, do the following:

1. Type the customer number (Cust #) **100** and press ⏎Enter.
2. The cursor moves down to the next field. Enter the customer's last name. Type **Blackadder** and press ⏎Enter.
3. The cursor is now located in the First Name field. Type **Edward** and press ⏎Enter.
4. Now enter Edward Blackadder's phone number. Type **503-255-5555** and press ⏎Enter.
5. Enter the street address. Type **7686 NW Shalimar Way** and press ⏎Enter.
6. Enter the city. Type **Portland** and press ⏎Enter.

87

Adding, Editing, and Viewing Data with a Table

Do not enter a comma after the city name. When you create a report, you will enter the comma on the report form.

7. Now enter the state, using the two-letter abbreviation. Type **OR** and press ⏎Enter.
8. Enter the zip/postal code. Type **97200** and press ⏎Enter.
9. Finally, enter the country. Type **USA**.

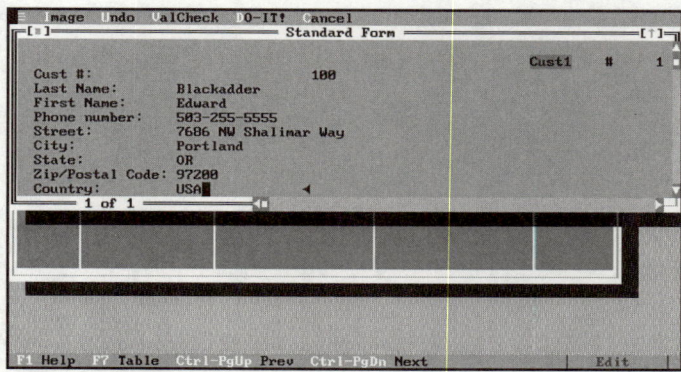

The customer form is now completed.

10. Press ⏎Enter.

    Notice that when you press the Enter key, the customer is accepted and a new blank form is displayed. The form is numbered 2.

11. Press F7 to return to Table View.

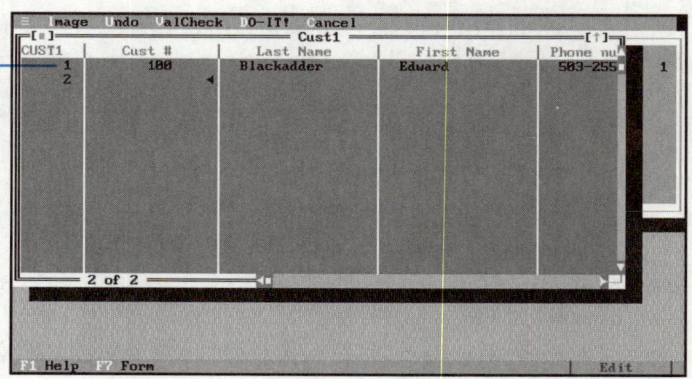

The Cust1 table is now displayed with record 1 inserted.

88

Working With Tables in Edit Mode

Notice that the table is displayed in the foreground and the form is still displayed in the background, or underneath the table.

Now you will use the Table View to enter another customer. The cursor is located in the first field of record 2. To enter the next customer, do the following:

1. Enter the customer number. Type **101** and press `Enter`.
2. Enter the customer's last name. Type **Phillpott** and press `Enter`.
3. Enter the customer's first name. Type **Phillip** and press `Enter`.
4. Enter Phillip's phone number. Type **503-999-9901** and press `Enter`.

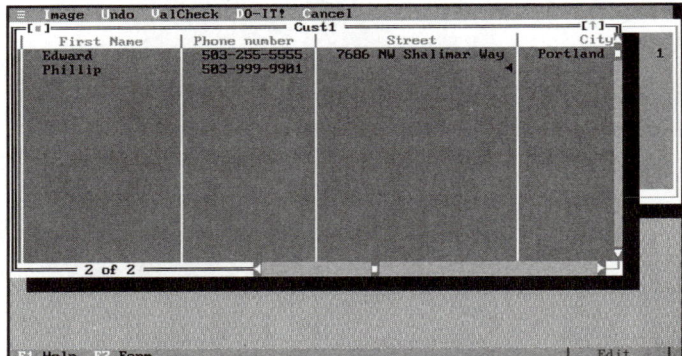

The Cust1 table is too wide to display all the fields in one screen. The table, therefore, scrolls to the right.

You will notice that when you press the Enter key, the table shifts to the left. The Record Number, Cust #, and Last Name fields all move out of view. Notice also that the bottom scroll bar's position box has moved from the far left end to about one-third of the way across the bar.

5. Now enter the street address. Type **Route 1, Box 48** and press `Enter`.
6. Enter the city. Type **Corbett** and press `Enter`.
7. Enter the state, using the two-letter abbreviation. Type **WA** and press `Enter`.
8. Enter the zip/postal code. Type **98633** and press `Enter`.
9. Enter the country. Type **USA** and press `Enter`.

After you press the Enter key in step 9, the cursor moves back to the first field and to the next available record.

89

Adding, Editing, and Viewing Data with a Table

Using Field View

As with any data entry function, whether using a database program or a pencil and paper, mistakes are made sometimes. Generally, when using Paradox, you can use ⬅Backspace and retype the information to replace the erroneous data.

Paradox gives you another method for correcting errors. This alternative method is Field View. Field View is helpful when you must correct a long entry that contains a minor error. Using Field View is similar to correcting a mistake within a word processing program.

Now that your cursor has moved to the Cust # field in record 3, you may notice that you misspelled Phillip Philpott's name. To correct it, do the following:

1. Move the cursor to the field in which you will make the correction by pressing ↑ once, and then → once. The cursor is now located at the end of the last name Phillpott.
2. To enter Field View you can:

   Press Alt-F5, or press Ctrl-F.

   Or

   Move the mouse pointer to the field to be corrected and double-click the mouse button.

   You will notice that the cursor changes from a blinking dash to a large block in reverse video.
3. Press ← until the cursor block is located on either of the *l*'s.

Here, you see the Field View cursor located on the second *l*.

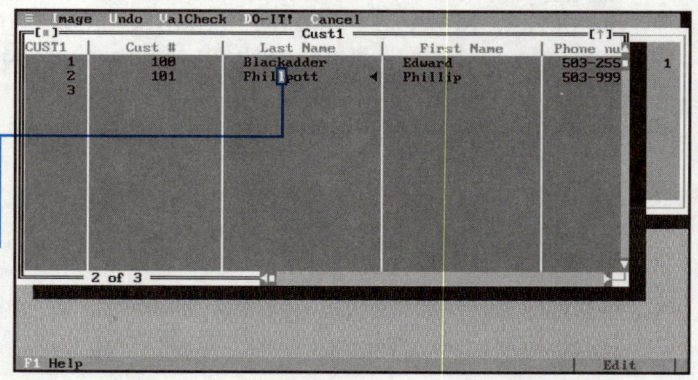

Working With Tables in Edit Mode

4. Press Del. The *l* is removed. The cursor is now located on the letter *p*.
5. To exit Field View, press Enter.

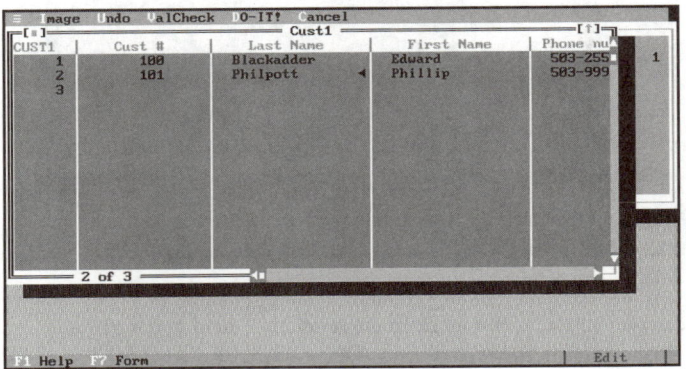

The field is corrected, and the cursor is now in Normal mode.

Using Undo

Paradox understands that mistakes sometimes happen, and for that eventuality Paradox maintains a transaction log of all changes you have made during an Edit or CoEditing session. Each transaction begins when you enter a record and either create the record or make a change to the record. The transaction ends when you leave the record.

To understand better how the transaction log works, do the following:

1. Move the cursor to record 3 and the Cust # field. Type the number **1** and press Enter.
2. Type the number **2** in the Last Name field and press Enter.
3. Type the number **3** in the First Name Field.
4. Now move the cursor down one row and type the numbers **4**, **5**, and **6** into the first three fields of record 4, and move the cursor down one row to record 5.

91

Adding, Editing, and Viewing Data with a Table

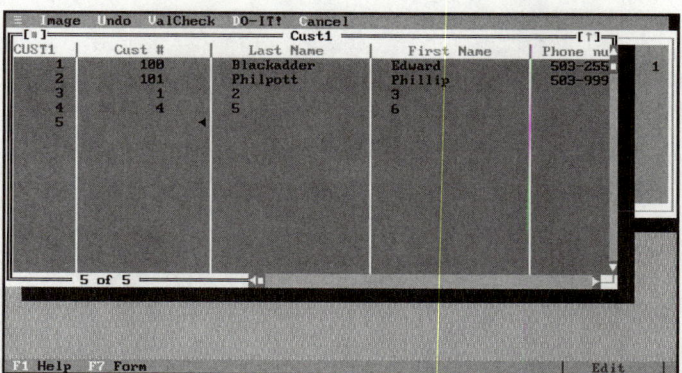

Your screen should now look like this.

5. Now move the cursor to the Cust # field in record 3, and type the number 7. The entry in this field is now 17. Press [↵Enter] and add the number 8 so that the Last Name field is 28. Press [↵Enter] and add the number 9 so that the First Name field is 39. Press [↓] three times so that the cursor is located in the Cust # field of record 6.

Several individual transactions have occurred. To understand how the Undo feature works, you must understand how the transactions have been recorded. The Undo command will reverse, or undo, each of your transactions, beginning from the one you just completed through the very first action you did upon starting the Editing session. In this section on Undo, your transaction log has the following transactions recorded:

1. Created record number 3, and made three entries.
2. Created record number 4, and made three entries.
3. Created record number 5, and made no entries.
4. Made three corrections to record number 3.
5. Created record number 6, and made no entries.

Working With Tables in Edit Mode

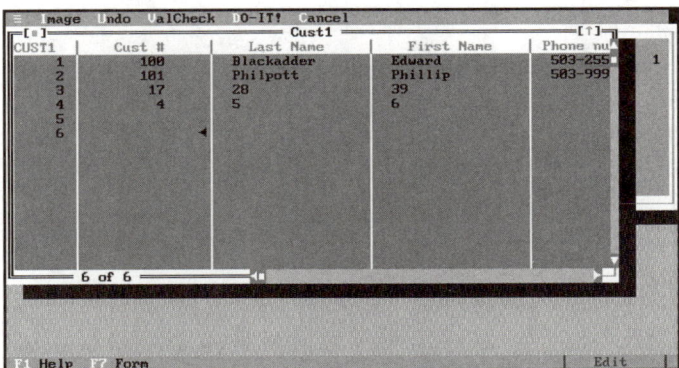

Your screen should look like this.

If you have now decided that the corrections made to record 3 were in error, you can use the **U**ndo command and undo the changes. In doing so, you will first have to undo transaction 5 before you can undo transaction 4. Or you can move the cursor to record 3 and manually change each of the fields. Since record 6 is empty, erasing it does no harm, nor does it cause you additional work. To undo the changes made to record 3, perform the following steps:

1. Press F10 to activate the menu bar.

2. Choose the **U**ndo option by pressing U, or by moving the menu bar highlight to the **U**ndo option and pressing ↵Enter.

   Again, with a mouse, choose the menu option with the mouse pointer and click once.

3. The **U**ndo pull-down menu is displayed. Select **Y**es to undo the last change made, or select **N**o to return to the menu bar. Choose **Y**es.

   The message `Record 6 deleted` is displayed in the message box.

4. To Undo the next transaction, press Ctrl-U.

   The message `Changes for record 3 undone` is displayed in the message box.

93

Adding, Editing, and Viewing Data with a Table

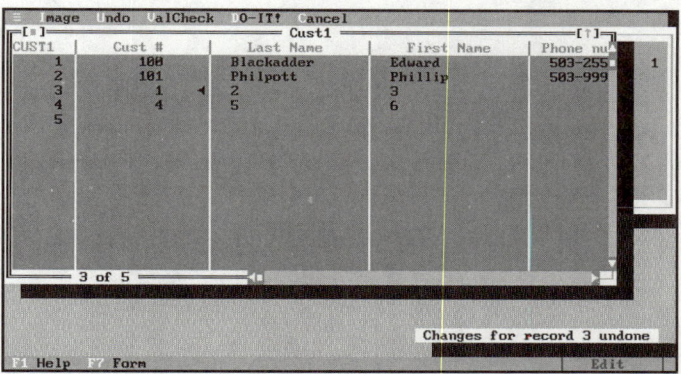

Here, you see that the Undo feature has removed the last two transactions.

The Undo command is an invaluable feature. If you accidentally press [Del], for example, you can use the Undo command to replace the deleted record.

Deleting a Record

If a record is no longer active or needed, Paradox makes removing the record very simple. To delete records from the Cust1 table, for example, do the following steps:

1. Move the cursor to record 5.
2. Press [Del] once. You will notice that record 5 is removed from the display.

   Again, you can use the Undo command from the menu bar, or press [Ctrl]-[U] to recover a deleted record.
3. Move the cursor to record 3.
4. Press [Del] twice to remove records 3 and 4.

The cursor is now located on record 2 in the Cust # field.

Using the Ditto Function

Paradox provides you with a shortcut feature called Ditto. The Ditto command enables you to copy the information into the field where the cursor is located from the record above the field. For example, do the following to use the Ditto feature:

Working With Tables in Edit Mode

1. Move the cursor to record 3 in the Cust # field and enter the following information into the indicated fields:

Cust #:	**103**
Last Name:	**Molinari**
First Name:	**Homer**
Phone Number:	**206-333-9999**
Street:	**P.O. Box 5432**
City:	**Vancouver**

2. After making the last entry and pressing [Enter], the cursor is located in the State field. Press [Ctrl]-[D].

   The contents of the State field from record 2 is copied into the field in record 3.

   This feature can save you much time and effort when you have entries that are the same. Use the Ditto command, for example, when entering identical cities and zip codes.

3. Now finish this record by entering the Zip/Postal Code and Country fields. Type **98331**, and then press [Enter]. Type **USA**, and then press [Enter].

Searching for Records

Paradox provides several ways to find single records or extract groups of records that meet certain criteria. In Edit mode, you may need to make a change to a single record out of hundreds and possibly thousands. The easiest way to find a single record among so many is to use Zoom and Zoom Next.

Zoom searches for an exact match to a given value. It searches only the field in which the cursor is currently located, starting from the first record. When Paradox finds a match, the cursor is placed on that record in the field you searched.

The only difference between Zoom and Zoom Next is that Zoom finds a specific value. In a large table that is not keyed or if you are not searching in the key field, you may have duplicate values. If the first instance of the value found by Zoom is not the correct one, then use Zoom Next to find the next occurrence of the value. To use the Zoom feature, do the following:

1. Move the cursor to the field you want to search. For this example, move the cursor to the Last Name field.

Adding, Editing, and Viewing Data with a Table

You can position the cursor on any record, so long as it is in the field you want to search.

2. Press Ctrl-Z.

   An alternative way to use Zoom is to select the **I**mage option from the menu bar. Then choose the **Z**oom option from the pull-down menu.

   When Zoom is selected, a dialog box appears asking for the value you want to find.

In the Zoom dialog box, enter the value you want to find.

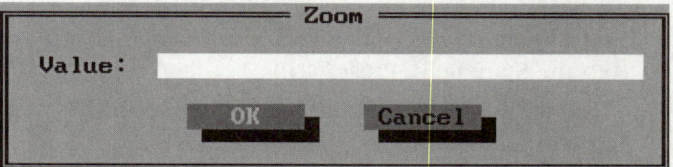

If you are working with a table that has a single key, as your Cust1 table does, Zoom will quickly find a record because there is only one record with that value. The only drawback is that in your Cust1 table the key field is Cust #. You must know the exact customer number of the record for which you want to search, in order to search on that field.

3. Enter the value for which you want to search. For example, type **JACOBY** and press ↵Enter.

   When Paradox finds the match, the value flashes in reverse video and then places the cursor at the end of the field.

4. Now use Search Next to find any other occurrence of the previous search value. Press Alt-Z.

As indicated in the message box, Zoom Next did not find a second match for the search value JACOBY.

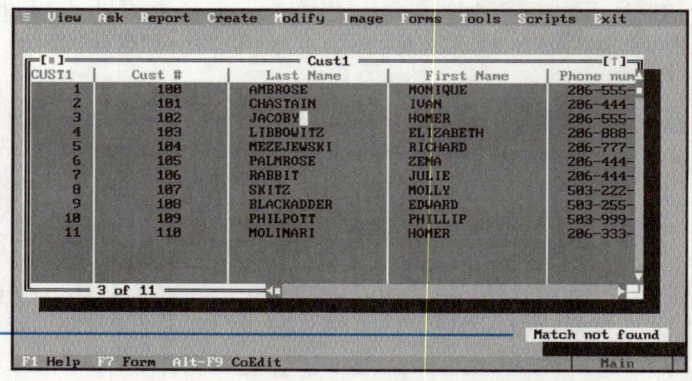

Working With Tables in Edit Mode

5. Now use Zoom once more. Press Ctrl-Z, enter the value **Blackadder**, and press Enter.

   The message Match not found is displayed in the message box. In the preceding figure, you can see that this name is located in record 9. Paradox, however, did not find this value because Paradox is *case sensitive*. In other words, lowercase letters and uppercase letters are not the same.

6. Press Ctrl-Z again, and type **BLACKADDER** in the Zoom dialog box. Press Enter again.

   Paradox quickly finds and moves the cursor to the correct record. Notice that you did not have to delete the previous entry in the Zoom dialog box. Typing the new entry automatically deletes the previous entry.

   Case sensitivity is one of the primary reasons you must be consistent in your data entry work. A good rule of thumb is to always use uppercase letters in any data entry. You should not allow one person to use a combination of upper- and lowercase letters if everyone else is using all uppercase letters.

Using Zoom with Wild Cards

You may not always know the exact spelling of a value you want to find. For such instances, Paradox provides a couple of tools you can use with Zoom and Zoom Next, even if you do not know the exact spelling of the value for which you are searching. These tools are called *wild cards*.

Paradox enables you to use the symbols .. (double period) and @ (at sign) to represent other characters. The double period can represent any number of other characters, but the at sign can represent only a single character. For example, to search for a last name beginning with the letter M, you would type **M..** in the Zoom dialog box. Paradox would then find all the customers with a last name beginning with M.

If you are almost sure of the spelling, you can use the at sign to represent a character. For example, if you want to find the record for Homer Jacoby, but you are not sure whether his last name ends with the letter Y or I, enter the value as **JACOB@**. Paradox will find the value; however, it also will find JACOB, JACOBE, JACOBI, and JACOBS, if they are in your database. Use Alt-Z, Zoom Next, until you find the record for which you are searching.

Adding, Editing, and Viewing Data with a Table

Inserting New Records

In an unkeyed table, you may want to insert a new record between two existing records. Without a key field to provide the sort order for a table, you must manually insert records in the order you want or use the **S**ort option located on the **M**odify pull-down menu. The **S**ort option is discussed in Chapter 6.

The process of inserting a new record is exactly like inserting a new field when you create a table structure. To insert a record, do the following:

1. Move the cursor to the location where you want to insert the new record. For example, if you want to insert a new record as the fifth record, place the cursor on the existing fifth record. You can position the cursor in any field.

    For this example, place the cursor on record 5, MEZEJEWSKI.

2. Press [Ins].

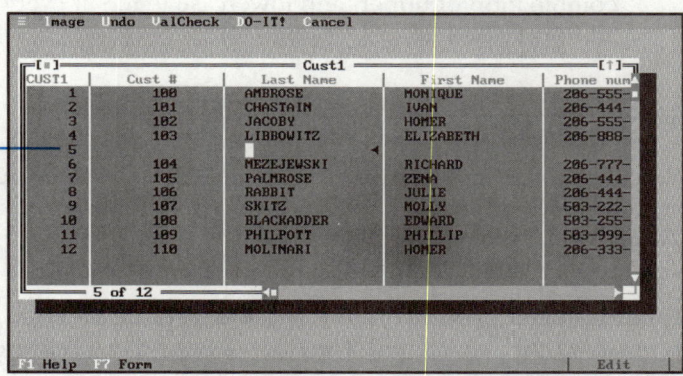

You now see the new, blank record 5 inserted above the record for MEZEJEWSKI.

You can enter data into each of the fields as you normally would. Notice that the cursor remains in the field where it was previously located. Also note that this table maintains the key field Cust #, so when you finish entering the new record and press [F2] or select **D**O-IT!, the record will move to its correct sorted position according to the key field.

Working With Tables in Data Entry Mode

Using Keys and Key Violations in Edit

In a keyed table, it is easiest to enter all your new records at the end of the table. When you save your changes, the table will automatically be re-sorted according to the key field(s).

When using Edit mode and entering new records, you run the risk of overwriting another record. For example, your Cust1 table is keyed on the field Cust #. If you duplicate a customer number when adding a new customer, Paradox will update the old record with the new information.

The possibility of overwriting is one of the primary arguments for using the CoEdit or DataEntry options instead of Edit for entering new records. As you read the sections "Working With Tables in DataEntry Mode" and "Using CoEdit Mode," you will understand why.

Saving or Canceling Changes

When you have completed your editing session, you must decide whether you are going to save your changes to the permanent file on the disk or cancel the changes and leave the file untouched.

To save your changes, select DO-IT! from the menu bar or press F2. All the changes you have made during the editing session will be saved.

To cancel and return the file to the condition that it was in before you started the editing session, select Cancel from the menu bar.

Remember, when you select either of these options, the transaction log is deleted. You will not be able to use the log to recover from a mistake. Instead, you will have to find the original information and use the Edit option to change the record.

Working With Tables in DataEntry Mode

DataEntry mode is the only one of the three Modify modes exclusively designed for data entry work. When you use DataEntry mode, Paradox displays a new table called Data Entry: *tablename* with which you can work. (Paradox replaces *tablename* with the name of the table with which you are working.) This table is a temporary Paradox table used by DataEntry, and so protects your data currently stored in the table. This table is identical to the table to

Adding, Editing, and Viewing Data with a Table

which you will add the new records. When you select **M**odify **D**ataEntry, you tell Paradox the table to which you will add the data. This table is the target table. Paradox then creates the temporary table, Data Entry.

Using DataEntry Mode

DataEntry mode is specifically designed for you to add new records into a table. If your intention is to add records during an editing session and not make any changes to existing records, then use DataEntry mode. When you select this mode, Paradox creates the temporary table, Data Entry. You add all the new records in the Data Entry table. Because you perform all the work in the Data Entry table, your existing records are protected from accidental changes. When you complete the new records, Paradox adds the records from Data Entry to the permanent table.

Adding Records

The Paradox DataEntry function is best suited for basic data entry work. To use the DataEntry mode, do the following:

1. Select **M**odify from the Main menu bar.
2. Choose **D**ataEntry from the pull-down menu.

This is the **M**odify pull-down menu, with the **D**ataEntry option highlighted.

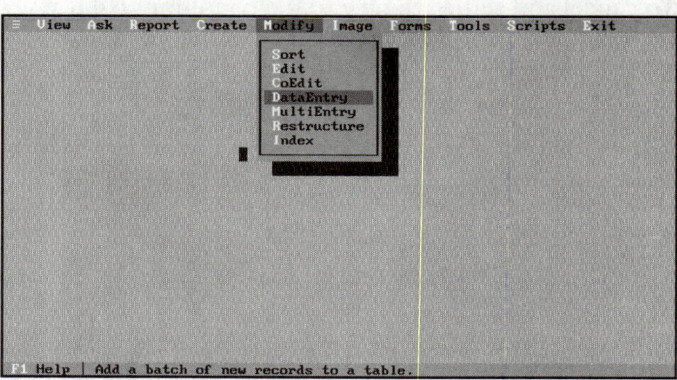

3. Type the name of the table to which you will add the new records. Type **Cust1** and press ⏎Enter.

Working With Tables in DataEntry Mode

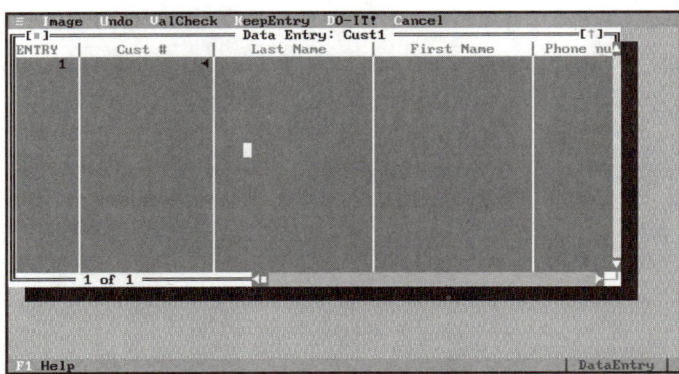

The Data Entry table is displayed.

Notice that the table has the identical structure of the Cust1 table. Paradox begins the data entry session with record 1, and places the cursor in the first field. As you enter data into the Entry table in DataEntry mode, you will find that all the cursor keys function in the same manner as when you were in Edit mode.

4. Press F7 to display the Standard form. Enter the following data for the first record. Remember, press Enter after entering the data into each field to move the cursor to the next field.

Cust #:	**100**
Last Name:	**GRAHAM**
First Name:	**PATEL**
Phone Number:	**604-555-2323**
Street:	**3984 E. 23RD ST.**
City:	**VANCOUVER**
State:	**BC**
Zip/Postal Code:	**V1B 2G4**
Country:	**CANADA**

Adding, Editing, and Viewing Data with a Table

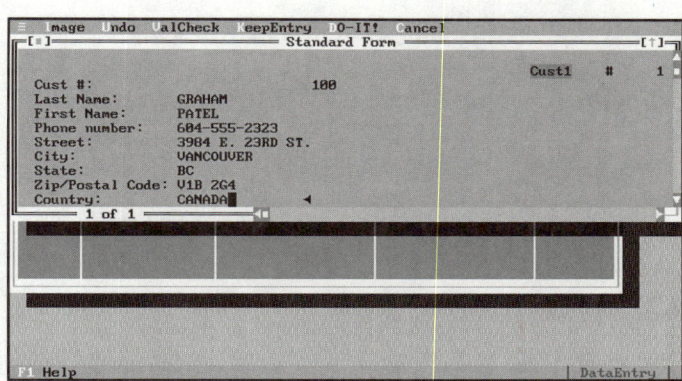

You can see the completed Standard form for the Entry table. Notice that the table is displayed behind the form.

5. Now press [↵Enter] to begin record 2.
6. Enter the following data for the second record:

Cust #:	**112**
Last Name:	**MARTIN**
First Name:	**CHANDA**
Phone Number:	**503-222-1133**
Street:	**1510 NW LOVEJOY #212**
City:	**PORTLAND**
State:	**OR**
Zip/Postal Code:	**97288**
Country:	**USA**

7. Press [↵Enter].

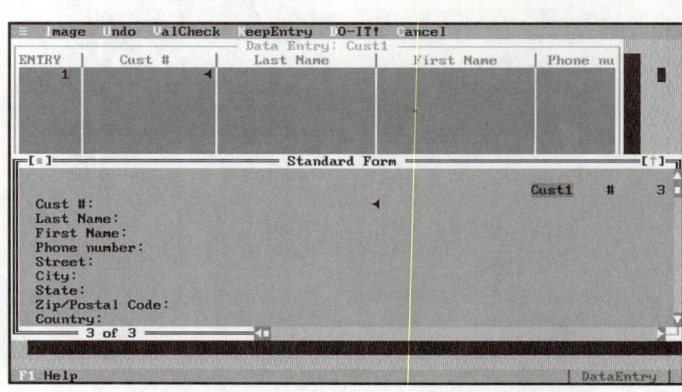

Paradox displays record 3—a blank record—in the Standard form.

102

Working With Tables in DataEntry Mode

You will notice in this figure that you have entered two records into the table using the Standard form, and neither are displayed in the Data Entry table in the background. The records do not appear because the table is not active. When you use a form to view, edit, or add records, you are in Form view. When you use a table, you are in Table view.

Your new records still exist. You can think of Form view as a pin printer loaded with continuous paper. Record 1 was printed on the first page of your paper and has now moved up and out of the printer; the same is true of record 2.

To view your records, press `PgUp` once.

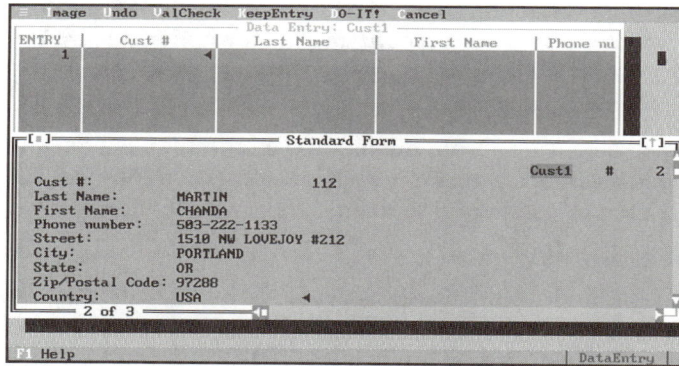

You now see record 2 displayed.

8. Now press `F7` (or click the mouse pointer on the table) to return to Table view.

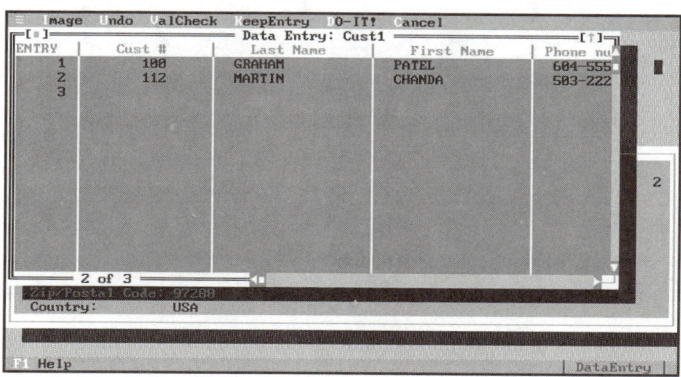

The new records are now displayed in the table.

Adding, Editing, and Viewing Data with a Table

You will also notice that the Standard form has now been moved to the background. The table, now active, is in the foreground. You also see that the cursor is located in the same field as it was in the form.

While in DataEntry mode, as in each of the editing modes, you still have use of the Paradox correction features. If you find that you have made an error on a record, you can move to the field and use `Backspace` to remove the data and then retype it. To delete an entire field, press `Ctrl`-`Backspace`. You can also use Field view by pressing either the combination of `Alt`-`F5` or `Ctrl`-`F`.

Using Undo

Paradox maintains the same transaction log that you used while in Edit mode. Each transaction begins when you enter a record and ends when you leave the record. Potentially, if you created a record and then edited it several times, a single record can have several transactions.

To use the Undo feature, select **U**ndo from the menu bar, and then choose the **Y**es option from the pull-down menu. Again, the shortcut method for Undo is using `Ctrl`-`U`. For example, to use the Undo feature, do the following:

1. Place the cursor on record 2, Cust # field.

    Suppose that your intention is to change the customer number from 112 to 113. You want to press `Backspace` and replace the number 2 with a 3. But suppose that you accidentally press `Del`. The result is a missing record.

Here is the Data Entry table, with a missing record.

Since this transaction has just occurred, you have an easy way to correct the problem: Undo.

Working With Tables in DataEntry Mode

2. Press Ctrl-U (or select **U**ndo from the menu bar, and then choose the **Y**es option from the pull-down menu).

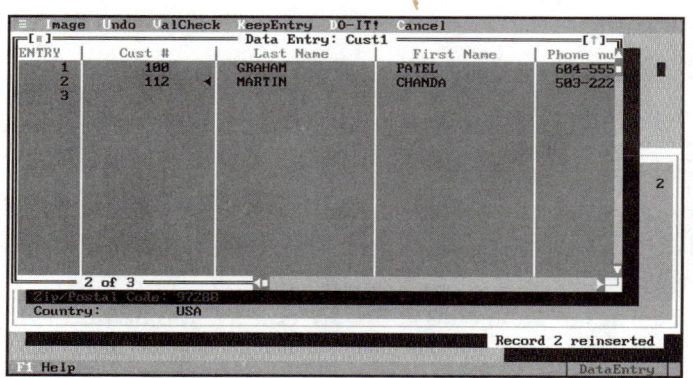

Here is the Data Entry table with the deleted record restored by the **U**ndo command.

Notice the message displayed at the bottom of the screen: Record 2 reinserted.

Again, be careful using the Undo feature. While it can be a lifesaver to correct a mistake (usually a deletion) you just made, it may be easier to reenter data that is several transactions in the past. Paradox starts with the newest transaction—the one you just completed—and works backward, undoing each transaction.

Using the Ditto Function

The Ditto function works the same way as described in the section "Working With Tables in Edit Mode." A great labor-saving command, use it as often as you can. Ditto copies the contents of the field in the record above with a single combination keystroke, Ctrl-D.

To use the Ditto function, do the following:

1. Enter the following data as record 3:

Cust #:	**113**
Last Name:	**BRADY**
First Name:	**CASEY**
Phone Number:	**503-223-9955**
Street:	**2133 NW MARSHALL**

105

Adding, Editing, and Viewing Data with a Table

Suppose that you now notice that the next several fields are identical to the record above.

2. Move the cursor to the City field and press `Ctrl`-`D`, then press `↵Enter`.
3. The cursor is now located in the State field. Press `Ctrl`-`D`, and then press `↵Enter`.
4. The cursor is now located in the Zip/Postal Code field. Press `Ctrl`-`D`, and then press `↵Enter`.
5. The cursor is now located in the Country field. Press `Ctrl`-`D`, and then press `↵Enter`.

By using the Ditto function, you have saved yourself much time and effort. Provided that the field entries in the record above are correct, you do not have to worry about typos.

Searching for Records

If you have entered a large number of records and need to find a specific one, use the Zoom and Zoom Next commands. To find a record, do the following:

1. Move the cursor to the field that contains the information for which you want to search.
2. Press `Ctrl`-`Z`.
3. Enter the value you want to find into the text box in the Zoom dialog box, and then press `↵Enter`.

    If Paradox finds the exact match, the cursor will be placed in that record. If no match is found, then Paradox will display the message `Match not found` in the message box.

For an alternative method of searching for data, use the **I**mage option on the menu bar. Under the **I**mage command, you will find another form of Zoom listed as an option. To use this form of Zoom, do the following:

1. Select **I**mage from the menu bar.
2. Choose the **Z**oom option from the pull-down menu.

Working With Tables in DataEntry Mode

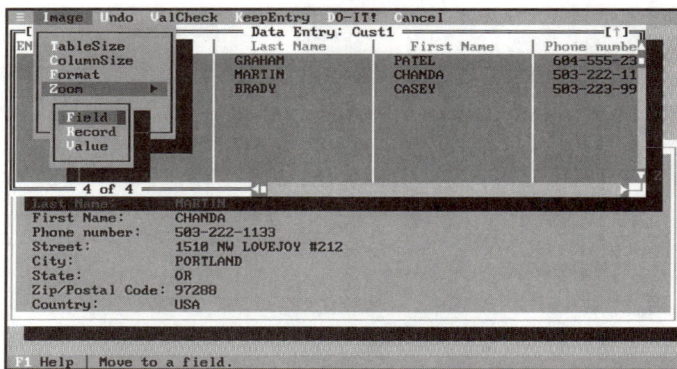

You can see the several alternative options available to you from the **I**mage **Z**oom command.

Image **Z**oom has three additional search options: **F**ield, **R**ecord, and **V**alue.

The **F**ield option enables you to Zoom to a specific field. When selected, a list box is displayed showing all the fields in the current table. A scroll bar is displayed on the right side so that you can view additional fields. Select the field to Zoom to, and then press ⏎Enter.

The **R**ecord option enables you to Zoom to a specific record. When selected, a dialog box is displayed. Enter the record number to Zoom to in the text box, and then press ⏎Enter.

When you use **F**ield or **R**ecord, the cursor will remain in the record (with the **F**ield option) or in the field (with the **R**ecord option) in which it started.

The **V**alue option enables you to Zoom to a specific value. When selected, a prompt is displayed at the top of your screen asking you the column in which to search. Select the column and then, in the displayed dialog box, enter the value for the computer to search; then press ⏎Enter.

To try the options, do the following:

1. Move the cursor to the Last Name field in record 1.
2. Select **I**mage from the menu bar. Choose **Z**oom from the pull-down menu. Then select the **F**ield option from the displayed cascading menu.

107

Adding, Editing, and Viewing Data with a Table

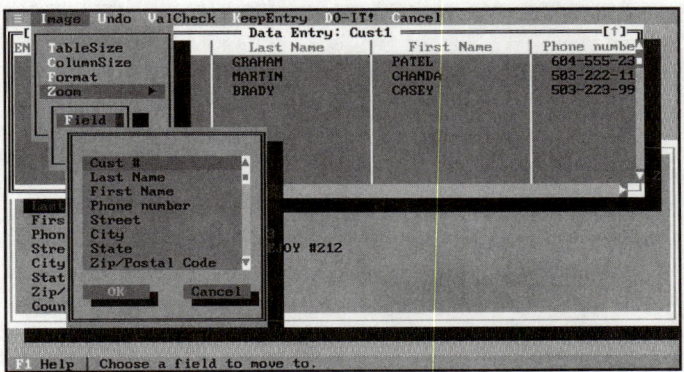

Here, you can see the list box displayed when using the **I**mage **Z**oom **F**ield command.

3. Choose the City field from the box and press ⏎Enter (or place the mouse pointer on the City field and double-click).

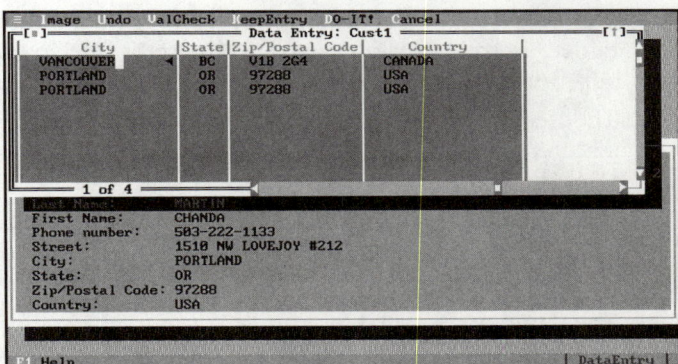

This table is Zoomed to the City field.

Notice that the cursor is still located on record 1.

4. Move the cursor back to the Last Name field in record 1.
5. Select **I**mage from the menu bar. Choose **Z**oom from the pull-down menu. Select the **R**ecord option from the displayed cascading menu.

108

Working With Tables in DataEntry Mode

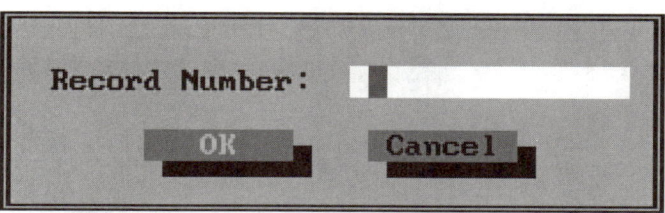

Here, you can see the Record Number dialog box.

6. Enter the record number for which you want to search. Type **15** and press ↵Enter.

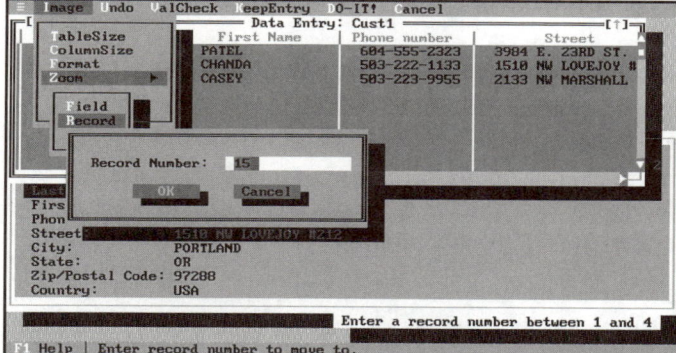

An incorrect value was entered for the record number.

Notice the message `Enter a record number between 1 and 4` in the message box. Paradox will allow you to enter only a value that is within the range of numbers of records that the table contains.

7. Press ←Backspace twice to delete the incorrect entry 15, and then type the number **3** and press ↵Enter.

The cursor moves to record 3 in the Data Entry table.

8. Select **I**mage from the menu bar. Choose **Z**oom from the pull-down menu. Select the **V**alue option from the displayed cascading menu.

109

Adding, Editing, and Viewing Data with a Table

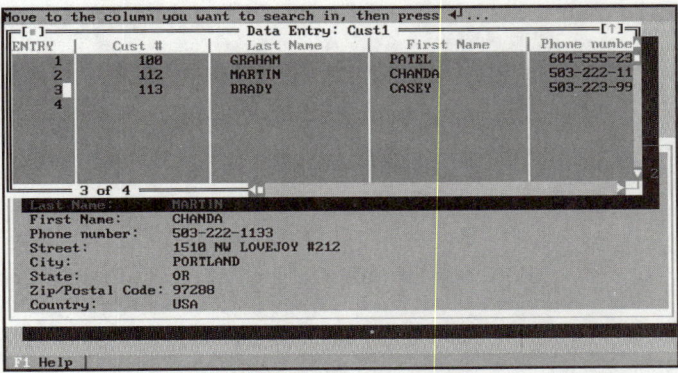

Paradox displays this screen after you select the **I**mage **Z**oom **V**alue option.

The cursor is now a large, solid, blinking block. The menu bar has been replaced with the message Move to the column you want to search in, then press ↵...

9. Move the cursor to the City field and press ↵Enter.
10. Enter the value for which you want to search in the Zoom dialog box text box. Type **PORTLAND** and press ↵Enter.

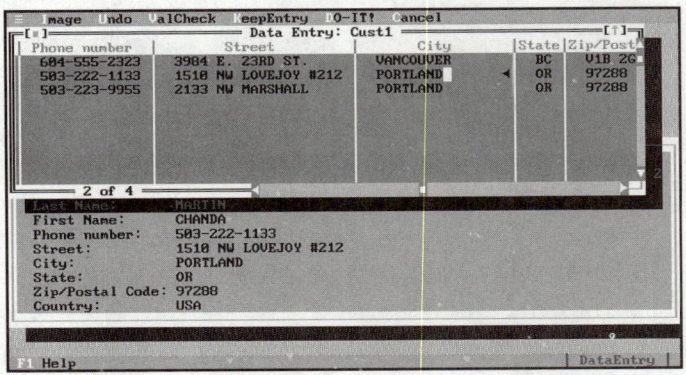

A match is found in the City field of record 2.

11. Press the Zoom Next key combination, Alt-Z.

110

Working With Tables in DataEntry Mode

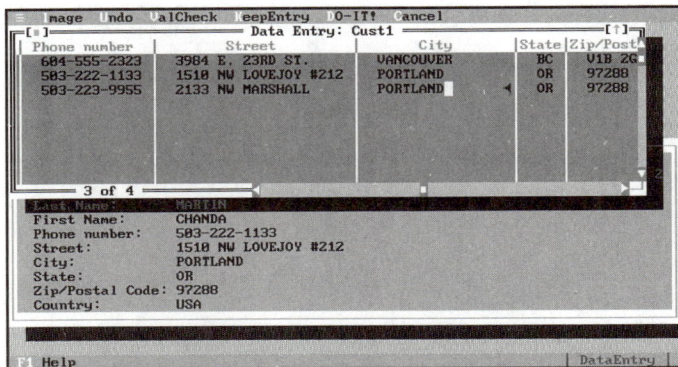

Zoom Next found the next occurrence of the value PORTLAND in record 3.

Inserting New Records

As you already learned in the Edit section of this chapter, when working a keyed table, using insert to place a new record between two existing records is unnecessary work on your part. Paradox will automatically re-sort and place all the records in order according to the key for that table.

In DataEntry mode, you can insert records between others in the Data Entry table. Remember, all of these records will be added to another table when you have finished. If the master or original table is a keyed table, all records both old and new will be sorted by the key field. If the original table is not keyed, then all of the new records will be added to the end of the table, in the order that you have placed them in the table.

If you must insert a record, do the following:

1. Place the cursor on the record that will drop below the newly inserted record.
2. Press [Ins].

111

Adding, Editing, and Viewing Data with a Table

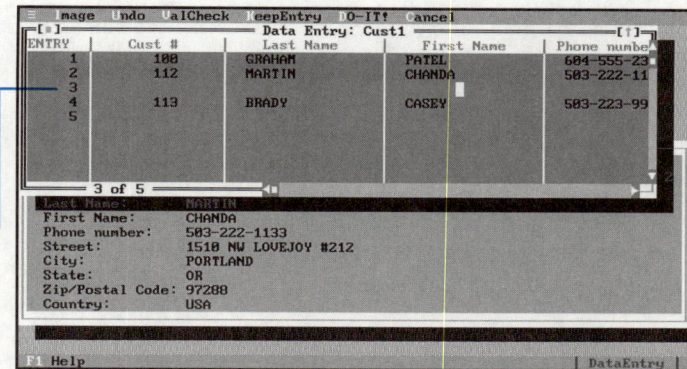

Here, you see the new blank record 3.

Deleting a Record

If you decide that a record you have created, or the blank record you have inserted, is no longer needed, you can delete it. To delete an entire record, do the following:

1. Place the cursor on the record you want to delete. Leave the cursor on the blank record 3.
2. Press Del.

The record is deleted from the table.

Remember, you can use the Undo command to reverse the deletion if needed.

112

Working With Tables in DataEntry Mode

Saving or Canceling Changes

When you have completed entering all the new records, you are ready to end DataEntry mode. If you are satisfied with the records, select **D**O-IT! from the menu bar or press `F2`. Either of these actions adds the new records to the original, or target, table. You will see the message `Adding records from Entry to Cust1...` displayed in the message box.

If you decide that you do not want to add the new records at this time, you can save the Data Entry table temporarily. To save the Data Entry table, select **K**eepEntry from the menu. You will see the message `Saving Entry table....`

Before you use DataEntry again, you must be sure either to add the records to the target table or rename the Entry table. If you do not do one of these actions, the next time you use the **M**odify **D**ataEntry option, the new temporary Entry table will overwrite the previously existing table.

If you do not want to add the new records, you also have the choice to select **C**ancel from the menu. This option cancels all the records you have entered in the DataEntry session and returns you to the main desktop.

Working With Keys and Key Violations in DataEntry

Key fields and their uses were discussed in Chapter 3. The main reason for using key fields is to keep records in order and to prevent duplicate records. While adding records in DataEntry mode, Paradox does not monitor the key field for either purpose. If you duplicate a record in the original table or the Entry table, Paradox will not find out until you press `F2` (**D**O-IT!). At that time, Paradox checks the new records against the existing records.

Paradox places the new records in the order dictated by the key field. Any of the new records created during DataEntry that duplicate the values in the key field(s) of an existing record are considered by Paradox to be key violating records and are then placed in the temporary table, Keyviol. Paradox then displays the target, or original, table on the desktop, and displays the Keyviol table, if created, below the original.

In the example you have been working on, selecting `F2` has created a key violation.

Adding, Editing, and Viewing Data with a Table

The Keyviol table is displayed after adding the new records from the Entry table into the target table, Cust1.

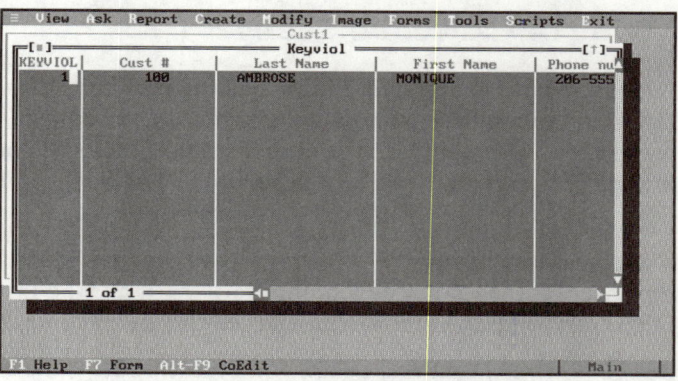

The Size/Move option enables you to view part of the Cust1 table.

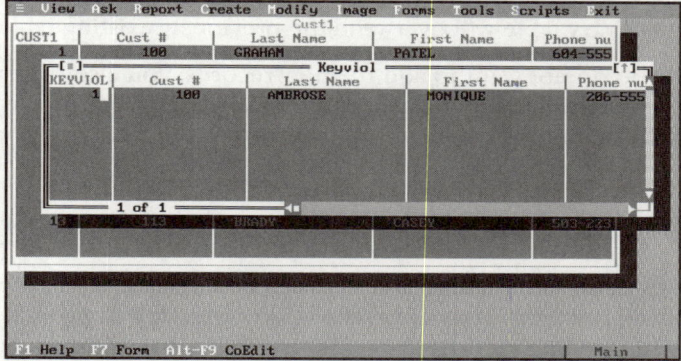

Having moved the Keyviol table, you can see the key violation that occurred. You accidentally duplicated the customer number 100. To correct this and add the record into the target table, do the following:

1. Press F9 to enter Edit mode.
2. Move the cursor to the Cust # field. Press ←Backspace twice to delete both of the 0's, and then type **11**. The entry should now read 111.
3. Press F2 (**DO-IT!**) to complete the edit.
4. Select **T**ools from the Main menu.
5. Choose **M**ove from the pull-down menu, and then choose **A**dd from the displayed cascading menu.
6. Enter the table name **KEYVIOL** as the source table, and press ↵Enter.
7. Enter the table name **CUST1** as the target table, and press ↵Enter.

114

Using CoEdit Mode

8. Select **N**ewEntries from the pop-up menu box, and press ⏎Enter.

    You will see the message Adding records from Keyviol to Cust1... displayed.

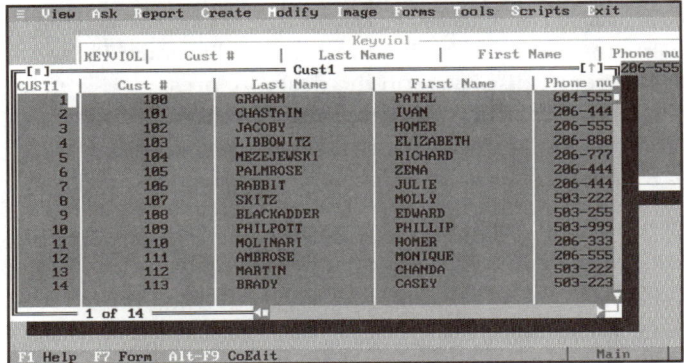

Now the completed table is displayed.

Using CoEdit Mode

The CoEdit function is designed primarily for using Paradox within a multi-user network system. Each user's screen is refreshed, or updated, with the changes made by other users. This feature helps to ensure that everyone is using the same data, and not working with and making decisions based upon data that may now be wrong.

You do not have to be tied in with a network in order to use the CoEdit function. It is designed to enable you to edit records within the actual table, not an Entry table as you did using DataEntry. The screen in CoEdit and Edit modes are very similar. The only differences are contained in the menu bar. The Edit menu bar contains a **C**ancel command and does not have the **A**utoRefresh option. With few exceptions, both commands work in the same way. The primary difference is that Edit mode updates automatically any changes made to a record with a duplicate key, even if the duplication was in error. CoEdit mode prompts you about a duplication when you have completed the record entry. You have the option to view the original record, and then you can confirm the new record.

115

Adding, Editing, and Viewing Data with a Table

Adding and Editing Records

The CoEdit option may be the best method for adding and editing records. Since Paradox prompts you when key violations occur, you do not run the risk of overwriting an existing record accidentally.

You can start CoEdit using the same methods you used in Edit mode. If the table you want to edit is currently displayed on the desktop, press Alt - F9. If you have more than one table displayed when entering CoEdit mode, all of the tables will be placed into CoEdit mode. If the table is not currently located on the desktop, do the following to display it:

1. Select **M**odify from the Main menu bar.
2. Choose the **C**oEdit option from the pull-down menu.
3. Enter the table name into the text box of the displayed dialog box. Type the table name **Cust1** and press ↵Enter.

   As always, if you do not know the name of the table, press ↵Enter or click the mouse pointer in the list box to see a list of available tables.

You see the Cust1 table displayed in CoEdit mode.

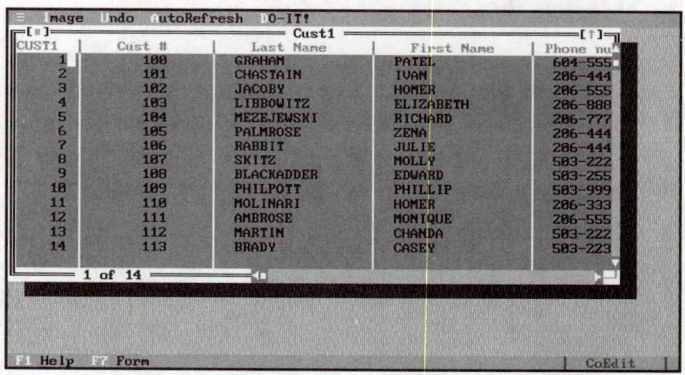

4. Press End. This moves the cursor to the last record, and then press ↓.

   This step starts the next new record. You will notice that the cursor moves from the record number column to the first field, Cust #.

5. Enter the following data as record 15.

Cust #:	**114**
Last Name:	**MARTINI**
First Name:	**MACK**

Using CoEdit Mode

Phone Number:	**206-777-1991**
Street:	**STAR RT 2, BOX 54**
City:	**LOPEZ ISLAND**
State:	**WA**
Zip/Postal Code:	**98856**
Country:	**USA**

Remember to press ⏎Enter after you enter data in each field.

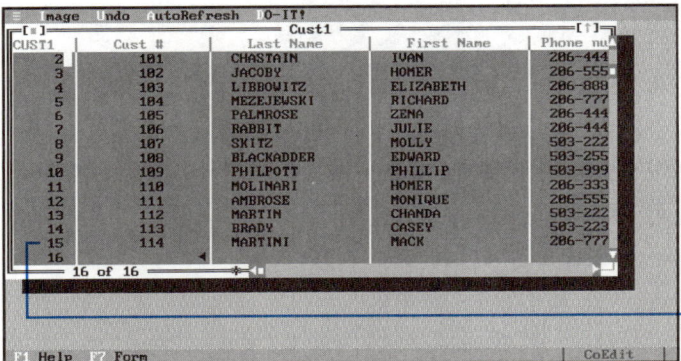

You can see the completed record now inserted into the table.

6. Now move back the cursor to the first field, Cust #, in record 14 and make the following change:

   Press ←Backspace and remove the customer number.

7. Now type the new customer number, **99**, and press ↓.

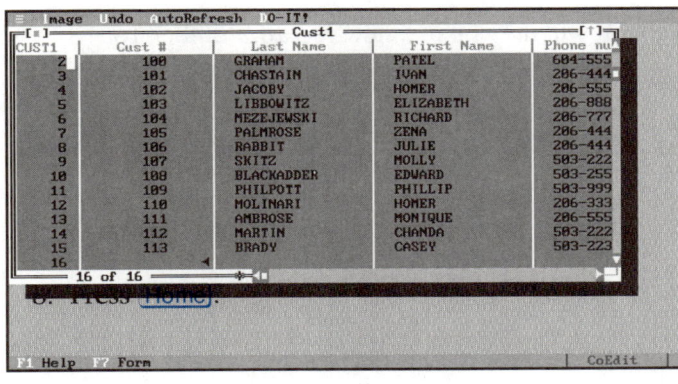

Notice that the record you just edited no longer appears in the table.

117

Adding, Editing, and Viewing Data with a Table

You now see the missing customer, Mack Martini.

When you complete a record in CoEdit mode, Paradox posts, or saves, the record immediately to the disk. Remember that while a keyed table prevents you from duplicating a record, it also sorts the files. When you complete a record by leaving it, Paradox automatically re-sorts the table and places the new record in its proper location.

Using Undo

As you have already learned, the **U**ndo command works by referring to the transaction log Paradox creates while you work. In CoEdit mode, Paradox maintains the transaction log for only a single record.

Unlike in Edit mode where you can reverse every transaction performed during an editing session, CoEdit mode limits you to only a single record. To see how **U**ndo works in CoEdit mode, do the following:

1. Press [End] and [↓]. You will now be in a new record, number 16.
2. Enter the following data:

    Cust #:   123

    Last Name: 456

3. Press [↓] again.

118

Using CoEdit Mode

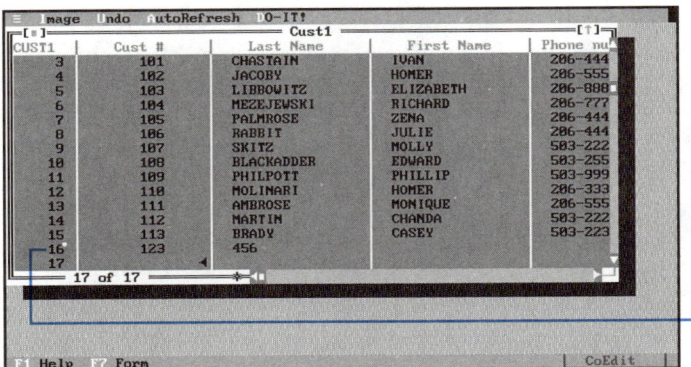

You can see the new record number, 16, inserted into the table.

Remember what a transaction is: a record of the keystrokes you perform from the time you enter a record until you leave the record. In steps 1 through 3 you have entered a record, added data, and then left the record. The transaction is complete.

4. Now use the **U**ndo command to remove the record. Press Ctrl-U (or select **U**ndo from the menu bar).

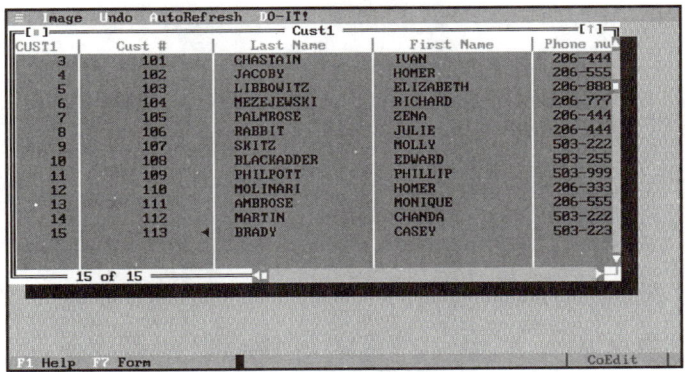

The **U**ndo command has reversed the last transaction and deleted record 16 from the table.

5. Now repeat steps 1 through 3 again.

   You should now have customer number 123 entered again, and the cursor is located in record 17.

6. Type **1** for the customer number.

7. Suppose that you now realize you did not want the previous customer added. Press Ctrl-U to undo the transaction.

Adding, Editing, and Viewing Data with a Table

Using the Undo command removed the 1 from record 17's Cust # field. Attempting to use the Undo command again will result in Paradox beeping at you. As soon as you typed the 1 into the Cust # field, you started a new transaction.

Deleting a Record

Deleting an unneeded record is a simple procedure. Do the following to delete record 16:

1. Move the cursor to any field in record 16.
2. Press `Del`.
   You will now see the cursor move up to record 15.

Inserting New Records

Just as in both Edit and DataEntry modes, you can insert records in CoEdit mode. Again, if you are using a keyed table, Paradox sorts the records for you and inserts new records into their proper location.

If you are working in an unkeyed table and need to insert a record, do the following:

1. Move the cursor to the record that will drop immediately below the inserted record.
2. Press `Ins`. A blank record line appears above the cursor location.
3. Enter the data required for the new record.

Using the Ditto Function

The Ditto function remains available to you. A shortcut feature, Ditto can save much time and effort. As in Edit and DataEntry modes, to use Ditto, press `Ctrl`-`D`. The contents of the field in the record above are copied to the current field.

Searching for Records

In CoEdit mode, you may need to verify a record's existence or the data contained in a record. When working with a large table, the Paradox Zoom (`Ctrl`-`Z`) and Zoom Next (`Alt`-`Z`) features are available to you, as are the

Using CoEdit Mode

Image **Z**oom options from the menu bar. These Zoom options are the same as those in Edit and DataEntry. To review the Zoom options, do the following:

1. Place the cursor in the field that contains the information for which you are searching. In this case, move the cursor to the Cust # field.

2. Press `Ctrl`-`Z`. Enter the value for which to search, **101**, and press `⏎Enter`.

   The cursor highlights in reverse video the value, if found, and then places the cursor at the end of the field.

3. To search for another duplicate value, use Zoom Next. Press `Alt`-`Z`.

   You will see the message Match not found displayed in the message box. If a duplicate value had been found, it would have been highlighted and then the cursor would have been placed at the end of the field.

4. Select **I**mage from the menu bar. Choose the **Z**oom option.

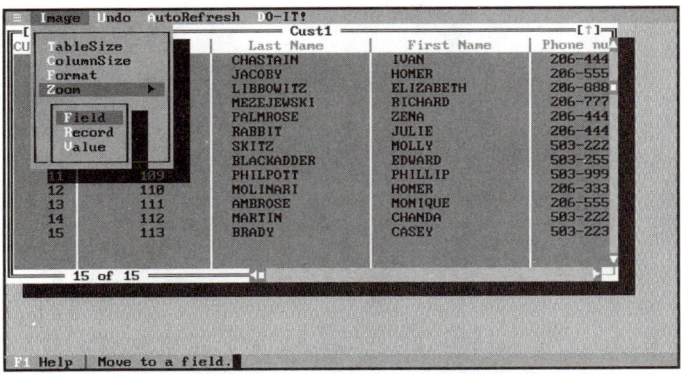

You again see the menu box with three options.

Select one of the options:

The **F**ield option searches for a specified field. When selected, a list box is displayed with all table fields shown. Select the required field and press `⏎Enter`. The cursor jumps to the indicated field.

The **R**ecord option searches for a specific record number. When selected, a dialog box is displayed. Enter the record number for which you want to search and press `⏎Enter`. The cursor moves to the indicated record. Remember, customer number and record number are not the same thing. The record number is the row number.

121

Adding, Editing, and Viewing Data with a Table

To use the Value option, move the cursor to the field in which to search and press [⤶Enter]. Then enter the value for which you want to search and press [⤶Enter].

Treating Keys and Key Violations in DataEntry

In a keyed table as Paradox posts each new record to disk, it sorts the record into the appropriate place as determined by the key field and then looks to see whether a key violation exists. If none does, you can go on to your next record.

If Paradox finds a key violation, you are unable to continue. Paradox immediately flags the violation and prompts you to correct the violation or to accept one entry as correct. To see how this works, do the following:

1. Move the cursor down to record 16, and enter the following data:

   Cust #:   **110**
   Last Name: **BLACKBIRD**
   First Name: **CEASER**

2. Press [↓] after the First Name field.

Here, you are prompted to correct the key violation or view the existing record.

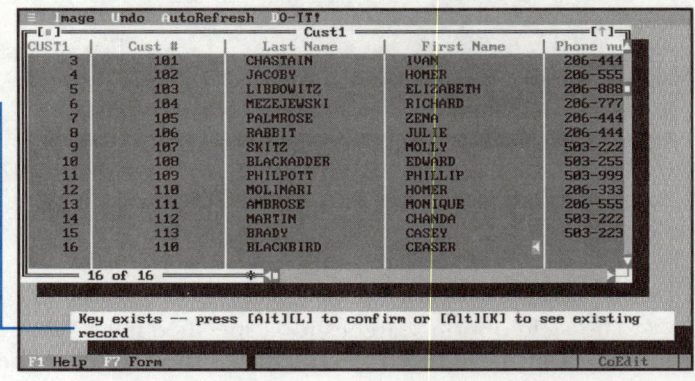

You are given two options. You can confirm that the new record is correct—in which case Paradox will delete the existing record and insert the new one. Or you can view the existing record, and then confirm the new record or the existing record.

3. Press [Alt]-[K] to view the existing record.

Using Paradox Table Images

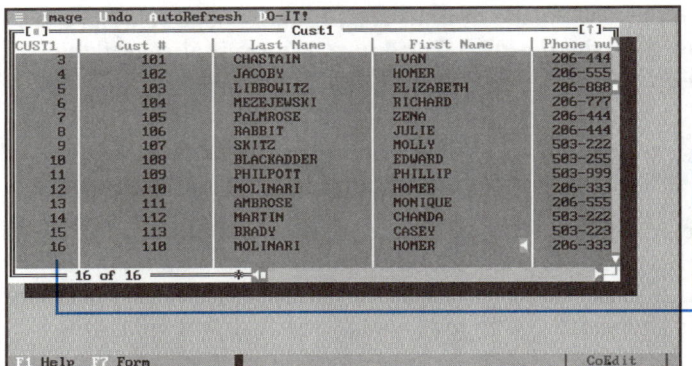

Here, you can see the existing record.

Notice that the existing record, 110 MOLINARI, is now being displayed both in record 16 and in its original location in record 12. Pressing any key at this point will redisplay the prompt.

4. Press Alt-L to confirm that the original record is the correct record. This action causes the key-violating record to be deleted. You will have to reenter this record without creating a violation.

Pressing Alt-K toggles between the new and existing record. Press Alt-L to confirm which record you want to keep. To edit the new record so that it does not violate the table key, display it by pressing Alt-K and then edit the key field as necessary. Paradox will then insert the new record into the table.

Saving Changes

When you use the CoEdit option, Paradox saves each new entry to disk as you finish a transaction. Because everything is already saved, there is no Cancel option in CoEdit. The only way to exit from CoEdit is to use the **F2 D**O-IT! option.

When the **D**O-IT! option is selected, the table's final changes are saved to disk and the session is closed. Paradox then displays an image of the completed table on the desktop.

Using Paradox Table Images

Each of the modes discussed in this chapter—Edit, DataEntry, and CoEdit— includes an option called **I**mage. You have already used a part of this menu

123

Adding, Editing, and Viewing Data with a Table

option, the Zoom option. The Image options are primarily used to adjust the way tables are displayed on the desktop. The Image option is also available from the Main menu bar.

Changing the Table's Size

The TableSize option enables you to change the number of lines or records a table will display. This option is almost identical to the System menu's Size/Move option that was discussed in Chapter 2—except that you can adjust only the table's height, not the width. To change a table's size, do the following:

1. Select Image from the menu bar.
2. Choose the TableSize option from the pull-down menu.

Notice the prompt at the top of the screen.

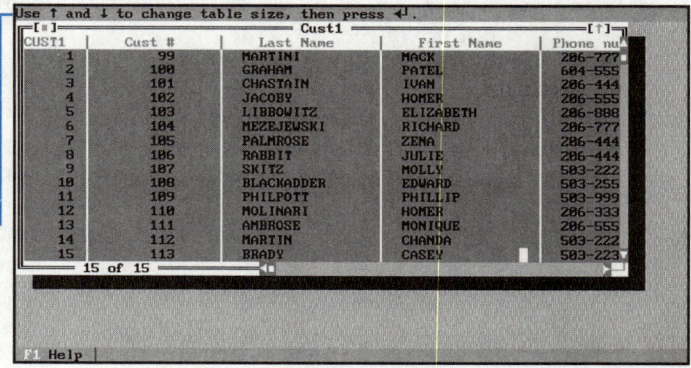

3. Use ↑ or ↓ to change the table to the required size.

    You will notice that the cursor jumps to the bottom of the screen, and is displayed as a large, fast-blinking rectangle.

    If you use a mouse, remember that you can resize a table by clicking and dragging the corner icon in the bottom right corner of the table.

Changing the Column Width

The width of a column is specified when you create the table definition. The ColumnSize command enables you to alter this set width as needed.

Using Paradox Table Images

To use the ColumnSize command, do the following:

1. Select the Image option from the menu bar.
2. Choose the ColumnSize command from the pull-down menu.

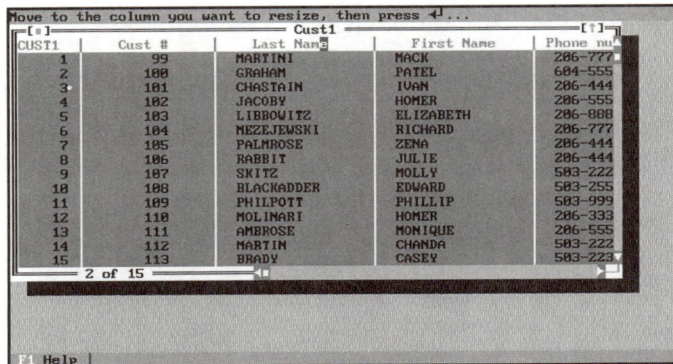

Paradox displays this screen after you select the Image ColumnSize command.

3. As prompted, move the cursor to the column you want to resize, and then press ⏎Enter. For example, move the cursor to the Last Name field and press ⏎Enter.
4. Use ← or → to move the right border line in or out. Press ⏎Enter when you have the required width.

If you are using a mouse, do the following to change a column's width:

1. Place the mouse pointer on the right-hand column dividing line.
2. Click and drag the border to the required position, and then release the mouse button.

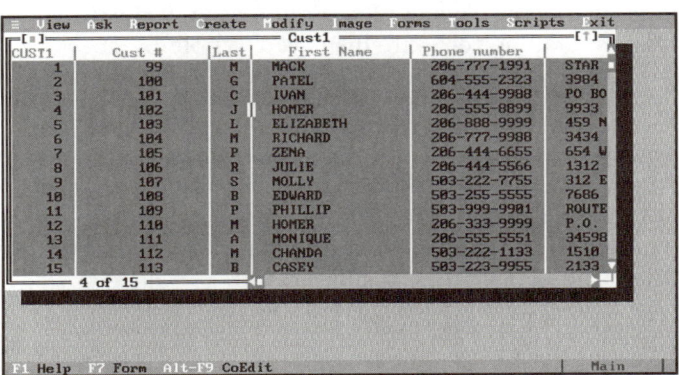

Here, you see the same field being resized with the mouse.

125

Adding, Editing, and Viewing Data with a Table

Choosing a Display Format

Using the Image Format command, you can reformat the default settings for the Number, Currency, and Date fields. When this option is selected, Paradox requires you to move the cursor to the field you want to reformat, and then press ⏎Enter. The available options are described in the following text.

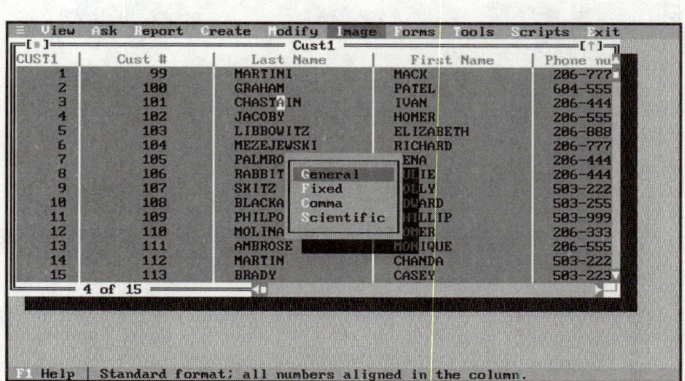

These are the Number and Currency field reformat options.

If you are reformatting a Number or Currency field, you will see a menu box with these four options:

General — This is the standard format. All the numbers are aligned on decimal points. As many decimal places as necessary are displayed. Numbers are displayed without whole number separators, or commas, and negative numbers are indicated by displaying a – (minus) sign.

Fixed — Enables you to display a fixed number of decimal places. Trailing zeros are displayed. Whole number separators are displayed as commas, and negative numbers are indicated by displaying a – (minus) sign.

Comma — This format displays a whole number separator, or comma, between each group of three numbers to the left of the decimal place. If the International format is chosen, the comma is replaced with a . (period), and the decimal position is displayed with a comma.

Scientific — All numbers are displayed in exponential notation.

Using Paradox Table Images

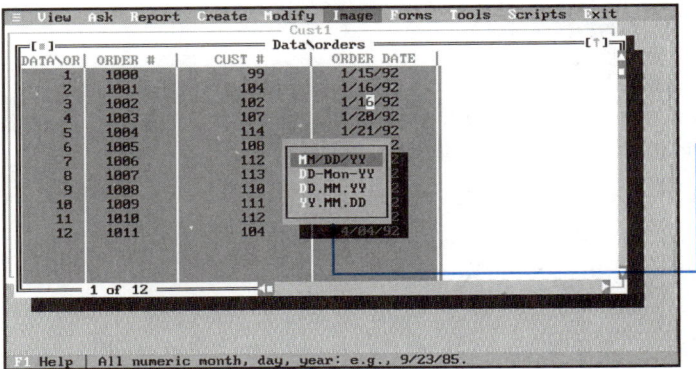

Here, you see the Date reformatting options.

If you are reformatting a Date field, you will see a menu box with the following options:

MM/DD/YY — Formats a date field to display the date with one or two digits for the month, two digits for the day, and two digits for a year in the twentieth century. The / (slash) is used as a separator. For example: 12/31/92.

DD-Mon-YY — Formats a date field to display the date with one or two digits for the day, three letters for the month, and two digits for the year. The – (minus sign) is used as the separator. For example: 31–Dec–92.

DD.MM.YY — Formats the date to be displayed with numbers separated by a . (period). For example: 12.31.92.

YY.MM.DD — Formats the date to be displayed with numbers separated by a . (period). For example: 92.12.31.

If a date is not within this century, Paradox automatically adds the century number to the date.

Moving Columns

At times you will want to rearrange the columns in your table without ending an editing session, restructuring a table, and then reentering the editing session again. Paradox gives you two methods for moving columns: the **I**mage **M**ove command and the Rotate Column command (Ctrl - R).

127

Adding, Editing, and Viewing Data with a Table

Using the Move Command

The **I**mage **M**ove command enables you to move a column to another location. This is an excellent tool if you need to compare data in columns. To use the **M**ove option, do the following:

1. Select **I**mage from the menu bar.
2. Choose the **M**ove option from the pull-down menu.
3. The list box showing the field names for the table is displayed. Select the field you want to move and press [↵Enter]. For this example, choose the Last Name field.
4. Now move the cursor to the location where you want to move the field. Place the cursor on the field that will be in front of (or to the right of) the field you're moving. For this example, you want to move the Last Name field so that it is after the First Name field and before the Phone Number field. Place the cursor on the First Name field and press [↵Enter].

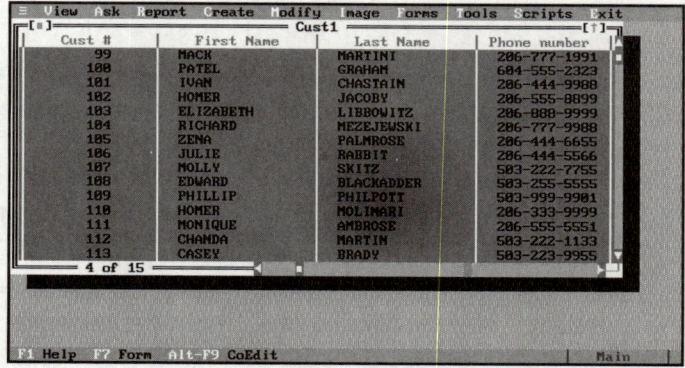

The Last Name field is now located after the First Name field.

Using the Rotate Command

The Rotate Column option will move the selected column from its current position to the last position in the table. You can rotate a column with the keyboard or with the mouse.

To use the keyboard to rotate a column, follow these steps:

1. Move the cursor to the Zip/Postal Code field.
2. Press [Ctrl]-[R].

Using Paradox Table Images

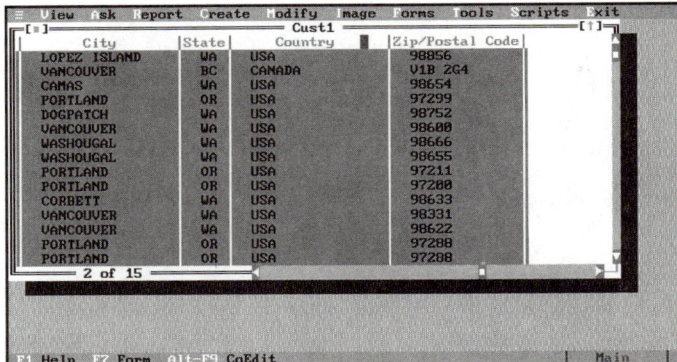

The Zip/Postal Code field is now the last column in the table.

You can also use the mouse to rotate a column. Do the following:

1. Place the mouse pointer in the column name area. Move the mouse pointer to the Country column and place it on the word Country.
2. Double-click the mouse.

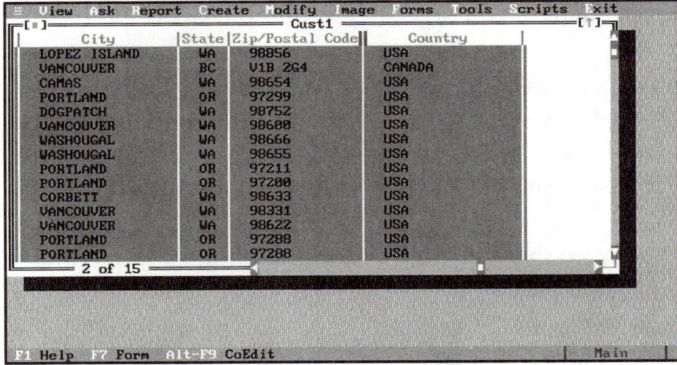

Now the Zip/Postal Code and Country fields are back in their original positions.

Saving the New Image Settings

The KeepSet option enables you to save the changes that you made with the Image options to the table. To use this option, select Image KeepSet. You will see the message Settings recorded... displayed in the message box area. When you next use the table, these settings will be the default view of the table. Before using KeepSet, changes made with the Image option are temporary.

129

Adding, Editing, and Viewing Data with a Table

Summary

In this chapter, you learned how to perform basic editing on individual tables, including using the Edit, DataEntry, and CoEdit modes. You also learned to alter the Table view, or image, using the Image options.

Specifically, you learned the following key information about editing, adding, and viewing data in tables:

- To use Edit mode for making changes to specific records, press F9 if the table is displayed on the desktop; or choose Modify Edit, and then select the table you want to edit.
- To add records in Edit mode, move the cursor to the end of the table and type the new record into the fields.
- To use the Form view, press F7. Form view ensures that you do not accidentally edit the wrong record.
- To use Field view, press Alt-F5 or Ctrl-F. You can edit a specific part of a field using text entry techniques.
- To use the Undo feature, press Ctrl-U. This key combination will undo, or reverse, the changes you made in the last transaction.
- The transaction log works differently in different modes. In Edit or DataEntry mode, you can use the transaction log to undo all the changes you made. In CoEdit mode, you can use the transaction log to undo only the last transaction.
- To delete a record, place the cursor anywhere in the record and press Del.
- To copy information from the previous record, place the cursor in the field you want to copy and press Ctrl-D.
- You can use Zoom and Zoom Next to search for records. Press Ctrl-Z to search for a specified value. Use Zoom Next by pressing Alt-Z to find the next occurrence of the same value.
- To insert a new record between two existing records, place the cursor on the record that will be below the new record and press Ins.
- In Edit mode, a new record that duplicates an existing record's key field(s) causes Paradox to replace the old record with the new information. In DataEntry mode, the Keyviol table is created. You must correct the key-violating records and add them to the target table. In CoEdit mode, a key violation causes a prompt to appear. You can view the original record by pressing Alt-K. To confirm either the new record or the old record, press Alt-L.

Summary

- To change the size of the table display, select **I**mage **T**ableSize from the menu, and then use the arrow keys to move the table to the required size. With a mouse, click on and drag the size corner on the table.

- To change a column width, choose the **I**mage **C**olumnSize command from the menu. Select the column, and then use `←` and `→` to resize the column as required. With a mouse, click and drag the right-hand column marker.

- You can specify different formatting characteristics for Number, Currency, and Date fields.

- You can use **I**mage **M**ove to move a column from one location to another. Select the column you want to move, and then select the new location.

- To use the Column Rotate command, press `Ctrl`-`R` or double-click on the field name. This command will move the selected column to the end of the table.

In the next chapter, you will learn to use the Paradox Standard form. You will become familiar with using a form to view and edit records.

Using the Standard Form

The Paradox form is an alternative way to view a table. When you use the Paradox form, you can perform all the functions that Table view allows—plus a few additional functions.

In this chapter, you will learn about the Paradox Standard form. Paradox creates this single-record form as the default form when you select Form view the first time. In this chapter, you will learn to view records with the Standard form. Then you will learn to add and edit records, search for records, and copy information from one record to another.

If you have not read the preceding chapter on using tables, do so before you read this chapter.

5

Parent versus child windows

Displaying the Standard form

Using the Standard form

Working with the Standard form

Closing a form

Using the Standard Form

> **Key Terms in This Chapter**
>
> *Form* — The Paradox form is a member of the table's family. The form is an alternative way to view data contained in a table. The form generally displays a single record instead of many records and the number of fields that fit in a single screen width.
>
> *Parent window* — The parent window is an independent window. A table window is a Parent window; the window is independent of other windows.
>
> *Child window* — The child window cannot exist if its parent window is not currently displayed on the desktop. A form window is a child window of a table window.

Parent Versus Child Windows

Paradox displays images of various types on the desktop. Many windows are dependent upon other windows for their existence. This concept is known as a *parent and child window relationship*. For example, a table is contained in a parent window. Forms or reports are contained in child windows. Forms and reports do not exist independently of the table window. If a form window is closed, there is no effect upon the report or table windows. On the other hand, if the table window is closed, then both the form and report windows also close.

Displaying the Standard Form

You can use the Standard form with Form view almost anytime you are displaying a table. The primary differences between the Table view and the Form view are:

- A table can show many records at a time, while a form generally displays a single record. The form can be constructed to display more than one record.
- A table can display only a limited number of fields, while a form often can display the entire record on a single form.

Displaying the Standard Form

- A table can be wider than its maximized window, while a form can be only as wide as its maximized window.
- A form can display calculated fields that are not contained by the table.
- A form can display the text of a field in more than one line, using a wrapped field format.
- While a table is always arranged in a row and column format, a form can be arranged in almost any way you require.
- A form can have multiple forms embedded within a master form. The embedded forms can display information from different tables.

The Form Window

As mentioned earlier, the form window is the child window to its parent, the table window. Regardless of the current mode Paradox is in—Main, Edit, or CoEdit—the form window will always be a child window belonging to the table.

To open the Standard form for your Cust1 table, do the following:

1. Select the **V**iew option from the Main menu bar.
2. Enter the table name into the dialog text box. Type **Cust1** and press ↵Enter.

   The image of the Cust1 table will be displayed in Table view on the desktop.
3. Press the Form toggle, F7, or click the mouse on F7 Form displayed in the status bar at the bottom of your screen.

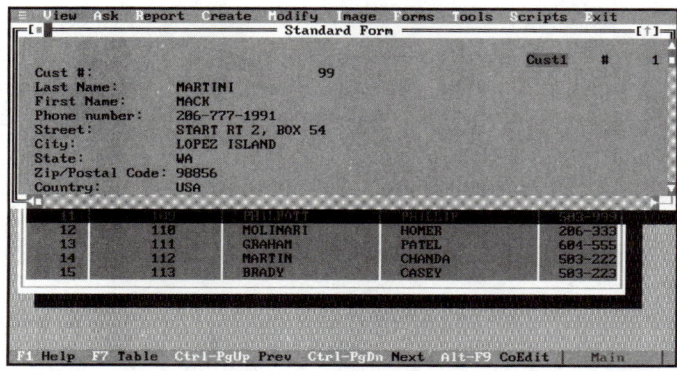

Here, you can see the first record displayed in the Paradox Standard form.

135

Using the Standard Form

As you can see in this figure, the form window has many of the same features as the table window. Because the form window is now the active window, Paradox displays the scroll bars and the Maximize/Restore and Close buttons.

Unlike the Table view, the form displays an entire record within it. Each field is labeled on the left-hand side, and the field data is displayed to the right of the appropriate field name. The record number is displayed in the upper right-hand corner.

Notice that all the fields except one are displayed in a left-justified mode. The only field that isn't left-justified is Cust #. Cust # has a field type of Number. Number, Currency, and Date fields are all right-justified. Right justification ensures that columns of numbers displayed in the Table view will be aligned on their right sides just as you would enter a column of numbers on paper.

If your table contains more than 19 fields, your form will become a multi-page form. To view the subsequent pages of the multi-page form, you can use either the arrow keys or PgUp or PgDn to display subsequent pages.

Here, you can see a record displayed that contains more than 19 fields.

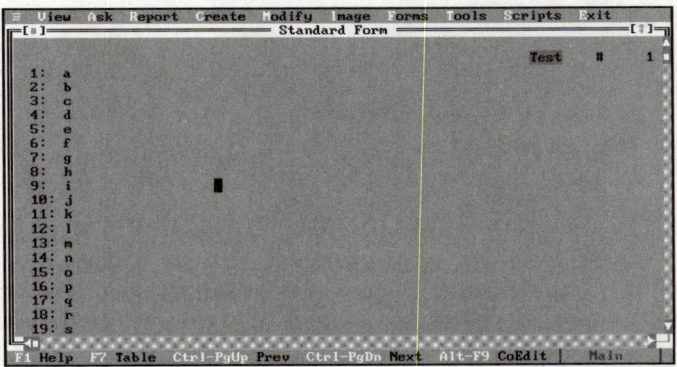

After pressing PgDn, the second page of the form is displayed. Notice that the page number is indicated for the subsequent pages. Only the first page of each record is not numbered.

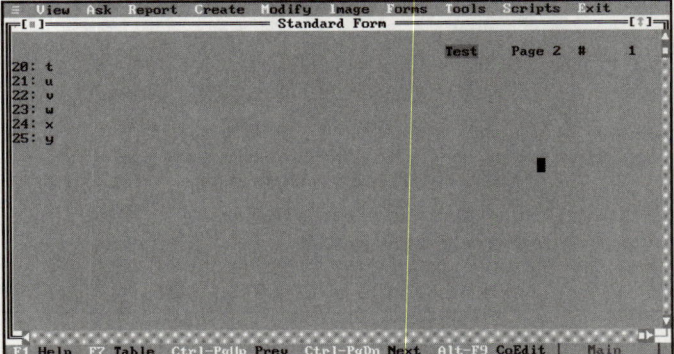

136

Displaying the Standard Form

Form Menus

Because the form window is a child window of the table, the form window shares the same menu bar that the table currently uses. Like the table, the menu bar and available options will vary depending upon the mode and other menu options selected.

One primary change you will notice are the options available to you on the status bar.

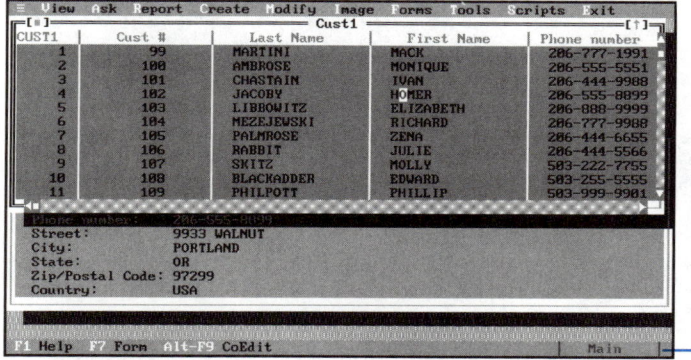

This is the Table view status bar.

On the Table view status bar, you have the following buttons, or hot-spots: **F1** Help, **F7** Form, and **Alt-F9** CoEdit.

The first option, **F1** Help, is available at all times.

The second option, **F7** Form, is the toggle to switch you back and forth between Table and Form view.

The third option, **Alt-F9** CoEdit, switches you from viewing the current table to the CoEdit mode.

137

Using the Standard Form

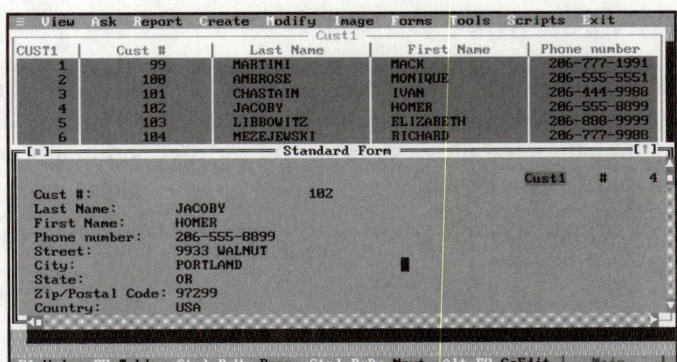

This is the Form view status bar.

Notice the difference in the status bar when using Form view. On the Form view status bar, you have the following options: **F1** Help, **F7** Table, **Ctrl-PgUp** Prev, **Ctrl-PgDn** Next, and **Alt-F9** CoEdit.

The first option, **F1** Help, is available at all times.

The second option, **F7** Table, is the toggle to switch you back and forth between Table and Form view.

The third option, **Ctrl-PgUp** Prev, moves you up one record. This option is similar to using PgUp except that the cursor remains in the same field. For example, if you had record #3 displayed in the form, pressing Ctrl-PgUp would move you to record #2.

The fourth option, **Ctrl-PgDn** Next, moves you down one record. This option is similar to using PgDn except that the cursor remains in the same field. For example, if you had record #4 displayed in the form, pressing Ctrl-PgDn would move you to record #5.

The fifth option, **Alt-F9** CoEdit, switches you from viewing the current table to the CoEdit mode.

Remember, if you are using a mouse, simply move the mouse pointer to the bottom of the screen and click the required option. The option will be executed immediately.

Using the Standard Form

To use a form, you must first open the table to which the form belongs. As with all Paradox objects that are child objects, you must open the parent before you can access the other.

To use the form while viewing a table, do the following:

1. Select the **V**iew option from the Main menu.
2. Enter the name of the table you want to open. Type the name **Cust1** or press `Enter`, or click the mouse inside the list box to see a list of available tables.
3. When the table is displayed on the desktop, you can open the form. Press `F7` or click the mouse on **F7** Form on the status bar.

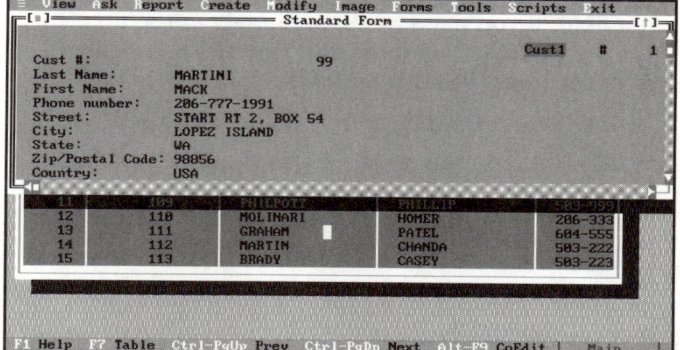

The Standard form is displayed.

When you open the table, the default cursor location is record number 1. The form opens, displaying the record in which the cursor was located, and with the cursor in the same field.

By default, the form window is sized so that either the entire record is displayed, or, if the record is more than 19 fields, the form is maximized. You can manually resize the window if you want to display a smaller window.

Moving among Fields

Movement within the form is the same as when you view a table. You can use the arrow keys and `Enter` to move from field to field and record to record. Using `Ctrl`-`Home` moves the cursor to the first field of a record. `Ctrl`-`End` moves the cursor to the last field of the record.

139

Using the Standard Form

You can use the mouse to immediately move to a selected field that is displayed in the current image of the form. To do this, move the mouse pointer to the field that you want the cursor to be in and click the mouse button. If the field is not visible, use the scroll bars to display another portion of the form.

Moving among Records

You can move from record to record in several ways. As mentioned above, you can use the arrow keys and [↲Enter] to move up or down the form. In the table, as you move through each field to the last field in the form, pressing [↓] or [→] or [↲Enter] moves you to the first field of the next record.

You also can use [PgUp] and [PgDn] to jump from record to record. You will notice that the cursor position changes when you use [PgUp] or [PgDn]. When using [PgUp], the cursor position changes to the last field of the record. When using [PgDn], the cursor shifts to the first field. If you need to move directly to the first record of your table, press [Home]. If you want to get to the last record of the table, press [End].

As already mentioned in this chapter, you can use [Ctrl]-[PgUp] to move from a record to the record above. The cursor will remain located in the same field as in the previous record. Alternatively, [Ctrl]-[PgDn] will move down a record.

The different key movements are listed in table 5.1.

Table 5.1
Key Movements

Key(s)	Movement
[↑] or [←]	Previous field up or left
[↓] or [→]	Next field down or right
[Ctrl]-[Home]	First field current record
[Ctrl]-[End]	Last field current record
[Ctrl]-[PgUp]	Previous record same field
[Ctrl]-[PgDn]	Next record same field
[Home]	First record same field

Working with the Standard Form

Key(s)	Movement
End	Last record same field
PgUp	Previous record last field
PgDn	Next record first field

Working with the Standard Form

Until you enter one of the Paradox editing modes, you can view records with the Standard form. For the remainder of this chapter, you use the Standard form in Edit mode. The form has the same characteristics and functionality in all editing modes.

The same restrictions that apply to tables within each of the modes apply to forms as well. For example, in the DataEntry mode, the Standard form still works with an Entry table, while in the CoEdit mode, the Standard form works with the actual table. The **U**ndo command in DataEntry is not limited to a single record as it is in CoEdit.

Adding Records

You can use the Paradox Standard form to add records to the table to which the form belongs. The Standard form is well suited for adding new records and editing existing records. The Form view has several advantages over the Table view. You can see the whole record at a glance, not just three or four fields. You also will not become distracted by adjacent records. The Form view is much easier for a new user who is not comfortable using a table, because the form is a more natural way of viewing information.

To use the Standard form to add new records to the table, do the following:

1. Press F9.

    Because you already have the Cust1 table displayed on the desktop, you can immediately go to the Edit mode without selecting **M**odify **E**dit to choose a table. If the table you wanted to work with was not displayed on the desktop, then you would use the **M**odify **E**dit command to select the table.

141

Using the Standard Form

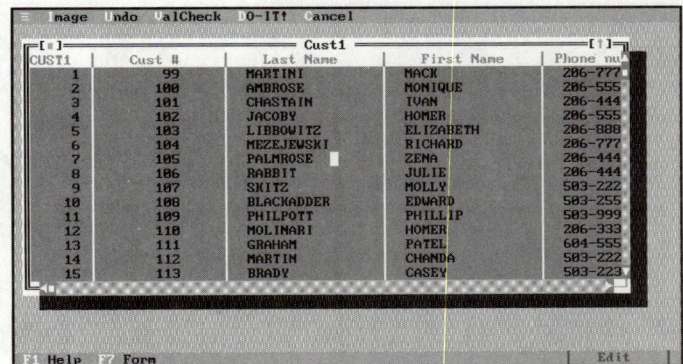

The Cust1 table is now in Edit mode.

The only obvious difference you will notice in Edit mode are the changes in the menu bar and the mode indicator, which changes from Main to Edit.

2. Press [F7] to display the Standard form.
3. Press [End] to get to the last record in the table, then press [PgDn] once. This opens a blank record and positions the cursor in the first field.
4. Enter the following data into the indicated fields. Remember to press either [⏎Enter], [↓], or [→] to move to the next field. Do not press any key after entering the data for the last field.

Cust #:	114
Last Name:	SWENSON
First Name:	IVAN
Phone Number:	503-222-7302
Street:	5567 NW HAVENHERST
City:	STHELENS
State:	OR
Zip/Postal Code:	97166
Country:	USA

Working with the Standard Form

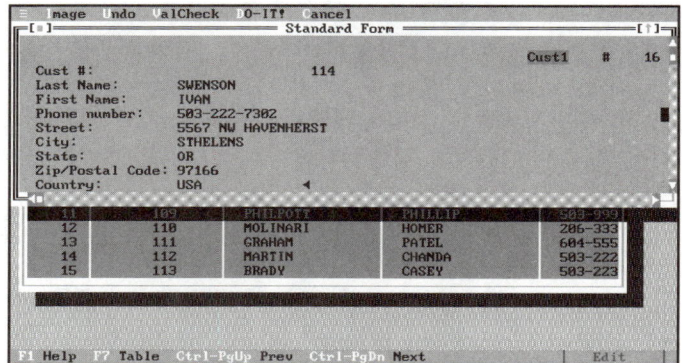

Here, you can see the completed record.

Changing Field Data

If you check over the information you just entered, you will probably realize that STHELENS is two words, not one. You can correct this error in two ways. You can simply erase the incorrect information and retype it, or you can use Field view.

Editing a Field

To edit a field, you can erase the data and retype it. For many corrections or changes, this is a quick and easy way to edit. To correct the error in your data, do the following:

1. Move the cursor to the City field.
2. Press `Backspace` six times, until the cursor has erased all the data except ST.
3. Type in the corrected data, **. HELENS**.

You can also make the same correction with a few less keystrokes. To do so, follow these steps:

1. Move the cursor to the City field.
2. Press `Ctrl`-`Backspace`. This key combination erases the entire field.
3. Retype the correct information, **ST. HELENS**.

143

Using the Standard Form

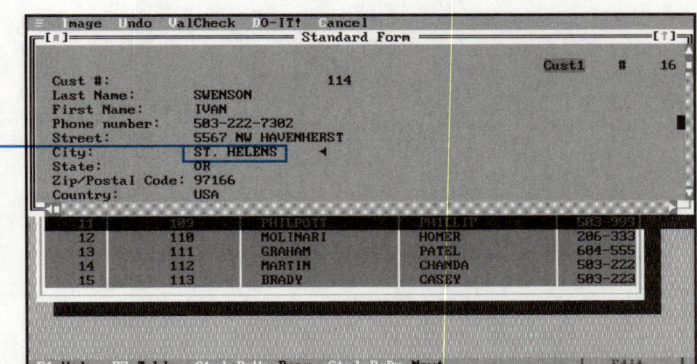

The City field is shown with the corrected data.

Using Field View

The alternative way to make this correction is with the Field view. When you would have a typo to correct, Field View is the most efficient method. To use the Field view technique, do the following:

1. Move the cursor to the City field.
2. Press [Alt]-[F5]. The cursor changes into reverse video.
3. Move the cursor to the H in HELENS. Press [.] and then the **space bar**.

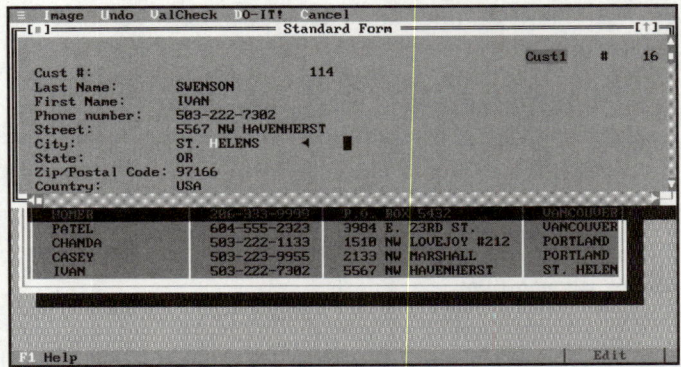

Your screen should now look like this.

Searching for a Record

Paradox enables you to search for a record while in Form view. You have the same options that are available to you in Table view: Zoom, Zoom Next, and **I**mage **Z**oom. Just as in Table view, the Zoom option is case-sensitive when

Working with the Standard Form

searching for a value. You also have the option to use the wild-card characters, .. (double period) and @ (at symbol), to search for an inexact match. Remember the differences between each of the following options:

Zoom
: Place the cursor in the field that contains the data you want to find. Access Zoom by pressing `Ctrl`-`Z`. Enter the exact value you want to search for in the text box of the displayed dialog box. Press `Enter` to start the search. If a match is found, the cursor moves to the record and field. If a match is not found, a message is displayed in the message box.

Zoom Next
: This option searches for the next occurrence of the value you found using Zoom. Zoom Next is accessed by pressing `Alt`-`Z`. If a duplicate value is found, the record is displayed in the form and the cursor is located in the field that was searched. If a match is not found, the message Match not found is displayed.

Image Zoom
: This menu bar option enables you to search for three different types of data. You can select the following three options:

    The **F**ield option enables you to jump to the selected field. When you choose this option, a list box is opened that contains a list of all the fields in the table. Select the required field name and press `Enter`. The cursor jumps, or zooms, to the selected field.

    The **R**ecord option enables you to zoom to a selected record number. Enter the record number in the displayed dialog box and press `Enter`. The cursor moves to the indicated record.

    The **V**alue option is similar to the Zoom option above. The only difference is that after you make this selection, Paradox asks you to select the column, or field, in which to search. Move the cursor to the required field and press `Enter`. The Search for Value dialog box is then displayed. Enter the value you want to find and press `Enter` again.

Using the Standard Form

To see for yourself how each of these different forms of Zoom work, do the following:

1. Move the cursor to the Zip/Post Code field and press Ctrl-Z.
2. Enter the value you want to search for—type 97288.

The Zoom dialog box is ready to perform the search.

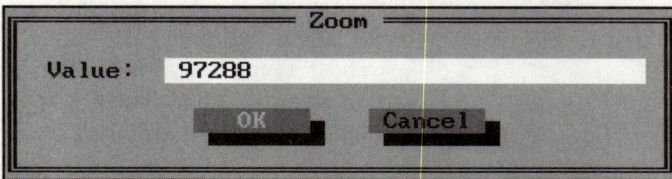

3. Press ↵Enter. You will see the message Searching... displayed as Paradox conducts the search.

Zoom finds a match. The record is displayed in the form, and the cursor is in the field you searched.

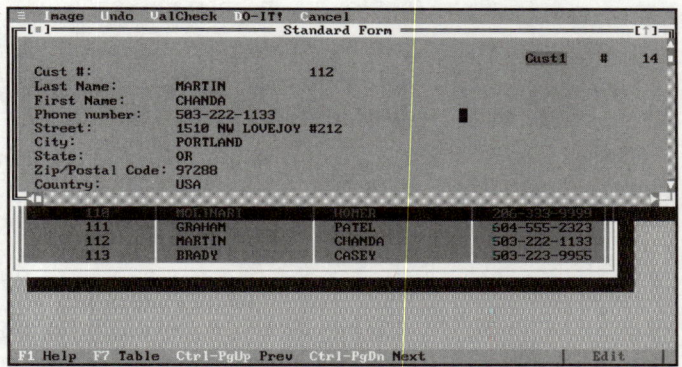

4. Now use Zoom Next to see if a duplicate value exists. Press Alt-Z. The message Searching... is again displayed in the message box (in some cases the message flashes).

Working with the Standard Form

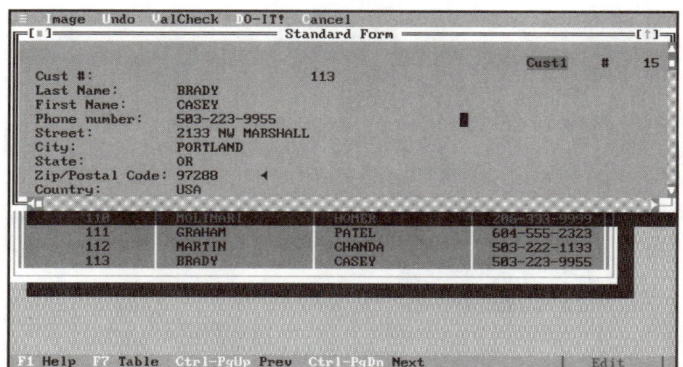

A second record is displayed after using Zoom Next.

5. Now choose the **I**mage option from the menu bar, and then select **Z**oom.

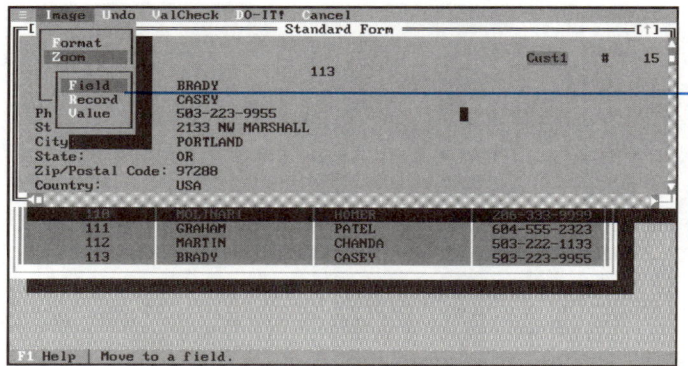

Here, you see the options available on the **I**mage **Z**oom menu box.

6. Select the **F**ield option.

147

Using the Standard Form

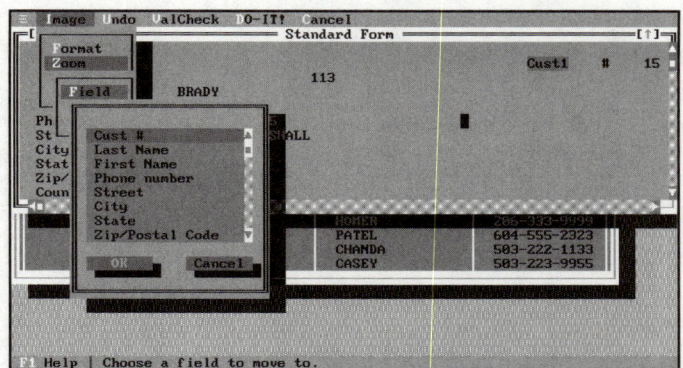

You now see the Field list box.

7. Choose the field to zoom to. Select Last Name and press ⏎Enter.

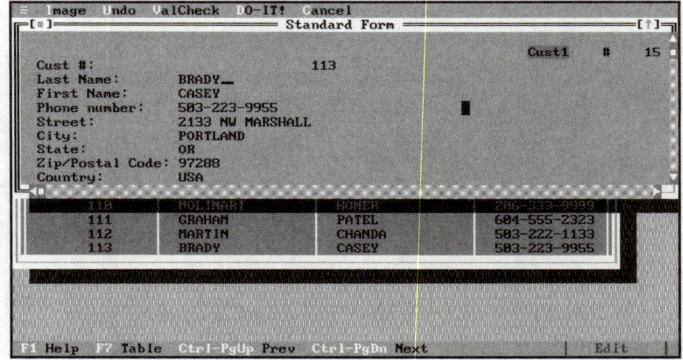

You will notice that the cursor has moved to the Last Name field.

When using the Form view, the **I**mage **Z**oom **F**ield command can be the quickest way to move within a single-page form. In Paradox, a form can be up to 15 pages in length. With a large form, using this command could be the easiest way to move directly to another field. Remember, this command moves the cursor to a selected field within the same record.

8. Select **I**mage **Z**oom, and then select **R**ecord.
9. Enter the record number to which you want to move. Remember, this is a record, or row number, not the customer number. Enter the value **100** and press ⏎Enter.

148

Working with the Standard Form

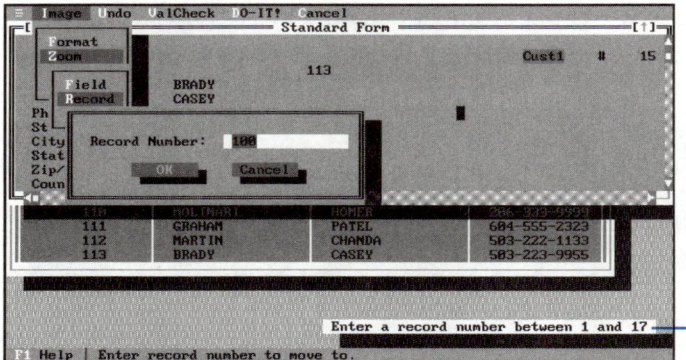

Notice the error message displayed in the message box.

Paradox allows you to enter only a value that is within the range of records in the table. Because you entered a value greater than the number of records, the message indicating the allowed range is displayed. As you enter more records into the table, the range becomes larger.

10. To enter a value that is within the range of record numbers, press Ctrl-Backspace to erase the current value, and then type **5** and press Enter.

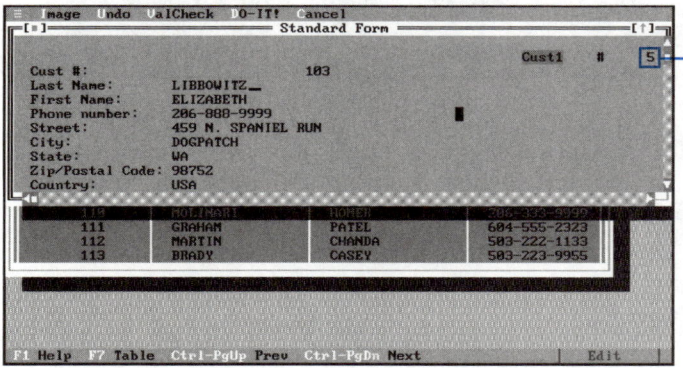

You now see that record number 5 is displayed in the form. Notice that the cursor remains in the same field where it was located in the prior record.

11. Select **I**mage **Z**oom, and then select **V**alue.

    Notice that when you select **V**alue, the cursor changes to a rapidly blinking rectangle. The menu bar disappears and is replaced by the prompt Move to the column you want to search in, then press ↵....

5

149

Using the Standard Form

12. Move the cursor to the Phone Number field and press ↵Enter.
13. Enter the value for which to search. Type **503-255-5555**.

The Zoom dialog box is completed.

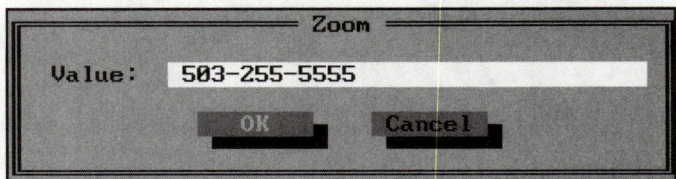

14. Press ↵Enter.

Here, you see the desired record.

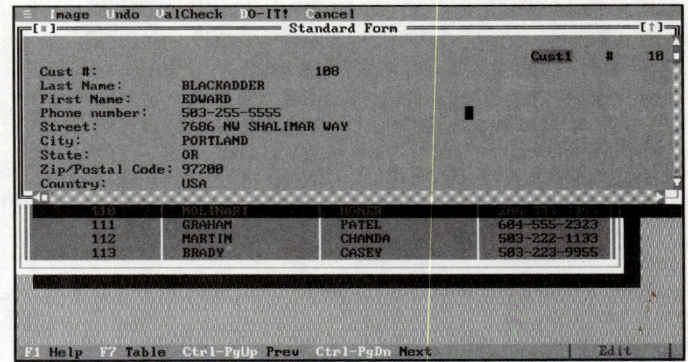

As you can see, Paradox provides you with a variety of ways to find data located in your table. In Chapter 7, which discusses using queries, you will learn another aspect of searching for and extracting data.

Closing a Form

If you complete your work using the form and finish using the table, you can close both by pressing F2. You will see the message Ending edit... displayed, and the image will return to the viewing mode. Both table and form windows will still be displayed on the desktop.

If you are temporarily finished with the form and want to return to the Table view, press F7. This step toggles the display back to the Table view. You will still see the image of the form displayed behind, or underneath, the table.

Summary

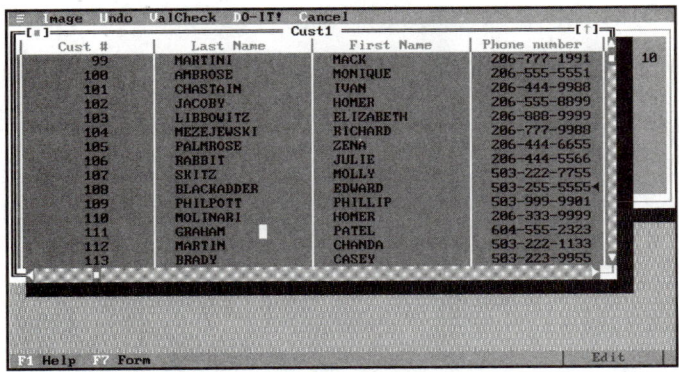

Here, you can see the form removed as the active window and the table moved to the foreground.

If you are using a mouse, you can accomplish the same result by moving the mouse pointer to any visible location on the table and clicking the mouse button. The table then becomes the active window.

You can also close just the form window by clicking on the close button, located in the upper left-hand corner of the window. The form window closes, leaving the Table view window active.

Summary

In this chapter, you have learned the differences between parent and child windows and how to use one of the child windows of a table, the form. You also learned to display records within a form and to add and edit records, using the form.

Specifically, you learned the following key points about Paradox 4.0:

- You must open a table before you can open the form that is associated with it.
- To view additional pages of a form, press `PgUp` or `PgDn` or use the arrow keys.
- You can use the **S**ize/Move option or the mouse to change the available view of the table.
- Press `Ctrl`-`PgUp` and `Ctrl`-`PgDn` to rapidly move from record to record and keep the cursor in the same field.
- You can use the arrow keys or `↵Enter` to move between fields in a form.

151

Using the Standard Form

- Use `PgUp` and `PgDn` to move from record to record.
- To edit a field while in Form view, move the cursor to the record and field. Press `◆Backspace`, and then retype the data.
- To use Field view to correct data, press `Alt`-`F5`, and then use text-editing techniques to change and add data.
- To use Zoom and Zoom Next to search for information, press `Ctrl`-`Z` to zoom to a specified value. Press `Alt`-`F5` to search for the next occurrence of the data in the selected field.
- Use the **I**mage **Z**oom **F**ield command to zoom the cursor to a selected field.
- Use the **I**mage **Z**oom **R**ecord command to jump to a specific record number.
- Use the **I**mage **Z**oom **V**alue command to search for a specified value.
- To close only the form, leaving the table open, click the mouse pointer on the close button at the top left-hand corner of the window.
- To switch from Form view to Table view, press `F7`.
- To close the table and form, press `F2`.

In the next chapter, you will learn to use the **M**odify **S**ort options. These options will enable you to re-sort the table into other orders, making some of your data more readily accessible.

Sorting a Table

With Paradox you can sort your data in almost any order you require. You can use the sort function to find trends in your data, or to group your data in different types of categories. You can even sort a keyed table in an alternative order as a new table.

This chapter will introduce you to the Paradox sort function, and show you how to use the **M**odify **S**ort option. You will learn to sort data into another table, and then to use the new table in sorting operations.

Paradox can sort records in up to four different orders. The type of sort order is selected when you first install Paradox and select the country options. Paradox has special sort options for international usage.

Using the standard sort order

Using the sorted table options

Sorting a Table

> **Key Terms in This Chapter**
>
> *Sort* — Arranging records, based on selected fields; records can be arranged in an ascending or descending order.
>
> *ASCII* — An acronym for American Standard Code for Information Interchange. This is the order Paradox uses as a default sort order.
>
> *Sort order* — Order in which characters are arranged alphabetically. Paradox supports several different sort orders. The order varies depending upon the country selected during installation of Paradox.
>
> *Ascending* — Sorting a field from lowest to highest value either alphabetically or numerically.
>
> *Descending* — Sorting a field from highest to lowest value, both alphabetically and numerically.

Using the Standard Sort Order

The standard, or normal, sort order for a table depends upon whether the table is a keyed table. A keyed table is sorted by the key field(s) in an ascending order. A non-keyed table is displayed in the order in which the records were entered.

When you initially install Paradox, you are asked to choose a country and a sort order. The standard default for the US is country equals US; the standard default sort order equals ASCII (American Standard Code for Information Interchange). The choices you make during the installation process determine how Paradox will sort your tables. For a few applications, this sort order is not appropriate. This type of order can be problematic because it is case-sensitive (upper- and lowercase letters do not sort together), and special international letters do not sort in their proper order.

Alternative sort orders include US dictionary, International dictionary, special dictionary order for Swedish-Finnish, and a special dictionary order for Norwegian-Danish languages. These special dictionary sort orders combine upper- and lowercase letters, along with special characters in a unified dictionary order, based upon the country selected.

Using the Sorted Table Options

When you choose the **M**odify **S**ort option, you will choose the table you want to sort. If you are working with a keyed table, you will then be prompted to supply the name of the table to which you will sort, or the Sort To table. The reason for this is that if Paradox allowed you to sort a keyed table in a different order, you may create a key violation of the table data.

If you are working with a non-keyed table, you are given the option to sort to the same table or to a new table. If you choose to sort to the same table, you must remember that the new sorted table will be the new order for this table. If you need to retain the original order of the table, then sort to a new table.

When you have made these decisions, you will see the Sort Questionnaire displayed on your screen. Here, you will make your choices for sorting the table. Selecting **D**O-IT! will perform the sort function and then display the sorted table.

Selecting the Sort To Table

Before you can perform any sort functions, you must choose the table with which you will be working. This is the table that will be sorted.

You will need to know whether the table is a keyed or unkeyed table. If the selected table is keyed, your sorted data will be placed into a new table. Paradox prevents you from re-sorting a keyed table, so that accidental key violations do not occur. When you save the sorted records into the new table, the new table is unkeyed.

If your table is unkeyed, you will be given the option to sort the records in the same table, or to save the sorted records into a new table.

In this chapter, you will sort your table, Cust1, into another table, saving the new table and performing other sort operations.

To perform a sort operation, do the following:

1. Select **M**odify **S**ort from the menu bar.
2. Choose the table to use in the sort operation. Type **Cust1** in the Table Selection dialog box.

155

Sorting a Table

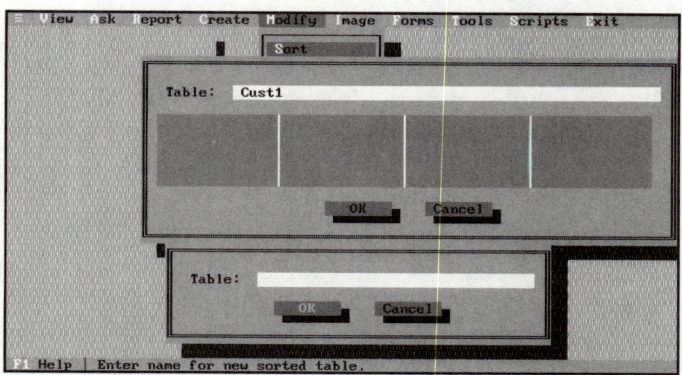

Here, you see the dialog box where you enter the Sort To table.

Because the Cust1 table is a keyed table, you are not given the option to sort to the same table. You must sort to a new table.

3. Press ⏎Enter and then enter the table name for the new Sort To table. Type in the name **Sortcust** for Sorted Customer, and press ⏎Enter.

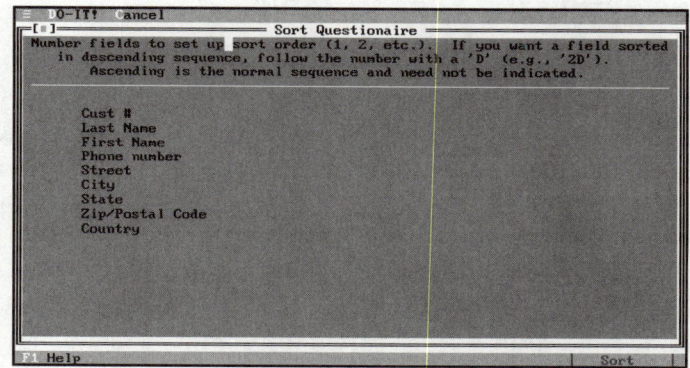

You now see the Sort Questionnaire displayed.

You use the Sort Questionnaire to tell Paradox how to sort the records in the table and in what order. The Sort Questionnaire is a simple list of all the fields that are contained in the chosen table. To the left of each Field Name is an area used to indicate the sort order for the table.

Using the Sort Menu

The Sort menu consists of only three options: the System menu (_), the **D**O-IT! command, and the **C**ancel command.

Using the Sorted Table Options

The System menu (≡) contains the generic menu that is available from all other menus. Many of the options are not active while in the Sort Questionnaire window. Because the Sort Questionnaire is specific to the Sort mode, you cannot move to another window while in this mode.

The **D**O-IT! option sorts the table in the specified order.

The **C**ancel option cancels the sort operation and returns you to the Main menu and the desktop.

Sorting By One Field

A table can be sorted by a single field. If you wanted to sort an unkeyed table by the value contained in the first field, with any duplicate value ties broken by sorting with the second field, and, if necessary, by the third field, you could select **F2 D**O-IT! now. Of course, this will also work with a keyed table, but because a keyed table requires unique values in the key fields, the sorted table will be identical to the original.

In this example, you will select an alternate sort order by the Zip/Postal Code field. This is the field you would select if you were doing a bulk-mailing of catalogs or literature to your customers.

To perform the sort operation, do the following:

1. Move the cursor to the Zip/Postal Code field by pressing ⬇ until you place the cursor to the left of the field name.

2. Because Paradox will use this field as the primary, or first, sorting value, type the number **1** here.

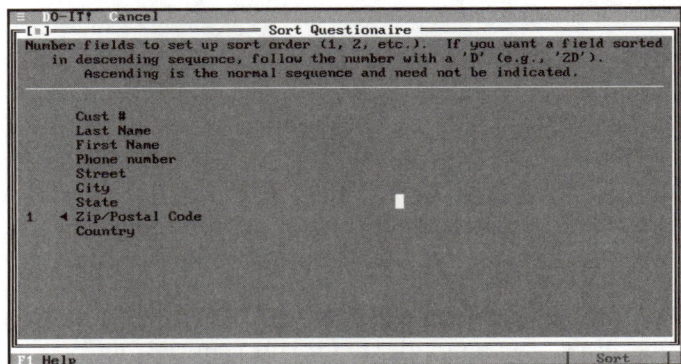

Here, you see the 1 beside the Zip/Postal Code field name. This will now be the primary sort order for the new table, Sortcust.

157

Sorting a Table

3. Press F2 or select **D**O-IT! from the menu bar.

   You will see the message Sorting... displayed as Paradox works on the sorting process. When Paradox has completed the sort, the new table, Sortcust, is displayed with the table sorted as you indicated.

Here, you see the first several fields of the new table, Sortcust.

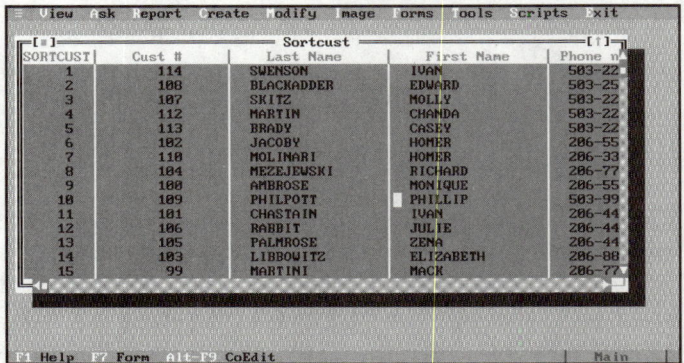

Notice that the Cust # field is now no longer in numerical order. This table is not keyed, nor indexed, by this field.

Now you see the remaining fields of the Sortcust table.

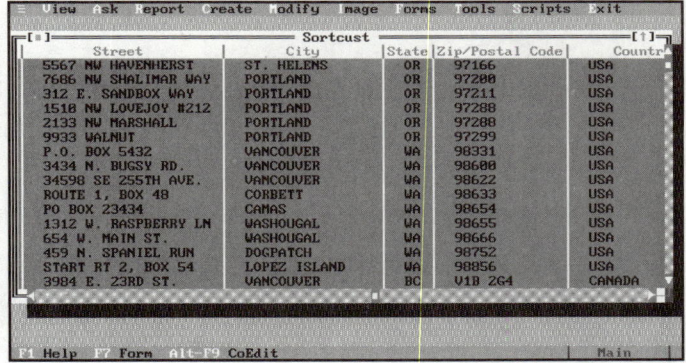

You can see in this view that the Zip/Postal Code field is now sorted in what appears to be numerical order. This field is actually sorted in ASCII order. Remember, this field is an alphanumeric field, not a number field. Generally, you should always use the alphanumeric field type for a zip code field because Paradox will drop leading zeros from a number field. This feature would invalidate ZIP codes such as 00212, which would include much of the

158

Using the Sorted Table Options

northeastern United States. Also, a number field would not permit many foreign postal codes, such as the one now displayed as the last record for Canada.

Sorting By Many Fields

Often when you sort an unkeyed table, you will have duplicate values within a field. Duplicate values are likely when you attempt to sort a name list of any size. In order to break ties when you have duplicate values, Paradox enables you to use additional indexes. Generally, using a primary and secondary index is sufficient for most databases. When you use Last Name as the primary index and First Name as the secondary index, however, you still may have ties. A large database can contain more than one John Smith, for example. You then will have to select an additional field to break these ties.

To sort your new table, Sortcust, using another sort index, do the following:

1. Select **M**odify **S**ort from the menu bar.
2. Enter the name of the table you want to sort. Type **Sortcust** or press Enter to see a list of all the available tables.

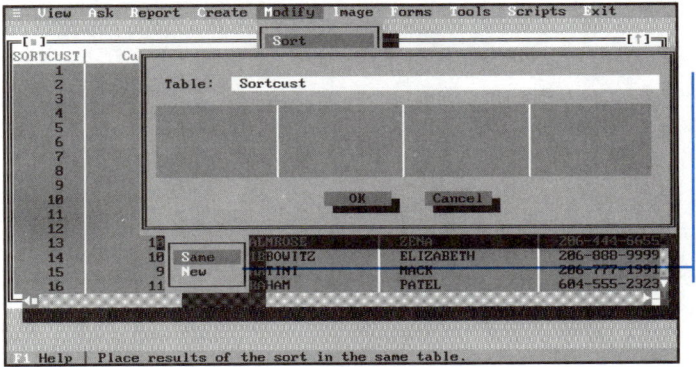

The Sortcust table is a non-keyed table, so you are given the option to sort to the **S**ame table or a **N**ew table.

3. Press Enter to accept the default value of **S**ame table.

159

Sorting a Table

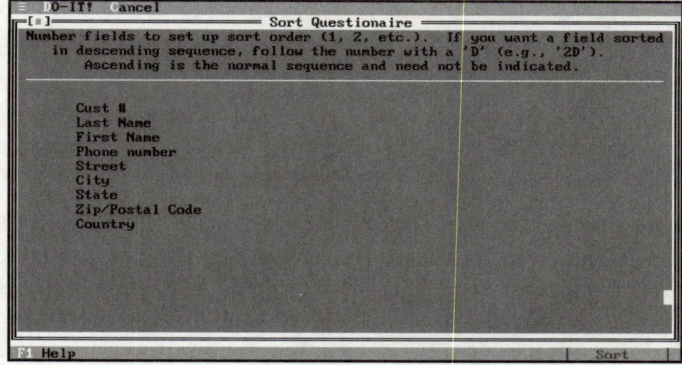

Here, you again see the Sort Questionnaire.

4. Move the cursor to the Last Name field and enter **1** to make the field the primary field.
5. Move the cursor to the First Name field and enter **2**. This field will be the secondary index.
6. Move the cursor to the Phone Number field and enter **3**. This will be the final tie-breaking field.

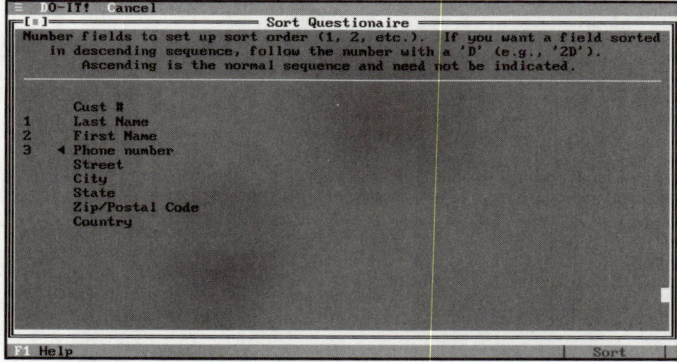

This is the completed Sort Questionnaire.

7. Press F2 or select **D**O-IT! from the menu bar.

The newly sorted table is displayed as soon as Paradox completes the sort operation.

160

Using the Sorted Table Options

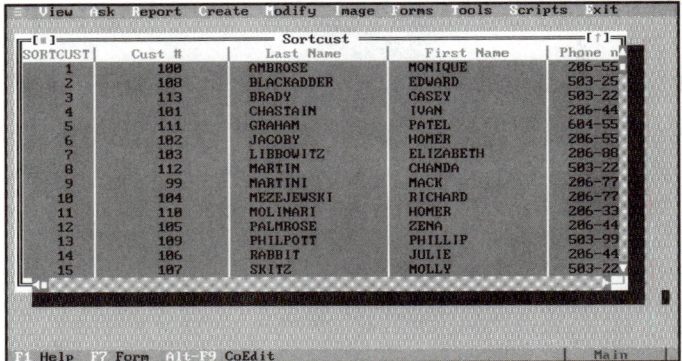

You now see the re-sorted Sortcust table.

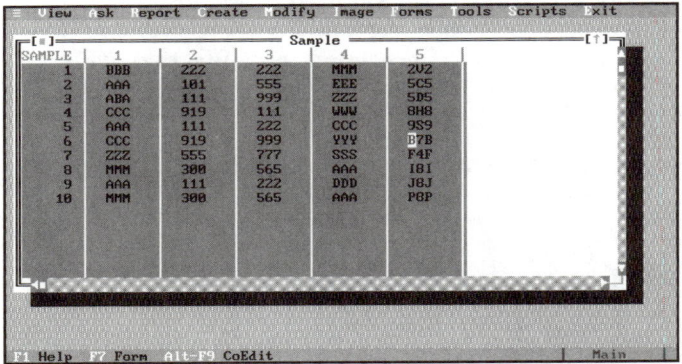

Here, you see the Sample table.

This table will illustrate the sort process to you more clearly. The Sample table contains five fields, and is an unkeyed table. You will notice that the table contains several duplicate values in fields throughout several records. This table will be sorted using the same steps you just completed on the Sortcust table to create multiple sort indexes.

Sorting a Table

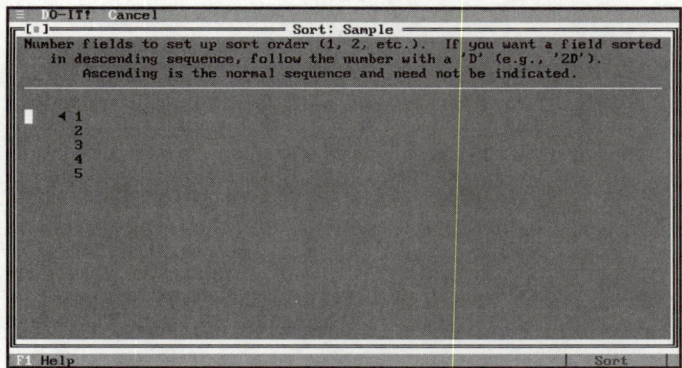

This is the Sort Questionnaire for the Sample table. For this example, no fields are selected to sort the table.

As mentioned, when you do not make a selection in the Sort Questionnaire, Paradox automatically sorts the table by the first field first; the second field breaks ties in the first field; the third field breaks ties in the first two fields, and so on until the last field.

Here is the final Sample sorted table.

You will notice in this example that the AAA values (in the first field of records 1, 2, and 3) are sorted first in the second field, and records 2 and 3 are finally sorted again in the fourth field. Records 8 and 9 are not sorted until the fifth field breaks the sort ties.

Defining the Sort Order

Most of the time you will sort a table as you have done in the preceding examples. You will choose the fields to use as the sort index, and then let

162

Using the Sorted Table Options

Paradox perform the sort operation. This type of sort is done in an ascending order. You also have the alternative method of sorting in a descending order.

Ascending Order

When filling in the Sort Questionnaire, you tell Paradox not only the fields to use for sorting a table, but also the order in which to sort the fields. As already mentioned at the beginning of this chapter, your choice of the basic sort order is determined when you install Paradox. The default sorted order when you fill in the Sort Questionnaire, or when a table is sorted by a key field, is an ascending order. Ascending order is:

   1, 2, 3, 4, ..., A, B, C, D, ..., a, b, c, d, ...

Descending Order

You can also choose to use a descending sort order when sorting a table. Descending order is:

   z, y, x, w, ..., Z, Y, X, W, ..., 9, 8, 7, 6, ...

Remember, that a key field is always sorted in ascending order. To choose a descending sort, do the following:

1. Select **M**odify **S**ort from the menu bar.
2. Select the table you want to sort. Type in **Sortcust** and press ⏎Enter.
3. Select **S**ame to sort the items in the new order to the original table.
4. In the Sort Questionnaire, type in **1** in the Cust # field. Paradox will sort the table by the first field.
5. Now, beside the 1, type in the letter **D**.

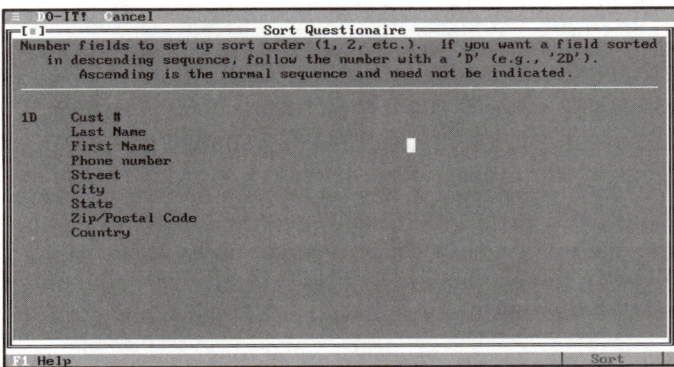

Your Sort Questionnaire should now look like this. The table will be sorted by the first field in descending order.

163

Sorting a Table

6. Press F2 or select DO-IT! from the menu bar.

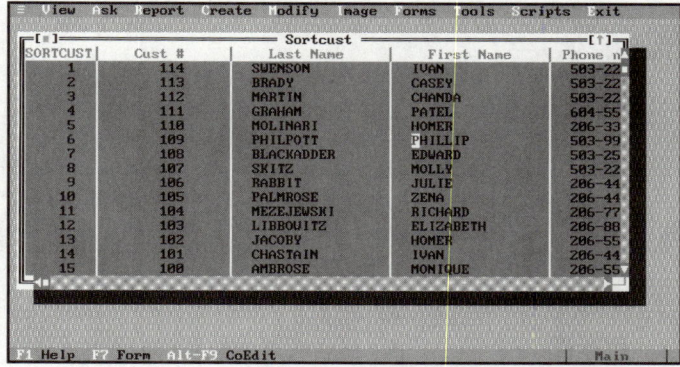

You now see the Sortcust table re-sorted by the first field in descending order.

Summary

In this chapter, you learned to use the Paradox sort options. You also learned how Paradox sorts a table and how to re-sort a table by alternate fields.

Specifically, you learned the following key points about Paradox 4.0:

- ■ To sort a keyed table, enter the name of the new table into the dialog box. This step prevents possible key violation conflicts.
- ■ Use the Sort Questionnaire to select the fields to use as sort indexes.
- ■ Paradox will automatically break any ties when sorting the table by using the left-most field first and working towards the right-most side of the table until a tie is broken.
- ■ To use a single index to sort a table, choose the field in the Sort Questionnaire and enter the number 1 beside it.
- ■ To select a secondary index to break ties in the primary sort index, select the required field in the Sort Questionnaire and enter the number 2 beside the field name. You can select additional indexes by entering the appropriate number (3, 4, ...) beside the field name.
- ■ To use the default ASCII sort order, select the table to be sorted and then choose F2 DO-IT! from the menu.
- ■ To use ascending order when sorting a table, complete the Sort Questionnaire and press the F2 DO-IT! key. Paradox automatically sorts the table in ascending order.

Summary

- To sort a table in descending order, select the field you want to sort in descending order in the Sort Questionnaire, enter the appropriate number beside the field name (**1** if this is the primary sort index, **2** if secondary, and so on), and then type the letter **D** beside the number. Paradox will use a descending sort order.

In the next chapter, you will learn to ask questions about your data by building a query. Using the query statement enables you to extract data that meets your stated requirements.

Querying the Database

7

So far you have created a table—or database—added records, changed records, and sorted records. You have also used a form to add and edit records. In short, you have worked with lists. Although using Paradox to create and sort lists is much easier than doing the task on paper, it is still a demanding task. One of Paradox's features, Query By Example, adds the power of the relational database to your data.

The center of the Paradox program is *Query By Example* (*QBE*). QBE is Paradox's capability to extract, or find, data for which you search. Many database programs require that you know the specific database language used by your program to retrieve specific data or records. For these programs, you have to know the proper syntax, or order, and the many commands.

QBE is the approach Paradox uses to help you query, or ask, questions about the data. To ask these questions, you use a form in which you place *check marks* and provide Paradox with *examples* of what you are looking for. Paradox then finds the best way to find the information you requested.

Asking the question

Querying a table

Working with special operators

Using comparison operators

Using the Answer table

Saving the query form

Querying the Database

> **Key Terms in This Chapter**
>
> *Query* — The method Paradox uses to retrieve selected information from a table.
>
> *QBE* — Query By Example, the process whereby you tell Paradox what information to find by providing an example of the data.
>
> *Query statement* — A question or request that details to Paradox where the data is, what data to extract, and how to display it.
>
> *Operators* — Used to define an operation you want to perform.
>
> *Pattern* — A model or picture of a value you want to find.

7 Asking the Question

With Paradox, you can ask a wide variety of questions about the data contained in your database. But why would you even need to ask questions about your data? After all, your data is already stored in your table, and you can see it.

For example, you can use a query to find all of your customers who bought a specific item in the last quarter. Or you can extract all of the invoices that are coming due this month. You also could list your employees who earn greater than a certain salary and who have been with the company for more than a certain number of years. You can construct a query that will supply you with many answers that you may not be able to get by looking at a list of your data.

As already mentioned in the introduction to this chapter, a Paradox table is basically a list—a list of customer information, orders, inventory, sales figures, and any other data you may need to keep. When you query Paradox about the data in a table, you construct a query statement using a query form. Paradox then shows you the answer to your query in a temporary table called *Answer*.

Forming a Query

You do not necessarily have to pose a query in a question format. You can also phrase a query as a request or statement, such as "I need X, Y, and Z." Some requests you might have regarding your data could include:

- Which of our customers live in the state of Oregon?
- List all customers whose area code is 206, and include only their name and phone number.
- Find all customers who do not live in the USA.

As you can see, a query may not be a question, but it is always a request from you to Paradox, asking for information that meets the criteria you have given in the form of your query.

Using Query By Example

QBE is the Paradox method of refining a query so that your request for information is as specific as possible. This method enables Paradox to find the data you need, and not to include extraneous data that might meet the general form of the query but not the example you give.

In this chapter, you will learn to use the various forms of QBE, and to construct your own query statements.

Querying a Table

In order to use QBE, you must first know what you are looking for, and where it will be located. You would not, for example, tell an employee to just "go and find the information." Because you are the one who knows what type of information you are looking for and have at least a general idea of where it is, you would give your employee more specific instructions.

The same is true of Paradox. You must tell Paradox where to look for the information, what you are looking for, and to include or not to include duplicates that may be found. When Paradox has completed your query, the results are displayed in the temporary table, or Answer table.

When you first use QBE, you may find it beneficial to write out your query. You can then refer to what you have written as you construct the query statement. A written query can help you to remember what it is you are looking for. For this first example, the question, or request, you will give to Paradox is:

   List the Names and Phone Numbers of all customers who live in Portland, Oregon.

Querying the Database

Selecting a Table

The first step in the query process is deciding on the *where*. Before you can construct a query, you must be familiar with the tables and the data contained in them. You cannot tell Paradox, for example, to search the inventory list table for all customers with phone numbers that begin with 3. Paradox would not find anything.

In this chapter, you will continue working with your Cust1 table. It is a good idea to display your table on-screen as you construct your query. Select **V**iew from the main menu, type **Cust1**, and press ↵Enter.

Here you see the Cust1 table displayed.

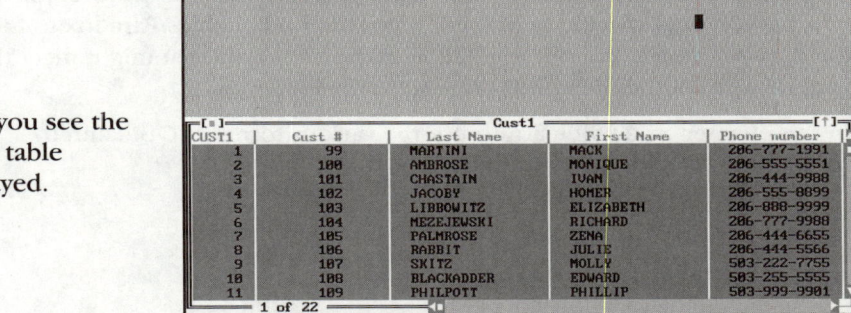

To create a query, you must select a table on which to base the query. To select the table, follow these steps:

1. Clear the desktop by pressing Alt-F8, and then select **A**sk from the Main menu bar.
2. Enter the table name you want to use for the query, or press ↵Enter to see a list of available tables. You can also click the mouse pointer in the list box to see the list of tables.

   Type **Cust1** and press ↵Enter.

Querying a Table

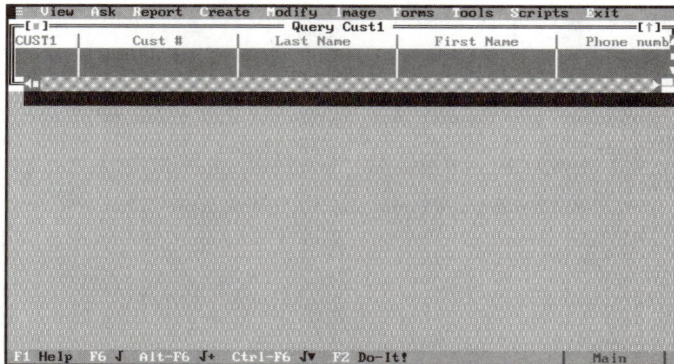

The query form for the Cust1 table is displayed.

When you select the table to use for the basis of the query, Paradox displays an empty copy of the table image. In this example, the query form contains the same fields that were contained in the Cust1 table.

You will also notice that while the menu bar has not changed, the status bar has. A new set of alternative function keys is displayed.

Choosing Fields

Now that you have selected the table on which to base your query, you must tell Paradox what data you are looking for. You will use the query form to indicate the fields you want to include in the Answer table.

To complete this part of the query, you must again refer to the request:

> List the Names and Phone Numbers of all customers who live in Portland, Oregon.

Looking at the written statement, you can see that you will need to look in the Name fields, the Phone Number field, the City field, and the State field. All the other fields in the table are not necessary to answer this query.

To create the query statement within the query form, do the following:

1. Move the cursor to the Last Name field. You can use any of the Paradox cursor movements within the query form. Press [F6].

   When you press [F6], you will notice the check mark placed within the field. Paradox uses the √ symbol to indicate a field to include in the Answer table.

171

Querying the Database

2. Move the cursor to the next field, First Name, and press F6 again.
3. Now move the cursor to the Phone Number field and press F6.

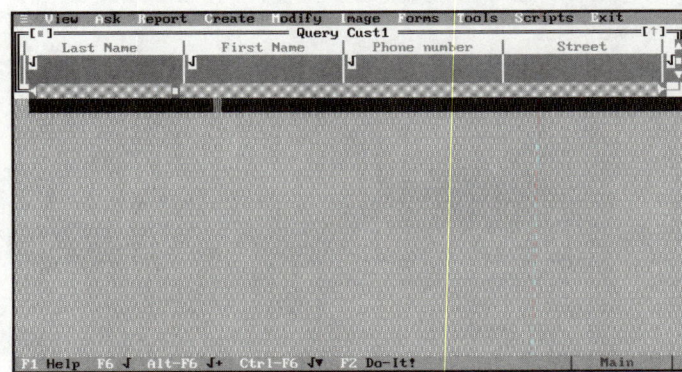

Here, you see the first fields of the query form with the appropriate check marks.

4. Move the cursor to the City field and press F6 again, placing a check mark in the field. Now enter the value for which you are searching. Type in the city name **PORTLAND**.

   Because you have entered your data in all uppercase letters, you must remember to use uppercase letters. In this type of QBE, Paradox is case-sensitive.

5. Move the cursor to the State field and press F6. Type **OR** as the value for which you are searching.

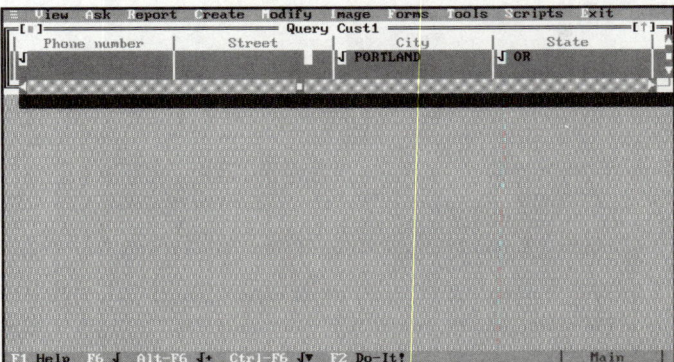

Now you can see the City and State fields completed, along with the values you want to find.

172

Querying a Table

6. Press F2 or select **DO**-IT! from the menu.

   Almost immediately after selecting **DO**-IT!, you see the message Expression makes no sense displayed in the message box. The message appears because the US Postal Service has reserved OR as the abbreviation for the state of Oregon, while Paradox also reserves OR as a special operator.

   To correct this error, you must tell Paradox that you mean OR as a word, not a special operator.

7. Press ◆Backspace to delete the value OR. Now type in "OR" as the replacement. Be sure to include the double quotation marks. The double quotation marks tell Paradox that what is contained between the marks should be interpreted literally and not as a command.

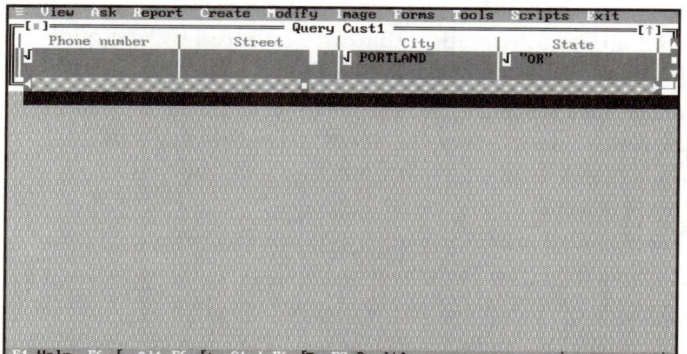

You now see the corrected State field.

8. Press F2 or select **DO**-IT!.

   The message Processing query ... is displayed as Paradox completes the query.

173

Querying the Database

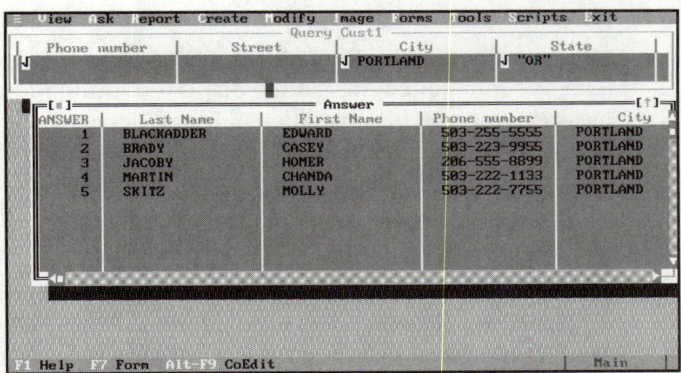

Paradox has found five records that match the query statement. They are displayed in the Answer table.

The Answer table is too wide to be displayed on the screen at one time. Ask yourself if all the information that was gathered by this query actually needs to appear in the Answer table.

The answer to the preceding question is No. While all the information is needed to perform the query, it is not necessary to display all the information in the Answer table. To further refine this query statement, go to the next step.

9. Close the Answer table by clicking the mouse pointer on the close button, or select **C**lose from the System menu.

   The query form is displayed as the active window.

10. Locate the cursor in the State field if the cursor is not already there. Press F6.

    The F6 key acts as a toggle, adding and removing the check mark ( ) from the field. If you remove the check mark, Paradox will still match the search criteria.

11. Move the cursor to the City field and press F6.

174

Querying a Table

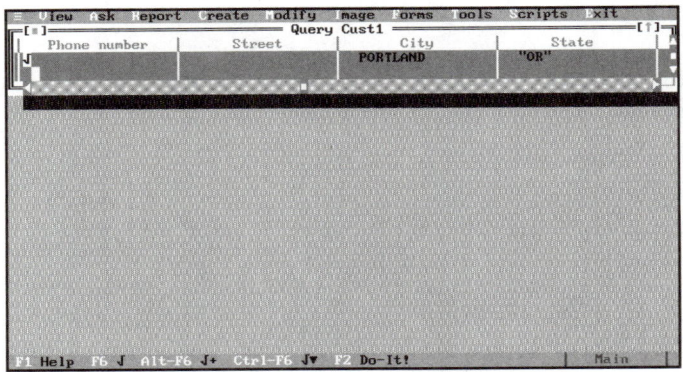

Your screen should now appear like this. Both check marks have been removed. Paradox will still use these search criteria when processing the query.

12. Press F2 or select **D**O-IT! from the menu bar.

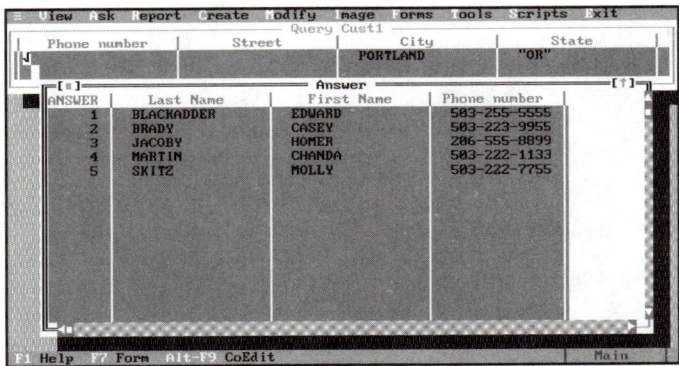

You now see a very similar Answer table as you did before, except that the City and State fields are not included.

While you did need to include the values in the query statement, you did not have to display them in the Answer table because they were redundant.

You should be cautious when using query forms. All query forms on the desktop are active. If you had simply closed the Answer table as you did in this section and then opened a new query form, Paradox would have tried to process both query forms at the same time. In this example, you made changes to the active query form and reused it, so there is no conflict. If you do not need a previous query form, press the Alt-F8 combination to clear the desktop before processing the next query. When the query form you want to remove is in the active window, you can press F8 to remove a single query form from the desktop.

175

Querying the Database

Displaying Duplicates

When processing a query, Paradox will not include duplicate values in the Answer table. To understand this concept, do the following:

1. Clear the desktop by pressing [Alt]-[F8], and then select **A**sk from the Main menu bar.
2. Enter the table name you want to use for the query, **Cust1**, and press [↵Enter].
3. Move the cursor to the First Name field and press [F6].
4. Press [F2] to process the query.

This query will include all the first Names of all customers in the Cust1 table, but will not include duplicates.

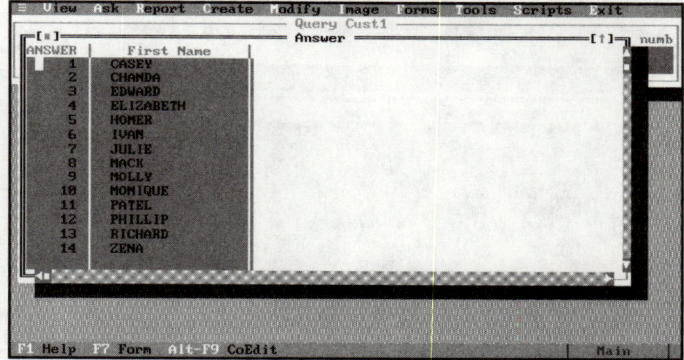

Here, you can see the new Answer table. Notice that there are 14 records displayed.

Your Cust1 table has a total of 16 records. In the First Name field, you have two sets of duplicate values: Homer and Ivan. When processing the query, Paradox does not include duplicate values in the Answer table.

To force Paradox to include all values within a field, including duplicates, you would do the following:

1. Close the Answer table by clicking the close button or selecting **C**lose from the System menu.
2. Move the cursor again to the First Name field.
3. Press [F6] to remove the check mark from the field.

Querying a Table

4. Press [Alt]-[F6]. You will see the √+ symbol displayed. This tells Paradox to include all values, including duplicates, in the Answer table.
5. Press [F2] to process the new query.

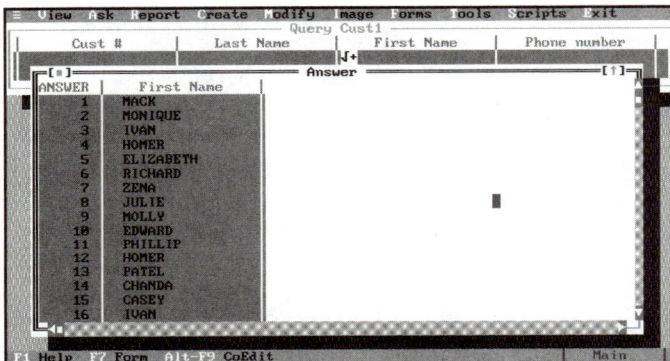

You now see the new Answer table with all 16 records, including the duplicate First Name values.

Matching Exact Values

In the previous examples, you have used QBE to search for exact value matches. You might have noticed that using an exact match query is similar to using the Zoom and Zoom Next commands you learned in the last chapter. The primary difference is that you can use the power of the query form to extract all the records that meet a match, and select specific fields to extract. You have all the records and the needed data in a single place, the Answer table, and you do not have to scroll through a record, find the information, and then move (Zoom Next) to the next match.

Finding Similar Values

At times you will need to find a value or group of values for which you do not know the exact match. Paradox provides you with two *wild-card* operators. A wild-card operator takes the place of another character. The Paradox wild-card operators are used to create a pattern for which you want to search. The two wild-card operators are:

- ..   The double period symbol takes the place of any other string of characters.
- @   The at sign takes the place of a single character.

177

Querying the Database

Table 7.1 lists some examples of the Paradox wild-card operators in pattern searches.

Table 7.1
Examples of Wild-Card Operators

Sample	Will Find	Will Not Find
M@L..	MELVIN MILLIE	MIKE
H..E	HASKLE HEBE	HELP HERBERT
2/../92	Will match all dates in the month of February 1992	

When you use the wild-card operators in a search pattern, Paradox becomes insensitive to case. If you are not sure whether the value in a field was entered in all uppercase, all lowercase, or mixed case, use the wild-card operators. The wild-card operators will ensure that you will find the value(s) you want regardless of case.

To use the wild-card operators, do the following:

1. Clear the desktop by pressing Alt-F8, and then select **A**sk from the Main menu bar.
2. Enter the table name you want to use for the query, **Cust1**, and press Enter.
3. Move the cursor to the Last Name field and press F6.
4. Type in the value for which you want to search, **m..**, and press Enter.
5. Place check marks in the First Name and Phone Number fields.

Querying a Table

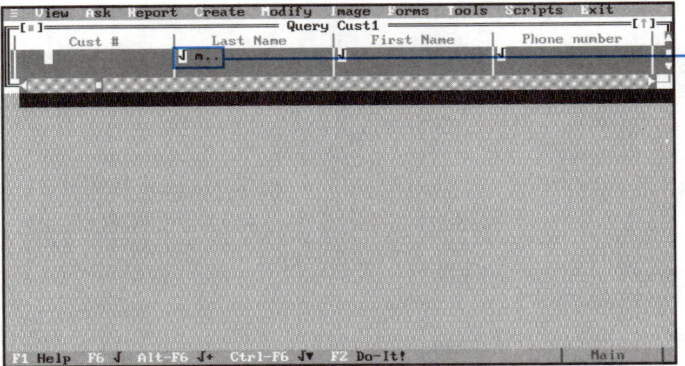

Here is the completed query form. The search pattern m.. is used to find all entries in the Last Name field that begin with the letter M.

6. Press F2 or select **DO-IT!** from the menu.

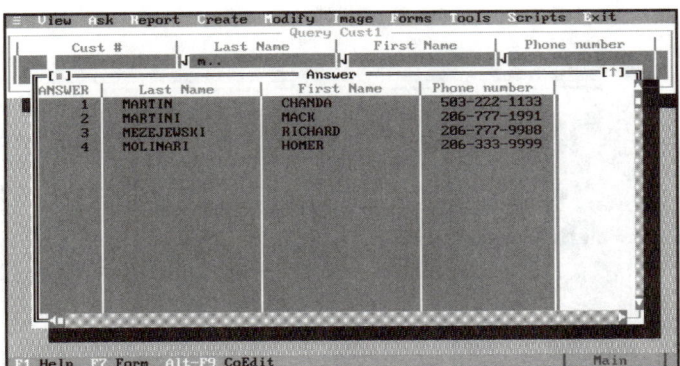

Here, you see the Answer table that results from the above query.

Here is an example of using the single character symbol, @. Do the following:

1. Close the Answer table and move the cursor to the Last Name field of the query form.
2. Delete the previous search pattern by pressing Ctrl-◆Backspace.
3. This time you want to search for the specific customer, Jacoby, but you cannot remember how to spell the name. Type in the search value **jacob@**.

179

Querying the Database

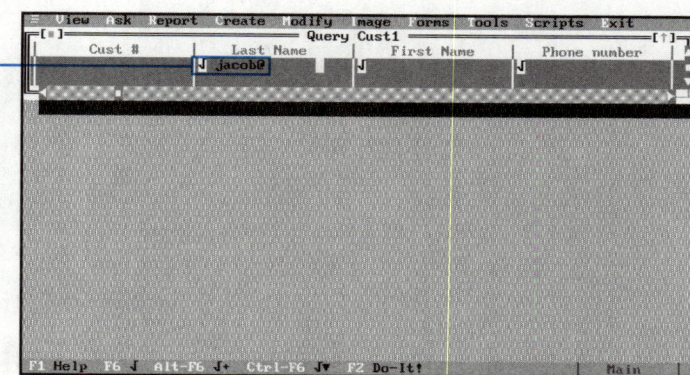

Here, you see the new search pattern with a single-character wild card.

4. Press F2 or select **D**O-IT! from the menu.

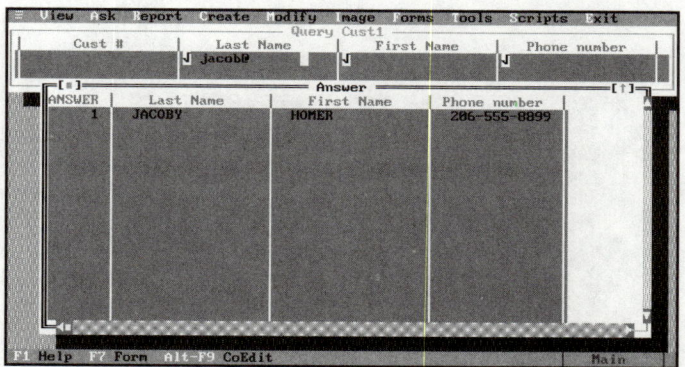

You can now see the new Answer table using the above search pattern.

As you saw in table 7.1, you can combine the search operators in almost any fashion. This feature enables you to find almost any value and display it in the Answer table.

Working with Special Operators

While you may be able to find any record you need using the preceding methods, Paradox provides some additional methods that may make some types of queries easier to construct.

Working with Special Operators

The special operators in this section are designed to help you find data you may not have found using the methods you have learned so far. You can use these operators in conjunction with the other methods already discussed.

Using AS

The AS operator is different from the other operators discussed in this section. AS is specifically designed to enable you to rename the field title in the Answer table.

Normally, when you tell Paradox to perform a query, the Answer table displays the same names that the query form and original table use. With the AS operator, you can rename the field so that it is more descriptive of the Answer table.

For example, to see how to use the AS operator to rename fields in the Answer table, do the following:

1. Clear the desktop by pressing **Alt**-**F8**, and then select **Ask** from the Main menu bar.
2. Enter the table name you want to use for the query, **Cust1**, and press **Enter**.
3. Move the cursor to the First Name field and press **F6**.
4. Now you will use the AS operator to rename this field in the Answer table. Type **AS NAME** and press **Enter**.
5. Press **F6** to select the Phone Number, and then type **AS PHONE** and press **Enter**.

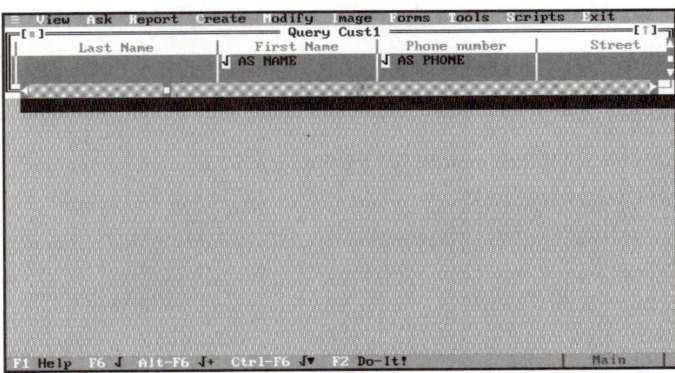

Here, you can see the query form with the AS operator used to change the Answer table's field names.

181

Querying the Database

6. Press F2 or select **D**O-IT! from the menu.

Here is the resulting Answer table. Notice that the field names are changed in the Answer table, but not in the query form.

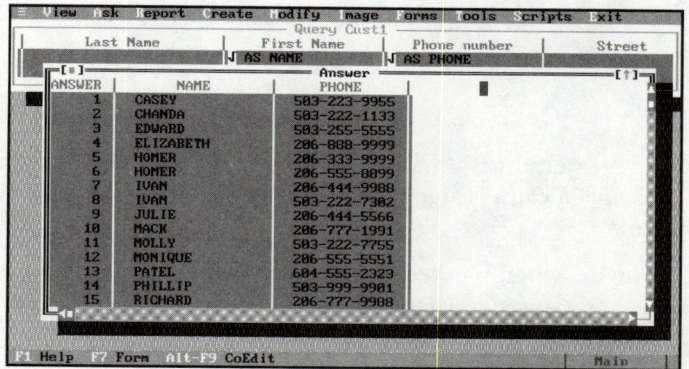

Using LIKE

The LIKE operator is an extremely useful tool. With this operator, you can locate information in a table based upon your best guess for spelling the value. This operator can help find information several people entered and, therefore, may not have been spelled exactly the same.

For example, suppose that your company takes a lot of orders over the phone. Occasionally someone will not hear a customer's name correctly and will enter a slightly different spelling of a name. You can use the LIKE operator to find this customer's orders under various spellings.

To see how the LIKE operator works, do the following:

1. Clear the desktop by pressing Alt-F8, and then select **A**sk from the Main menu bar.
2. Enter the table name you want to use for the query, **Cust1**, and press Enter.
3. Move the cursor to the Last Name field and press F6.
4. Type in the special operator and the value, **LIKE MARTIAN**.
5. Place a check mark in the First Name and Phone Number fields.

Working with Special Operators

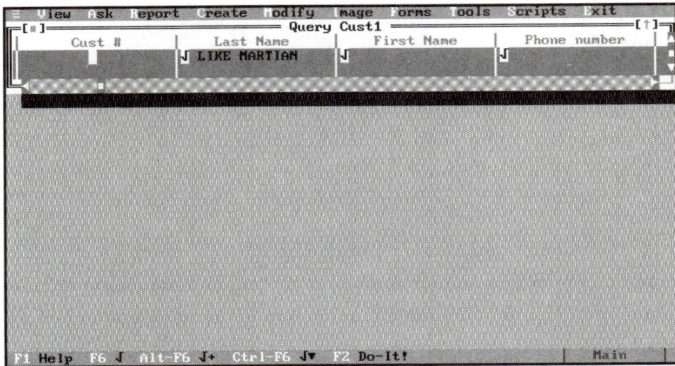

You see the query form completed with the LIKE operator.

6. Press F2 or select **D**O-IT! from the menu.

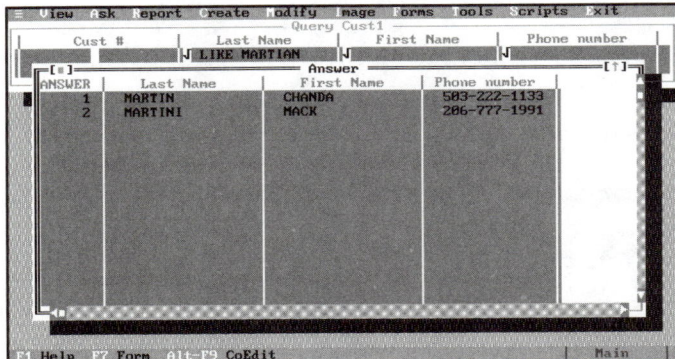

Here are the results of the query using the LIKE operator.

The only requirement for using the LIKE operator is that you must get the first letter correct or Paradox will not find the match you are seeking.

Using NOT

The NOT operator is an excellent way to filter out records you do not want to see in the Answer table. If you are searching for, or extracting, data and you know that there is a group or range of records you do not need for the answer, use the NOT operator.

In the above query, if you knew that the individual you were seeking did not live in the state of Washington, you could use the NOT operator to narrow the search criteria.

183

Querying the Database

To narrow a search criteria by eliminating selected records with the NOT operator, do the following:

1. Close the Answer table, using either the mouse or the System menu.
2. Move the cursor to the State field, and type **NOT WA**.

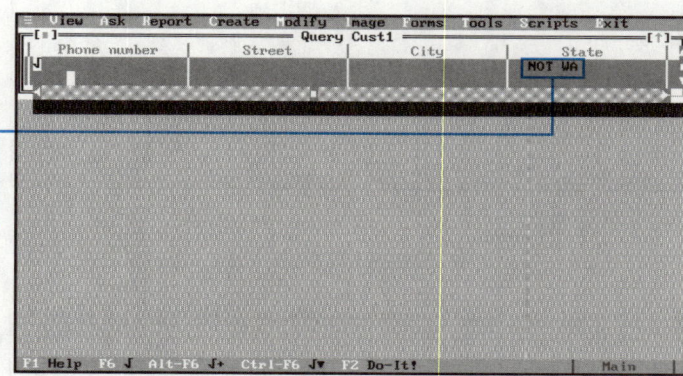

Here, you see the NOT operator in use.

3. Press F2 to process the new query.

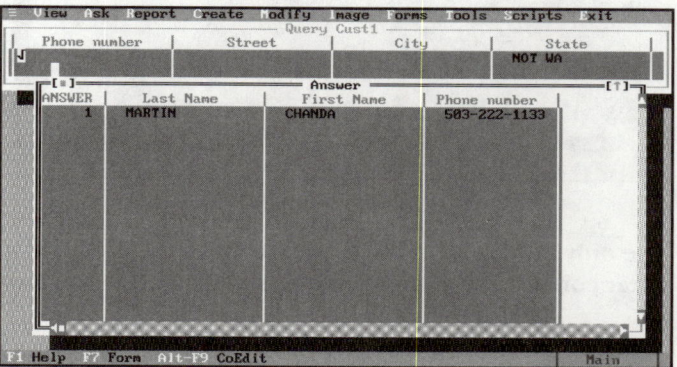

You now see the results of the new query and the NOT operator.

The second record MARTINI that was included in the last Answer table, has now been eliminated because this person lives in Washington.

Using BLANK

QBE requires you to provide Paradox with an example of the data you want to find. An exception to this rule is the blank or empty field. When creating a

184

Working with Special Operators

query, if you place a check mark in a field and do not enter an example, Paradox assumes that you want to see all the values in that field, provided the record meets all other criteria of the query form.

Suppose that you are interested in a record that contains a blank entry in a field. Leaving the field blank in the query form tells Paradox to display all records. Paradox provides a solution with the BLANK operator.

If part of your query is looking for an empty value in a field, then use the BLANK operator in the field. Use the BLANK operator just as you would the other special operators—but do not provide an example; BLANK is its own example.

To see how the BLANK operator is used, try the following example:

1. Clear the desktop by pressing Alt-F8, and then select **A**sk from the Main menu bar.
2. Enter the table name you want to use for the query, **Cust1**, and press Enter.
3. Move the cursor to the Last Name field and press F6.
4. Place a check mark in the First Name and Phone Number fields.
5. For this example, you are looking for any customers without a phone number, so type the operator **BLANK** in the Phone Number field.

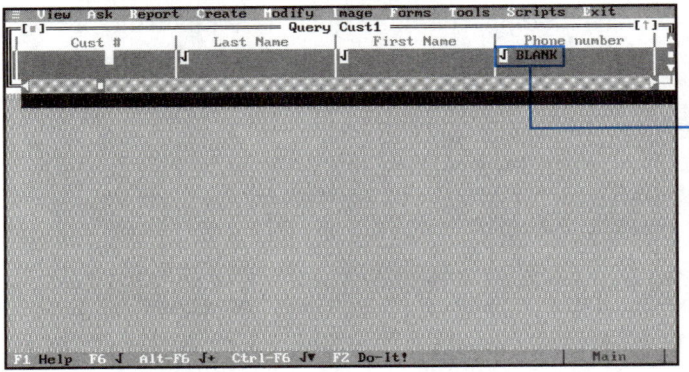

You now see the query form with the BLANK operator.

6. Press F2 or select **DO-IT!** from the menu.

185

Querying the Database

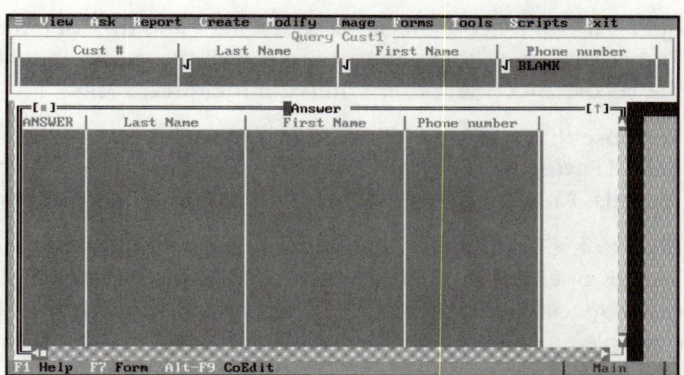

The resulting Answer table for this example is an empty table because no customers are without phone numbers.

The use of the BLANK operator can tell you whether your database is complete or information is being left out during data entry. The resulting empty Answer table tells you that you have no customers without phone numbers. If customers were listed in the Answer table, you would know that your data entry work is not complete.

Using Multiple Conditions

Most often when you construct a query statement, your answer must meet several conditions. Creating a multiple condition query is not difficult, but it does take a little time and thought.

So far in this chapter you have been working with multiple criteria within a record, in what is known as the *logical AND* format. As you enter a separate criteria in different fields on the same line, you are saying to Paradox, "AND this AND that." The records displayed in the Answer table must meet each of the criteria before they will be included.

When you construct a multiple AND criteria within a single field in a query form, each separate part of the criteria must be separated by a comma (,). This form of the logical AND criteria is most generally used in combination with range operators and is fully discussed in the next section of this chapter.

You also can use the opposite of the *logical AND*, which is the *logical OR*. Before the record can be selected for the Answer table, the record must meet one or the other of the criteria. It can also meet both and be included. An example of an OR criteria is searching in the State field for either WA or OR.

Working with Special Operators

Remember the error message received earlier in this chapter. The OR in Oregon is also used by Paradox as the reserved OR operator.

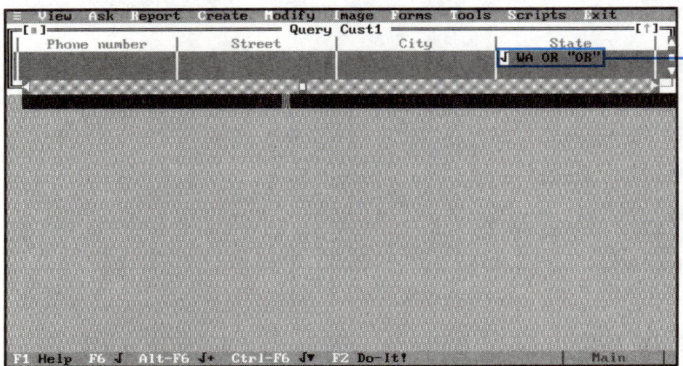

The OR operator within this field indicates that either of the two alternatives, WA or OR, is acceptable for inclusion in the Answer table.

Although you can combine the OR operator in a single field, as shown in the preceding illustration, you cannot create an OR statement using several fields in one line of a query. Each OR expression in the query statement that is contained in a separate field must also be separate lines. Paradox enables you to construct a query statement with up to 22 lines. An example of an OR expression that covers two fields and must be separated into two lines is: Find all customers that live in the city of Portland OR in the state of Washington. This query creates an OR expression over two fields. Generally, when constructing a multiple-line query, you must place check marks in each field you want to include in the Answer table, in each line.

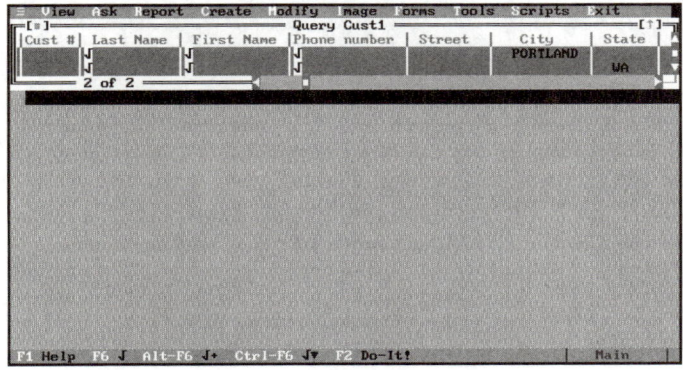

Here, you can see a two-line logical OR expression in a query statment.

187

Querying the Database

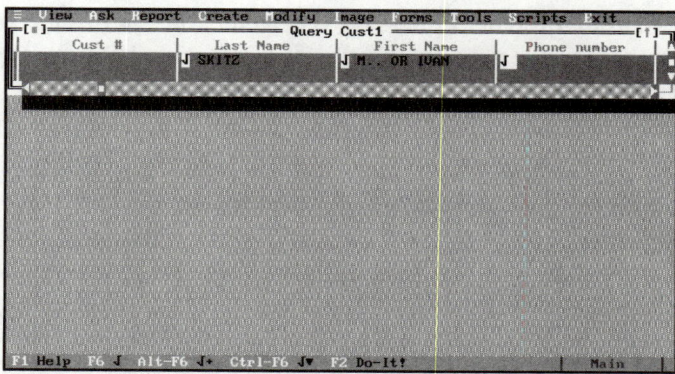

This is a logical AND query statement.

This query says, "Find the customer with the last name of Skitz *and* a first name that either begins with the letter M *or* is equal to Ivan, *and* include the phone number in the Answer table."

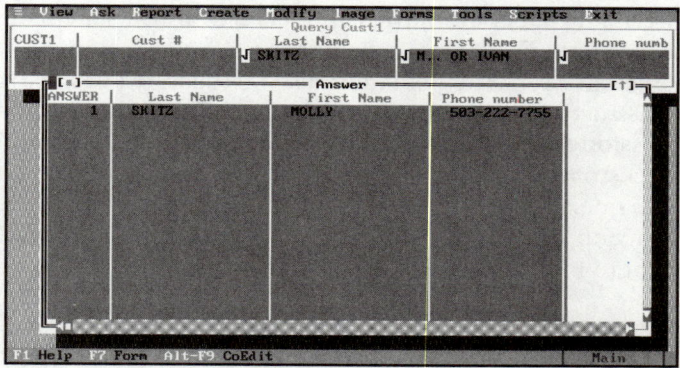

Here is the resulting Answer table from the query.

You know that your Cust1 table has two customers with the first name of Ivan. Why were they not included in the Answer table? The reason is that the logical OR operator cannot be used across fields within a single row. While the criteria statement within the First Name field was an OR statement, the OR did not reach back to the criteria in the Last Name field. In other words, your query actually said:

> Find the customer with the last name of Skitz *and* a first name that begins with the letter M, *or* a customer with a last name of Skitz *and* a first name of Ivan, *and* include the phone number.

Working with Special Operators

The logical OR operator can be used across fields if you construct the query in two lines.

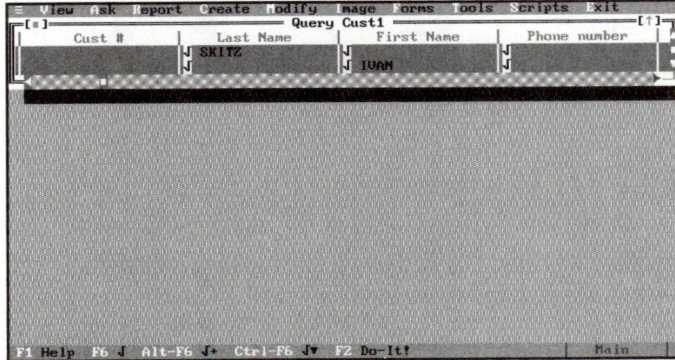

Here, you see a two-line logical OR query statement.

This query says, "Find a customer with the last name of Skitz, *or* find a customer with the first name of Ivan, *and* include the phone number for any matches."

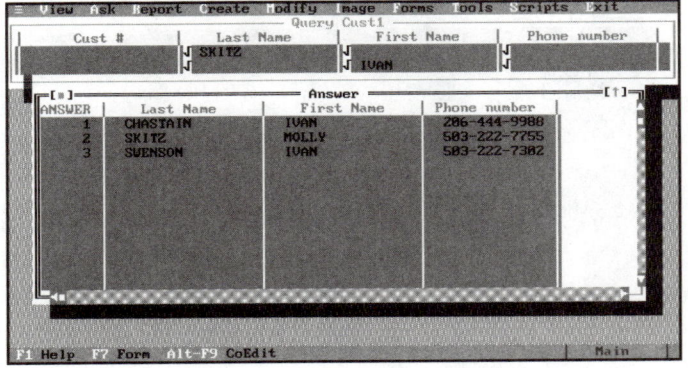

The Answer table from the preceding query finds three records that meet the criteria.

Here is an example of a written, multiple-condition query:

> Search for the customer whose first name is like Milly, but *not* the customer Monique, *and* who does not live in Washington, *or* the customer whose first name is Richard.

189

Querying the Database

The query contains several conditions that must be met. To construct this query, do the following:

1. Clear the desktop by pressing [Alt]-[F8]. Select **A**sk from the menu.
2. Choose the Cust1 table.
3. Place a check mark in the Last Name field of the query form.
4. Move the cursor to the First Name field and place a check mark.
5. Now enter the first criteria. Type:

   LIKE MILLY, NOT MONIQUE and press [←Enter].
6. Move the cursor to the Phone Number field and place a check mark.
7. Move the cursor to the State field and type **NOT WA** to create the criteria of not living in the state of Washington.
8. Now move the cursor down one row and back to the Last Name field, and place a check mark.
9. Move to the First Name field and place a check mark, and then enter the next criteria OR RICHARD by typing in **RICHARD**.

Here, you see the completed query statement. So that you can view the entire query statement, the field columns have been resized using the mouse.

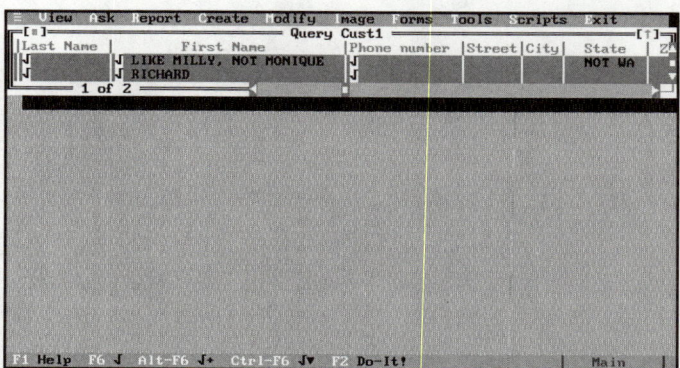

10. Press [F2] or select **D**O-IT! from the menu to process the query.

Using Comparison Operators

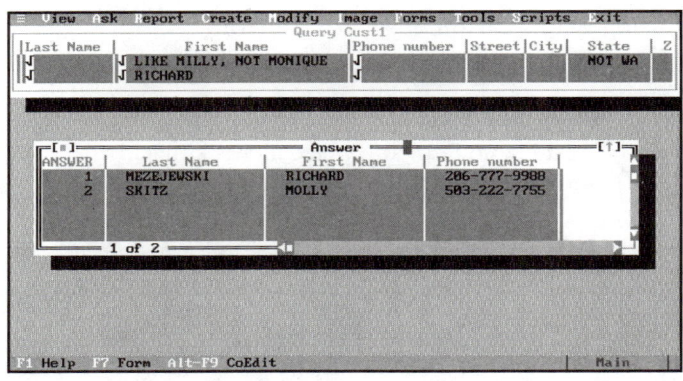

Here, you can see the results of the query statement.

Using Comparison Operators

Comparison operators, or range operators, are often used to find values within number fields. These operators can be used successfully in alphanumeric fields as well. Often the data you may be seeking is a range of information such as:

- All the sales made between 1/1/92 and 1/31/92
- All the customers whose last names start with the letter K to and including the customers whose last names start with the letter Q
- All the customers who bought an item X between 1/1/92 and 1/10/92
- All the employees whose gross pay is between $1000 and $1750 per month

These are all examples of looking for a range of records. Table 7.2 lists the five types of comparison operators Paradox uses.

Table 7.2
Comparison (Range) Operators

Operator	Meaning
=	Equal to a specific criteria, usually optional
>	Greater than the specified criteria
<	Less than the specific criteria
>=	Greater than *or* equal to the criteria
<=	Less than *or* equal to the criteria

191

Querying the Database

Here is an example of using a comparison or range operator:

1. Clear the desktop by pressing Alt-F8. Select **A**sk from the menu bar.
2. Choose **Cust1** as the table to query.
3. Move the cursor to the Last Name field and place a check mark.
4. Enter the criteria **>M**.

Here, you see the range criteria in the query form.

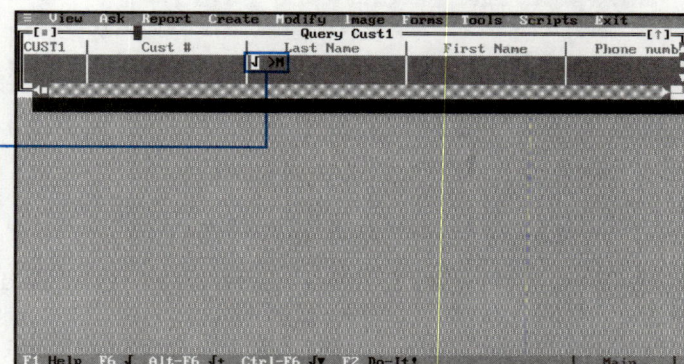

5. Press F2.

Here, you see the results of the query statement in the Answer table.

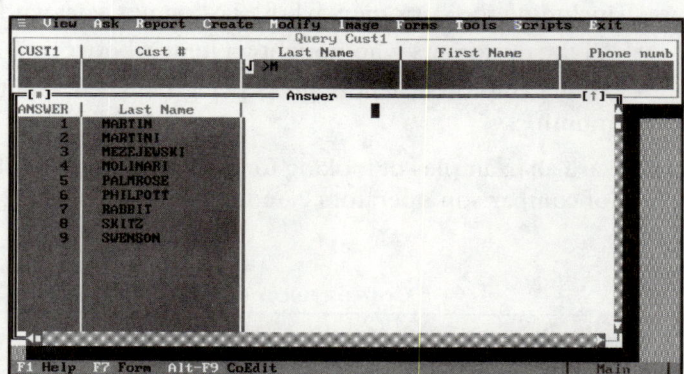

Notice that four customers with a last name beginning with the letter M are included. Doesn't the criteria statement in step 4 say to include only last names greater than M? Why are these included?

Using the Answer Table

Remember that Paradox sorts using ascending ASCII order (... 1, 2, 3, ... A, B, C, ... a, b, c, ...). In the U.S. dictionary order, *greater than M* means through the last name of Lz and includes any last name of M. You must remember that Ma is greater than M in almost any sort order.

Using the Answer Table

All query results are placed in the temporary Paradox table, Answer. You must remember that the Answer table is a *temporary* table. If you create and process another query, new data will overwrite the previous query. If you exit from the Paradox program and later return, the temporary table is not saved.

If you plan at a later time to use the data generated by the query, you must use the Tools Rename Table command to rename the table Answer and to create a permanent table for the data.

Within these restrictions, the Answer table is the same as any other Paradox table. You can edit the data, insert additional records, sort the records, and print reports. The query statement and Answer table are often used to extract and consolidate data for reports and graphs. These uses are discussed in Chapters 11 and 13.

Sorting the Answer Table

The Answer table is an unkeyed table. When the table is created by the query statement, it includes only the fields that have a check mark in the query. The table fields are in the same order that they were in the query statement.

The records are sorted automatically by Paradox in ASCII order. Paradox starts with the left-most field and works toward the right-most field, breaking any ties in the sort order.

To sort a field in descending order in the Answer table, press Ctrl-F6. Paradox then displays the √▼ symbol in the field. The Answer table field with this check mark is sorted in descending order.

If a different sort order is required for the data, use the Modify Sort option. Select the Answer table from the table list. You also should select the New table option and rename the table now. Then use the Sort Questionnaire as you did in Chapter 6.

Querying the Database

Editing the Answer Table

As already mentioned above, you can edit, add to, and use the Answer table like any other Paradox table. Be careful not to revise an Answer table too much. After all, you did go to the trouble of extracting specific data from the master source table to make significant changes to the resulting Answer table.

Saving the Answer Table

If you find that you will need to use the data extracted by the query later, you must save the Answer table as a permanent table. As mentioned earlier, if you create and run another query, the existing Answer table will be overwritten and you will lose the data.

To save the Answer table as a permanent table, do the following:

1. Select the **T**ools option from the Main menu bar.
2. Select the **R**ename option from the pull-down menu.
3. Choose **T**able.
4. Type the table name into the selection box and press [⏎Enter], or press [⏎Enter] to see the list of tables.

Here, you see the list box with the available tables. The Answer table is highlighted.

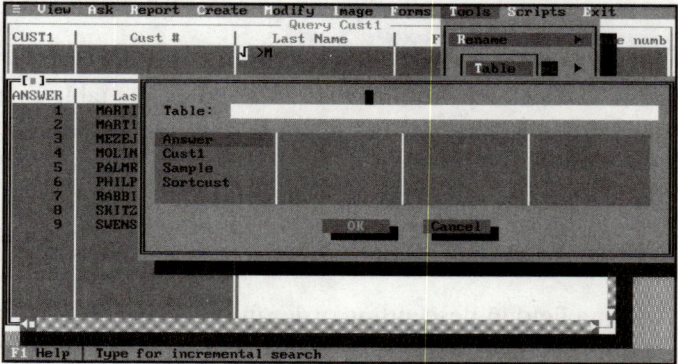

5. Press [⏎Enter] again to select the Answer table.
6. Enter the name you want to give the permanent table. Type in **PERMANSW** for Permanent Answer.

Saving the Query Form

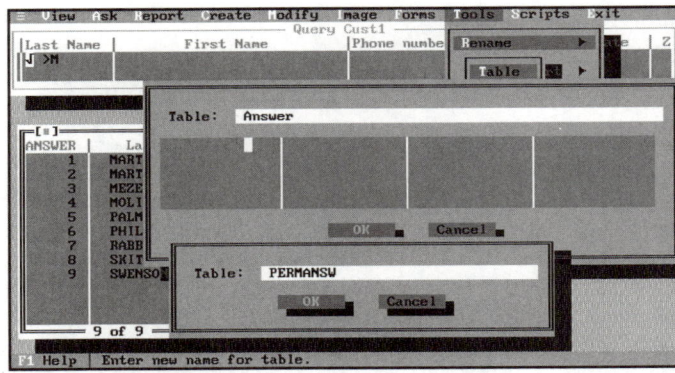

Here, you see the second Table dialog box completed with the new permanent table name.

7. Press Enter] to rename the Answer table. You see the message Renaming Answer to PERMANSW ... displayed in the message box.

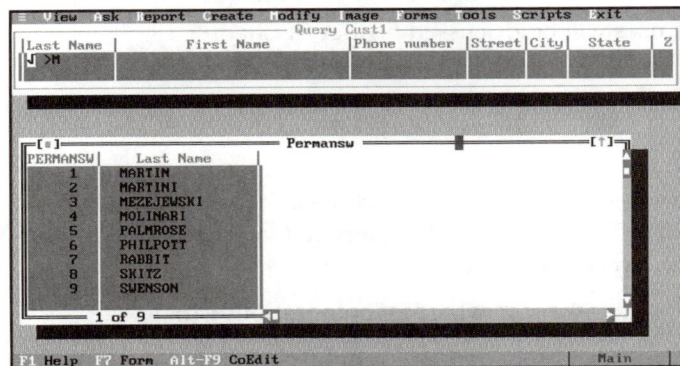

You now see the new permanent table, Permansw. Notice the table name at the top of the window.

Saving the Query Form

Paradox can save a query so that you do not have to re-create the query form each time you need to use it. When you have perfected your query statement, you can save your query form as a *script*. The Paradox script is a recording of keystrokes you can replay as needed.

To save a query, do the following:

1. Display on-screen the query statement you want to save. Then select **S**cripts from the Main menu.
2. From the pull-down menu, select the **Q**uerySave option.

Querying the Database

3. Enter a unique name for this query.

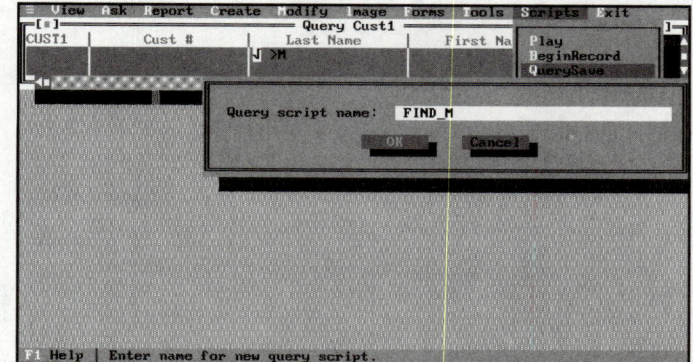

For this example, type **FIND_M**.

4. Press `↵Enter` to complete the command and save the query as a script. The script process and uses will be discussed further in Chapter 14.

Summary

In this chapter, you have learned to use the Paradox Ask command and a query statement. You have learned to use the query statement to extract and find specific data and records in a selected table.

Specifically, you have learned the following key points about Paradox 4.0:

- To use a query when searching for a group or a specific record(s), select **A**sk from the menu bar and enter the name of the table to use in the query.

- Write out the query, and then use the query form to create the query statement.

- To select a field to include in the Answer table, press `F6` to place a check mark in the field.

- To clear the desktop so that Paradox does not attempt to run several conflicting queries on the data, press `Alt`-`F8` between queries.

- To clear a single query form, activate the query forms window, and then press `F8`.

- To include duplicate values within a field, use the `Alt`-`F6` check plus option.

Summary

- To select inexact values, use the wild-card operators .. and @. The double periods replace a string of characters of any length, while the ampersand replaces a single character.
- Use the AS operator to change the field name in the Answer table.
- Use the LIKE operator to find similar information.
- Use the NOT operator to include all data in a field—except selected data.
- Use the BLANK operator to include only fields that do not have a value entered.
- Use the logical AND to create multiple criteria across fields in a single line query.
- Use a two-row query to create the logical OR expression across fields. Logical OR can be used within a field to define multiple criteria.
- Use the comparison or range operators, such as > (greater than), in extracting a range of data.
- To sort a field in descending order, press Ctrl-F6.
- When you use the temporary Answer table, use the **T**ools **R**ename **T**able option to rename the Answer table as a permanent table.
- To save a query form, use the **S**cript **Q**uerySave option.

In the next chapter, you will learn to construct a report. You will learn to use the Report menus and create a tabular report.

Constructing a Report

8

Up to now, you have created a database, entered data, changed records, used forms, and asked questions of the data. Although this is all well and good, it does not help the front office in the next town when the employees are trying to put the year-end financial reports together and need your input.

Keeping the data complete and accurate is an important part of database management, but presenting the data in an understandable format is equally important. For many people, the raw data contained in a Paradox table is neither meaningful, nor usable.

You use a *report* to tell someone about your table and what it contains. Just like when you created the query statement, lay out what you want your report to tell or show another person, and then bring together the necessary parts to create that report.

In this chapter, you will learn to use the Paradox Instant report. You will then learn the basics of creating your own report specification. Building your own report is much like building the table specification. You will use this information for creating more complex tabular and free-form reports in Chapter 12.

Creating an Instant report

Creating other types of Paradox reports

Understanding the Report Designer and Previewer

Using the Report Designer

Specifying the output

Constructing a Report

Key Terms in This Chapter

Report
Usually information printed from a table. A report also can be viewed on-screen or sent to an ASCII text file.

Report specification
A pattern or template specifying information's placement in a report. It includes all information for printing a report, including header and footer data.

Setup string
A series of control characters sent to your printer for features like boldface fonts and alternative sizes. These are specific to your own printer.

Band
A horizontal band in the report specification that controls the elements contained within it. A page band controls the repeated elements for each page: page number, title, date, and so forth. A table band contains fields, field titles, and some calculated fields. A group band specifies how records should be grouped within the report.

Creating an Instant Report

Unlike many other relational database programs, Paradox provides you with a Standard or Instant report, just as it provides you with a Standard form. The Paradox Instant report gives you a quick printout of the data in your table.

The Paradox Instant report is a simple, tabular report based on the table that is currently active. A tabular report prints the field names across the top of each page and then prints the records, with the appropriate data under each field name.

You can use the Paradox Instant report for any table. The table, however, must be displayed in the active window. You can also use the Instant report while viewing a table. To print the Instant report, do the following:

Creating Other Types of Paradox Reports

1. Use the **V**iew option to open the table that will be used to create the report. Select the **V**iew command from the Main menu.
2. Select the Cust1 table and press ⏎Enter.

    With the selected table displayed, you can now use the Paradox Instant report.
3. Check that your printer is on and ready to print. Now press Alt-F7.

Here, you can see the Paradox Instant report for the Cust1 table.

You can effectively use the Instant report for checking a table's accuracy or for listing inventory quickly when you want to do a physical inventory.

Creating Other Types of Paradox Reports

In the Paradox vocabulary, a report refers to any type of data output. A report is usually in printed form, although Paradox also can output, or display, a report on your computer's screen. Or, you can save a report as a separate file you can incorporate into your word processing program.

With Paradox, you can create a report that contains data from several tables, using a *multi-table report*. You also can create fields that calculate totals or subtotals for groups or pages, averages, and many other forms of calculations. A familiar example of a report you can create is the sales invoice. An invoice can be tabular or free-form, contain calculated fields, and draw information from several tables. In short, Paradox gives you a wide variety of tools with which to create almost any type of printed output for effectively communicating your message.

201

Constructing a Report

When you begin experimenting with the Paradox report options, you do not have to begin from scratch after making a test print. Paradox saves your report design as a *report specification*. If you need to alter the report design, you can edit the report specification.

Paradox saves a report specification as part of the table's family. An individual table can have up to 15 report specifications associated with it. Paradox saves each report specification with the table's name and the extension R*xx*, where *xx* is the number for the report. For example, when you create your first report specification for the Cust1 table, Paradox names the report Cust1.R1. The fifteenth report specification would then be Cust1.R15.

Understanding the Report Designer and Previewer

Paradox has two modes you use while creating and using reports: the Report Designer and the Report Previewer. Each of these modes has its own menus and functions. The primary difference between these modes is that the Report Designer works and manipulates the report format or specification itself while the Report Previewer mode provides a view of the actual live data displayed in the format of the report specification.

The Report Designer

You enter the Designer mode when you choose either **D**esign or **C**hange from the **R**eport pull-down menu. Report Designer is an extremely interactive and visual mode. As you begin to design a report specification, you start with either a tabular or a free-form standard specification. With this as your template, you alter it to meet your individual requirements. Generally, a tabular report contains the report fields across the page and is very similar to the actual table. The free-form report enables you to place fields in any location in the report.

As you make changes, you can test each phase by displaying the report on your screen or printing a copy. You can continue adjusting and modifying the specification until the report is just what you need. When you're satisfied with the report, you can save the specification.

Understanding the Report Designer and Previewer

After the report specification has been saved, it becomes part of the table's family of objects. If you make a change to the table, such as adding, deleting, or changing a field type, Paradox deletes the altered field from the report specification. You have to edit the report specification to replace the field.

The Report Previewer

You enter the Previewer mode each time you display a report on your screen, using the Output or RangeOutput options from the Report pull-down menu, or when you select Output from the Report Designer window. The Previewer mode enables you to view a copy of your report on your computer's screen before you create the actual hard copy.

The view of the report displayed with the Report Previewer is not a permanent Paradox object. When you leave the Previewer, this image of the report is gone. If you change any of the data on which the view was based, the next time you use the Preview mode, the view will be based on the new data.

When using the Preview mode, notice there is no cursor. Paradox hides the cursor because you are viewing an image of the actual report. If you find errors in the data, you must edit the table. If you find errors in the report format, you have to edit the report specification.

An Overview of the Report Menu Options

To create a report or to redirect the Standard report to the screen or a file, you need to navigate and use the Paradox Report menu system.

The Paradox Report option contains all the necessary tools for you to create and customize your own report. The options available on the Report pull-down menu are organized so that you can easily find and use the group of tools needed for a task.

You will find that the Paradox Report menu is easy to use and understand. Within a short time, you create and use your own report specifications. Table 8.1 contains a quick overview of the Report menu.

Constructing a Report

Table 8.1
Report Menu Options

Option	Description
Output	This option sends the selected report to your choice of printer, the screen, or an ASCII text file.
Design	This option enables you to create a new report specification. It contains all of the tools needed to design and save a new report specification.
Change	With this option, you can change or edit a selected report specification. You have access to all the tools available with the **D**esign option so that you can make the required changes.
RangeOutput	This option enables you to specify selected pages. You have the option to print, display, or send to a file only the pages you require.
SetPrinter	With this option, you can specify a selected printer port (if you have more than one printer), or select a *setup string* for your printer. The setup string is discussed later in this chapter.

Using the Report Designer

In this section you will learn how to use the Report Designer to create your own tabular report. The tabular report is very much like the image of the table. All of the fields are arranged in rows and columns. You have the options of which fields to include, and in what order.

As mentioned above, the report specification is the format of the report. Another way to think of the report specification is as a template or pattern. In the report specification, you lay out the way you want a report to appear, create any groupings, define fields to be calculated, assign page titles, and design page layouts. You use the **D**esign option to create a new report specification. This option is illustrated in this section and covered in more depth in Chapter 10.

Using the Report Designer

Working with the Tabular Report

The tabular report is useful for many types of lists. For many business reports, this is the report of choice. All the fields are displayed in columns, with a single record for each row. You can make summary calculations for groups or pages if needed.

Planning the Report Layout

Before you start to use the Paradox Report Designer, plan what you are trying to do. If you are creating a report that already exists on paper, look at it and see what is there.

What can be taken from the table? What types of headers or footers are on the report that you may need to create? Are there summaries of certain types of data, or are records grouped in certain ways?

When you can answer these questions, you are halfway to building your own report specification. Before creating a report specification, you need to know what you want the report to say, and how to say it.

Understanding Report Bands

A solid understanding of how Paradox lays out a tabular report is necessary before you begin this section. Paradox lays out a report specification in distinct bands or layers that run horizontally across the entire width of the report specification.

Each band is separated by a thin line running across the report specification. The band name is displayed on the line at the far left side of the first page width of the report specification. Each band name is displayed twice, once at the top, or beginning, of the band and then again at the bottom of the band. A down-pointing triangle is displayed to the left of each band name, indicating the beginning of that particular band. An up-pointing triangle beside the band name indicates the end of the band.

Constructing a Report

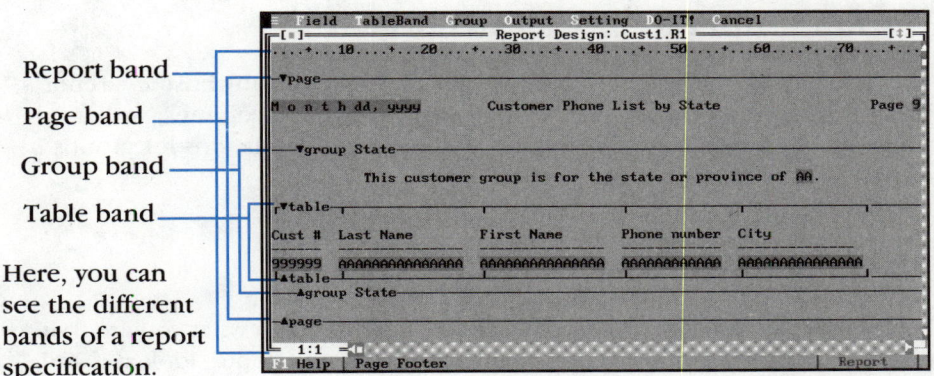

Here, you can see the different bands of a report specification.
- Report band
- Page band
- Group band
- Table band

Each band serves to divide the report into parts. You can place either literals—text or fields—into any of the bands of the report specification. Depending on the band in which you place the literals, they will print in the location specified for the specific band. Table 8.2 describes the kinds of bands.

Table 8.2
Types of Bands

Band	Description
Report band	Think of this band as the base of the report. Paradox lays all other bands on top of the report band. All information contained in the top of the report band, the report header, prints once at the beginning of the report. Information in the bottom of the report band, the report footer, prints at the very end of the report, but before the last page footer. You can use the report band for company information or final summary data.
Page band	The page band is the next band of the report specification. The top of the page band, the page header, prints at the top of each page of the report; the bottom of the page band, the page footer, prints at the bottom of each page. You can use the page band to print on each page the report name, page numbers, and page summaries.

Using the Report Designer

Band	Description
Group band	The group band, an optional feature, is the next layer of the report. A group band groups table information by specific fields. Paradox enables you to specify a maximum of 16 different groups per report specification. The top of the group band, the group header, prints once at the beginning of each group; the bottom of the group band, the group footer, prints at the bottom of the group.
	You can use the group bands to group records together by a specific field. For example, you can group employees by department, or customers by state. You can print specific group information in the header or footer for each group.
Table band	Use the table band to print the basic data extracted from the table. By default, the top of the table band, the table header, contains the field titles. The table header prints once at the top of each page. The bottom of the table band, the table footer, contains the report body. The layout of this part of the report specification determines how each record prints in the report—which fields will be included, and the line spacing between each record.

Designing a Report Specification

The **Report Design** option opens the Report Designer. You first tell Paradox which table to base the report on and then give the specification a name. Use the Cust1 table to design a report that will print a phone list of customers, grouped by state, and include the city and state that they live in.

To create this report specification, do the following:

1. Select the **R**eport option from the Main menu.
2. Choose the **D**esign option from the pull-down menu.
3. Select the table for which to design the report. Type the table name **Cust1** and press ⏎Enter. (If you know the name of the table, you can type it in the text box and press ⏎Enter; otherwise, just press ⏎Enter to display a list of tables.)

207

Constructing a Report

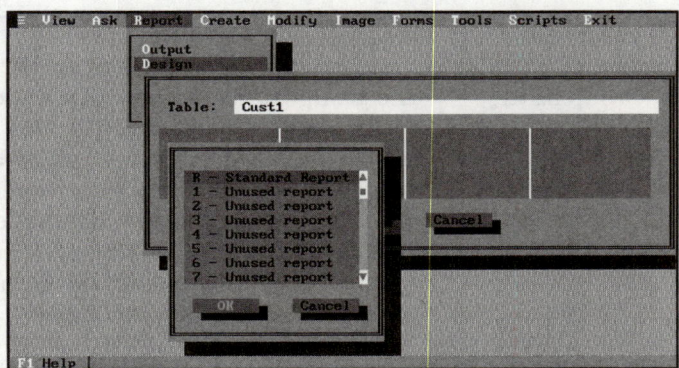

You now see the Report list box.

Notice that eight reports are listed in the Report list box, most of which are numbered and named Unused report. As you create new reports, you give each one a descriptive name. That name then appears here and also in the Report list box when you select the **R**eport **O**utput option. You can have up to 15 report specifications, including the R - Standard Report, for each table.

4. Select report 1. Move the cursor down one place by pressing ↓ once and then ⏎Enter. You also can do the same with the mouse by placing the mouse pointer on the required report (1) and double-clicking the mouse.

5. Enter a description for the report. Type **Customer Phone List by State** and press ⏎Enter.

You can use up to 40 characters to describe this report. This description will appear in all Report list boxes for this table. This description also will appear as the default report title. You can change the report title later if necessary.

If you are using several reports in a table, place those used most often at the beginning of the list. Use the space Paradox gives you to describe the report so that you or someone else has no problem identifying the report's function.

Using the Report Designer

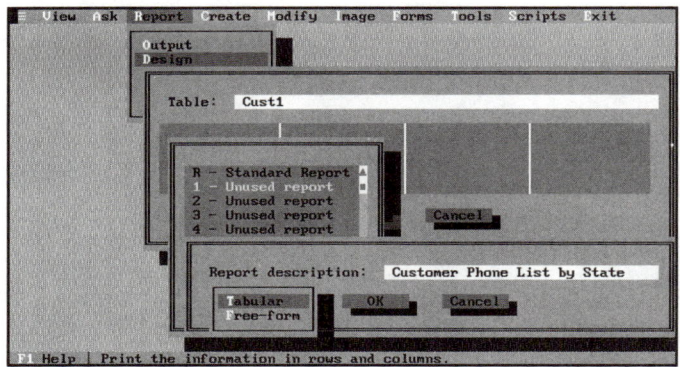

A pop-up menu is now displayed. You can choose between a **T**abular or **F**ree-form report.

6. Select the **T**abular option and press ⏎Enter.

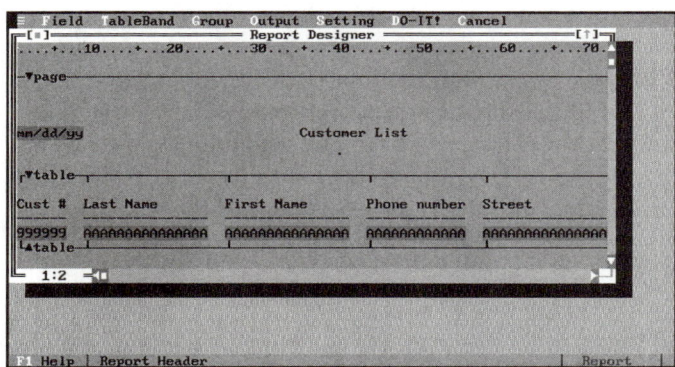

Here, you can see the basic Report Designer window.

7. Increase the window size to maximum. Select the **M**aximize/Restore option on the System menu, or click the mouse on the Maximize button [↑] in the upper right-hand corner of the window.

209

Constructing a Report

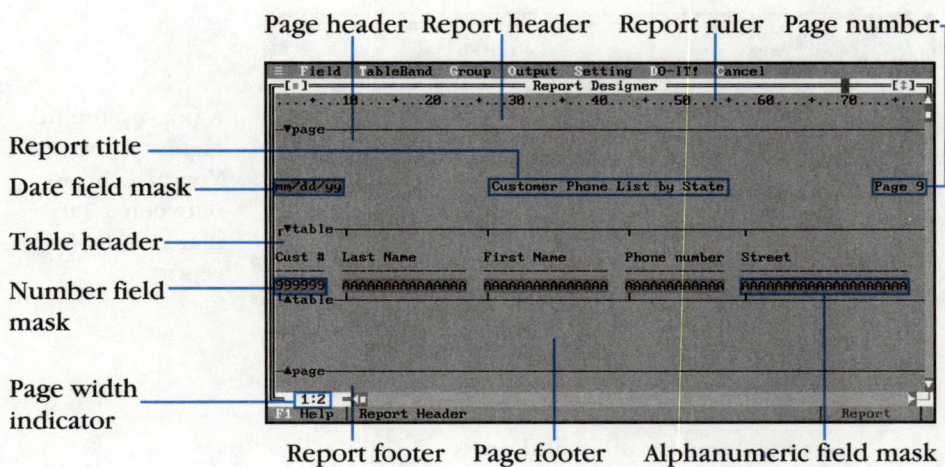

You now see the window in its maximized view. This view is easier to work with when designing a report.

You will notice that the cursor has changed its shape to a rapidly blinking rectangle.

The maximized window is helpful when designing a report. A general rule of thumb is that if a report's width fits within the window, then it should fit on an 8 1/2-by-11-inch paper. Using the maximized window can help you to judge the report size.

Notice also that the window does not display all the fields. This is because the default report is the same as the Standard report. It displays all the fields in a single row, as they are in the table. You can see the remaining fields if you scroll the screen to the right.

Within a report specification, Paradox does not display a field's live data. Field masks, such as those in the last figure, indicate field types. The letter A indicates alphanumeric fields, and 9 's appear in number fields. A Date field displays the mask for the selected date format. Field widths for alphanumeric and memo fields appear at their maximum, as designated by the field type or as needed for the field title. When you move the cursor, now a rapidly blinking rectangle, onto a field mask, the field name is displayed on the status bar at the bottom of your screen.

All items shown in unhighlighted black, such as the report description title and field names, are called *literals*. Paradox adds these for the report reader's convenience. You can change or add literals as needed.

Using the Report Designer

Removing Page Widths

When you create a table, you are concerned primarily with getting the required information into each record and field. You do not have to consider how the table will fit on a page later. Often, you will have a table with many fields, each having so many characters. Paradox enables you to have a maximum record length of 4000 characters for an unkeyed table. Needless to say, 4000 characters do not fit across an 8 1/2-inch page.

Paradox automatically creates the necessary additional page widths for an entire record. Paradox uses an assumed default page size of 8 1/2-by-11 inches, a 10-character per-inch font, and 6 lines per inch. If you are using a different size, you must tell Paradox. For the Cust1 table, Paradox creates a default report specification of 135 characters in width. For the report specification, Paradox uses the longer of the field type length or the field name length, plus two spaces at the end of each field.

The page width indicator is in the bottom left corner of the Report Designer window. At this time it reads 1:2, which tells you that the cursor is located on the first page of a two-page wide report.

To move the cursor to the next page width, do the following:

1. Press Ctrl-→. The cursor jumps one-half page width. Press the Ctrl-→ again.

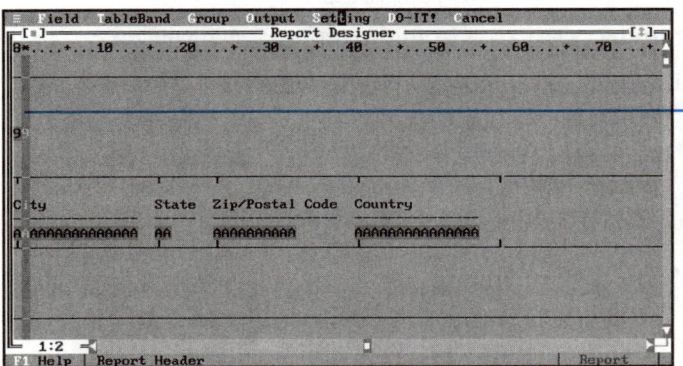

You can now see the page width bar, which indicates the beginning of the second page width.

Notice that the numbers on the ruler at the top of the window end at 80 and start again. Also, the cursor is still located in the first page width, so the page width indicator continues to display 1:2.

2. Press → twice.

Constructing a Report

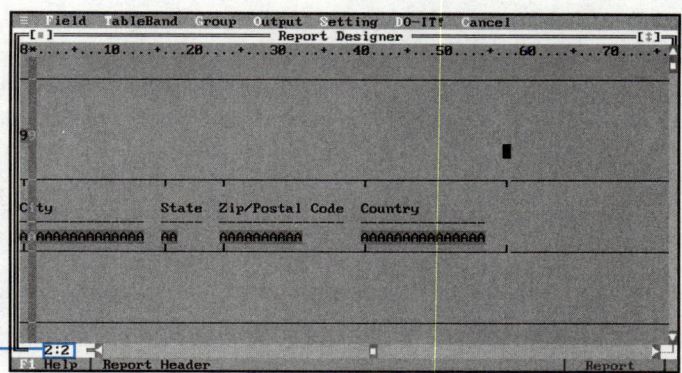

Now you see that the page width indicator has changed to 2:2.

If your report specification is more than one page width, Paradox prints all the first page width and then goes back to the top of the table and prints the next page width. You then have to put the pages together with tape if you want the report on a single page. You do have a couple of alternatives to running up your tape bill:

- If your printer supports a compressed font, or smaller pitch, like 12 or 15, you can fit more data onto an 8 1/2-inch line. Use the Settings PageLayout Width command and increase the page width to an appropriate value.
- You can use wider paper if it fits in your printer.
- You can remove unnecessary data from the report specification.

In most cases, removing unnecessary data from the report is the best alternative. For the average report, you do not want to clutter it with unneeded detail. For the report you are now creating, several fields are not needed: Street, Zip/Postal Code, and Country.

To remove an unneeded page width, do the following:

1. Select Setting from the menu bar.
2. Choose the PageLayout option.
3. Select the Delete option on the cascading menu.

212

Using the Report Designer

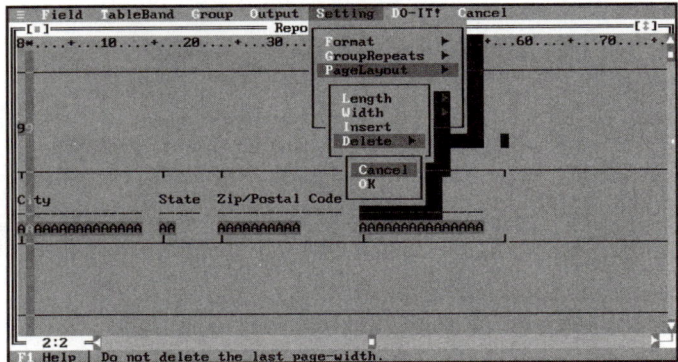

Here, you can see the menu options for deleting the last page width.

4. Select **OK**.

You can see that the cursor moves back to the first column of page 1. Notice that the page indicator now displays 1:1, telling you this is the first page of a one-page wide report.

Be cautious in your use of the **S**etting **P**ageLayout **D**elete command. This command always deletes the *last* page width, not a selected page width. It also deletes any columns and fields on that page width.

Removing Columns

Paradox also enables you to remove single columns. This can be a more accurate method of removing unnecessary fields than deleting the page width. In the page width displayed in the Report Designer window, one additional column is unneeded: the Street field.

To delete the column, do the following:

1. Select the **T**ableBand option from the menu bar.
2. Choose **E**rase from the pull-down menu.
3. Move the cursor to the Street column in the report specification.

213

Constructing a Report

You now see the cursor in the Street column.

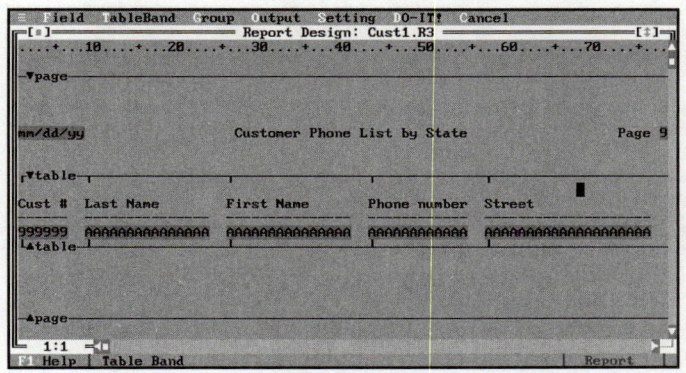

4. Press ⏎Enter.

8

Now you see that the literal street and the Street field have been deleted.

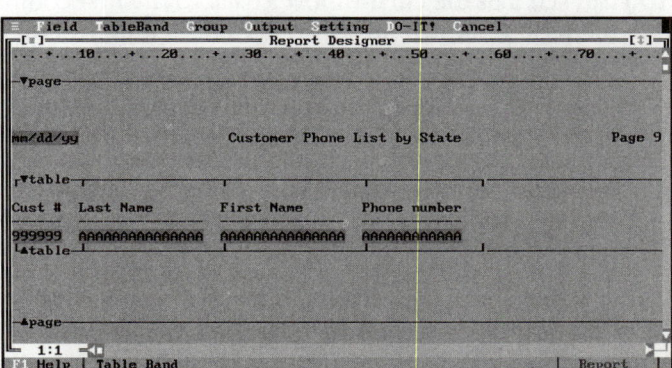

Adding Columns

You also can add a new column to a report specification. If you remove a field you need when deleting a page width, or if you want to insert a calculated field, you then need to insert a column.

To insert a column, do the following:

1. Select **T**ableBand from the menu bar.
2. Choose the **I**nsert option and press ⏎Enter.
3. At the top of the screen, Paradox displays this prompt: Move to the position for the new column, then press ⏎. Move the cursor to the table band at position 65 on the ruler and press ⏎Enter.

214

Using the Report Designer

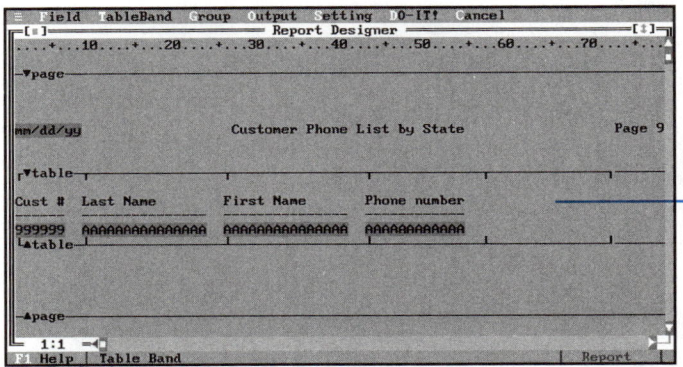

You can see the new blank column.

Using Literals

When the report specification is first created, Paradox enters several text items into it. These text items are called *literals*. Any character you enter into the report that will print or be displayed and is not a field is also called a literal.

You can type text into the report specification. This text can clarify points on the report, or add other information. When you add a field to a table, Paradox does not automatically supply the field title. If you have erased a field and now are placing it in a new position, you have to enter the field title.

The location of the literal (and of a field) is very important. If you type a literal in the page header band and above any group band, then this literal prints at the top of every page. If you type the literal in a group footer band, it prints at the end of that group. A literal placed inside the table band and on the same line as the field's values prints once for every record.

You can edit literals by using Del or Backspace. Pressing Ctrl-Y deletes everything from the cursor to the right side of the report. If you use Ctrl-Y with the cursor located at the far left of a line, then the entire line is deleted.

You now need to label the new column you added. Do the following to enter a label:

1. Move the cursor so that it is below the left column mark for the new column and beside the literal Phone number. Type the field title **City**.
2. Move the cursor to the beginning of the literal City, and then down one line. Type dashes (–) across the column.

215

Constructing a Report

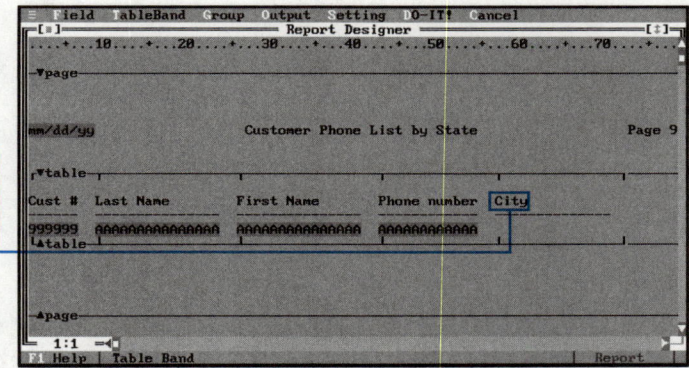

Here, you can see the new column's literal title.

Adding Fields

You can add many different field types to a report specification. The various field types serve different functions. Table 8.3 lists the field types you can use.

Table 8.3
Field Types

Type	Description
Regular	This field type is a table field. Use this option to move or replace a field.
Summary	This field type calculates summaries for regular or calculated fields.
Calculated	This field type calculates (adds, subtracts, multiplies, or divides) data from one or more regular fields.
Date	This field type is for dates listed within a report.
Time	This field type enters the time the report is printed.
Page	This field type enters a page number into each page of a report.
# Record	This field type numbers each record in the report. You can specify that the numbering is for the whole report or by group.

Using the Report Designer

Now add a field to your new column by doing the following:

1. Choose the **F**ield option from the menu bar.
2. Select the **P**lace option
3. Select **R**egular field.

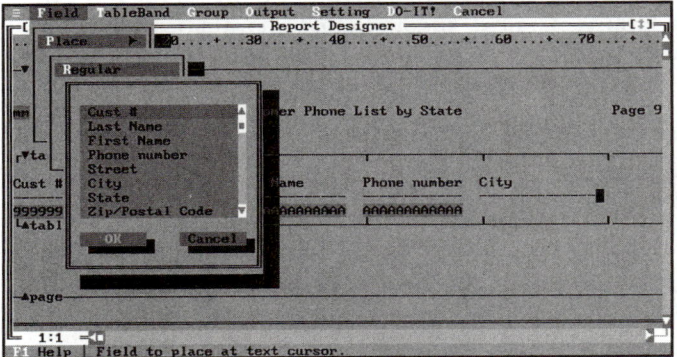

You now see the Field list box.

Use this set of commands to place any regular field. You can place a field more than once on the same report.

4. Choose the City field from the menu list and press ⏎Enter.
5. Move the cursor to the location for the new field. Place the cursor in line with the other fields in the table band, below the dashed line under the C in City, and press ⏎Enter.

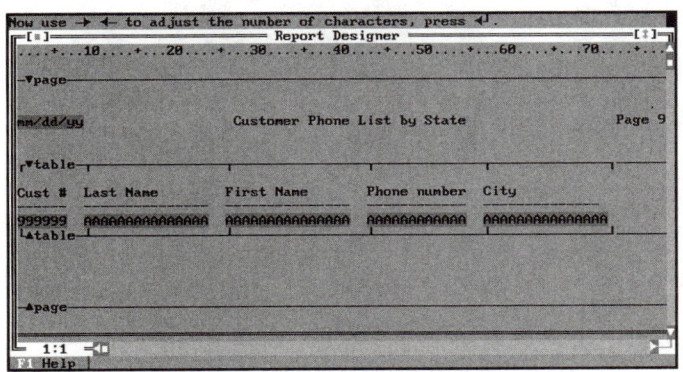

Now you can see the field mask for the City field.

6. Press ⏎Enter again to accept the default field length. If you want a longer or shorter field, you can use ← or → to change the length.

217

Constructing a Report

Reformatting and Editing Fields

Within the Report Designer, the only field type you can edit is the calculated field. By selecting **F**ield **C**alcEdit and then placing the cursor on the calculated field, you can edit the calculation.

On the other hand, you can reformat most field types. For instance, you can reformat the size of an alphanumeric or memo field. Other field types can be reformatted to display their data differently. To see how reformatting a field works, reformat two different field types, as follows.

To reformat two different field types, follow these steps:

1. Select **F**ield **R**eformat from the menu bar.
2. Move the cursor to the newly placed City field mask and press ⏎Enter.

   If you placed the cursor in the middle of the field mask, you probably noticed the cursor jump to the right end of the field when you pressed ⏎Enter.
3. Move the cursor to the left one place and press ⏎Enter.
4. Select **F**ield **R**eformat again. Now move the cursor to the Date field in the page band. The Date field is currently displayed as mm/dd/yy. Press ⏎Enter.

Here, you can see the Date Reformat list. These are the alternative date formats you can use in a report. Although the list displays only 8 format choices, you can use the scroll bar or press ↓ to display all 12.

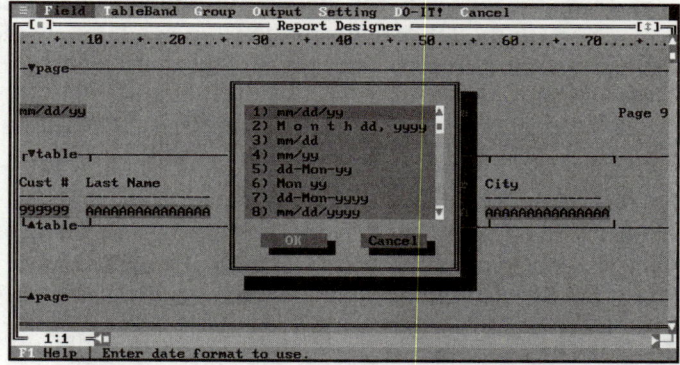

5. Select format 2 and press ⏎Enter.

Using the Report Designer

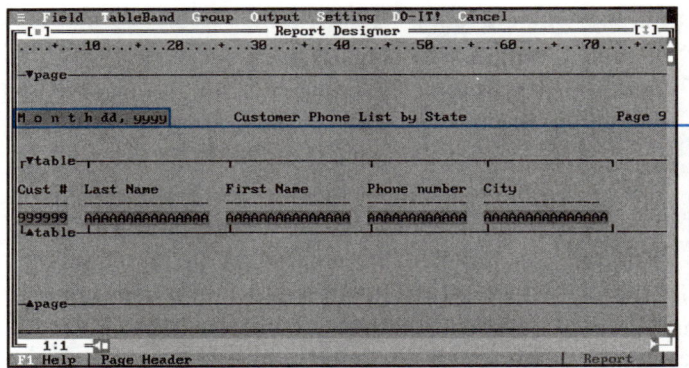

Now you can see the new date format displayed in the window.

Table 8.4 lists the various options for report date formats, using the date January 31, 1992. As already mentioned, Paradox has 12 date formats you can use in the report specification.

Table 8.4
Report Date Formats

Date Mask	Date Displayed in Report
mm/dd/yy	1/31/92
Month dd, yyyy	January 31, 1992
mm/dd	1/31
mm/yy	1/92
dd-Mon-yy	31-Jan-92
Mon yy	Jan 92
dd-Mon-yyyy	31-Jan-1992
mm/dd/yyyy	1/31/1992
dd.mm.yy	31.01.92
dd/mm/yy	31/01/92
yy-mm-dd	92-01-31
yy.mm.dd	92.01.31

Constructing a Report

You also can reformat number and currency fields with the Field Reformat option. Instead of the date options you saw above, however, you will see a different pop-up menu box.

Using Groups

You can often format a report to display certain groups of records together. This can make for easier reading of a report and is useful for creating summary totals of some information. Using group bands, you can organize your report into a maximum of 16 distinct group levels. You can divide groups based on a field value, a range of values, or a specific number of records. You can add group headings and specify the sort order for a group. By default, Paradox sorts each group in ascending order. You can use the Group Sort Direction option to select either Ascending or Descending sort order.

You can group records alphabetically, by location, by item, or by date. You also can use a range to group records. For example, a group may consist of all records with the customer last name beginning with the letters A through C, or all records for sales grouped by days, weeks, months, or years. The latter can be especially helpful when you are trying to correlate sales trends.

To create a group that divides the report by the field state, do the following:

1. Select Group from the menu bar.
2. Choose the Insert option.
3. Select Field from the cascading menu.
4. From the Field list box, choose the State field and press ⏎Enter.
5. Move the cursor to the location for the group band, just below the Date field, and press ⏎Enter.

Here, you can see that the State group band has been included.

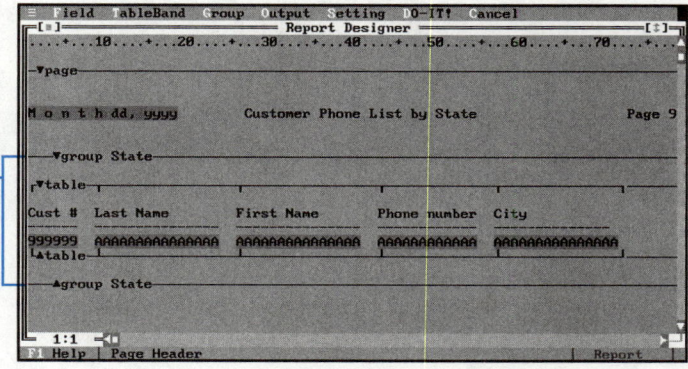

220

Using the Report Designer

6. Move the cursor down one line and then to position 25 in the State group band header section and type **This customer group is for the state or province of** . Be sure to leave three spaces between of and the period.
7. Select **F**ield **P**lace **R**egular from the menus.
8. Choose the State field from the Field list box and press `Enter`.
9. Move the cursor to the space between of and the end period, and press `Enter`.

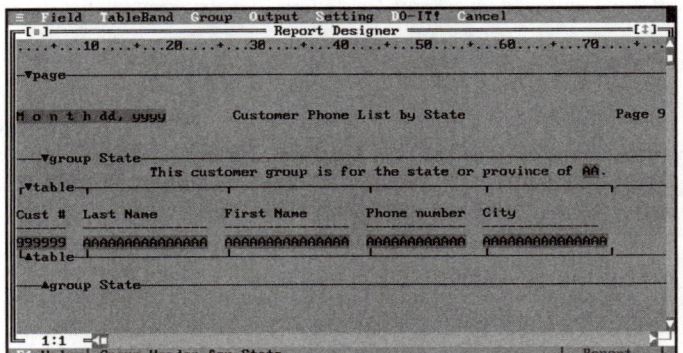

Your screen should now look like this.

You must place a group band outside the table band. The actual placement of group bands is not as important as their relative placement compared to other group bands. The outermost band, the one closest to the page band, is the primary group. As the groups move closer to the table band, they become less significant. For example, suppose that you divide your employee table by State (the primary group), then City, then Division, and finally Department. As your report is sorted, each group contains fewer and fewer records until each of the subgroupings by Department will contain the fewest records.

Adjusting the Table Bands

The only adjustments you can make in the table bands, other than changing literals, is to remove empty lines or insert additional lines. Adjusting lines can be helpful if you feel there is too much or too little space between the page headers or footers and the group or table headers or footers.

221

Constructing a Report

To remove a line from the report specification, do the following:

1. Move the cursor to the far left side of the report specification, position 1. When Paradox beeps, you are there.
2. Paradox also provides a vertical ruler to help in positioning. Press the toggle Ctrl-V to display the ruler.
3. Now move the cursor up until it is positioned directly below the page band on line 3 of the vertical ruler.

You can see the cursor beside the row 3 indicator, just below the page band line.

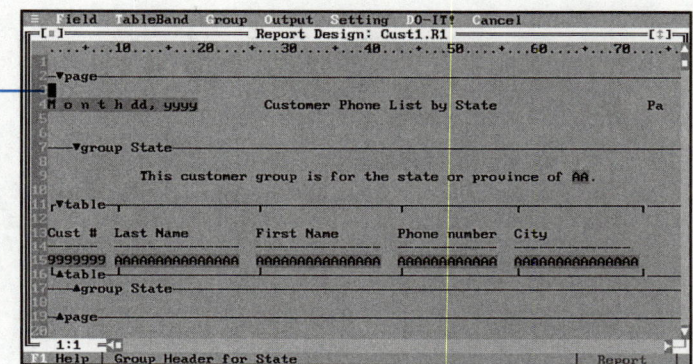

4. Press Ctrl-Y.

Here, you can see that the entire report specification has moved up one line.

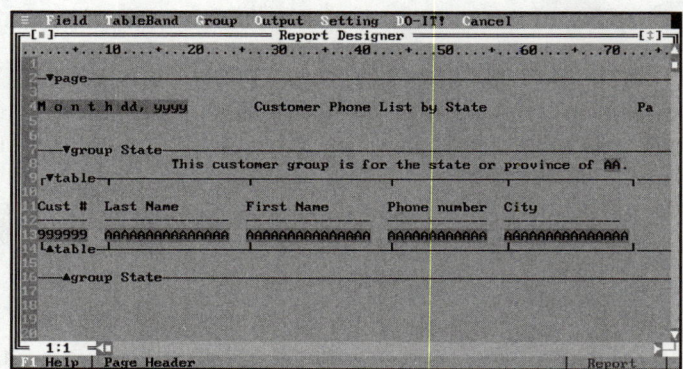

5. Now move the cursor down to line 9.
6. Press Ins, and then press ↵Enter.

222

Using the Report Designer

Note: To insert blank lines into the report specification, you must be in Insert mode; otherwise, pressing ⏎Enter only moves the cursor down a line.

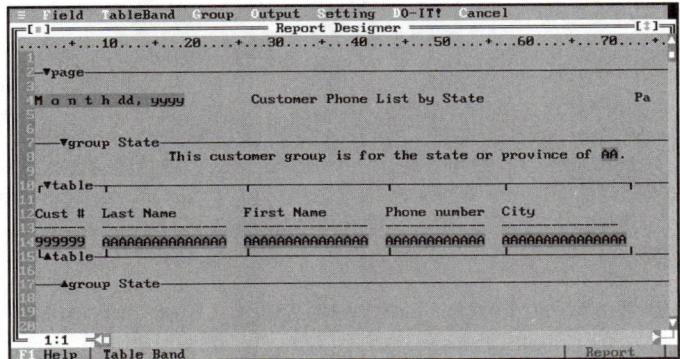

You can now see that an extra line has been inserted into the State group band. The report specification below the insertion point is moved down one line.

7. Press Ctrl-V to remove the vertical ruler, and then press Ins to switch out of the Insert mode.

Previewing the Report

Before you save the report specification, you will want to test it to see whether it works as you planned. You can print a copy of the report, but first you should use the **O**utput **S**creen option to view the report on your screen. This generally enables you to catch any gross errors before you commit your report to paper.

To preview a report before creating a final hard copy as a printout or a file, use the Report Previewer. To activate the Previewer mode, do the following:

1. Select the **O**utput option from the menu bar.
2. Choose the **S**creen option.

    You should see the message Sending report to screen... displayed as Paradox creates the report. Depending on the size of the table and the number of fields included, this can take as long as several minutes.

3. Click the Maximize button or select the **M**aximize/Restore option on the System menu so that you can view as much of the report as possible.

223

Constructing a Report

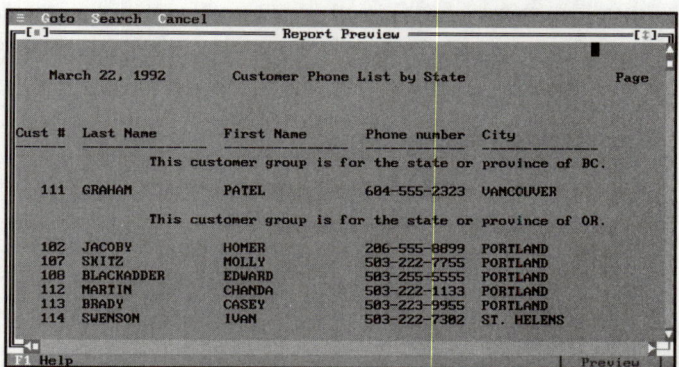

Here, you can see the report displayed in the Report Previewer window. This report is sorted first by the State group band and then by the first field, Cust #.

Notice that the cursor is not visible in the Previewer window. This is because you are viewing a report, and editing options are not available while you are previewing a report. You must return to the Report Designer to edit the report specification. The mouse pointer is still visible, so you can use the scroll bars to view other parts of the report. To see the bottom half, use ⬇ or the scroll bars.

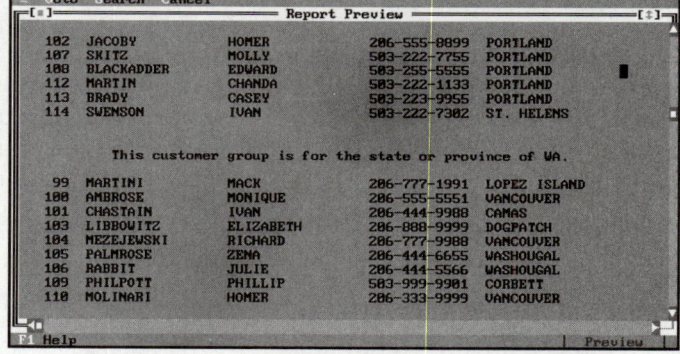

You can now see the remaining portion of the report.

Notice that the field names are not included. In the first picture of the report, the field names appear above the initial group title. In the default setting, Paradox displays the field titles once per page. This type of setting is called TableOfGroups.

224

Using the Report Designer

To display the field titles for each group, select Cancel from the Report Previewer menu bar, or click the mouse on the close button. This returns you to the Report Designer window.

Changing Settings

Paradox enables you to adjust many of the default settings for a report. You can use the Settings option to make many final adjustments to your report specification, including how to print headings and group calculations, page layouts, margins, and setup strings for your printer. To change the settings, do the following:

1. Choose the Settings option on the Report Designer menu bar.
2. Select the Format option.
3. Select the GroupsOfTables option.

    You should see the message Settings changed displayed in the message box.

4. Now use the Output Screen option to view the report again. Remember to maximize the Report Previewer window.

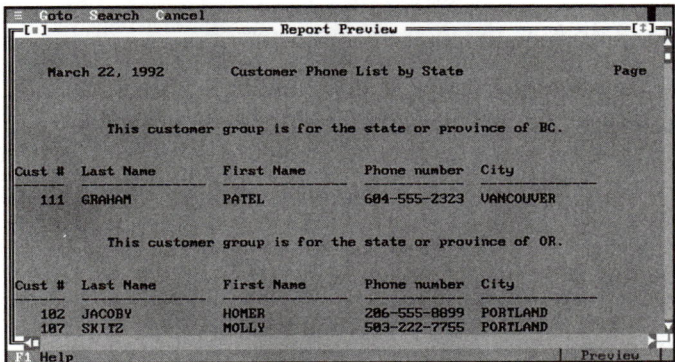

Here, you can see the new settings. Notice that the table headings (field titles) are now listed above the fields within each group.

5. Use the scroll bar or ⬇ to view the rest of the report.

225

Constructing a Report

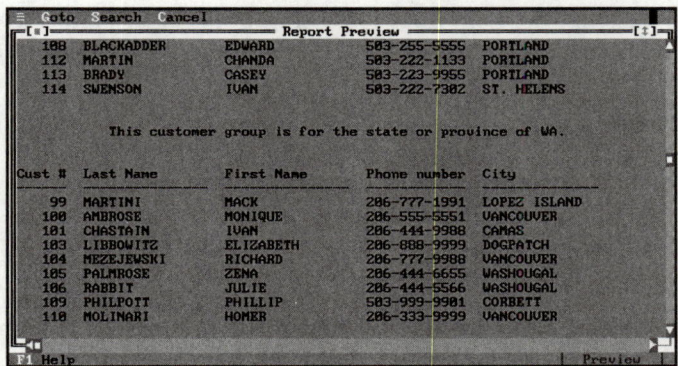

Now you can see the table headings listed above the Washington group, which makes the report much easier to read.

Saving the Report Specification

Now the report specification meets the original requirements:

> A list of customers, with phone numbers and cities, grouped by the state in which they live.

You are ready to save the report specification. To save this specification, do the following:

> Select the **D**O-IT! option from the menu bar, or press F2.

You have now saved the report specification as part of the family of objects belonging to the Cust1 table. The report specification is cleared from the desktop, and you return to the point you were at before you began designing this report.

Specifying the Output

To produce a hard copy of your report, you use the **R**eport **O**utput option. This option enables you to print your report, view it on your screen (Previewer mode), or send it to an ASCII text field. The **O**utput option creates a complete report, using the selected report specification. If you need only a partial report, use the **R**angeOutput option.

Specifying the Output

Printing a Report

When you select the **O**utput option, you then must tell Paradox which table to use, and select the report specification. Remember that a report specification belongs to a specific table. If you have not yet designed a new report specification for your table, the only option given to you is the Standard report specification. This is the same report that is generated when you use the Instant report (Alt - F7).

To print the report, do the following:

1. Select **R**eport from the Main menu bar.
2. Choose the **O**utput option.
3. Choose the table for the report. Type in **Cust1** and press ⏎Enter.

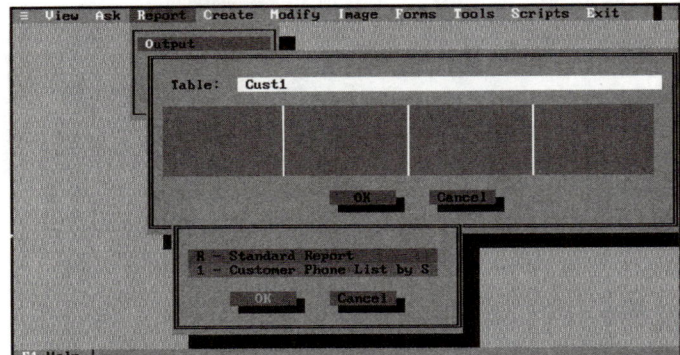

Here, you can see that the new report specification has been added to the report listing.

You now see R - Standard Report and 1 - Customer Phone List by S. As you design more of your own report specifications, they are displayed in this list box and, for example, look like this:

```
R - Standard Report
1 - Mailing Labels
2 - Telephone List
3 - Invoice
```

4. Select the 1 – Customer Phone List by S report by clicking the mouse on it, or pressing ↓ once. Then press ⏎Enter.
5. Select the **P**rinter option. You should see the message Sending report to printer... displayed in the message box. Again, just like when the report is sent to the screen, this function can take several minutes.

227

Constructing a Report

Here, you see the final printed report.

8 Previewing a Report

If instead of printing your report, you want to preview it on your computer screen, select the **S**creen option. To see how this is done, do the following:

1. Select **R**eport from the Main menu bar.
2. Choose the **O**utput option.
3. Choose the table for the report. Type in **Cust1** and press ⏎Enter.
4. Select the Standard report.
5. Select the **S**creen option from the pop-up menu box.

   You should see the message Sending report to screen... displayed in the message box.

228

Specifying the Output

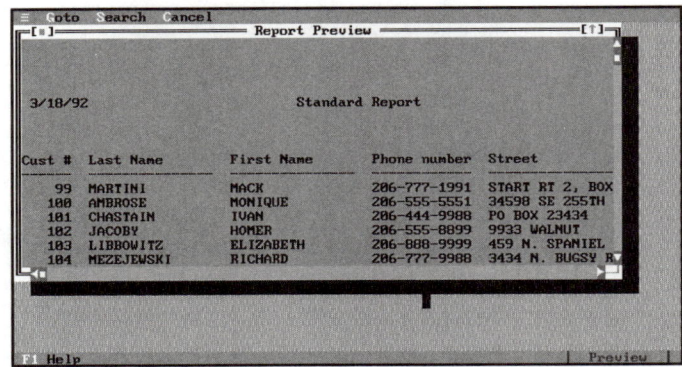

Here, you see the Report Preview window.

Notice that the mode indicator now displays Preview. Your menu bar at the top of the screen also has changed, and the cursor is no longer visible on the screen.

You can use the mouse and the scroll bars or the various menu options to view parts of the report that are not on the screen. To use the menu options, do the following:

1. Select the **G**oto option.

   This option displays a pull-down menu with two options. The first, **P**age, moves you to a selected page of the report. The second, **E**ndOfReport, moves you to the end of the report.

2. Select **E**ndOfReport. See how the last record in the report is now displayed on the screen.

   You also should see the message End of report! displayed in the message box.

3. Select the **S**earch option, and then choose the **F**ind option. This displays a dialog box. Enter the value for which to search.

   You can use the following *wild cards* to help set up a search pattern: @ and .. (double period). The @ sign takes the place of any single character, whereas the .. (double period) takes the place of any group of characters.

   For this example, type **..SPANIEL..**.

229

Constructing a Report

The pattern searches for a value that has anything in front of the word SPANIEL and anything behind it.

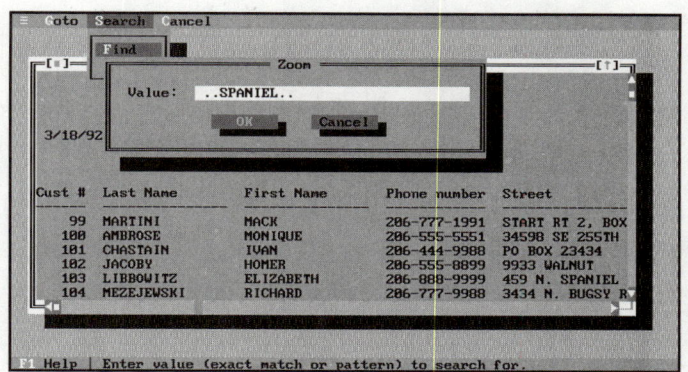

4. Press ⏎Enter to start the search.

You now see that the searched for value has been found and highlighted.

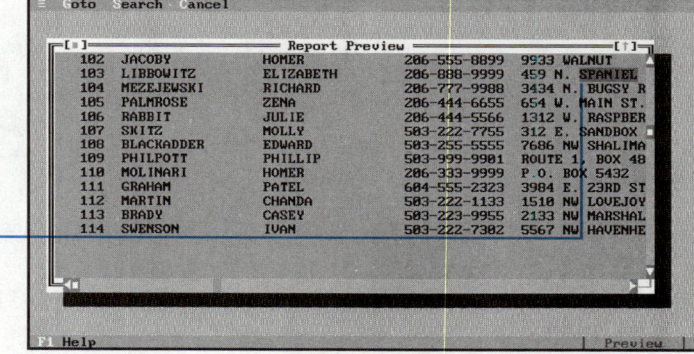

If you need to find the next occurrence of this value, select the Search option again. Use the second option, Next. This operates in the same manner as Zoom Next.

5. Select Cancel to exit the Preview mode and return to the desktop.

Saving a Report as a Text File

Finally, Paradox gives you the option to send the report data to an ASCII text file. This enables you to include the report in a word processing file, so you can include the data in a larger report. To use this option, do the following:

1. Select Report from the Main menu bar.
2. Choose the Output option.

230

Summary

3. Choose the table for the report. Type **Cust1** and press ⏎Enter.
4. Select the Standard report option.
5. Select **F**ile from the pull-down menu.
6. Enter the file name under which this report should be saved. If needed, include the drive and path for the file.

   In this example, type **TEST1.RPT**. This file will be saved in the current working directory.

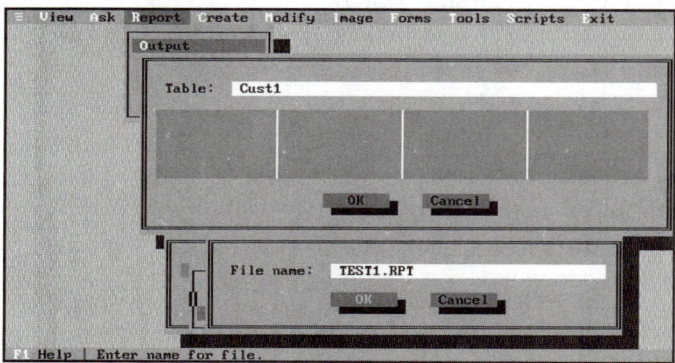

Here, you see the File dialog box completed. The report will be saved as the ASCII text file TEST1.RPT.

As Paradox creates the report, you should see the message Sending report to TEST1.RPT... displayed in the message box.

You can use this file with most word processing programs. With minor reformatting, you can easily include table data into a final report.

Summary

In this chapter, you learned to design your own report specification using the Paradox tabular report format. You also viewed, made changes to, and then printed the report. Finally, you saved the report specification.

Specifically, you learned the following key points about Paradox 4:

- ■ To use the Paradox Instant report, view the table from which to print a report and press Alt-F7.
- ■ To print a report in a customized format, you must first create a report specification or pattern for Paradox to use.

Constructing a Report

- To send a selected report to the printer, the screen, or an ASCII text file, use the **O**utput option.
- To create a new report specification, use the Report Designer window. To open the Designer window, use the **R**eport **D**esign option. Select the table on which to base the report, and choose the report number for the specification. Then enter a descriptive name for the report and select the **T**abular or **F**ree-form option.
- To remove an unneeded page width, select the **S**etting **P**ageLayout **D**elete option from the Report Designer menu, and then choose **OK**. This removes the last page width in the report specification.
- To add a page width to a report specification, choose **S**etting **P**ageLayout **I**nsert. This adds a blank page width to the report specification.
- To delete a column, select **T**ableBand **E**rase.
- To add a new column, select the **T**ableBand **I**nsert option.
- To add a literal, explanatory text or any other figures to print with the report, move the cursor to where you want the literal and type it in. Depending on the location of the literal, Paradox prints it with every page, each group, or each record.
- To add a field, select the **F**ield **P**lace option and then choose the type of field you want to add. Move the cursor to the location for the new field and press `Enter`.
- To delete a field, select the **F**ield **P**lace **E**rase option and then choose the field you want to delete by placing the cursor on the field mask. Press `Enter` to complete the erasure.
- To reformat a field, select **F**ield **P**lace **R**eformat. Select the field you want to reformat by placing the cursor on it, and then press `Enter`.
- To sort a report by a selected group of records, you must insert a group band. Select the **G**roup **I**nsert option from the menu. Then select the type of group: **F**ield, **R**ange, or **N**umberRecords. Paradox sorts the records first, by groups, and then the fields. You can have up to 16 different group selections within a table.
- To increase the size of a report specification band, you can add lines within the band. To add lines, press `Ins` and then `Enter`. A blank line is added each time you press `Enter`.
- To decrease the size of a report specification band, you can delete lines within the band. Move the cursor to the far left side of the report and press `Ctrl`-`Y`. This deletes a line.

Summary

- To view the vertical ruler, press `Ctrl`-`V`. This displays the ruler containing line numbers on the left side of the window.
- To display table headings (field names) within each group, select **S**etting **F**ormat **G**roupsOfTables option. This causes the table headings to print below each group title.
- To display the table headings (field names) only at the top of each page, select the **S**etting **F**ormat **T**ableOfGroups option.
- To test a report specification with live data before saving, use the Report Previewer by selecting **O**utput **S**creen from the Report Designer menu.

In the next chapter, you will learn to restructure a table and to link tables to create a basis for a multi-table database. Here is where you begin to learn the real power of a relational database.

Restructuring a Table

9

As you continue to work with Paradox and your data, you will realize that a database is never quite finished. You will continue to find more tasks for your database as you become more familiar with Paradox.

When your table needs updating, or maybe even renovation, you will need to restructure it. For example, you may find some fields you do not use in a table, or some fields that are not the right size or type. Maybe you have created additional tables and find yourself duplicating information in several of them. Or, perhaps you are asked for information you do not currently keep. If you find that your information needs have changed and you need to keep additional data within a table, you can add a new field or fields. Likewise, when you are ready to link tables together, you may need to restructure the table to add the needed links.

In this chapter, you will learn to change a table's structure. You will also learn how to change records that don't fit the new table structure so that you can add them back to the original table. And, finally, you will learn how to use the Paradox editing aids called validity checks.

Rules regarding restructuring

Changing a table's structure

Using the Key Violations table

Using the Problems table

Using validity checks

Restructuring a Table

Key Terms in This Chapter

Restructure — The process of altering a selected table's structure. This process can include changing a field's name or type, or adding or deleting fields.

Concatenated key — A table key that uses more than one field to create the key.

Source — The table that currently contains a set of records you want to add to another table.

Target — The table to which you will add records.

Validity check — A system of checks that are placed on fields to ensure the accuracy and consistency of the data entered.

Picture — A form of validity check that creates a template for data.

TableLookup — A form of validity check that requires a field value to exist in another table.

Autoconfirm — Enables Paradox to automatically move the cursor to the next field when a field is appropriately completed.

Rules Regarding Restructuring

To change the table itself, not just the data contained within it, you must restructure the table. Although restructuring a table is not difficult, you must understand some of the potential hazards.

As you restructure a table, Paradox may create two temporary tables: *Problems* and *Keyviol*. Paradox creates these tables when necessary, and places all records that no longer fit into the new table structure into one of these temporary tables. They act as a safety net for your data. Both of these tables are discussed later in the chapter.

If you have previously restructured another table and created either of the temporary tables, Paradox warns you that you may overwrite them if you proceed further. This warning gives you the chance to edit the records and add them to the original table, or to rename the temporary table to permanently save the records. These temporary tables can be created by actions

Rules Regarding Restructuring

other than restructuring a table. For example, if you import data into a table from a spreadsheet or another database, Paradox may create these tables because of inconsistencies between the data and the table.

You must follow some general rules when you begin to plan to restructure a table. Most of these rules are actually warnings you need to keep in mind.

The primary rules concerning restructuring a table include the following:

- You cannot restructure a table with a *compatible* file structure if your table contains memo fields. Use the compatible file structure only if you will use a table with Paradox 3.5 or an even earlier version of Paradox, because these versions do not support the memo field type.

- If you delete a field, you delete all the information contained in that field, for all records in the table. If you are unsure at all, save the original table and its records on a separate disk or with another name before you restructure the field. Paradox prompts you to confirm the deletion of the field before you save the new table structure.

- If you create a keyed field in a previously unkeyed table, you may cause key violations within records. This error causes Paradox to delete the records that violate the key and place them in the Keyviol table.

  For example, you restructure an unkeyed table so that the Last Name field is now the key field. If your table contains the last name MARTIN more than one time, Paradox moves duplicate MARTIN's to the Keyviol table. Paradox considers the entire records to be duplicates, even if all the other fields are not duplicated.

- If you change keys in a table, you may create key violations. Again, Paradox removes the key violating records and places them in the Keyviol table.

- In some cases, changing a field's type, including field length, causes records to be removed and saved in the Problems table. If, for instance, you change a field's type from alphanumeric to number, any record that has alphanumeric characters in that field is removed and placed in the Problems table. Again, Paradox asks for confirmation when you save the table's new structure.

  For example, if you were to restructure your Cust1 table by changing the Zip/Postal Code field from alphanumeric to number, Paradox would remove the record for PATEL GRAHAM, whose postal code is V1B 2G4, because this field contains characters other than numbers.

9

237

Restructuring a Table

Changing a Table's Structure

As already mentioned, changing a table's structure is a very simple process. With only a few minor exceptions, altering an existing table's structure is almost the same process you used when you first created the structure.

Two additional tables have now been created: Invnty and Orders. Use what you learned in Chapter 3 to create these two tables. In this chapter, you will learn to make changes to the structures of these two tables and to create the foundation to link all three tables together into a related database.

The Invnty table is a table of current inventory. It contains fields for item code, description, quantity on hand, and cost.

Here, you can see the structure of the Invnty table.

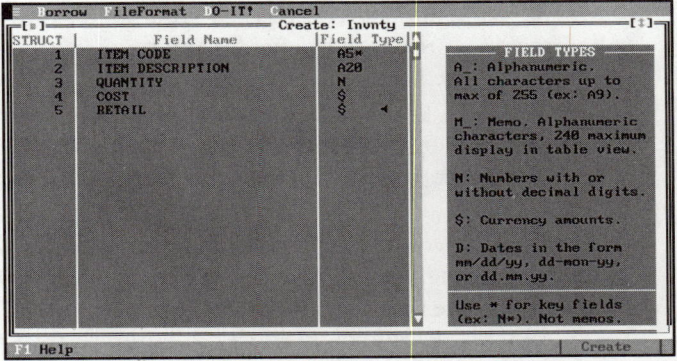

The Orders table includes each of the items ordered by a customer. It contains fields for invoice number, item code, quantity, cost, and retail price.

Here, you can see the structure of the Orders table.

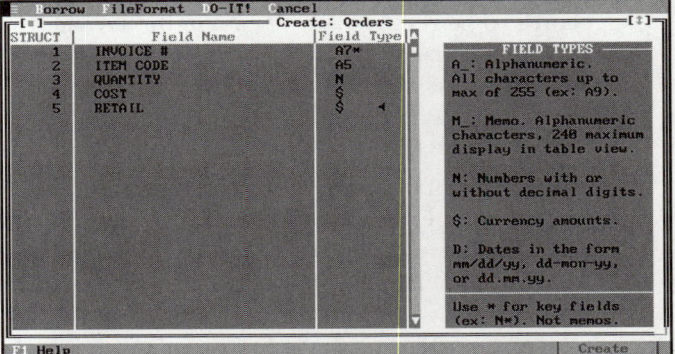

Changing a Table's Structure

As it stands now, you use your three tables primarily as lists. You have a list of your customers, a list of your current inventory and value, and a list of invoices with what was sold. You have to maintain each list individually.

The current process goes like this. A customer buys an item, and an invoice lists the items sold, their retail cost, and the quantity. Then you check the Cust1 table to see whether the customer is in the database. If they are not, you add them. After you add them, or if they were there, you enter the invoice into the Orders table. You type in the invoice number, item code, quantity sold, cost, and retail price for each item. Finally, you go to the Invnty table and subtract the number of items sold from the quantity on hand.

Although this process does work, it is time-consuming, and the potential for errors is relatively high. In this section, you will restructure these tables with the final intention of linking them together.

To start the process of restructuring a table, do the following:

1. Select the **M**odify option from the menu bar.
2. Choose the **R**estructure option.
3. Select the table you want to restructure. Type **Orders** into the text box in the dialog box and press ⏎Enter.

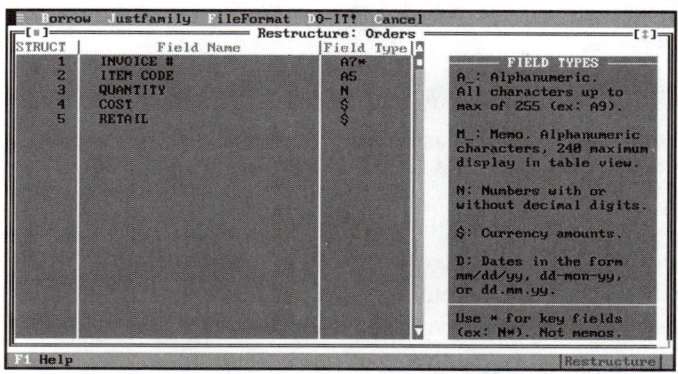

Here, you can see the structure of the Orders table in the Struct table. Notice that the mode indicator in the bottom right corner now indicates that the mode is Restructure.

Adding and Moving Fields

At this time, you are planning to add a field to the Orders table. You have found that frequently you want to match a customer name with a specific invoice. With the information currently kept in the Orders table, you can get this information only by referring back to the original invoice through the invoice number. This, of course, assumes you keep a file of sequential invoices.

239

Restructuring a Table

Adding a new field to a table during the restructure process is very easy. Depending on your requirements, you can insert a field between existing fields, or add the new field at the end of the table.

To insert a field, do the following:

1. Move the cursor to the field where you want the new field to appear. For this example, position the cursor on field 3, Quantity.

   You can place the cursor in any of the fields of the Struct table.

2. Press Ins.

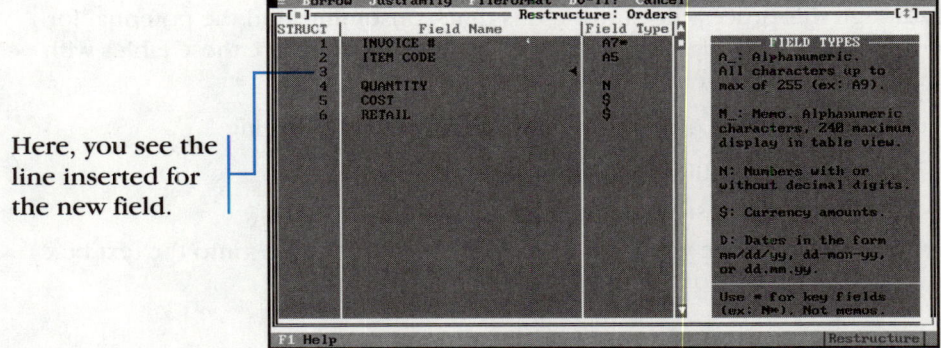

Here, you see the line inserted for the new field.

3. Enter the field name to use for the customer reference.

   Remember, you want to be able to easily reference a specific invoice to a specific customer without having to go back to find a copy of the invoice. You could use the customer's name, but what if you have two Fred Smiths? You would still have to look at the original invoice to see which Smith ordered the product. However, you do have a unique identifying field within the Cust1 table: the Cust # field. This would be the best field to use to identify an invoice with a customer.

   For this example, type the field name **Cust #** and press Enter.

4. Now enter the field type. Use the same field type for this Cust # field as you did in the original table. Press N for number field, and then press Enter.

Changing a Table's Structure

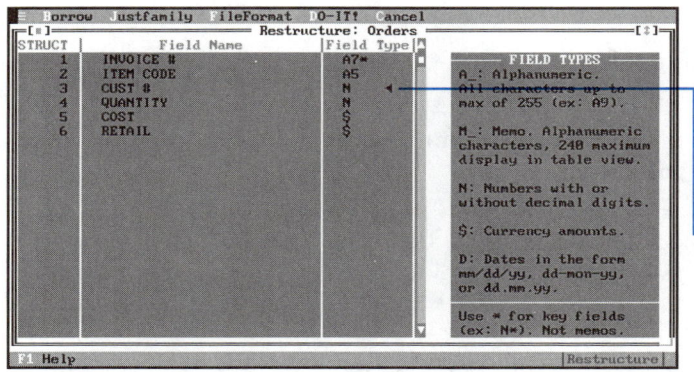

Now you can see the completed field.

5. Move the cursor to the last field. Press End.
6. Press ↓ to create a new line in the Struct table. The cursor should move to the Field Name column.
7. Enter the name for the new field. Type **QTY SHIPPED** and press ↵Enter.
8. Enter the field type. Press N, and then press ↵Enter.
9. Move the cursor down another line. Paradox inserts a new blank line. Type **INVOICE DATE** and press ↵Enter.
10. For the field type, press D for date field.

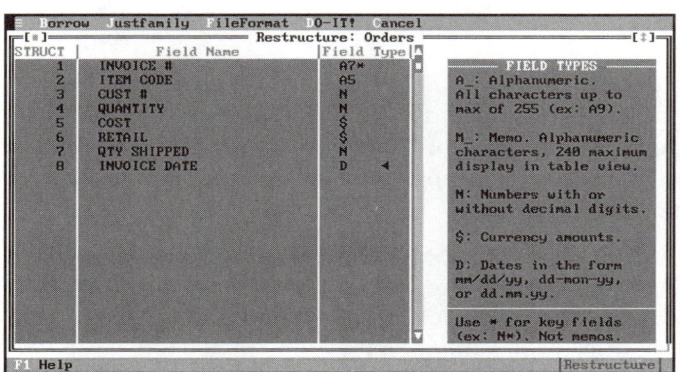

Here, you can see the new field specifications QTY SHIPPED and INVOICE DATE.

Paradox enables you to move a field from one location to another. If you decide that a field would be better located in another position, you only have to insert a line for the field and type its field name. Paradox then copies the field type for you and deletes the field specification in the old location.

241

Restructuring a Table

To move a field specification, do the following:

1. Move the cursor to line 5, COST, and press [Ins].

    You should see a blank line open.

2. Enter the name of the field you want to move on the blank line. Type **QTY SHIPPED** and press [↵Enter].

    Note that Paradox is not case-sensitive when moving fields. If you enter "qty shipped" instead of "QTY SHIPPED," Paradox displays the new field name as Qty shipped, moves the field type data, and erases the old field.

Here, you can see the new field and the old field. Notice the message Moving QTY SHIPPED field... in the message box.

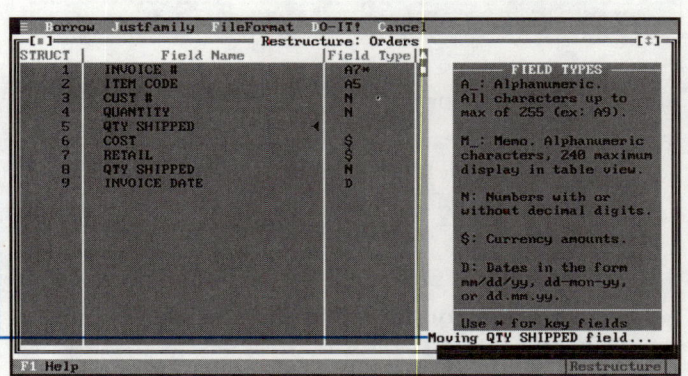

Erasing Fields

With Paradox, you can remove unneeded fields from a table structure. You may decide to remove a field because the data in the field is not used, or you may keep the data in another table. One of the reasons to use several small tables within Paradox is to keep them simple and not duplicate unnecessary information in the tables.

When you erase a field, you must remember that deleting a field specification from the table structure also deletes all the data contained in that field. You cannot recover it later. If you have any calculated fields within forms or reports that are based on the erased field, then they too are deleted.

If you decide a field can be deleted from a table, and from any of the table's family members, then do the following:

1. Move the cursor to the field you want to delete. Place the cursor on the Retail field.

Changing a Table's Structure

Just like when you inserted a new field, you can position the cursor in any column of the field specification.

2. Press [Del]. The field specification is erased.
3. Move the cursor to the Cost field and erase it also.

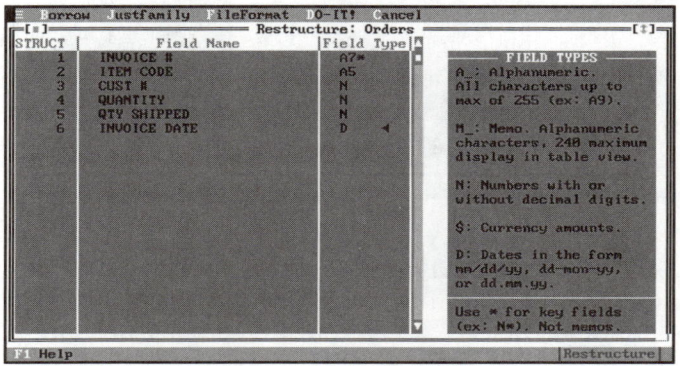

Your Orders table structure should now look like this.

Changing Existing Fields

Changing an existing field specification is just like editing a newly created specification. You only have to delete and/or add the needed text changes for the new field names. In this section, you will change both field names and field types.

To edit a field specification, do the following:

1. Move the cursor to field 4, Quantity, and then to the Field Name column.
2. Press [←Backspace] to delete all the letters up to the letter Q.

   Remember, you can use any of the editing techniques you learned in Chapter 4, including Field view.
3. Type **TY ORDERED**.

243

Restructuring a Table

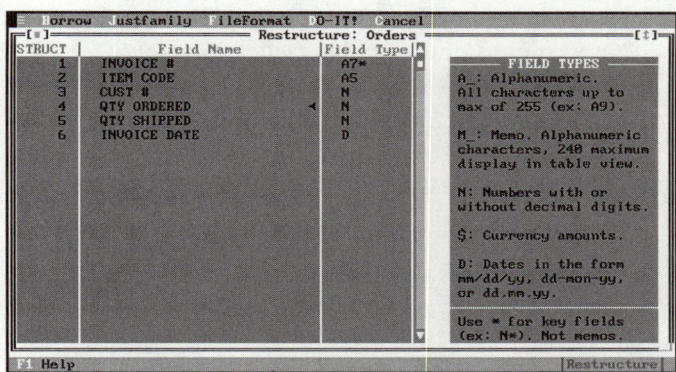

Now you can see the edited Qty Ordered field.

Alternatively, you can erase the entire field name by pressing Ctrl-Backspace and then typing the new field name. If you are correcting a small part of a field name or type, using Backspace is quicker. When you are replacing an entire field, Ctrl-Backspace is faster.

You also can change an alphanumeric or memo field's length. Changing a memo field's length only changes the number of characters displayed in Table view. The actual memo data still exists regardless of the length of the field display. Shortening an alphanumeric field, on the other hand, can cause loss of data.

If you shorten an alphanumeric field, several things happen. To see the results of shortening an alphanumeric field, do the following:

1. Move the cursor to the field type column of the Item Code field.
2. Press Backspace twice. Type 4*.
3. Press F2 or select DO-IT! from the menu bar.

Here, you see the pop-up menu box and a message displayed.

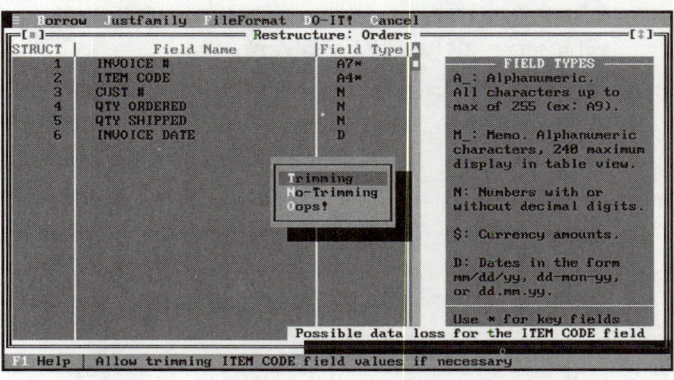

244

Changing a Table's Structure

Paradox identifies the field that is causing problems with the message `Possible data loss for the ITEM CODE field`. You are given three options for correcting the problem:

The **T**rimming option truncates, or shortens, all the data in the field to fit the new field length. If you choose this option, you lose all the trimmed data.

The **N**o-Trimming option moves all the offending records to the Problems table. You have to correct the records manually or save them as a separate file.

The **O**ops! option cancels the **DO**-IT! command and enables you to change the field type again.

4. Select **O**ops!.
5. Reverse the change you just made by changing the field type back to **A5***.

Modifying Key and Non-Key Fields

Paradox also enables you to add key fields or change an existing field to a keyed field. You may find, for instance, that a previously unkeyed table now needs a key field.

Up to now, you have only used tables containing a single key. Paradox also enables you to use a multi-field, or *concatenated*, key. Your Cust1 table uses the single key field, Cust #. Customers have their own unique numbers to identify them. As discussed before, you cannot use the Last Name field as a single key field because many people have the same last name. You can create a concatenated key by using both the Last Name and First Name fields. But again, someday your database will grow to the point where you have two people with the same first and last name. You may be more successful with a three-tier concatenated key, by using Last Name, First Name, and Street. Having two records that are identical in all three fields is highly unlikely.

Although this approach may be workable, it is also cumbersome and comparatively slow with queries and sorting. Additionally, attempting to link this table with another may prove extremely awkward. The single key field is preferable, but at times not completely practical.

To add a key field to a table you only have to place an asterisk (*) beside the field type. Remember, the primary key must be the first field listed in the table. Secondary keys follow the primary one in the order you require. Paradox uses secondary key fields to break any ties in the primary key field when sorting a

245

Restructuring a Table

table and determining whether duplicate records exist. You cannot have a regular, unkeyed field between two keyed fields.

To see how Paradox requires you to place key fields, do the following:

1. Move the cursor to the field type column of the Item Code field.
2. Press [◆Backspace] once to remove the asterisk (*).
3. Move the cursor down one field and place an asterisk (*) beside the field type of the Cust # field.
4. Press [F2].

Here, you can see an unkeyed field between two keyed fields.

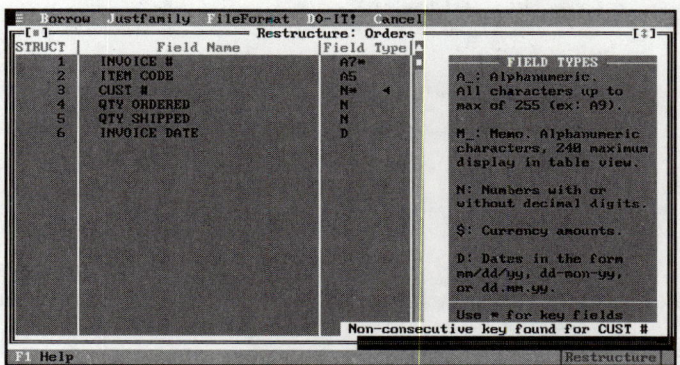

Paradox displays the message Non-consecutive key found for CUST #. This tells you the location of the unkeyed field, and you can correct the error. You can key the problem field or move it below the last keyed field.

5. Press [◆Backspace] once to remove the asterisk (*).
6. Press [F2] or select **D**O-IT!.

246

Changing a Table's Structure

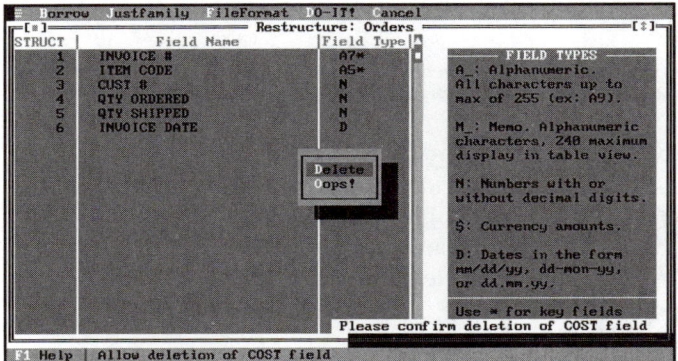

Here, you see Paradox prompting you to confirm the deletion of the COST field.

The pop-up menu box that is displayed gives you two options: Delete and Oops!. The message displayed in the menu box, `Please confirm deletion of COST field`, tells you specifically which field to confirm.

The Delete option deletes the field and all the data contained in each record. You cannot recover any of this information. If you are not sure of this choice, select the Oops! option.

The Oops! option cancels the DO-IT! command. You can then add the field back to the table specification. Selecting this command does not automatically reinsert the deleted field.

7. Select the Delete option.

    You should now see the same pop-up menu box again with the message `Please confirm deletion of the RETAIL field` displayed.

8. Select the Delete option again.

    As Paradox restructures the table, you should see the following messages displayed:

    `Updating report R — modified fields will be deleted from report...`

    `Updating form F — modified fields will be deleted from form...`

    These messages are repeated for each report or form that is part of the table's family.

Changing a field's type can cause various problems. Table 9.1 gives you a short overview of what potentially can happen when changing different field types.

247

Restructuring a Table

**Table 9.1
Changing a Field Type**

Original	Change To	Potential Consequence
Any field	Alphanumeric	No problems should occur here provided the field type width is long enough to contain the data. Otherwise, you are prompted to trim data to fit the field, move records to the Problems table, or edit the field width.
Any field type	Memo	No problems should occur in this conversion because a memo field is variable in length. Only the number of characters displayed in Table view is fixed.
Alphanumeric or Memo	Numeric (N, S, $)	If all the records contain only numeric data, no problems should occur. Any records that do contain data other than numbers are moved to the Problems table.
Alphanumeric or Memo	Date	If all the records contain only date information, in a format recognized by Paradox as a date, then no problems should occur. Any records containing information that is not a date, or not in a recognized date format are moved to the Problems table.
Numeric (N, S, $)	A different numeric format	No problems should occur when converting between the numeric formats, except to a Short number field if the number is not between -32,767 and 32,767, or is not a whole number. In such cases, the data is trimmed or the record is moved to the Problems table.
Numeric (N, S, $)	Date	All records are moved to the Problems table.
Date	Numeric (N, S, $)	All records are moved to the Problems table.

Using the Key Violations Table

When you insert or change key fields in a table, any record that is in violation of the duplicate record rule is removed from the table and placed in the Keyviol table. If this happens, you have four options:

- Edit the records in the Keyviol table so that they conform to the new table structure; then add them back to the table.
- Rename the Keyviol table so that it becomes a permanent table.
- Ignore the Keyviol table and the data it contains. The next time you create this table, change working directories, or end the current Paradox session, the Keyviol table is deleted.
- Restructure the table again, either to its original form or so that the records conform to the new key, enabling you to add the figures back to the table.

You probably noticed that when you completed the previous section and selected **D**O-IT!, the Struct table was replaced with the Keyviol table.

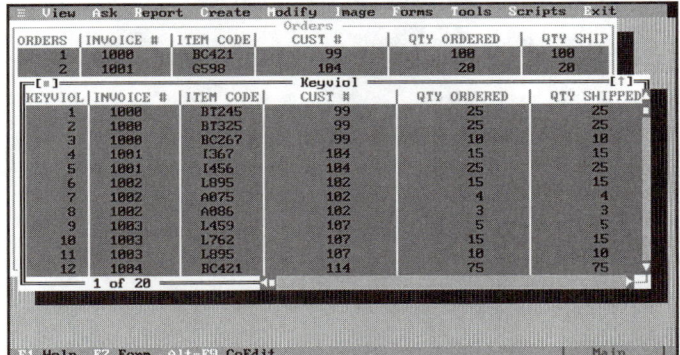

Here, you see the Keyviol table displayed on the desktop.

These records were in the table before. To understand why they became key violating records, look again at the actions in the previous sections.

You inserted a new field into the table specification. This causes a key field problem if you insert the field before a key field and do not designate the new field as a key field. Remember, Paradox warned you to avoid this type of mistake and would not let you save the table until you corrected the problem.

You added a new field to the end of the table specification. This only causes a problem if you designate it a key field and do not move it to the beginning of the table. Had you done this, Paradox would have again warned you of the error.

249

Restructuring a Table

You deleted two field specifications. This also causes a key violation if you delete a key field from a multi-key table. However, the two fields that were deleted were not among the table's key fields.

You then deleted the key field designation, the asterisk (*), from the Item Code and Cust # fields. The Cust # field was a field just added to the table, so it should not have been the problem. But, the Item Code field was part of a concatenated key. (The Invoice # and Item Code fields together created a concatenated key. When you deleted the key field designation from the Item Code field, you created a single key table. Only the first occurrence of a unique invoice number can be considered a unique record. Paradox considers all other records duplicates and places them in the Keyviol table.)

You want to add the records contained in the Keyviol table back to the Orders table because you may need them later. The records also are needed to keep the data in the Orders table accurate. To correct the problems, do the following:

1. Select the **M**odify **R**estructure option from the menus.

Here, you see the list of available tables. The table currently on the desktop, Keyviol, is the highlighted default selection.

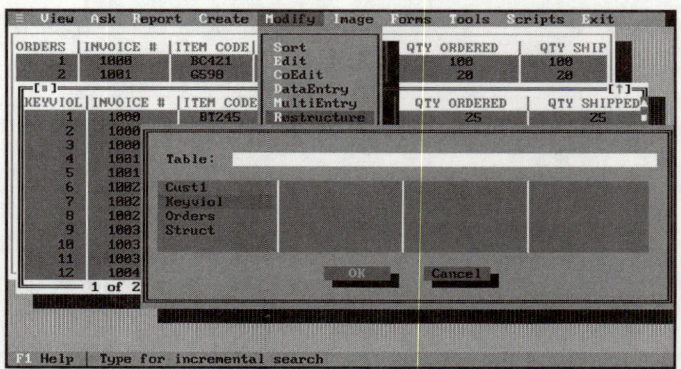

2. Choose the Orders table from the Table list box.

250

Using the Key Violations Table

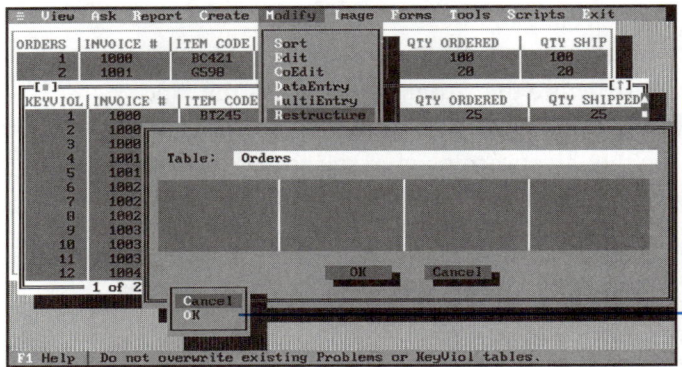

Here, you see the pop-up menu box displayed. Notice the message displayed on the status bar.

Remember, if any of the commands you initiate while again restructuring the Orders table causes the Keyviol table to be created, the new table overwrites the old. To ensure that you do not lose the data you are now attempting to save, you need to rename the Keyviol table. The same is true when you have a Problems table.

3. Select **C**ancel, and then press Esc twice to go to the Main menu.
4. Select the **T**ools option from the Main menu.
5. Choose the first option, **R**ename, and then the **T**able option from the cascading menu.
6. From the Table list box, select the Keyviol table.
7. Enter a name under which to save the table. Type **Tempord** for Temporary Orders table.

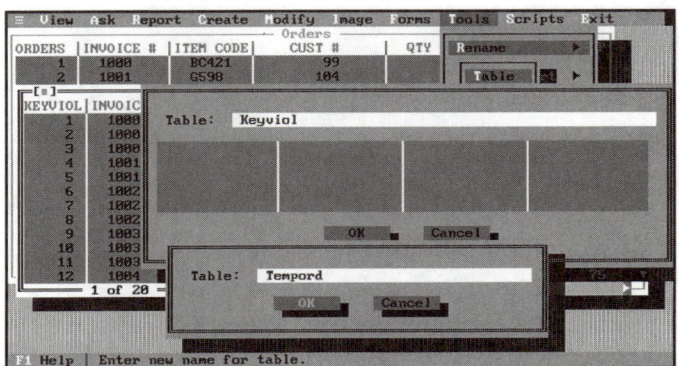

Here, you see the dialog box with the new table name entered.

Restructuring a Table

8. Press [↵Enter].

   The new Tempord table displays on the desktop.

9. Now, again try to restructure the Orders table. Select the **M**odify **R**estructure option from the menus, and then choose the Orders table.

   You should not see the same warning message about overwriting the Keyviol or Problems tables because you have renamed the Keyviol table.

10. Move the cursor to the Field Type column and down to the second field.

11. Type an asterisk (*) beside A5.

Your screen should now look like this. The Item Code field is again part of a concatenated key.

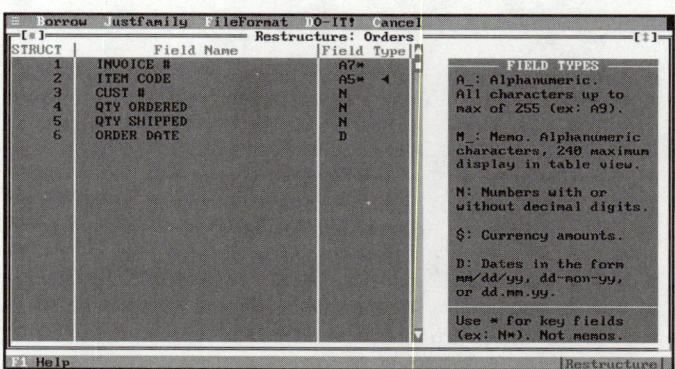

12. Press [F2], or select **D**O-IT! from the menu.

Here, you can see the restructured Orders table displayed on the desktop. Notice that it currently contains only six records.

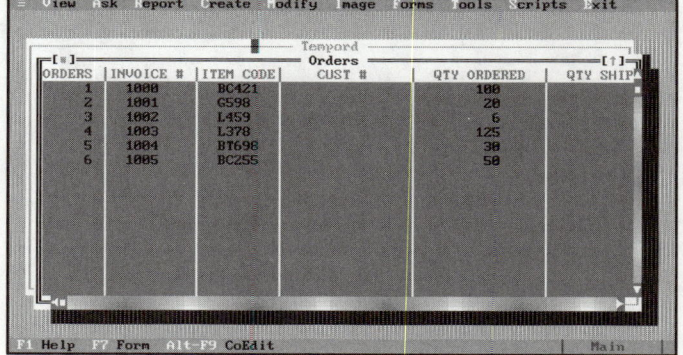

Using the Key Violations Table

To complete the job, you must now add the records contained in the Tempord table back into the Orders table. To do this, do the following:

1. Select the **T**ools **M**ore **A**dd command from the menu bar and cascading menus.
2. Press ⏎Enter to see the list of tables.

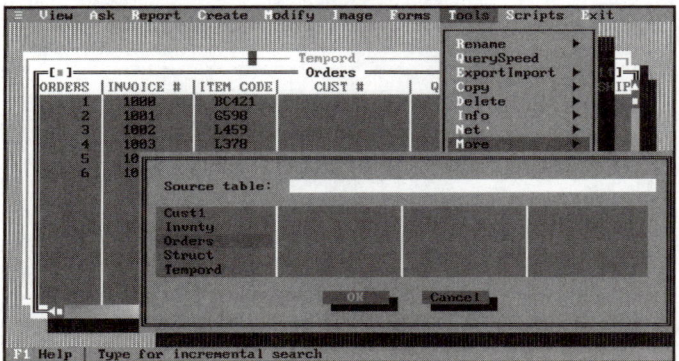

Here, you see the list of available tables.

You also see a Source Table dialog box. The source table is the table that contains the records you want to add to the target table.

3. Select the Tempord table and press ⏎Enter.

You now see the Target Table dialog box. The target table is the table to which you want to add the records.

Again, the source table is the table the records come from, and the target table is the one to which they are added.

4. Type in the target table, **Orders**, and press ⏎Enter.

You now have two new options: **N**ewEntries and **U**pdate. You see these menu options only when you add records to a keyed table.

The **N**ewEntries option adds those records that are new to the table. A record is considered new if it is not currently duplicated in the target table, according to the key fields. Duplicates are not added to the target table, but are placed in the Keyviol table.

The **U**pdate option adds all records to the target table. If a duplicate exists, the new information from the source table "updates" the record in the target table. The old data from the target table moves to a temporary *Changed* table. This enables you to check for any errors.

5. Select the **N**ewEntries option, and press ⏎Enter.

253

Restructuring a Table

Select this option because all the records were previously in the table and should not cause any further key violations.

You should see the message `Adding records from Tempord to Orders...` displayed in the message box as Paradox adds the records from one table to the other.

Here, you see the Orders table displayed on the desktop.

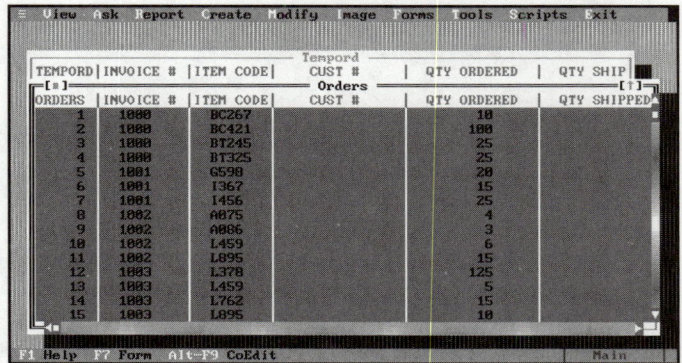

This table is now complete and has all its records back. You can delete the Tempord table by using the **T**ools **D**elete **T**able option.

Using the Problems Table

In many ways, the Keyviol and Problems tables are the same, although they occur for different reasons. The Keyviol table occurs only if a record no longer fits the rules of the key fields. This generally happens when you add a record to a table or change the key fields while restructuring.

The Problems table contains records that for some reason are no longer consistent with the current table structure. The record may have the wrong type of data in a field or data too long to fit within the field length.

For example, you have an alphanumeric field containing dates for meetings. You then restructure the table so that this becomes a date field. You have no problems, as long as all the records use a date format that Paradox recognizes. If, however, you have two meetings that always occur on days like First Tuesday of the month and Third Friday of the month, Paradox does not recognize these as valid dates and places both records into the Problems table.

Using Validity Checks

You then have to edit the data in the Problems table to make it compatible with the new format and add the records back into the table. This involves a process like the one you learned in the previous section on the Keyviol table.

Using Validity Checks

Validity checks are a system of controls you can use to make data entry easier and ensure the accuracy of the entered data. Using the **V**alCheck option on the menu, you can add validity checks to a table while in the Edit or DataEntry mode. Once established, the checks also are valid in the CoEdit mode.

Although Paradox does provide minimal forms of validity checking, such as not allowing you to enter text in a number field or an invalid date into a date field, validity checks go far beyond this form of checking. With some validity checks, you can have data entered automatically from a lookup table, or a set value entered into a field when you do not enter a value. You can set fields so they do not accept data that does not fit within a predefined range.

When you create validity checks, they are valid only for the current table. Any settings you have created are saved as an object in the table's family when you end the edit or data-entry session. These settings are then valid the next time you use the table. Table 9.2 lists the various validity checks and their uses.

Table 9.2
Validity Checks

Validity	*Check Uses*
LowValue	Defines the lowest acceptable value in a field. Most often used in number or date fields.
HighValue	Defines the highest acceptable value in a field. Most often used for number or date fields.
Default	The specified default value entered into a field if you leave it blank.
TableLookup	Requires that the value entered into a field exists as a value in the first field of the designated lookup table.
Picture	Lets you create a format or template for a value in a field. Helps to ensure consistency in data entry.

continues

255

Restructuring a Table

Table 9.2 Continued

Validity	Check Uses
Required	Requires that you enter a value into the field before you can enter another record.
Auto	Moves the cursor to the next field when you have entered all the information required for the field, based on its type and other validity check requirements.

A word of caution about assigning validity checks: Paradox does not check the consistency of the checks you define. You can do things such as assign a Low Value of 10 and a High Value of 5 for the same field. Needless to say, entering any value into such a field is difficult.

Using LowValue and HighValue Checks

You generally use the **L**owValue and **H**ighValue validity checks for fields that contain numbers. Although Paradox enables you to enter any size number into a **N**umber or **$**Currency field and a wide range of sizes in the **S**hort number field, most values entered in a field are within a narrow range. For example, in the Invnty table, which contains data about inventory items including cost and selling price, you know that none of the items has a cost of less than 25 cents or more than $25.50. The same is true of the selling price in the Retail field: your lowest value is 45 cents and the highest is $42.50.

Using a combination of **L**owValue and **H**ighValue validity checks ensures that costs and selling prices are entered only within a set range of appropriate values. To see how this is done, do the following:

1. Open the Invnty table in the Edit mode. Select the **M**odify **E**dit option, and choose the Invnty table.
2. Select the **V**alCheck option from the menu bar.
3. Choose the **D**efine option.

    You should see the prompt `Move to the field for which you want to set check, then press ↵...`.

4. Move the cursor to the Cost field and press ⏎Enter.

Using Validity Checks

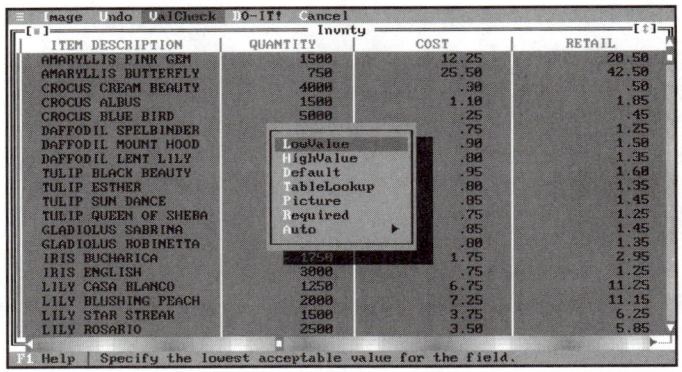

Here, you see the pop-up menu box containing the validity check options.

5. Select the first option, **L**owValue.
6. Enter the lowest allowed value for the Cost field into the dialog box. Type **.25**.

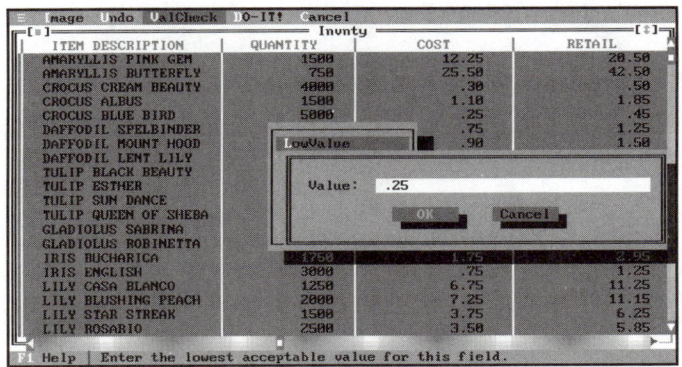

You now see the low value entered into the dialog box.

Remember, even though this is a currency field, do not include the dollar ($) sign.

7. Press ⏎Enter to save this low value validity check.

   You should see the message Low value recorded displayed in the message box.

8. Now select the **V**alCheck **D**efine option again. Leave the cursor in the Cost field and press ⏎Enter.

9. This time select the **H**ighValue option. Enter the highest value you want to be able to enter into the Cost field.

257

Restructuring a Table

You probably do not want to use the current highest cost and then have to alter this validity check later if your costs go up or you bring in a higher cost item. At the same time, you do not want to set the **H**ighValue too high and defeat your purpose for using it.

Type **30** and press ⏎Enter.

You should see the message `High value recorded` displayed in the message box.

To see how the validity check works, try to change the cost of the first record from 12.25 to 31, as follows:

1. Press Ctrl-⬅Backspace five times to delete the current value, 12.25.
2. Enter the new value. Type **31** and press ⏎Enter.

Here, you can see that the entered value, 31, is displayed in reverse video and an error message is displayed.

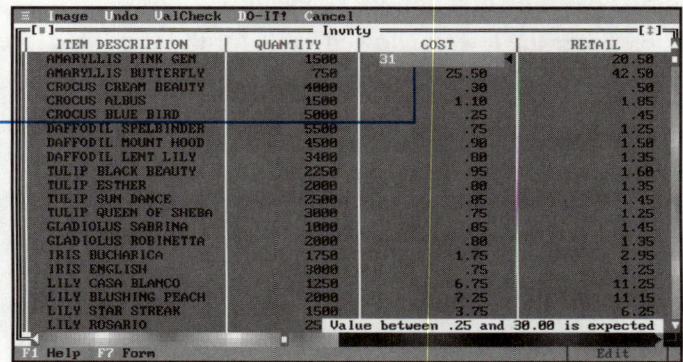

Paradox displays the message `Value between .25 and 30.00 is expected`. Paradox supplies the valid range that is acceptable for this field.

3. Correct the value by pressing ⬅Backspace twice and typing in the original value of **12.25**. Then press ⏎Enter.

You can use the **L**owValue/**H**ighValue option with alphanumeric fields, but this is not common. A possible application may be a ZIP code field if you do not use foreign postal codes. You can set a **L**owValue of 0 and a **H**ighValue of 99999 and avoid invalid ZIP codes.

You also can specify low and high values for a date field. You can use the reserved word TODAY as the low or high value and exclude dates earlier or later than the current date set in your computer's clock. If you set the high and low values as TODAY, you are doing the same thing as if you set the

Using Validity Checks

Default value for the date field as TODAY. See the next section for more information concerning default values.

Using Default Values

By definition, all records within a table should be unique, even though this may not always hold true if you are using an unkeyed table. Although a record should be unique, each individual field within the record does not have to be unique.

Often, the actual data within some field may be repeated throughout a table. For example, if you have a table containing employee data, which includes addresses, you may have a table in which the state field is identical for all the records. This is a perfect example of when to use a Default validity check value.

To see the use of the Default value, do the following:

1. Open the Cust1 table in Edit mode. Select **M**odify **E**dit and choose the Cust1 table.
2. Select the **V**alCheck option from the menu bar.
3. Choose the **D**efine option. Then move the cursor to the Country field and press ⏎Enter.
4. Choose the **D**efault option from the pop-up menu box.
5. Type the default value **USA** into the dialog box.

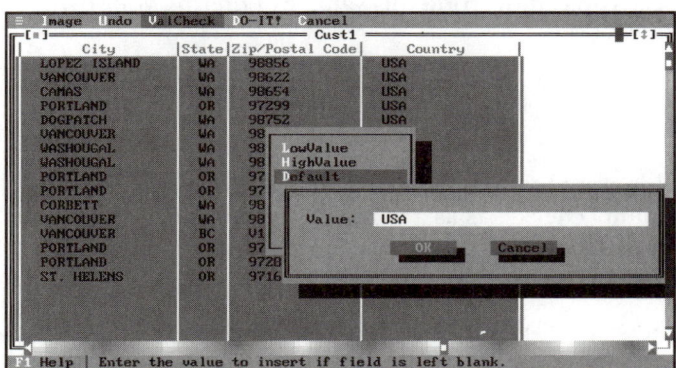

Here, you can see the default value USA added to the Country field in the Cust1 table.

Use the default value for fields usually filled in with identical values. If you need to enter a value other than the default value, just type in the alternative value.

259

Restructuring a Table

6. Press ⏎Enter to accept the default value.

   You should see the message Default value recorded in the message box.

7. Press F2 or select **D**O-IT! to complete this edit session and save the new validity checks.

Many times when using a date in a field, you may want to automatically fill in the current, or today's, date. To use a default date, do the following:

1. Open the Orders table in Edit mode. Select **M**odify **E**dit, type the table name **Orders** in the dialog box, and press ⏎Enter.
2. Select **V**alCheck **D**efine from the menu, move the cursor to the Invoice Date field, and press ⏎Enter.
3. Select **D**efault from the pop-up menu box, and press ⏎Enter.
4. Enter the reserved word **TODAY** as the default value.

Here, you see the dialog box with the reserved date value of TODAY entered.

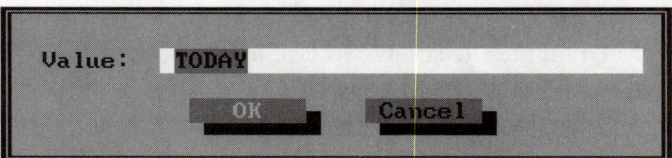

5. Press ⏎Enter to complete the operation.

Now each time you enter this field, Paradox fills in the current date according to your computer's clock. You can override this value by entering your own date.

Using Picture Fields

You can use picture fields as a tool to make data entry easier and more accurate. The **P**icture validity check acts as a template for the data entered into a field. Paradox also can use the specified picture format to check the accuracy of entered data.

Remember, Paradox does not consider lower and uppercase letters to be the same. Suppose that you want to sort the Cust1 table by the Last Name field and you have entered two customers with the same last name as follows:

   Martin

   MARTIN

Using Validity Checks

Paradox may not sort them together because one uses lowercase letters. A picture field can help to ensure that your data is entered consistently. Table 9.3 lists the various characters you can use as pictures, and table 9.4 shows you some examples of picture fields.

Table 9.3
Picture Field Characters

Character	Used for
#	Numbers.
?	Any letter, either upper or lowercase.
&	Any letter, converted to uppercase.
@	Any character.
!	Any characters or letters converted to uppercase.
;	Interpreting the next picture character literally instead of as a picture character.
*n	Allowing the next picture character to be used *n* times. Enter the number of times to use the picture code. If you do not enter a number, then any number of repetitions, including zero, is allowed.
[]	Optional characters. Any literal value or picture characters enclosed in brackets are optional.
{}	Grouping operator.
,	Alternative choices. Values separated by a comma are interpreted as alternative choices.

Table 9.4
Examples of Picture Fields

Picture	Description	Format Created
#####[-####] *5#[-*4#]	Standard U.S. ZIP code with optional ZIP+4	46033 46033-0001
[(###)]###-####	Normal U.S. phone number with optional area code	555-5555 (555)555-5555

continues

Restructuring a Table

Table 9.4 Continued

Picture	Description	Format Created
&*&	Converts any size alphabetic string to all uppercase	PHILPOTT O'TOOLE'S TOOLS
Yes,No	Allows choice of alternative values	Yes or No

Add several picture fields to the validity checks in the Cust1 table by doing the following:

1. If the Cust1 table is not currently open in Edit mode, use the **M**odify **E**dit option to open it.

2. Select **V**alCheck from the menu bar. Then choose **D**efine, place the cursor on the Last Name field, and press ⏎Enter.

3. Select **P**icture from the pop-up menu box.

4. Enter the required picture in the dialog box. Type **&*&**.

Here, you can see the Picture dialog box completed with the picture for converting any letter values to all uppercase letters.

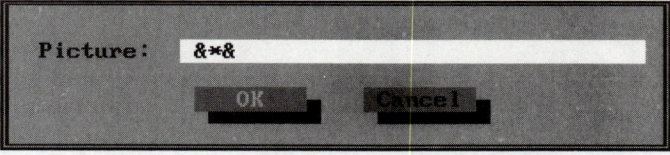

5. Press ⏎Enter to complete the operation.

   You should see the message `Picture specification recorded`.

6. Select **V**alCheck **D**efine again. Move the cursor to the Phone Number field, and press ⏎Enter. Select **P**icture from the pop-up menu box.

7. Enter the picture type for phone numbers. For example, type *(###)###-####*.

262

Using Validity Checks

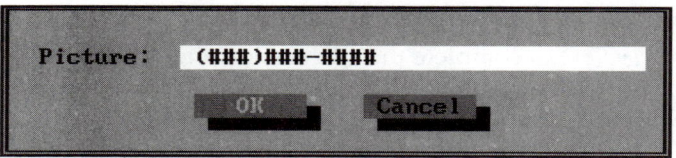

Now you see the Picture dialog box filled in with the picture for phone numbers. Notice that the square brackets ([ ]) are not used. In this picture, the area code is required, not optional.

8. Press `Enter` to complete the operation.
9. Select **V**alCheck **D**efine again. Move the cursor to the State field and press `Enter`. Select **P**icture from the pop-up menu box.
10. Enter the picture characters **&&**. Now the State field will display only two uppercase letters.

Entering Required Fields

Within a table, some fields must have a value entered into them. For example, a key field should have a value entered, or you may not be able to retrieve a record.

The required field designation is the only validity check you can place in a memo field.

To enter a required field in the Cust1 table, do the following:

1. Select **V**alCheck from the menu bar and **D**efine from the pull-down menu box.
2. Move the cursor to the Cust # field and press `Enter`.
3. Select the **R**equired option, and then choose the **Y**es option.

   When you select the **R**equired validity check, a cascading menu is displayed with **Y**es and **N**o options. Selecting the **Y**es option requires a field to be filled in with a value. Selecting **N**o allows the field to be left blank.

   When you select the **Y**es option, you should see the message `Required status recorded` displayed in the message box.

263

Restructuring a Table

Now when you enter this field in the Edit, CoEdit, or DataEntry mode, you must enter a value before you can leave the field. If you attempt to leave, the message `A value must be provided in this field; press [F1] for help` is displayed in the message box.

4. Press `F2` or select **D**O-IT! to complete the edit session and save all the validity checks for the Cust1 table.

    If you accidentally open a new record and enter a required field, you can get out of it only by entering a value into the field, which then creates a new record, or by pressing `Del` to delete the record.

Using TableLookup Fields

Sometimes, for data to be entered into a field, it must not only be the right type and within a specified range, but also exist already in another table. For example, the Orders table uses values that exist in the Invnty and Cust1 tables. You can use the **T**ableLookup validity check to require that a value exists in another table.

A lookup table must meet certain requirements:

- The field that is being "looked up" must be the first field in the Lookup table, but cannot be a memo field.
- The Lookup field and the field that is being checked must have the same field type. They need not have the same field name.
- For the fastest search, the Lookup table field should be keyed, but this is not required.

To use **T**ableLookup validity checks with a table, do the following:

1. Select **M**odify **E**dit from the menu bar. Choose the Orders table and press `Enter`.
2. Select the **V**alCheck option from the menu bar, and then choose **D**efine from the cascading menu box.
3. Move the cursor to the Item Code field and press `Enter`.
4. Select the **T**ableLookup option.

    You now must choose the table to "look up" for a valid entry. Remember, the Lookup table must have the looked for value contained in the first field.

Using Validity Checks

5. Choose the Invnty table by typing **Inv**nty in the dialog box and pressing ⏎Enter, or press ⏎Enter and select Invnty from the Table list.

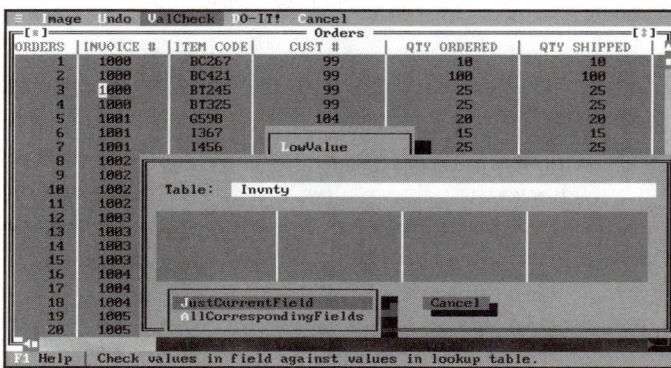

Here, you see the pop-up menu for the **T**ableLookup option.

The pop-up menu box has two choices: **J**ustCurrent Field and **A**llCorrespondingFields. See table 9.5 for descriptions of the options.

6. Select the option **J**ustCurrentField and then **H**elpAndFill.

   You should see the message `Table lookup recorded` displayed in the message box.

7. Now select **V**alCheck **D**efine, move the cursor to the Cust # field, and press ⏎Enter.

8. Choose the **T**ableLookup option, select the Cust1 table, and press ⏎Enter.

9. Select the **A**llCorrespondingFields option and then the **H**elpAndFill option. You again should see the message `Table lookup recorded` displayed in the message box.

Table 9.5 describes the **T**ableLookup options you select in step 6 of the preceding procedure.

265

Restructuring a Table

Table 9.5
TableLookup Options

Option	Description
JustCurrentField	In the **T**ableLookup menu, enables you to check only the values for the current field.
PrivateLookup	In the **J**ustCurrentField menu, requires you to enter a value into the field. Paradox then checks the value against the first field in the Lookup table to validate it. If the entered value is not valid, the message Not one of the possible values for this field is displayed. You must then correct the data.
HelpAndFill	In the **J**ustCurrentField menu, also requires that the entered value be contained in the first field of the Lookup table. Paradox enables you to browse the Lookup table to find the value you require; you then can enter the correct data or let Paradox fill it in for you. If you do not remember the correct valid entry for the field, pressing [F1] displays the Lookup table on the desktop.
AllCorrespondingFields	In the **T**ableLookup menu, enables you to check for the values in the current field and then fills in all values for fields with the same name.
FillNoHelp	In the **A**llCorrespondingFields menu, is similar to **P**rivateLookup. When you enter a valid entry into the field, Paradox then enters all of the data from the Lookup table that corresponds (has the same field name) with the current table.

Using Validity Checks

Option	Description
HelpAndFill	In the **A**llCorrespondingFields menu, enables you to enter a value into a field, and if valid, Paradox enters the data from corresponding fields into the table. Or, you can select Help, browse the Lookup table to find the required value, and then fill it and the corresponding field values into the table. If you do not remember the correct valid entry for the field, pressing F1 displays the Lookup table on the desktop.

Now, to see how the Lookup table function works, add a new record to the Orders table. Do the following:

1. Move the cursor down to the bottom of the table and press ↓ to open a new record.
2. Type **1006** for the next consecutive invoice number and press ↵Enter.
3. Now you must enter the item code, but because you have so many different items and cannot remember the specific code for the item ordered, press F1, the Help key.

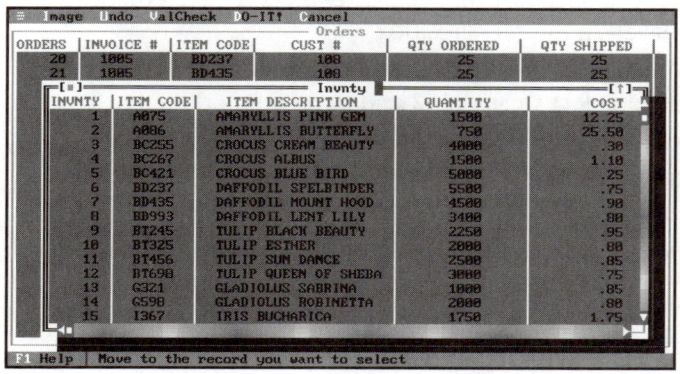

Here, you can see the Invnty Lookup Table displayed.

You can find the specific record value you are searching for by scrolling through the table until you find it.

You also can use the Zoom (Ctrl-Z) and Zoom Next (Alt-Z) commands to find the value for which you are searching.

9

267

Restructuring a Table

You can return to the table you are editing without automatically filling in a value and then enter it yourself.

Press F2 or select DO-IT!, and the value on which the cursor is located in the Lookup table is entered into the table you're editing.

4. Move the cursor down to record number 4, Item Code BC267, and press F2.

Now you see that the Lookup table has been removed from the desktop, and the selected value is entered into the Orders table.

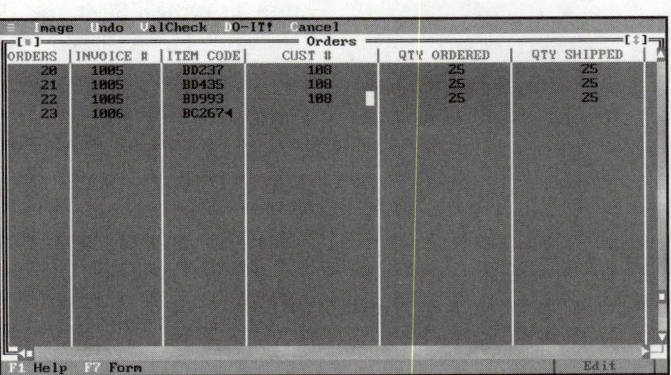

5. Press Enter to move to the next field. Then type **120** and press Enter again.

   You should see the message `Not one of the possible values for this field` displayed in the message box.

6. Press F1, the Help key, to view the Cust1 Lookup table, and select a valid customer code. Select Cust # **112** and press Enter.

7. Complete the record by entering the following data:

QTY ORDERED	**30**
QTY SHIPPED	**30**
INVOICE DATE	Press Enter to fill in the default date.

Creating Auto Fields

The term *Auto Fields* stands for Autoconfirm. In this type of field, Paradox moves the cursor from the field when you have completed a valid entry.

When you choose the **A**uto option, you have three options: **F**illed, **P**icture, and **L**ookup.

Using Validity Checks

Select the **F**illed option for fixed length fields. When you have filled the field, Paradox moves the cursor to the next field. If the value you enter does not completely fill the maximum field length value, then you have to move the cursor manually to the next field.

Use the **P**icture option in conjunction with a picture field. When you have satisfied the requirements of the picture field, Paradox moves the cursor to the next field.

The **L**ookup option functions in combination with an associated lookup table. After you have selected a value from the lookup table or entered a valid value, then Paradox moves the cursor to the next field.

To see how the **A**uto validity check is used, do the following:

1. Open the Orders table. Select **M**odify **E**dit **Orders**.
2. Select **V**alCheck **D**efine, move the cursor to the Item Code field, and press ⏎Enter.
3. Choose the **A**uto option.

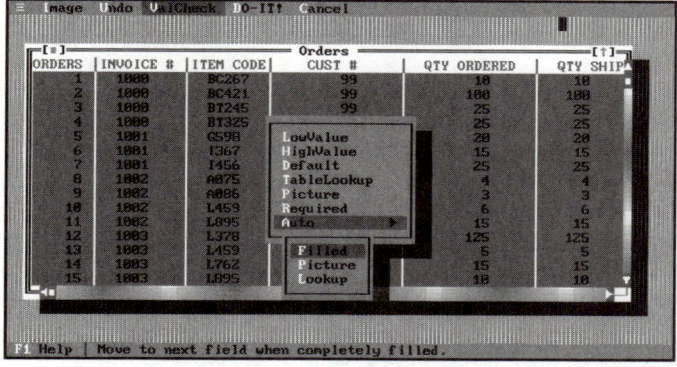

Here, you can see the **A**uto option menu.

4. Because the Item Code field is a lookup field, select the **L**ookup option.
5. Select **Y**es to enable the autoconfirm option.

   For each of the three autoconfirm options, you are given the choice to enable (**Y**es) or disable (**N**o) the option.

6. To enable Paradox to move the cursor automatically to the next field, repeat steps 2 through 5, using the Cust # field.

269

Restructuring a Table

To test how the autoconfirm function works, do the following:

1. Move the cursor to the bottom of the table and then down to the next blank record.
2. Enter the invoice number **1007** and press `↵Enter`.
3. Press `F1` to view the Lookup table. Move the cursor to record number 12, Item Code BT698 and press `F2`.

You now see the Item Code field has been filled in and the cursor automatically advanced to the next field.

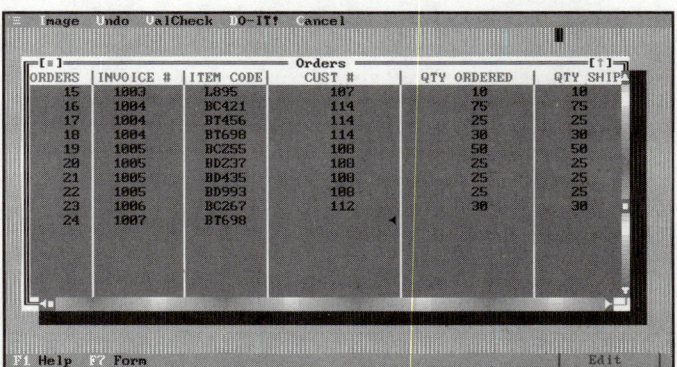

4. Press `F1` to view the lookup table. Move the cursor to record number 15, Cust # 113 and press `F2`.

Here, you can see that the Cust # field has been filled in and the cursor again moved to the next field.

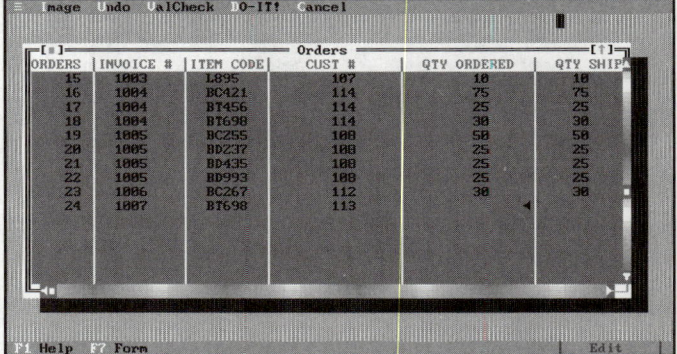

5. Enter the following values for the next fields:

QTY ORDERED	**20**
QTY SHIPPED	**20**
INVOICE DATE	Press ⏎Enter to enter the default date.

You use the Autoconfirm option primarily as a step saver. It enables the data-entry clerk to save time and effort. If a field is complete, Paradox moves the cursor to the next field.

Summary

In this chapter, you learned how to modify a table's structure to meet changing needs. You then learned how to change records that did not fit the new table structure so they can be added back to the original table. And, finally, you learned to use the Paradox editing aids called validity checks.

Specifically, you learned the following key information about Paradox 4:

- To restructure a table, use the **M**odify **R**estructure option on the Main menu. Select the table to restructure.
- Use a unique field to refer to a record in another table.
- To move a field when restructuring, use Ins and then type the field name. Paradox adds the field type and erases the old field specification.
- Be careful when you change a field type. Some field types may cause key violations and others may cause records to no longer meet a field requirement, placing the record in the Problems or Keyviol table.
- To create a multi-field, or concatenated, key in a table, you must place asterisks (*) beside the field type designations. The key fields must be the first fields in the table.
- Rename the Keyviol and Problems temporary tables before attempting to correct a restructuring problem. This step ensures that the data is not overwritten. Use the **T**ools **R**ename **T**able option.
- Edit records placed in a Keyviol or Problems table and then use the **T**ools **M**ore **A**dd option. The source table is the table currently holding the records to add to another table; the target table is the table to which to send the records.
- Use validity checks to ensure accuracy of data entry.

Restructuring a Table

- To create validity checks, a table must be open in the Edit or DataEntry mode. Validity checks are saved as a member of the table's family. Validity checks are valid then in the CoEdit mode.
- To use Default values for repetitive field entries, use the **V**alcheck **D**efault option. Then enter the value to be used as the default value in the dialog box.
- Use the reserved word TODAY in date fields for a default value or a **L**owValue/**H**ighValue. This step ensures that the current date is used in a report or form.
- Use a picture field for ensuring accuracy and consistency in data entry. The picture acts as a template for data.
- Use the required field to ensure that a value is placed in a field.
- Use **T**ableLookup fields when a field value must exist in another table.
- Use the **A**uto field option to move the cursor to the next field when the field is appropriately completed.

In the next chapter, you will learn to create a free-form form and use a multi-table form and report. With these devices, you will create a relational database.

Creating Free-Form and Multi-Table Forms

10

Up to now, you primarily have used the Paradox table. Although you can accomplish most of your work using the table format, it may not always provide the best way to perform a required task. In most Paradox tables, some data fields are not visible on your screen. Using Form view, you can see and use the entire record of data. But while the Paradox Standard form can work well for some applications, it is not the most user-friendly view.

The alternative is to create your own form. Using the Paradox Form Designer, you can create a form that contains special on-screen prompts, calculated fields, borders surrounding fields, multi-record forms, multi-page forms, and finally multi-table forms.

An overview of the Paradox form

Designing a free-form form

Working with the form design features

Designing a multi-record Form

Designing a multi-table form

Strengthening your form design

Editing an existing form

Creating Free-Form and Multi-Table Forms

When you use forms, you can unlock many of Paradox's most powerful features. You can enter data in several tables at a time, and you can view data both in several tables and in multiple records.

Key Terms in This Chapter

Detail form	The form that has fields embedded in a master form. The master form subsequently owns the records of the detail form.
Master form	The form created for the master table that has detail forms embedded within itself.
Embedded form	A form that has been placed in and linked to a master form.
Referential integrity	A special relationship between master and detail records. When you are using the master form and make a change in a record, the change is reflected in all the tables that contain or need this information.

An Overview of the Paradox Form

The Paradox form and report share many similarities in their construction. As you build your form, you will use the Form Designer just as you used the Report Designer. Fields and text are placed within the Form Designer window according to your requirements. As you plan the form, keep the average user of your database in mind. For some users, the Form view may be all they ever see. Keep your form focused on its task, and provide any necessary on-screen prompts.

The Paradox Form

The Paradox form is an alternative view of your data. For many users, this is the preferred view. You can design the form to resemble an existing paper form. A Paradox form is most often used for data entry work. You can also use the form to view data, especially single records.

You can build a Paradox form that displays several records; the form does not have to show a single record only. In the same manner, a form can display

Designing a Free-Form Form

information concerning several tables. With properly constructed tables, you can use a form to display and edit data from several records in several tables.

As you plan your new form, try to create a picture of it on paper. If you are replacing an existing form, use the features that work for the job and then make any required changes. When you design the form, you need to know if you can create the form from a single table, or if you will have to use a multi-table approach. While the single table form is the simplest to design, with proper planning of both the form and the tables, you can design your own multi-table form.

You can access the Paradox form by pressing F7 (Form Toggle) or by selecting **I**mage **P**ickForm from the menu. Using F7 will display the preferred form for the table. When you use F7 the first time, Paradox creates the standard form, F. Until you select an alternate form as the preferred form, form F will automatically be selected in Form view. Use the **I**mage **K**eepSet option to select a form as the new preferred form.

The Paradox Form Designer

With the Form Designer, you can build a form to meet any need you may have. Paradox enables you to customize a form for a table, and enables you to build up to 15 forms per table. You do not have to create a single general purpose form for each table.

Working in the Form Designer window, you can draw lines around fields and create prompts to draw the users' attention to some detail or help users fill in required information. You can also use colors to highlight areas or fields within a form.

Designing a Free-Form Form

As you begin to build your first form, give it the same careful consideration you gave to your first report. As you begin the process, ask yourself several questions:

- For whom are you creating the form?

    If you are building this form for your own use, you may want to leave off some of the amenities you might otherwise place for another user.

- What is the skill level of the average user of this form?

Creating Free-Form and Multi-Table Forms

If you are designing this form for users who are not familiar with Paradox or your database, you will want to make liberal use of on-screen prompts and instruction.

- Are you replacing a form that is currently in use?

    If the old form has a usable design, copy as much of it as possible. Using an existing design can help to ensure the new form's success and acceptance.

- Are all the fields necessary for the form contained in one table or in multiple tables?

    If your form is based on a single table, the design job can be relatively simple. If you need to use several tables, then you must ensure that they are properly keyed.

- Do you need to view more than one record within a form?

    Using a multi-record form enables you to view more than one record. A multi-record form enables users to view the last record, for example. You might use a multi-entry form to view the line items of an invoice.

As you begin the planning stage of your form, keep the preceding list in mind. A carefully planned form will be successful and will perform its required tasks.

Working with the Form Design Features

Now that you have determined your needs for a form and planned the layout, you are ready to begin. The form you will build is a customer order form. You can use the form to create an order with information contained in the customer table, Cust1, and the inventory table, Invnty.

In order to create this form, you will build several forms. Each table will require a form to display its part of the information. Later in this chapter, you will embed the detail form into a single master form.

To create the form, you need to create a new table. This table will act as an intermediary between your Orders and Invnty tables. This table will contain the detail records of each order.

Working with the Form Design Features

Table name:	LINEITEM	
Structure:	*Field Name*	*Field Type*
	ORDER #	A7*
	ITEM CODE	A5*
	ITEM DESCRIPTION	A20
	QTY ORDERED	N
	QTY SHIPPED	N
	RETAIL	$

If you need help creating this table, see Chapter 3. After you create the table, you can build the detail form. You will use this form to maintain the detail line items from the order form. This form will contain a calculated field and display multiple records.

Opening the Form Designer Window

With a multi-table form, you start with the detail forms and work to the master form. With a single table form, you begin with the table on which the form is based. Your detail form will use the new intermediate table, Lineitem.

To create a form, you must open the Form Designer window. Complete the following steps:

1. Select **F**orms from the Main menu bar.
2. Select the **D**esign option.

   You use the **D**esign option to build a new form. You use the **C**hange option to alter an existing form.

3. Enter the name of the table on which you want to base the form. Type in **Lineitem** and press ⏎Enter.

   Again remember, you can press ⏎Enter to view the list of tables available, or click the list box with the mouse.

10

277

Creating Free-Form and Multi-Table Forms

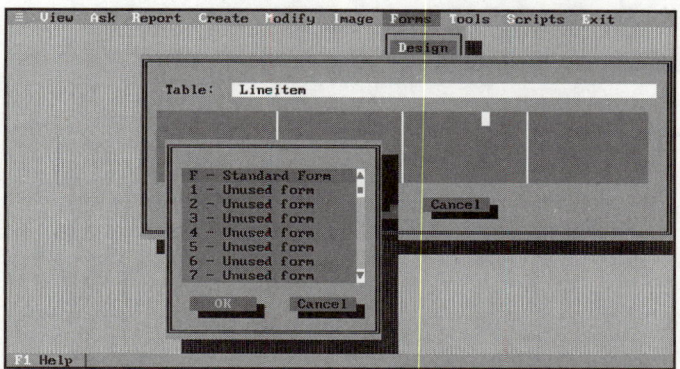

Here, you see the list of available forms displayed. Remember, Paradox can support up to 15 forms.

4. Select the form **1 - Unused form** and press ⏎Enter.
5. Enter a description for the new form. Type **Line Item Detail**.

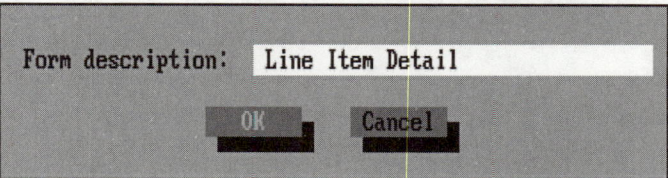

The Form Description dialog box is completed.

6. Press ⏎Enter.
7. Click the Maximize button with the mouse pointer, or select the System menu (≡) and choose the **M**aximize/Restore option.

Just like the Report Designer, the Form Designer is easier to use in its maximized size.

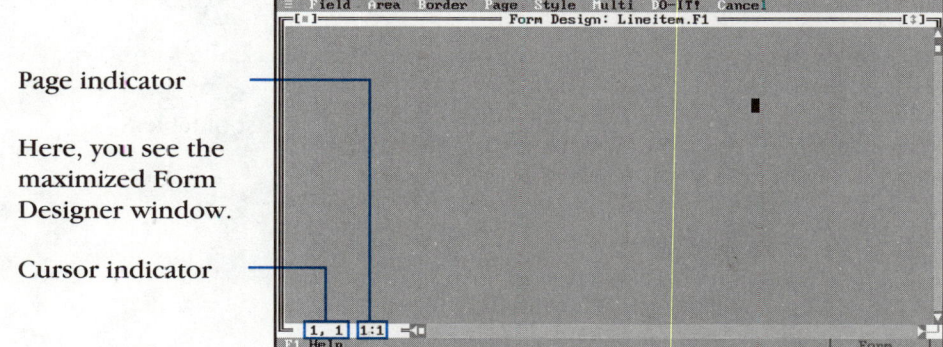

Page indicator

Here, you see the maximized Form Designer window.

Cursor indicator

278

Working with the Form Design Features

The cursor position indicator shows you the current location of the cursor, using an x,y coordinate system. The first number, or the x, indicates the row position. The second number, or the y, indicates the column position.

The second group of numbers comprise the page indicator. The indicator works on an x:y system also. The x is the current page number, while the y indicates the number of pages for the form. The maximum number of pages per form is 15.

As you begin to use the Form Designer, you will see additional information displayed in the status bar. When the cursor enters a field, several items of information about that field are displayed in the status bar. These items include the field name, type of field, and, if a wrapped field, how many lines the field can wrap.

As you begin to design your detail form, you must understand how Paradox will embed this form into the master form. Paradox uses a rectangular area that begins in position 1,1 and extends to include all fields and literals placed on the form. Any blank areas at the top and left side of the form are included in the embedded form. These blank areas can cause some possible positioning problems. Always begin a detail form that will be embedded into another form at position 1,1.

Using Field Labels and Prompts

Literals are used to identify fields, form titles, and provide on-screen prompts and instructions. When you enter a literal, Paradox displays the text as you enter it—just like when you entered a literal in the Report Designer.

If this form is only for your use, you may want to use prompts and field names sparsely. If someone else who is unfamiliar with your database will use the form to enter data, you may want to liberally place field names and on-screen prompts. On-screen prompts are discussed later in this chapter in the section "Using On-Screen Prompts."

This form will use two rows for field titles. To enter field names for your form, do the following:

1. Make sure that the cursor is positioned in row 1, column 1. The cursor position indicator will be displayed as 1, 1. Type the first field name, **ITEM**, and press ⏎Enter.

2. Move the cursor to the right to position 1,15, using → or the mouse. Type **ITEM** and press ⏎Enter.

Creating Free-Form and Multi-Table Forms

3. Add the remaining field titles at the positions indicated:

Field Position	Field Title
1,31	QUANTITY
1,41	QUANTITY
1,51	SELLING
1,64	EXTENDED
2,1	CODE
2,12	DESCRIPTION
2,32	ORDERED
2,42	SHIPPED
2,52	PRICE
2,65	PRICE

Here, you see the field titles entered onto the form as literals.

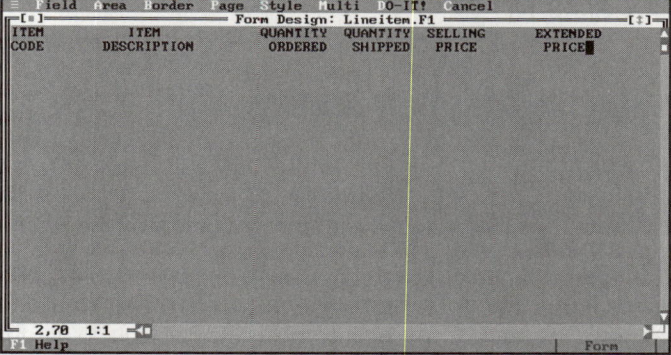

Any other literal value you want to place on the form is entered in the same manner. If you feel that an on-screen prompt or line of instruction is needed, type it on the form in a position that users will see clearly.

4. Move the cursor back to position 3,1. You will now draw a line across the form between the fields and the field titles.
5. Select Border Place Other. Type a dash (or minus sign) in the displayed dialog box.

Working with the Form Design Features

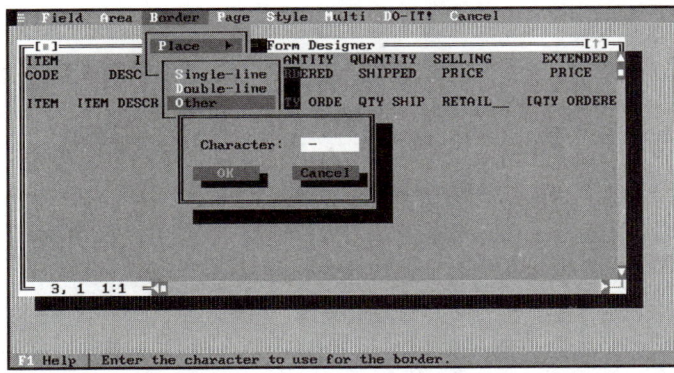

Here, the dash is entered into the dialog box.

6. Press ⏎Enter twice. (The second time you press ⏎Enter, you accept the new location where you have placed the cursor, 3,1.)

   If you want the line in another location, move it and press ⏎Enter.

7. Move the cursor to position 3,80. You will see a highlighted bar across the form. Now, press ⏎Enter again.

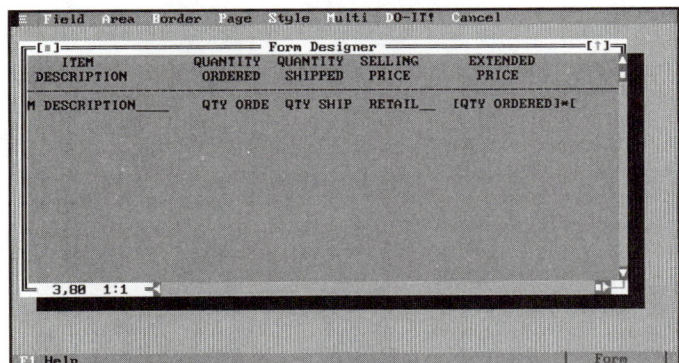

The dashed line is displayed across your form.

Placing Fields

The next step in completing your form is to place *regular* fields on the form. Again, just like with the Report Designer, you can place several types of fields on a form. The most common type is the regular field.

A regular field is contained within the table, and the data within the field can be edited. Paradox also enables you to place a field from the table as a DisplayOnly field. This type of field displays the field information on the form, but the information is in a read-only version so you cannot edit it.

281

Creating Free-Form and Multi-Table Forms

To place fields on the form, do the following:

1. Select **F**ield from the menu bar, and then select **P**lace from the pull-down menu.
2. From the cascading menu box now displayed, select the **D**isplayOnly option.

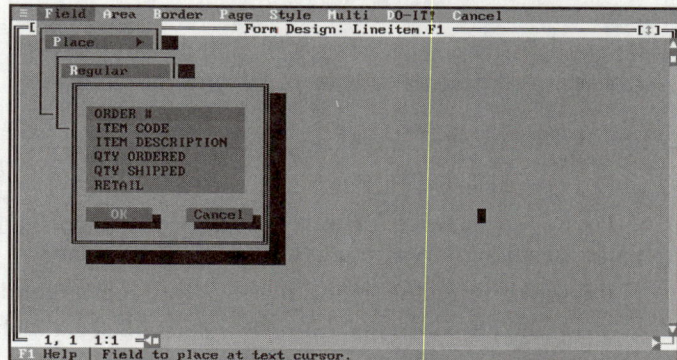

You now see the list of all available table fields.

3. Select the Item Code field and press ⏎Enter.
4. Move the cursor to position 4,1 and press ⏎Enter.

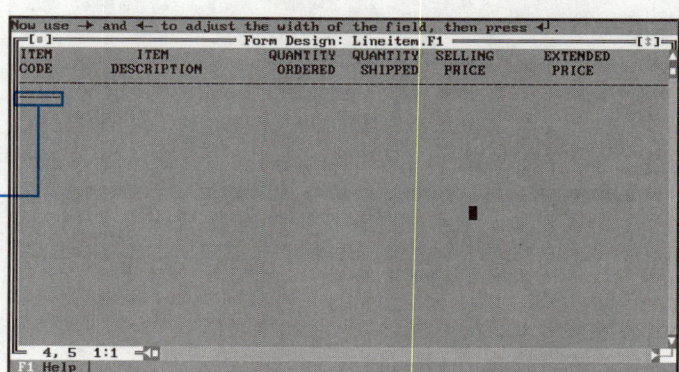

The field is in the indicated position. Paradox displays a field at its maximum size.

Notice the message at the top of your screen `Now use → and ← to adjust the width of the field, then press ⏎`. If a field is too long, such as this field, use ← to make the field smaller. You can use → to make the field larger again if necessary. You cannot make a field

282

Working with the Form Design Features

larger than the maximum size allotted by the table structure for that particular field.

5. Press [↵Enter]. The field is inserted into the form.
6. Move the cursor to position 4,5 to locate it on the field.

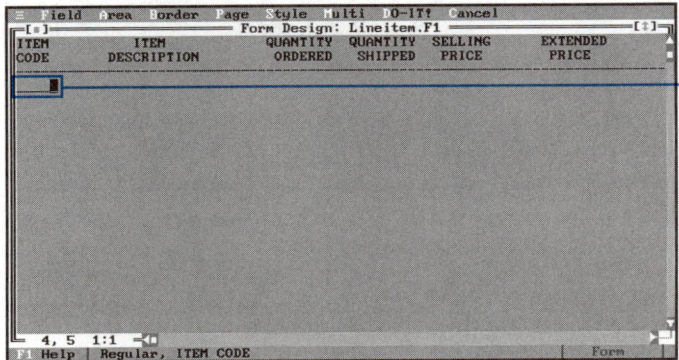

You now see the field inserted into the form.

Notice that the status bar area of your screen displays the message Regular, ITEM CODE. This message tells you both the field type and the name of the field.

When you actually use your form, the dashed lines that indicate a field will not be displayed. As you are building this form, you may not find the dashed lines that indicate the field very helpful. Unless you move the cursor onto the field so that the status bar displays the field information, you have to remember which dashed line represents which field. The Paradox option, Style FieldNames Show, helps you in this regard.

7. Select the Style option from the menu bar.
8. Choose the FieldNames option.
9. Select Show. Notice this message displayed in the status bar: Show the names of placed fields. Press [↵Enter].

Creating Free-Form and Multi-Table Forms

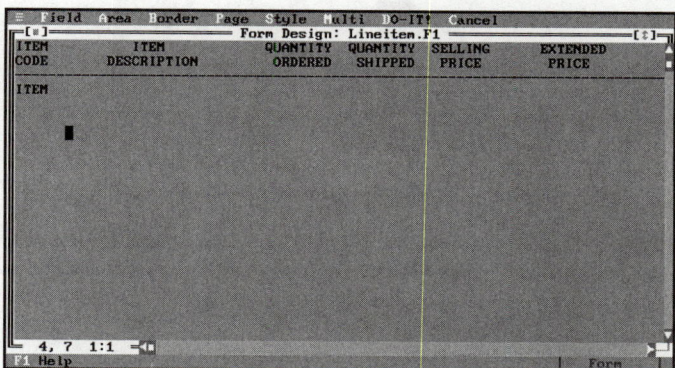

Here, you see the dashed line indicating that the placed field now displays the field name.

This new field indicator is only an aid for field placement and helping you remember where a field has been placed. The field will not be displayed like this when you use the form. Paradox will display the field name and dashes to represent the field width. If you have specified a field width less than the number of characters in the field name, Paradox will display as much of the field name as possible. You can hide the field name by selecting Style FieldName Hide.

10. Place the next field on the form. Move the cursor to position 4,7. Select Field Place Regular. Choose the field to be placed, Item Description, and press ↵Enter.

11. Press ↵Enter again to accept the default field length. Now move the cursor to the right two positions so that the cursor is located at 4,31.

12. Repeat steps 10 and 11, placing the indicated fields at the cursor positions shown; the end point of the field is indicated.

Position	Field To Place	Field Length
4,31	Qty Ordered	4,38
4,41	Qty Shipped	4,48
4,51	Retail	4,58

Notice how the Field Name list box displays fewer names each time you place a field on the form. Because the names disappear from the list box, you cannot accidentally place a field twice on the same form.

284

Working with the Form Design Features

This feature ensures that you do not enter data into a field on one part of a form and then enter conflicting data for the same field and record. The Cust # field, however, remains in the Field Name list box because you placed it as a DisplayOnly field. You can place a field as a DisplayOnly field as often as required. This feature enables you to place needed information, such as a customer name, on a multi-page form.

Paradox does not allow you to place as a regular field any field you will use to embed the detail form to the master form. The linking field is always the first key field contained in the detail table. This table uses the Order # field to link this detail form to the master form from the Orders table. You can place the linking field as a DisplayOnly field within the embedded detail form. For the detail form you are now constructing, this is not a necessary feature.

Now all the necessary fields from the Lineitem table have been placed on the form. Remember, you can use any of the fields again as DisplayOnly fields. Paradox enables you to do this because a DisplayOnly field cannot be edited.

Using Calculated Fields

With Paradox, you can create specialized fields that calculate values based on data from one or more actual table fields. You can use a calculated field to calculate a value from fields of the same type. Memo fields cannot be included as a field.

As you work with calculated fields, keep these points in mind:

- You can perform calculations on alphanumeric fields, number fields, and date fields.
- A calculated expression can contain a maximum of 175 characters.
- Field names must be enclosed by square brackets ([ ]) and must be spelled exactly as they are in the table structure.
- You can use arithmetic operators such as +, –, * , /, and ( ).
- Depending upon the calculation and the fields involved, you can use constant values such as "Dear", 1/31/92, and 1.5. Literal values must be enclosed within double quotation marks.
- You can also use many of the Paradox PAL functions. See the PAL user manual for more information on this subject.

Table 10.1 shows some simple calculated fields and their resulting calculations.

Creating Free-Form and Multi-Table Forms

**Table 10.1
Expressions and Their Resulting Values**

Expression To Be Calculated	Resulting Value
"Dear"+[First Name]+" "+[Last Name]	Dear MACK MARTINI.
2.5*[Price]	Multiplies the value in the Price field by 2.5.
[Invoice Date]+30	Displays a date 30 days from the date in the Invoice Date field.

You will now place a calculated field. This calculated expression will multiply the number of items ordered by their price. To create this calculation, do the following:

1. Move the cursor to position 4,61. Select **F**ield **P**lace **C**alculated.

You now see the dialog box in which to place a calculated expression.

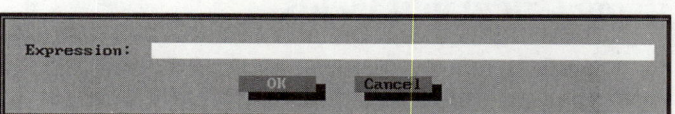

2. Type the following expression: **[QTY ORDERED]*[RETAIL]**.

The calculation dialog box is completed.

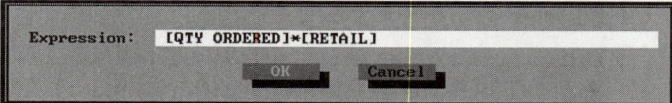

3. Press ⏎Enter.

   You see this message at the top of your screen: `Move to where you want the field to begin, then press ⏎`.... Because you already have the cursor where you want this field to begin, press ⏎Enter again.

4. Use → to move the cursor until the position indicator reads 4,75, and press ⏎Enter.

Working with the Form Design Features

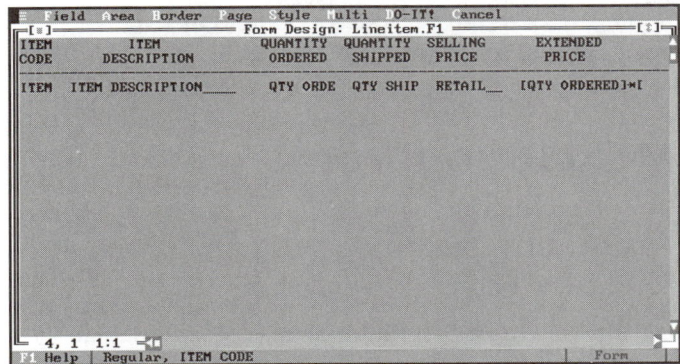

Now you can see each of the fields entered into your form.

Resizing a Field

As you create your form, you may find that a field is too large to fit in the form. Conversely, you may find that you have too much room and can expand a field. Paradox enables you to resize a field you have already placed without deleting and replacing it again. Remember, you can expand a field only to the maximum size that is specified in the table structure.

To resize a field, do the following:

1. Select the **F**ield **R**eformat options on the menu.

    You will see the message `Move to field you want to reformat, then press ↵...` displayed at the top of the screen.

2. Move to the field you want to reformat, or resize. Move the cursor to the Item Description field and press ↵Enter.

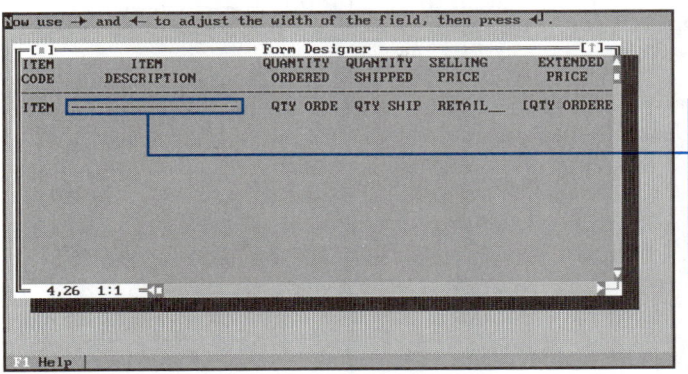

The field indicator changes to the dashed line. Use ← or → to resize the field as required.

10

287

Creating Free-Form and Multi-Table Forms

3. Use ← to decrease the size of the Item Description field by two spaces, and then press Enter to accept the new field length.

Designing a Multi-Record Form

Sometimes you will want to view more than one record on a form at a time. Paradox enables you to have the best of both views: a form that can view the entire record on a single screen, as well as view multiple records.

To create a multi-record form, you must first build the master, or original record. The fields do not have to be placed in a single line for each record. Build the form as you would any other—you should try to place the fields as close together as possible. The closer you place fields, the more records you can fit on a single screen.

The form you are now creating, Line Item Detail, for the Lineitem table illustrates a case in which a multiple record form is needed. This form is meant to show all the items ordered by a customer in a single order. Each line in the order for an inventory item is itself a single record. To display many items ordered, you must use a multi-record form.

To duplicate the original record on the form, do the following:

1. Select the **M**ulti option from the menu.
2. Choose the **R**ecords option.
3. Choose **D**efine from the cascading menu. This option lets you specify the area of the form you want to replicate.

   When you select the area of the form, you can include text, lines, and fields. Whatever you include in the definition of the original record will be duplicated. Be conservative with the nonfield text and other literals.
4. Move the cursor to position 4,1 and press Enter.
5. Move the cursor to position 4,80.

Designing a Multi-Record Form

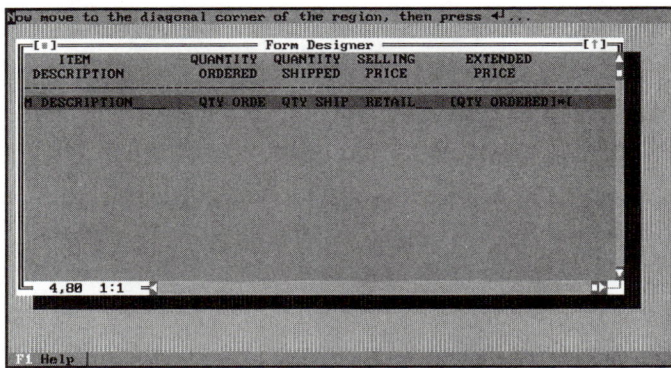

Here, you can see the highlighted area that will be included as the original record.

If you had included the dashed line or the field titles, these would have also been repeated for each of the replicated records you create. The dashed lines and titles would clutter the screen and enable you to place fewer records.

6. Press ⏎Enter to mark the end of the original record.

   You will see the message Use ↑↓ to add or delete repeating rows, then press ⏎ displayed at the top of your screen.

7. Use ↓ to add records. Press ↓ six times. You now have seven records to be used.

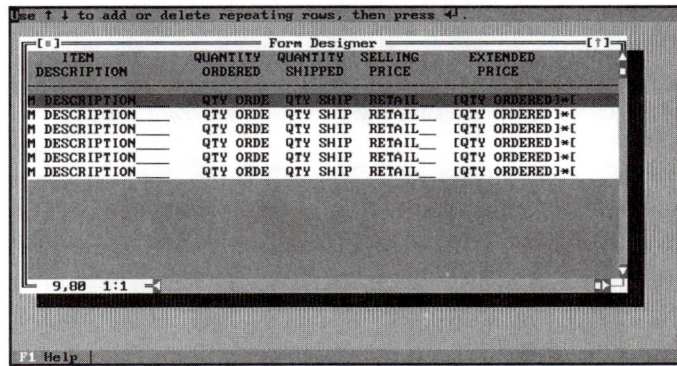

Here, you can see the replicated records in the form.

8. Press ⏎Enter to accept this format.
9. Press F2 or select **D**O-IT! from the menu to save this design as a form.

10

289

Creating Free-Form and Multi-Table Forms

For some applications, you may need a blank line between the records of a multi-record form. You can easily accomplish this in step 5 by moving the cursor to position 5,80. This step makes the highlighted area two rows wide. When you replicate the records in step 7, they appear with a blank line between them.

Here, you see what the addition of a blank line between records looks like.

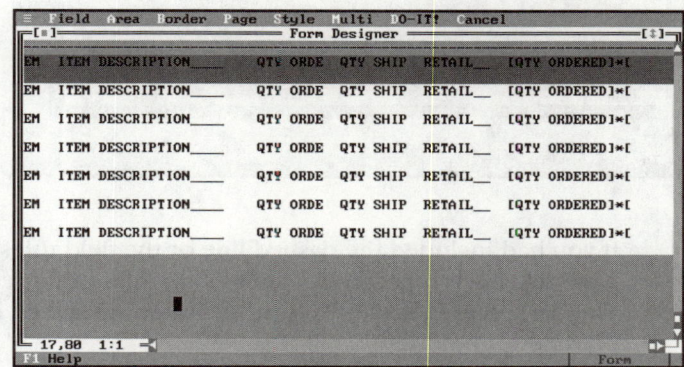

The use of a blank, or separating, line is especially useful when the record itself has multiple lines. Blank lines then help to distinguish the records.

If you need to remove the multiple records from the form, select the **M**ulti **R**ecords **R**emove option. Paradox then removes the copies, leaving only the original.

To make an adjustment to a multi-record form, select **M**ulti **R**ecords **A**djust from the menu. The copied records are removed, and the original record is highlighted again. Use the arrow keys to adjust the size and shape of the original record, and then press ↵Enter to accept the new size. You must then add the duplicates by using ↑ or ↓.

Designing a Multi-Table Form

You now have four tables, three of which are linked with the Paradox Tablelookup feature. The fourth table, Lineitem, has not yet been linked to the other tables. The multi-table form enables you to enter information into several tables at one time. Without the use of the multi-table form, you would have to make an entry into the Orders and Lineitem tables at the very least. If a customer had also changed an address, you would have to make that change in the Cust1 table also.

Designing a Multi-Table Form

Understanding Table Relationships

The records of two linked tables are related. A multi-table form can link a detail table to a master table if the first keyed field of the detail table exists in the master table. Paradox enables you to use these four different relationships between tables:

One-to-one	The master table record is linked to a single record contained in the detail table.
One-to-many	The master table is linked to many records contained in the detail table. Only a single master table record is linked to this group of detail records.
Many-to-one	A group of master table records is linked to a single record maintained by the detail table.
Many-to-many	The master table record is part of a group of records that is linked to a group of records contained in the detail table.

You will find that the first two relationships can be represented using a multi-table form. If you use the many-to-many or many-to-one relationship in a multi-table form, referential integrity cannot be enforced.

Referential Integrity

Paradox uses referential integrity to ensure that the changes you make to the master table are reflected in the detail table. For example, if you enter an order into the Orders table, you must also enter the items ordered into the Lineitem table. If later the customer calls and cancels the order, you must not only delete the master record in the Orders table, but you must also delete each of the detail records in the Lineitem table.

When the link between tables is either one-to-one or one-to-many, Paradox applies the concept of referential integrity. If you make a change in the master table, Paradox will ensure that the change is also made in a linked detail table when linked by either of these relationships. Paradox will not allow you to delete a master record if the detail records that depend on the master record still exist. You must first delete the detail records and then the master record.

The relationship between the Orders and Lineitem tables is one-to-many, which enables Paradox to maintain referential integrity between them.

The Orders table has been restructured to delete Cost and Retail and to add fields from Cust1, as shown below. Remember to use the **B**orrow option when

Creating Free-Form and Multi-Table Forms

restructuring the Orders table to borrow the new field names from Cust1. Use the validity checks, **T**ableLookup and **R**equired, to fill the customer information automatically into the table from the data already entered in Cust1.

Orders

Order # (key)

Cust #

Order Date

Last Name

First Name

Phone Number

Street

City

State

Zip

Country

Understanding Multi-Table Forms

A multi-table form is a master form with one or more detail forms embedded into it. When creating the master multi-table form, you must keep the following rules in mind:

- You can embed a maximum of nine detail forms into the master form.
- Your master form can be multi-page but not multi-record.
- A detail embedded form can be multi-record but not multi-page.
- You cannot embed a form into a form that will be embedded into another form.

Creating the Master Form

The master form is based on the table you can link most easily to the detail tables. This table is the master table. In order for a table to be used as the master table, it must contain direct links to the tables on which the detail forms are based.

Designing a Multi-Table Form

The most logical choice of a master table is the Orders table. It contains direct links to both Cust1 and to Lineitem. The table is indirectly linked to Invnty through Lineitem.

The master form uses the same techniques you have already used when you created the detail forms for the Cust1 and Lineitem tables.

To build the master form, do the following:

1. Select **F**orm **D**esign from the Main menu bar, and then select the Orders table.
2. Choose unused form 1 and press [Enter].
3. Enter the description for this form, type **ORDER FORM**, and press [Enter]. Then maximize the Form Designer window.
4. Move the cursor to position 2,33 and type **ORDER FORM**.
5. Now move the cursor to position 3,1 and type **ORDER #:**.
6. Place the cursor at 4,1, type **Customer #:**, and then move to 4,50 and type **Order Date:**.
7. Place the appropriate regular fields beside their respective titles.
8. Place the following literals at the positions indicated:

Position	Literal Value
5,1	Customer Name:
6,1	Street Address:
7,1	City,State,Zip:
8,1	Country:
9,1	Phone:

9. Move the cursor to position 6,17 and select **F**ield **P**lace **D**isplayOnly. Select the Street field from the displayed list and press [Enter] three times.
10. Use the **D**isplayOnly option to place the Country and Phone fields at positions 8,10 and 9,8 respectively.
11. Move the cursor to position 5,16 and select **F**ield **P**lace **C**alculated. Enter the expression **[First Name]+" "+[Last Name]** into the dialog box. Press [Enter] three times to place the field.

Creating Free-Form and Multi-Table Forms

12. Move the cursor to position 7,17 and select **F**ield **P**lace **C**alculated. Enter the expression **[City]+", "+[State]+" "+[Zip/Postal Code]** into the dialog box. Press ⏎Enter three times to place the field.

Here, you can see the master form, ORDER FORM.

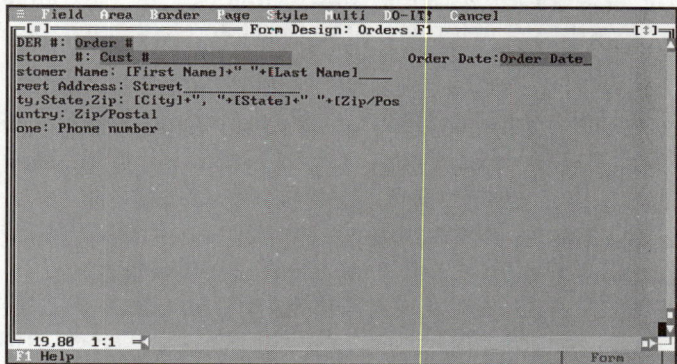

Using Linked Tables

To create a multi-table form that can automatically display and update records from several tables, you must properly link the tables. To link tables and forms together, you must ensure that the tables are related through the key fields of the detail table. This creates a logical association between the tables. You then create the actual link through the master form to the detail form.

The links created then define the value or record that is displayed in the detail table's embedded form. To see how this works, do the following:

1. Select the **M**ulti option on the menu.
2. Choose the **T**ables option, and then select **P**lace **L**inked.
3. Select the table that has the detail form you want to use in this link. Choose the Lineitem table, and then select the 1-Line Item Detail form.

   You now see a dialog box with a list of three field names. These are the field names from the master. You must choose the field that you want to use to link the master and detail tables together. The linking field must be the first field from the detail table, and this field must be keyed. You then choose the logical field to link to. In this case, you are linking the Order # field from Lineitem to a field in the Orders table. Neither Cust # nor Order Date are a match to Order #, while the Order # field matches both tables.
4. Select the Order # field and press ⏎Enter.

294

Designing a Multi-Table Form

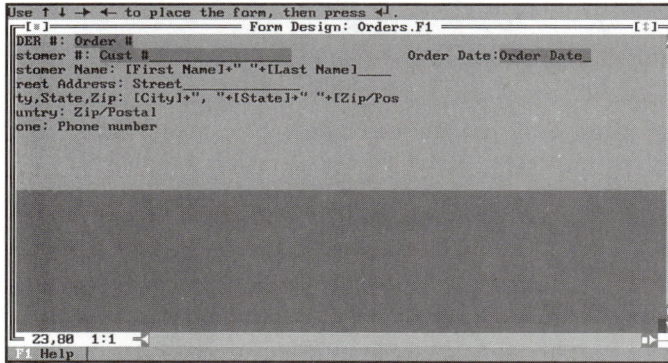

You now see a highlighted block appear at the bottom of the Form Designer window.

This highlighted block is a representation of the detail form's *natural* size. As mentioned earlier, the detail forms you created are sized from position 1,1 and extend in a block down and to the right, encompassing all fields and literals placed on the detail form.

5. Using the arrow keys, move the block to the position required for this form. When the position indicator reads 23,80, press ⏎Enter to place the detail form.

   The detail form is now *embedded* into the master form. You will notice that the block representing the detail form does not display the fields. Paradox only shows this image of the detail form because you cannot make any changes to the detail form from the master record.

You have now created a detail form and a master form, and then embedded the detail form into the master. Using this master form, you can link all your tables together. The link to the Invnty table is an indirect link through the Lineitem table.

Using Unlinked Tables

Embedding a form from an unlinked table creates a more familiar relationship. When you create a form and then add an unlinked detail form, you are creating a windowing type of relationship.

Neither form depends on the other(s) for any information. You can move from form to form using F3 (Up Image) and F4 (Down Image). You can enter data into any field of any form. You can use unlinked forms to add data to several tables that may be related, but do not have to be linked. This method provides an easy way to update several tables without having to complete all the changes for one table and then move to the next.

295

Creating Free-Form and Multi-Table Forms

Fortunately, because Paradox is a "forgiving" program, you can remove fields you have placed on a form. In many ways, deleting a field is easier than placing it. To remove a field from the form, do the following:

1. Move the cursor onto the field you want to delete. The specific location on the field is not important. Once you see the field name and type displayed in the status bar, you have the cursor positioned properly. Place the cursor on the Phone field at position 9,11.
2. Select **F**ield from the menu bar.
3. Choose the **E**rase option and press ⏎Enter.

You now see that the Phone field has been deleted from the form. To maintain the form and the required information, replace the field in its previous location.

Strengthening Your Form Design

You have now learned to place regular, calculated, display-only fields into a form. You learned how to move fields and to add text to the form. You have also learned to create a master form and to embed the detail forms into it.

In these next sections, you will learn to use some of the display features and to strengthen the appearance of your form.

Drawing Lines or Boxes

Using the Paradox **B**order option, you can draw lines or boxes around different parts of your form. Lines and boxes can help make different sections stand out. You could, for example, draw a box around an embedded form.

In this section, you will place boxes and draw lines to emphasize various parts of your master form. Do the following:

1. Move the cursor to position 1,25, and then select **B**order from the menu. Choose the **P**lace option, and then **O**ther.
2. Enter the character to use for the border. Type an asterisk (*) into the dialog box, and press ⏎Enter.
3. If you have not already moved the cursor to position 1,25, then do so now. If you have, press ⏎Enter to designate this position as the first corner.
4. Move the cursor to position 3,50.

Strengthening Your Form Design

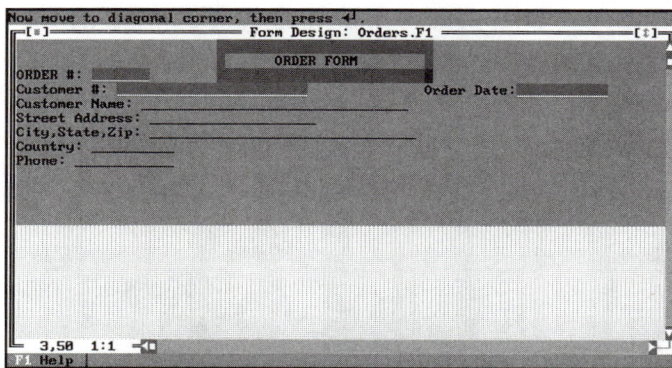

You can see a highlighted box around the form title.

5. Press ↵Enter. The highlighted box is now replaced with the character you used for this box, *.
6. Now move the cursor to position 5,1 and select the **A**rea **M**ove option.
7. Press ↵Enter to select the corner 5,1, and then move the cursor to position 9,48.

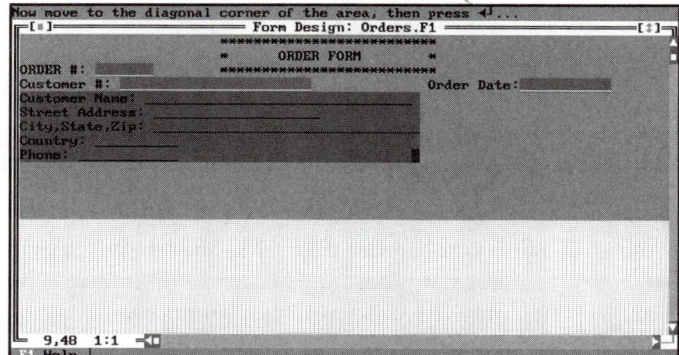

Here, you see the highlighted block to move.

8. Press ↵Enter to select the block. Notice the message at the top of your screen. Use the arrow keys to drag the block to its new location. Press ↓ and → so that the position indicator now reads 10,49.

    The selected block is placed in its new position. Notice that the selected block does not drag the text literals nor the fields with it.

9. Press ↵Enter. The text and fields move to the new location.
10. Now move the cursor to position 5,1 and select the **B**order **P**lace **D**ouble-line options, and then press ↵Enter again to select this position as a corner of the box.

297

Creating Free-Form and Multi-Table Forms

11. Move the cursor down and then right until the embedded Customer Address form is surrounded. The position should be 11,50, and then press Enter.
12. Select the **B**order **P**lace **D**ouble-line options, and then move the cursor to position 13,1 and press Enter.
13. Move the cursor to 13,80 and press Enter again.

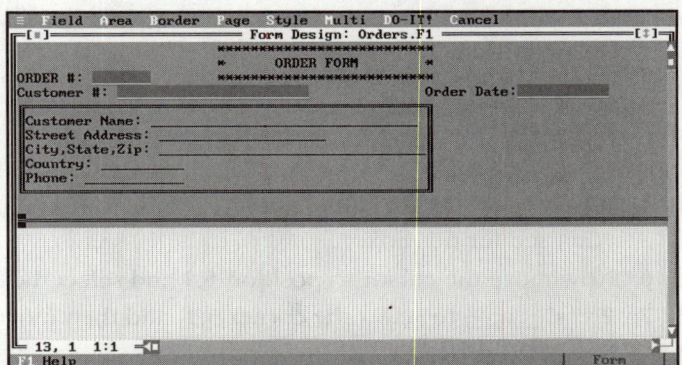

You now see the border lines placed on the master form.

Working with Multiple Line Fields

Often database fields are difficult to work with because they are too long to display on a form. For example, if you had a remark or comment field in your Cust1 table, you could allow someone to enter 255 characters of data. This much data will not fit in a form that is 80 characters wide.

Using the Paradox word wrap feature, you can break a field into several lines on a form. Then you can view and enter data that may be too long to fit in a single line across the form. You can only use this feature on memo and alphanumeric fields. Paradox will not allow number or date fields to be wrapped.

To wordwrap a field, select the **F**ield **W**ordwrap option from the menu. Then select the field you want to wrap and press Enter to designate it. You will then see a dialog box displayed on the screen. Enter the number of lines to allow the field to wrap. You must have enough space below the field for the number of lines you specify. If you tell Paradox that you want a field to wrap up to five lines and you have another field only two lines below the field's current position, you will see the message `The area designated for the word wrap must be clear` when you attempt to save the form with **D**O-IT!.

Strengthening Your Form Design

Using Color

If you are using a color monitor, you can create your own unique form through color. Paradox can display up to 128 possible color combinations on your screen. Use color to accent an area, a border, a field, or an on-screen prompt, but do not overwhelm your form by making it a work of art.

To change the color of some areas of your form, do the following:

1. Select the **S**tyle **C**olor **A**rea options, move the cursor to position 3,10, and press ⏎Enter. Move the cursor to the end of the field at position 3,16 and press ⏎Enter again.

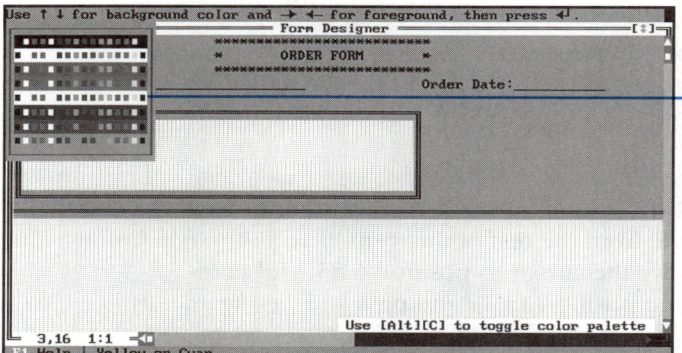

Here, you can see the Paradox color palette.

Notice that the color palette is composed of 8 lines with 16 boxes in each line. The color of the line is the background color, and the box is the foreground color. You can also see the current color option displayed in the status bar. Use the cursor keys to move around the color palette. The selected color spot will blink.

2. Move the cursor to the color option Blue on Cyan and press ⏎Enter.
3. Use this same color option to highlight the Customer # and Order Date fields.
4. Select the **S**tyle **C**olor **B**order options. Move the cursor to position 6,1 and press ⏎Enter. Then move to the opposite corner of the border at 12,49 and press ⏎Enter.
5. Choose a good contrast, such as Blue on Red. This option highlights this area as another form. Press ⏎Enter.

299

Creating Free-Form and Multi-Table Forms

Using On-Screen Prompts

Depending upon both the form and the people who will use it, you may want to provide information through on-screen prompts or help. If you are the only user of the form, you would not need to provide prompts or help.

To place on-screen prompts, do the following:

1. Move the cursor to 5,53 and type the following:
   Enter the Order # and
   Customer # into the fields.
   To use today's date, press
   Enter. Press F3 or F4 to
   move to the linked forms.
   If you need help finding a
   Customer or Item, press F1.
   Press F2 to select it.

2. Place a colored box around this on-screen prompt to highlight it and to keep it separate from the rest of the form. Select the **S**tyle **C**olor **A**rea options, move the cursor to position 5,53, and press [Enter]. Move the cursor to position 12,79 and press [Enter] again.

3. Choose a color to highlight the help box. Red on Blue may be a good choice. Then press [Enter] again.

4. Press [F2] or select **D**O-IT! to save the form.

Editing Screen Characteristics

Paradox also accommodates various screen attributes for monochrome screens. Blinking is the only attribute that can also be used by color screens. You can apply these monochrome attributes to either a border or to an area. The attributes are:

Attribute	Description
Normal	Changes any attribute setting back to the setting original.
Blink	Causes the area or border to blink.

Attribute	Description
Non-Blink	Removes the blink attribute without changing other settings.
Intense	Displays foreground in intense video.
Reverse	Displays the area or border in reverse video; the fore- and background colors are reversed.
Intense-Reverse	Foreground is intense video with fore- and background reversed.

To apply these video attributes select, **S**tyle **M**onochrome and then choose either **A**rea or **B**order. Select the area or border and press `Enter`. You then see the video attributes listed in the status box. Use `←` and `→` to rotate the different choices. Press `Enter` again to apply the video attribute that is currently displayed in the status box.

Editing an Existing Form

If needed, you can change any form you have created. If you add fields to a table, you may want to add them to a form. Any time you change a field type when you restructure a table, Paradox deletes the field from all associated forms. You will have to add them back to the forms.

To use the Form Designer to edit an existing form, do the following:

1. Select **F**orms **C**hange from the Main menu.
2. Choose the table to which the form belongs, and then select the form you want to edit.
3. If the purpose of the form has also changed, you may want to change the form description. If so, press `Ctrl`-`Backspace` to delete the old description, and then enter the new description. Press `Enter`.

The selected form is now displayed in the Form Designer window.

Make any required changes to the form, and then save it by selecting **D**O-IT!. If you decide not to keep your changes at this time, choose **C**ancel **Y**es to exit back to the desktop.

Creating Free-Form and Multi-Table Forms

Summary

In this chapter, you learned to create a detail and master form, and then to embed the detailed form into the master form. You then learned how to use key fields to link forms using the relationships between the master table and the key fields of the detail table. You also learned to use color and other screen attributes to highlight areas of a form.

Specifically, you learned the following key points about Paradox 4:

- To build a free-form form, use the Paradox Form Designer by selecting **F**orms **D**esign and then choosing the table on which to base the form. Select the form and give it a description.
- To accurately place fields and literals, use the cursor position indicator located in the bottom left-hand corner of the Forms Designer window.
- Use text literals for on-screen prompts and instructions by typing the required information in the needed location.
- When building a detail form that will be embedded into a master form, the first key field or linking key field cannot be included in the form.
- To display a field's name while building a form, use the **S**tyle **F**ieldNames **S**how options.
- To move a block of text or border literals or fields, select **A**rea **M**ove, select the block you want to move by highlighting it, and then press `Enter`. Now move the block with the arrow keys.
- To add a calculated field, select the **F**ield **P**lace **C**alculated options. Enter the expression you want to use in the calculation in the dialog box, and then indicate the field's position on the form.
- To adjust the size of a field, select **F**ield **R**eformat. Move the cursor to the field you want to resize and press `Enter`. Then use the ← or → to increase or decrease the field's size.
- To make a multiple record form, choose the **M**ulti **R**ecords **D**efine options. Select the area of the form you want to replicate, and then use ↑ or ↓ to replicate the original record above or below as needed.
- To embed a detail form into a master form, select the **M**ulti **T**ables **P**lace **L**inked options from the master form. Choose the detail table and form, and then the field to use as the linking field.

Summary

- To draw boxes around fields, titles, or forms, select **B**order **P**lace, and then choose the type of border to create. Highlight the area to place the border, and then press [⏎Enter].
- To add color to a form, use the **S**tyle **C**olor **A**rea or **B**order options. Select the area or border you want to color, and then choose the color from the color palette.
- To add video attributes to a monochrome display, select **S**tyle **M**onochrome **A**rea or **B**order. Select the area or border to which you want to apply the attributes, and then select the type of video display.
- To edit an existing form, select **F**orms **C**hange from the Main menu bar. Select the table and then the form. The form will be displayed in the Form Designer window.

In the next chapter, you will learn to use the more advanced concept of Query-By-Example. You will learn to group and summarize data from single and multiple tables using query statements, and to perform calculations with table data.

10

303

11

Using Advanced Queries

This chapter will further develop your understanding of Paradox Query By Example (QBE). As your grasp of this concept strengthens, you will become more satisfied with Paradox and your own use of your database.

Chapter 7 introduced you to the fundamentals of using Paradox QBE. You learned to retrieve data from a single table. In this chapter, you will learn to retrieve selected data from multiple tables using example elements. Using grouping techniques and calculations, you will be able to summarize data that you can then use to create reports.

Querying multiple tables

Using calculations

Executing table operations

Using groups

Creating inclusive link queries

11

Using Advanced Queries

Key Terms in This Chapter

Example element — In a query, a set of letters or numbers that shows Paradox how to link query forms.

Inclusive — The use of example elements in a query to retrieve records that do and do not match the criteria.

Exclusive — The use of example elements in a query to retrieve only records that match the criteria.

Querying Multiple Tables

You learned in Chapter 7 how to construct a single table query, and then in Chapter 10, you learned how to create multiple table forms. In this chapter, you will learn to query multiple tables. As you have created your database, you have kept certain types of information in their own tables. For example, all your customer information is kept in the Cust1 table, whereas all the information about each inventory item is kept in Invnty.

To query multiple tables, you use the heart of the Paradox query: QBE. With QBE, you provide Paradox with an example of the information you want to find. You do not have to use a highly structured command line and proper syntax to find the data you require.

With QBE, you can query multiple tables by constructing a query statement using a query form for each table. By placing a matching example element into linking fields, you tell Paradox to find records that match in both tables. Paradox then displays the results of your query in the Answer table.

Choosing Tables for the Multi-Table Query Statement

When constructing your query statement, you must have a good idea of the structure of your table. Just as you use key fields to link tables in a multi-table form, you use example elements to link tables in a multi-table query statement.

The order of your table selection in a multi-table query is not important. Paradox performs the query selecting the chosen records, regardless of the order in which you select tables. The only effect the order of table selection has is that the table chosen first has its fields listed first in the Answer table.

Querying Multiple Tables

You can rearrange the order of the fields by using the **I**mage **M**ove option or Ctrl-R to rotate the field order.

To see how a multi-table query works with QBE, construct the following query statement:

> Create a list of customers, by last name, who have purchased any item. Include with this list the name of the items purchased, how many, and the invoice number.

To construct this query statement, do the following:

1. Select **A**sk from the Main menu bar.
2. Select the Cust1 table and press Enter.

    You now see the query form for the Cust1 table.
3. Select **A**sk again, and choose the Orders table this time.

    You now see a second query form displayed.
4. Use **A**sk once more and choose the Lineitem table.

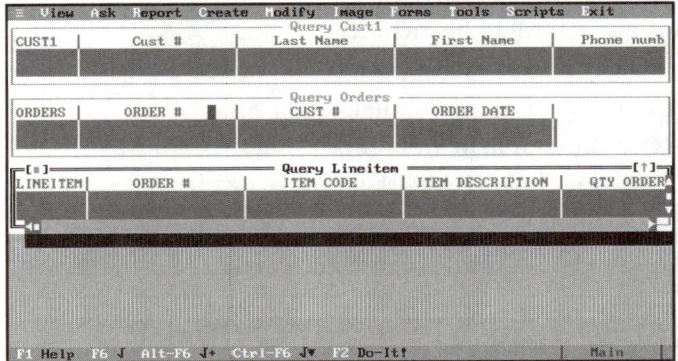

You can see all three query forms displayed. The last form selected, Query Lineitem, is the current active window.

Selecting Fields for the Multi-Table Query

Now that you have selected the tables to be used in the construction of your query statement, you need to choose the fields you want to include in the Answer table.

The Orders table is a linking table between Lineitem and Cust1, so it has fields from both tables. As you select fields, do not place the check mark in the same field in both tables. Doing so causes Paradox to include two copies of the field in the Answer table.

307

Using Advanced Queries

11

To select fields for the query statement, look at the written query statement and then compare it to the fields you have available from these tables:

> Create a list of customers, by last name, who have purchased any item. Include with this list the name of the items purchased, how many, and the invoice number.

Choose the fields that will answer the query by doing the following:

1. Move to the Query Cust1 window. You can do this by moving the mouse pointer to the window and clicking once or by pressing F3 (Up Image) twice. The window now becomes active.

2. In the query statement, you want a list of customers by last name. Move the cursor to the Last Name field and press F6.

   You are not including any other information from the Cust1 table.

3. Press F4 (Down Image) once to move to the Query Orders window. Or you can move the mouse pointer to the window and click once.

4. Move the cursor to the Order # field and press F6.

   Again, looking at the written query statement, you can see this is the only field from this query form to be included.

5. Press F4 (Down Image) to move to the Query Lineitem window.

6. Move the cursor to the Item Description field and press F6.

7. Now move to the Qty Ordered field and press F6 again.

Here, you can see all the fields the Answer table will include.

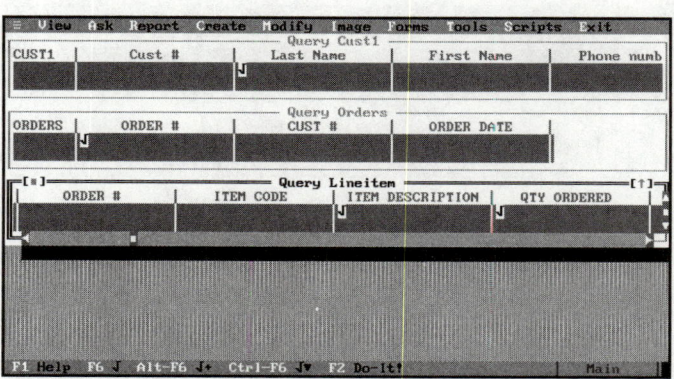

Notice that the Order # field was not checked in the query form for Lineitem. As already mentioned, you select a field from only one query form. If you check the Order # field in the Orders query form and in the Lineitem query form, the Answer table displays this field twice. It does not matter to Paradox which of the query forms you use to select the field.

308

Creating Table Links with Examples

You have now completed half of the job. You have told Paradox which fields to include in the Answer table. You now have to tell Paradox how to find the information. In essence, you must draw Paradox a map.

If you attempt to process the query at this point, Paradox displays the message Query appears to ask two unrelated questions in the message box. You must now show Paradox how to relate your query between these query forms. You can link query forms with example elements even if you do not include the field as part of the Answer table.

To create example elements for Paradox, do the following:

1. With the cursor still located in the query form for Lineitem, move it to the Order # field and press F5.

   The F5 key tells Paradox that the element entered into the field is an example. You can use any letter (A through Z, upper- or lowercase) or any number to represent an example element, but not any other type of character. You do not have to match the example element to the field type. This means you can use the example element *xyz* in a number field. As long as the example elements you use in a query form are identical to those in the other form you are matching it to, Paradox is not concerned about field type.

2. Now type **1111** as the example element.

3. Press F3 (Up Image) to move to the query form for Orders.

4. With the cursor in the Order # field, press F5. Then enter the example element, **1111**.

   Because Paradox uses this element to match records from Orders and Lineitem, you must be sure that the element matches exactly the element you just placed in the Lineitem query form's Order # field.

5. Move the cursor to the Cust # field in the Orders query form and press F5. Now enter the example element to link the Orders table and the Cust1 table. Type **AAA**.

6. Press F3 (Up Image) to move to the Cust1 query form.

7. Place the cursor in the Cust # field and press F5. Type the example element **AAA**.

   Notice that Paradox displays your example elements in reverse video.

Using Advanced Queries

Here, you can see the completed query statement.

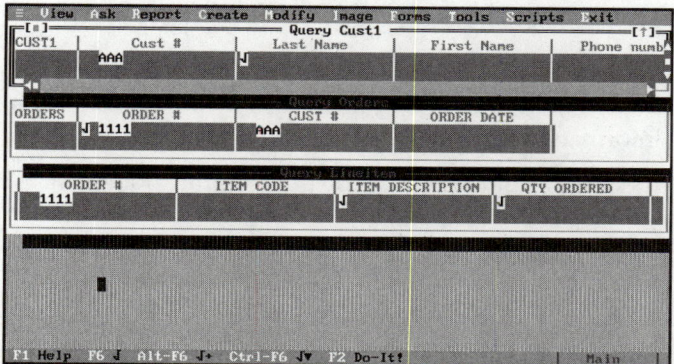

You have linked the three query forms together using example elements. Quickly compare the original, written query statement with the query statement you have constructed on-screen.

The query statement you have constructed says to include the Last Name field for all orders placed, the order number, the item bought, and the quantity of items ordered.

8. Because your written query statement seems to match the query statement you have constructed, press F2 to process the query.

Now you see the Answer table.

The Answer table displays the results of the query. As mentioned, you can use the Rotate command, Ctrl-R, or Image Move to move the columns and re-sort the table. Remember, the Answer table is an unkeyed table.

Querying Multiple Tables

Refining the Query Statement

To further refine your query statement, you can keep the current Answer table displayed on the screen. As you learned in Chapter 7, you can use the logical AND and OR operators when constructing your query. You can also use the arithmetic operators =, >, <, =>, and =<.

For example, alter your query to read as follows:

> Create a list of customers, by last name, who have purchased more than 20 of any item, or more than 5 of any item in the last 30 days. Include with this list the name of the items purchased, how many, and the invoice number.

Because the logical OR part of the statement, "or at least 5 of any item in the last 30 days," covers two different fields, you have to make this a two-line query:

1. Move the cursor to the Lineitem query form by pressing `F3` (Up Image), and then move to the Qty Ordered field.
2. Enter the following logical AND statement: type **>=20**.
3. Move the cursor down one row, and enter the first part of the logical OR statement: type **>5**.
4. Press `F3` (Up Image) to activate the Orders query form. Move the cursor to the Order Date field.
5. Now enter the second half of the logical OR statement: type **>=today–30**.

   Because you have added a second row to the query statement to include the logical OR statement, you now must place check marks in the second row of all the fields to be included in the Answer table. You also must provide different example elements in the linking fields for the second row.
6. Move the cursor to the Cust # field in the Orders query form, and enter an example element into the second row. Press `F5`, and then type **bbb**.
7. Move the cursor to the Order # field and down to the second row. Press `F6` to place a check mark and include this part of the query in the Answer table. Then press `F5` and enter the example element **2222**.
8. Press `F3` (Up Image) to move to the Cust1 query form. In the Cust # field's second row, press `F5`, and enter the example element **bbb** to match the field to that in the Orders query form.

311

Using Advanced Queries

9. Move to the Last Name field and place a check mark in the second row by pressing F6.
10. Press F4 (Down Image) twice to move down to the Lineitem query form. In the second row of the Order # field, enter the example element to match it to the field in the Orders query form. Press F5, and then type **2222**.
11. Now place check marks in the second row of the Item Description and Qty Ordered fields.

Here, you can see the new query statement.

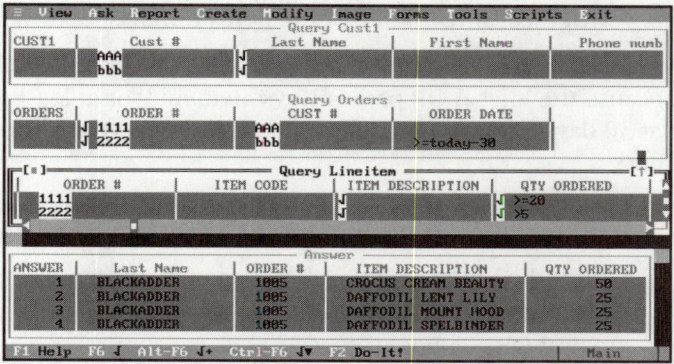

12. Press F2 to process the query.

You now see the refined Answer table.

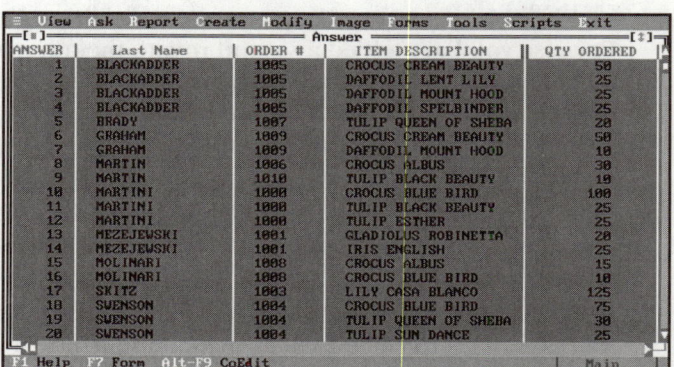

You can use this means of refining the query statement to get an answer or a group of responses you need. If your query does not return the answer you are expecting, then refine the query statement.

312

Using Calculations

Paradox can perform a surprising array of number-crunching functions. Many computer users export data to a spreadsheet program to perform numerical calculations. Paradox's CALC operator, however, provides you with much of the calculating power you may need.

Paradox can do two general forms of calculations: those involving numbers and alphanumeric fields with specific records, and summary calculations performed on groups of records. In this section of the chapter, you will learn about using CALC with individual records. To learn about using CALC with groups of records, see the section "Using CALC on Groups" later in this chapter.

Paradox enables you to choose the field in which to locate a CALC expression. You should locate the expression in or near fields that are included in the calculation. CALC creates its own new field in the Answer table for the results of the calculation. Paradox gives the field a default name based on the calculation performed. You can use the AS operator to give the field a name you feel is more appropriate.

CALC with Arithmetic Values

Generally your tables contain the basic data. Paradox does not perform or store calculations of any sort in a table's records. For example, your Lineitem table contains fields that keep data for the number of items ordered and their price. The table does not contain a field with the extended price of each item.

To construct a CALC expression in a query form using arithmetic values, do the following:

1. Using the same query forms as in the preceding section, delete all the check marks and example elements from the second row in each query form. Place the cursor in any field of the second row and press [Del]. This step deletes the entire row.
2. Move the cursor to the Lineitem query form and then to the Qty Ordered field in the first row. Press [F6] to remove the check mark. Enter the example element **QTY**.
3. Move the cursor to the Retail field and enter the example element **PRICE**.
4. Now, to enter a calculation expression in the Retail field, do the following:

313

Using Advanced Queries

11

Type **,CALC**.

Press F5 and type **QTY**.

Type *****.

Press F5 and type **PRICE**.

The expression you just entered should look like this:

PRICE,CALC QTY*PRICE, with PRICE, QTY, PRICE displayed in reverse video.

Here, you can see the resulting query statement with the CALC expression in the Retail field.

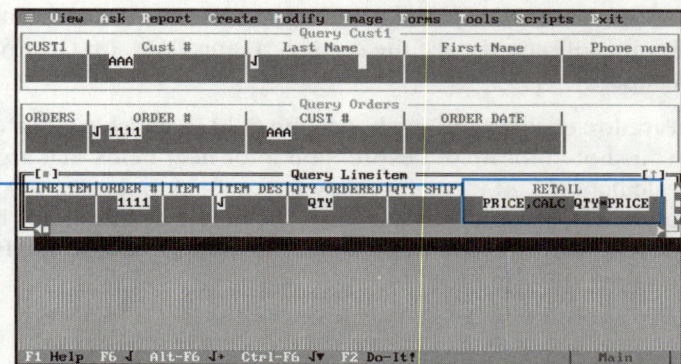

The above figure contains field columns resized using **I**mage **C**olumnSize, providing a display of all the fields together.

5. Now press F2.

You can see the resulting Answer table.

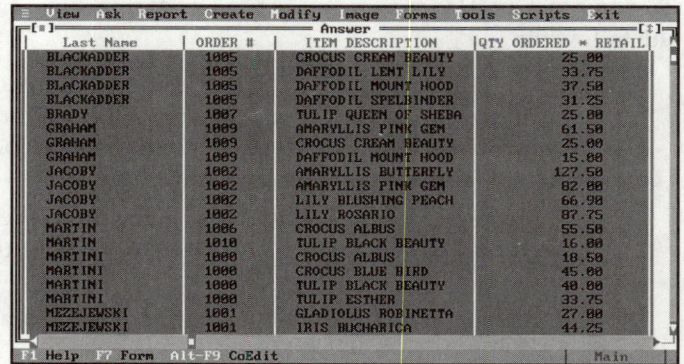

314

Using Calculations

Notice that Paradox has named the calculated field QTY ORDERED * RETAIL. Also notice that Paradox formats the field as currency (with two decimal places) because one of the fields used in the calculations, Retail, is a currency field.

If you want to apply your own name to this field, use the AS operator. In the expression you just entered in step 4, you could have used the AS operator to rename the resulting calculated field. The expression in the Retail field then appears as follows:

PRICE,CALC QTY*PRICE AS Extended Price

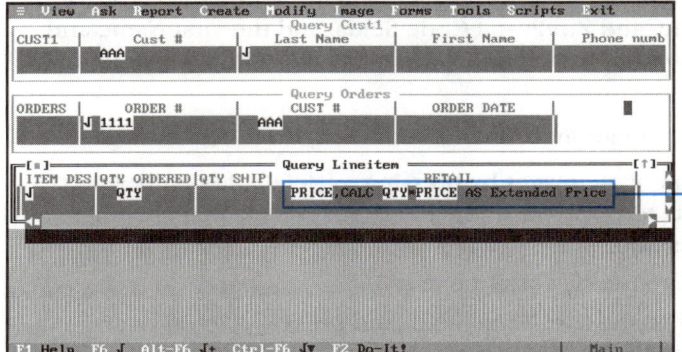

Here, you see the change made to include the AS operator.

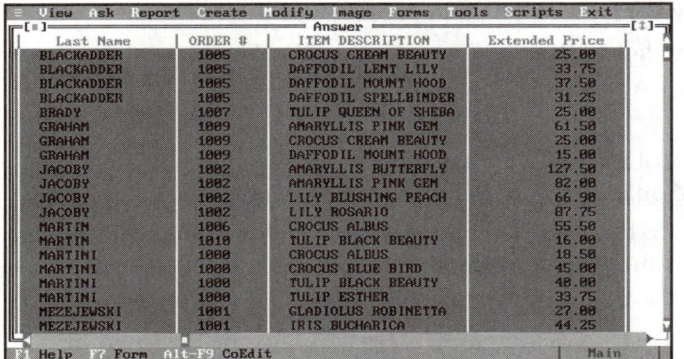

Here, you see the Answer table with the calculated field renamed Extended Price.

If you are performing calculations on more than two fields, you can use ( ) to combine calculations that should be performed together and separate them from others. If you do not use any type of grouping operators in a calculation, then Paradox performs all multiplication and division, and then addition and subtraction calculations.

315

Using Advanced Queries

11 CALC with Alphanumeric Values

Often a table contains fields for first name, last name, city, state, and zip code. Breaking this type of information into separate fields enables you to perform various sorts and queries on each of these fields. If you combine a person's first and last names in a single field, Paradox sorts the names by the first letter of the first name. This makes alphabetizing a list very difficult, and is the primary reason that you have used separate First Name and Last Name fields in your Cust1 table.

You can use CALC to combine fields containing alphanumeric data. (You cannot use CALC to combine data from a memo field.) Using the Cust1 table, combine the City, State, and Zip/Postal Code fields, and the First Name and Last Name fields together. You may use such information in this way in many types of reports.

To combine the fields containing alphanumeric data, do the following:

1. Clear the desktop of all images by pressing [Alt]-[F8]. Remember that Paradox attempts to combine all the query statements that are currently on the desktop.
2. Select **A**sk and choose the Cust1 table.
3. Move the cursor to the Last Name field, and press [F5] to enter an example element. Press [L] for Last Name.
4. Move to the First Name field, press [F5], and press [F] for First Name.
5. Move to the City field, press [F5], and press [C] for City.
6. Move to the State field, press [F5], and press [S] for State.
7. Move to the Zip/Postal Code field, press [F5], and press [Z]-[P] for Zip/Postal Code.

   Notice that none of the fields contain check marks. This is because Paradox will use only the CALC fields for the Answer table.
8. Move the cursor to the First Name field. Enter the following expression after the example element already there:

   ,CALC F + " " + L

   The literal values of "," (comma) and " " (space) must be enclosed in double quotation marks, or Paradox interprets them differently. The first comma in the expression is not a literal and, therefore, is not enclosed by double quotes; the comma is used to separate the example element from the expression. For clarity, spaces have been added to the example shown above between each element.

Using Calculations

9. Move the cursor to the City field and enter the following expression after the example element:

   ,CALC C + "," + " " + S + " " + ZP

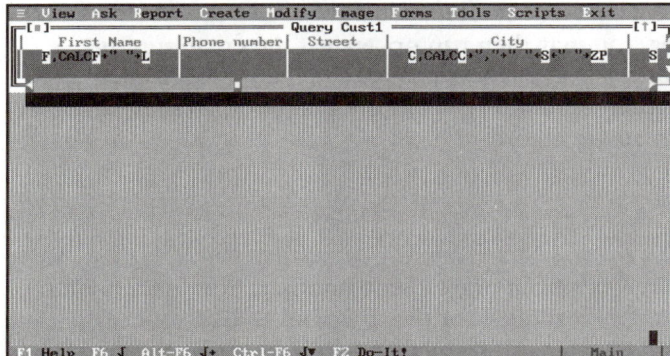

Here, you can see the CALC expressions entered in the First Name and City fields.

10. Press **F2**.

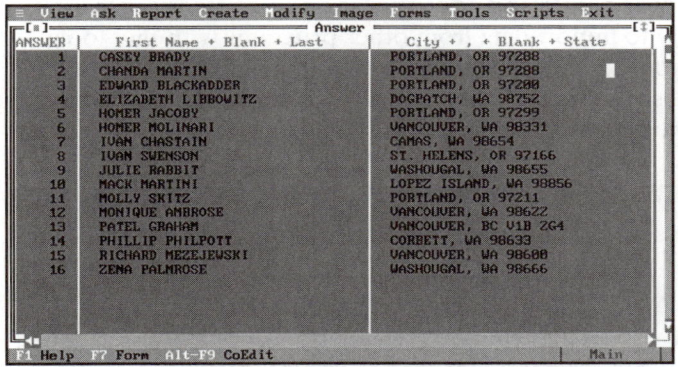

Now you can see the Answer table resulting from the query statement you just created.

Notice how this table is sorted: alphabetically, by first name. You also can shorten the CALC statement placed in the City field by combining two of the literals within a single set of double quotation marks:

   From this   **,CALC C + "," + " " + S + " " + ZP**

   To this   **,CALC C + ", " + S + " " + ZP**

Again, remember to use the AS operator if you want to use a field name that is more descriptive than "First Name + Blank + Last Name."

317

Using Advanced Queries

11 Executing Table Operations

All of the functions you have performed using query forms have used records and placed answers in a separate Answer table. If you want to add the records from the Answer table to a permanent table, you have to use the Tools More Add command. However, you may then run up against the error message Answer and "Other table" have incompatible structures. Fortunately, Paradox provides you with a set of query operators that perform their functions on a table, not on a single record.

INSERT Queries

The INSERT query adds records from one table to another, even if the tables have unlike structures. A good example for the use of an INSERT query is when you want to add a customer or product list you have received from another source. The data may be in another database format or in a spreadsheet format.

For example, suppose you have bought a mailing list from another company. You now want to add these names and addresses to your own customer list. Using Paradox's capacity to import data from other programs with the Tools ExportImport option, you can include the information in your database as a table with its own table structure. Paradox makes its best attempt to convert the field names from the original program.

Here, you can see both Cust1 and the new Customer table. Although the lists look similar, you cannot just add the new names to your own customer list.

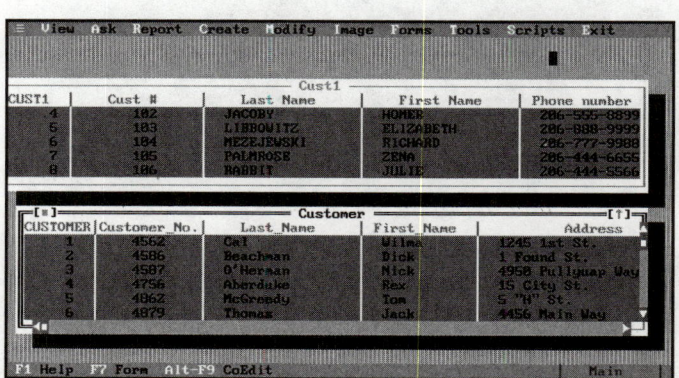

After converting the list into a Paradox table, do the following to add the names to your customer list, using an INSERT query statement:

318

Executing Table Operations

1. Open a query form for the new table. Select ^Ask, and then choose the Customer table.
2. Now open a query from your own customer table. Select ^Ask, and then choose the Cust1 table.

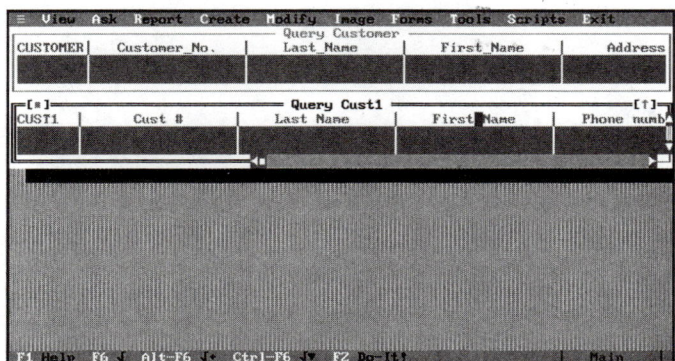

You now see the query forms for both customer tables.

3. Press F3 to move back to the query form for Customer.

   You now enter example elements for each field that is to be placed in the Cust1 table.

4. Move the cursor to the first field, Customer No., press F5, and type **CN** for Customer Number.

   Remember, you cannot use other characters, such as #, or spaces when placing example elements.

5. Now place the following example elements into the indicated fields:

Field Name	Example Element
Last Name	**LN**
First Name	**FN**
Address	**ADDRESS**
City	**CITY**
State/Prov.	**STATE**
Postal Code	**ZIP**
Telephone	**PHONE**
Discount %	Leave blank. Do not place an example element in this field.

319

Using Advanced Queries

6. Now press F4 to move back to the query form for Cust1. Enter the following example elements into the indicated fields:

Field Name	Example Element
Cust #	CN
Last Name	LN
First Name	FN
Phone Number	PHONE
Address	ADDRESS
City	CITY
State/Prov.	STATE
Postal Code	ZIP
Country	Leave blank. Do not place an example element in this field.

Here, you see parts of the two completed query forms.

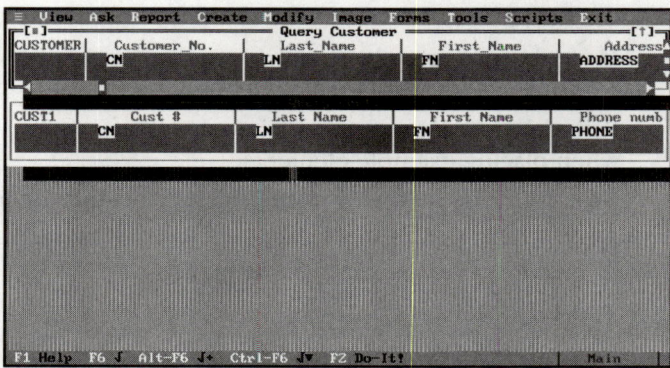

7. Move the cursor to the column marked CUST1, the very first column in the Cust1 query form.
8. Type the reserved word INSERT.

Executing Table Operations

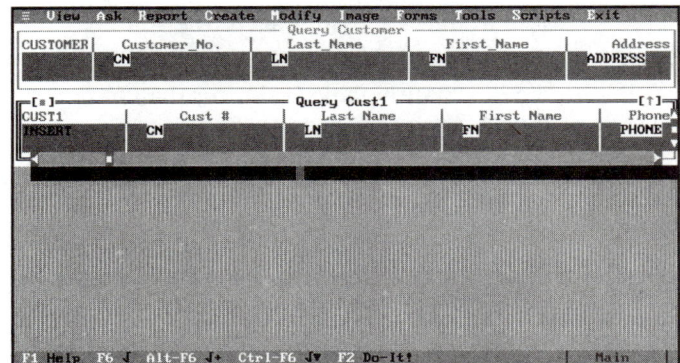

Here, you can see the Cust1 query form ready to have the new records inserted.

9. Press F2 to process the query and insert the new records.

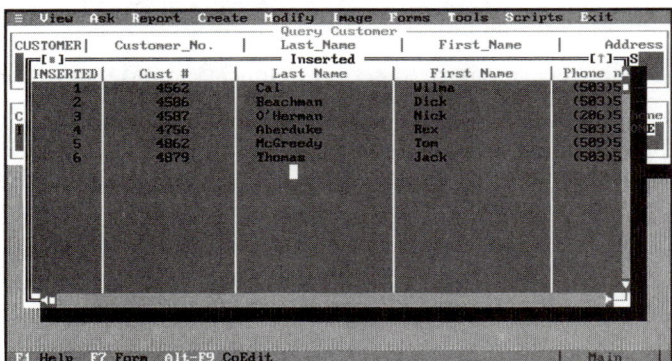

When the operation is completed, Paradox displays the temporary Inserted table, showing you the records that have been inserted into the table.

You can use the Inserted table to identify the new records if you decide to remove them from the table.

A few rules to remember when you use the INSERT query include the following:

- All corresponding fields must be the same type. For instance, you cannot have a number field in one table and a corresponding alphanumeric field in the other table.
- An empty field in the destination query form results in a blank field in the new record. For example, because you did not use an example element in the Country field, this field is blank for all of the new records.

321

Using Advanced Queries

11

- You can use a CALC expression to make adjustments to the source data before adding it to the destination table.
- If an alphanumeric field in the destination table is shorter than in the source table, some values may be truncated, or cut off, to fit.

DELETE Queries

Paradox provides you with several methods for deleting unnecessary or out-of-date records. If you have just a few records to delete, using Edit or CoEdit is safest and quickest. If, however, you are removing a large group of records and can construct a query statement that will select only those records, then you can use a DELETE query.

Before using a DELETE query, be sure to make a backup copy of the table and its records. Use the Tools Copy Table options. This step ensures the integrity of your data in case you make a mistake.

If you want to delete all sales records that are earlier than a specified date, you can do the following:

1. Select Ask from the Main menu and choose the Orders table. Select Ask again and choose the Lineitem table.

2. With the cursor located in the query form for Lineitem, move it to the Order # field, press F5, and type the example element 111.

3. Press F3 and place the cursor on the Order # field. Press F5 and enter 111 as the matching example element.

4. Move the cursor to the Order Date field and enter the following expression: <=1/31/92. This should now select all orders with an order date of less than and equal to 1/31/92 and the corresponding records from Lineitem.

    As an additional precaution, before actually performing a DELETE query, continue with the next few steps.

5. Move the cursor to the column marked ORDERS and press F6. This places a check mark in all the columns.

6. Press F4, and then repeat the operation in the column marked LINEITEM.

Executing Table Operations

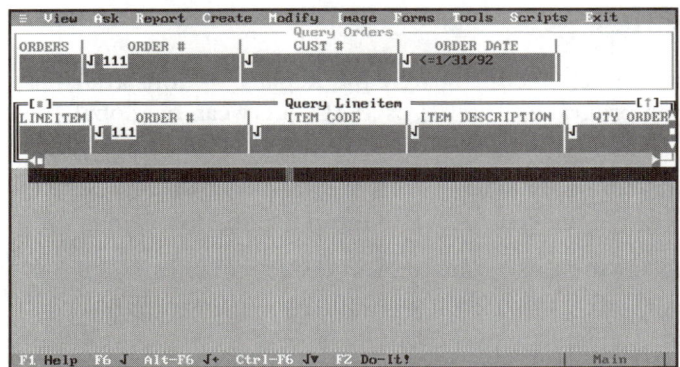

You should now have query forms like these.

7. Press F2 to process the query.

   Now check the Answer table. If the query has been properly constructed, you should see only the records you want to delete. If you see unexpected records, then you need to refine this query *before* you use the DELETE query. If the Answer table contains only orders dated 1/31/92 or earlier, you can continue.

8. Move the cursor to the Lineitem column, and type **DELETE**. Then press F3 to move to the Orders query form, and type **DELETE** in the Orders column.

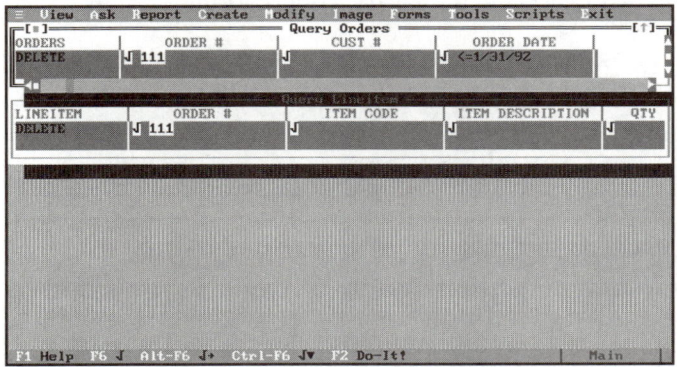

Here, you can see the query forms ready to delete the selected records.

9. Press F2 to process this query.

Paradox places all the deleted records in a temporary Deleted table. If you decide you want to keep the records, you can add them back into the table. You also can rename the Deleted table to keep a copy of these records filed. Remember, the Deleted table is a temporary table.

323

Using Advanced Queries

11

CHANGETO Queries

The CHANGETO query is much like the Search and Replace options available in most word processing programs. The CHANGETO query can be global, affecting all records of the table; the CHANGETO query can also be selective.

To see how the CHANGETO query works, add a 5 percent sales tax to all orders for people who live in the state of Washington. Do the following:

1. Open query forms for the Cust1, Lineitem, and Orders tables.
2. In the query form for Cust1, place the example element **111** in the Cust # field to link the table with the Orders table.
3. Move the cursor to the State field and enter the expression **=WA**. Then press F4 to move to the Lineitem query form.
4. In this query form, place the example element **2222** into the Order # field. Then move to the Retail column and enter the following expression:

    PRICE, CHANGETO PRICE * 1.05

    Remember that in the above expression "PRICE" is an example element, so be sure to press F5 before you type it.
5. Press F4 to move down to the Orders query form. Move the cursor to the Order # field and enter the matching example element from the Lineitem query form, **2222**. Then move to the Cust# field and enter the example element **111** to match the Cust1 query form.

Here, you see the CHANGETO query statement to add a sales tax to the Washington state orders.

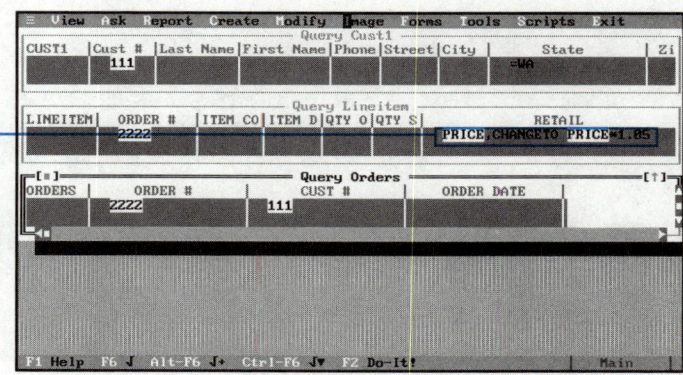

6. Press F2 to process the query.

324

Using Groups

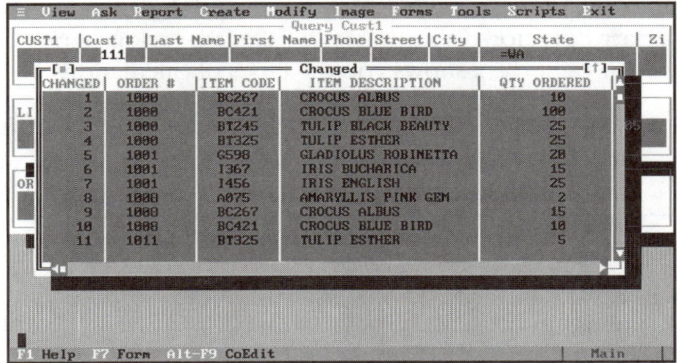

Here, you see the Changed table.

The temporary Changed table keeps all the original records as they were before the query was processed. If you decide the change is not what you want, you can add these records back to the table.

FIND Queries

The FIND query locates a specific record in a table. It has a very similar function as the Zoom and Zoom Next commands that you have already learned to use. FIND is much more powerful, however. You do not have to search only a specific field. You can be very selective with this type of query and search for a record that meets various criteria covering several tables.

To use FIND, construct a query statement as though you want to display the record in the Answer table. Then enter the word **FIND** in the far left column and press F2 to process the query.

Paradox places the cursor on the actual record in the table in which it is located. Paradox also creates the Answer table with the same information, but does not display it at this time.

Using Groups

So far all of your queries have asked questions about individual records. Although you have received answers with many records meeting your criteria, each record answered the questions on its own merits.

325

Using Advanced Queries

11

Paradox also enables you to group records and ask questions of the group. Paradox has several summary operators you can use to calculate various types of information from a group. Table 11.1 shows you the types of calculations you can perform.

Table 11.1
Types of Calculations

Operator	Outcome	Field Types	Default Grouping
AVERAGE	Average of values in group	N, $, D, S	All
COUNT	Number of values in group	All	Unique
MAX	Highest value in group	All	Unique
MIN	Lowest value in group	All	Unique
SUM	Total of values in group	N, $, S	All

The Default Grouping indicates whether an operator ignores or uses a duplicate value. AVERAGE and SUM use all values in the group, whereas MAX, MIN, and COUNT normally disregard duplicate values. By placing the word ALL after the operator in the same column, you can override the default setting.

Creating Query Groups

You can use summary operators to group records in a variety of ways. You can use summary operators to select records based on specific criteria for a group of records, or to calculate statistics (averages, counts, etc.) across a group of records. Summary operators can also compare certain aspects of a group to another group.

For example, if you want to find which customers have bought more than three items, you can scroll through the Lineitem table and then compare that to the Orders table. Or, you can create the following query:

1. Open query forms for Cust1, Lineitem, and Orders.

Using Groups

2. Link the query forms with example elements, and place a check mark in the Last Name field in Cust1 and in the Order # field in Lineitem.
3. In the Lineitem form's Qty Ordered field, enter the following expression:

   COUNT >=3

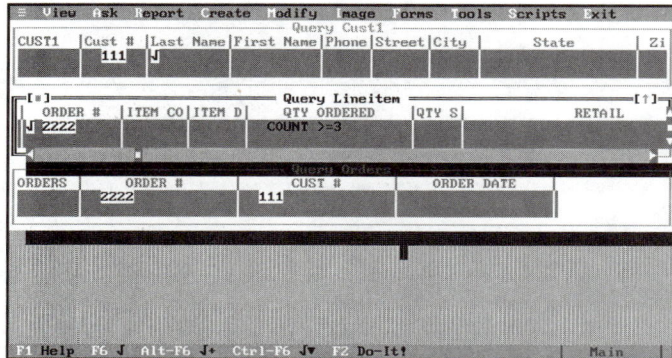

Your query statement should look like this.

4. Now press F2 to process the query.

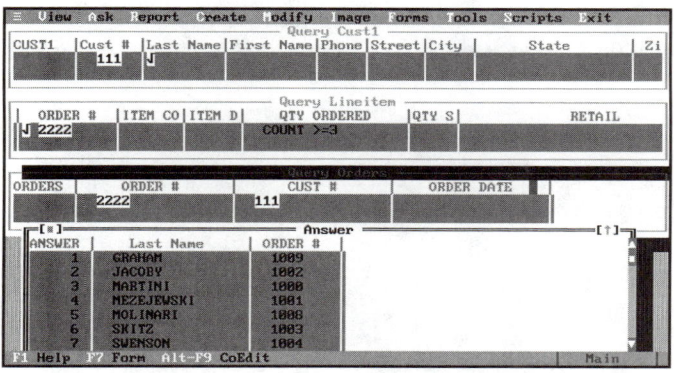

Here, you can see the results of the query statement.

Using CALC on Groups

You also can combine summary operators with the CALC operator to perform summary calculations. Such combinations of operators can calculate various statistics on a group of records.

327

Using Advanced Queries

11

For example, you can use the CALC SUM operator to calculate the total number of items sold. The CALC COUNT operator can tell you the number of customers who have placed orders. To see how summary operators can work with CALC, do the following:

1. Open a query form for Lineitem.
2. Move the cursor to the Qty Ordered field and type **CALC SUM**. Press `F2` to process the query.

Here, you see the query statement and the results of the query. You have sold 813 items.

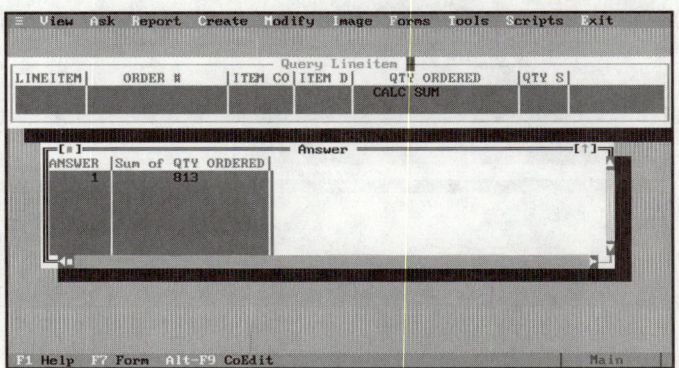

3. To find out how many orders have been placed, move the cursor to the ORDER # field, type **CALC COUNT**, and press `F2` again.

You now see the new query statement and the results of the query. You have received 12 orders.

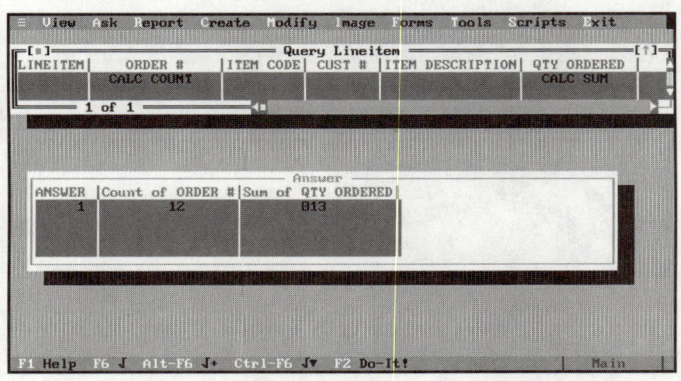

You can use the MIN, MAX, and AVERAGE operators in a similar manner to calculate statistics for a group minimum, maximum, or average.

328

Creating Inclusive Link Queries

Typically, a query asks Paradox to find records that match specific criteria. This type of query matching, using an exclusive link, is called an *inner join* and generally produces the type of results for which you are looking.

At times, you will look not only for the records that match the criteria, but also for the records that do not. This type of query matching is called an *outer join*, or an inclusive link. Paradox provides an *inclusion* operator you can use to create the outer join query. Paradox uses the exclamation point (!) to represent the inclusion operator. When using the inclusion operator, you must place it in the query column just after the example element.

Single Inclusive Links

When using the inclusion operator, you often can see data that you may not see otherwise. For example, if you credit sales to specific salespeople, you can use a regular query to find the salespeople who have made sales and gather various statistics concerning these sales. On the other hand, you have to use an outer join query to find both the salespeople who have been selling and those who have not.

In the following example, you will construct a query to ask the following:

> Create a list of all customers and show the dates of the orders they have placed.

To see the use of an inclusion operator, do the following:

1. Open a query for the Cust1 and Orders tables.
2. Press `F3` to activate the query form for Cust1. Enter the example element **111** in the Cust1 field.
3. Because you want to include all customer records, place the inclusion operator after the example element in this field. Enter an exclamation point (**!**).
4. Place check marks in the Last Name and First Name fields.
5. Press `F4` to activate the Orders query form. Enter the example element **111** in the Cust # field.
6. Place a check mark in the Order Date field.

Using Advanced Queries

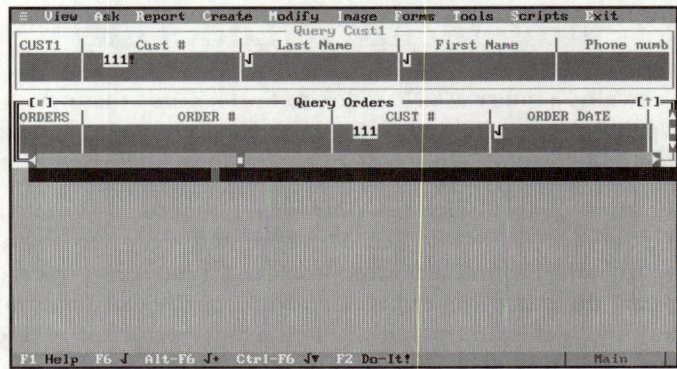

Here, you see the completed query statement with the inclusion operator.

7. Press F2 to process the query.

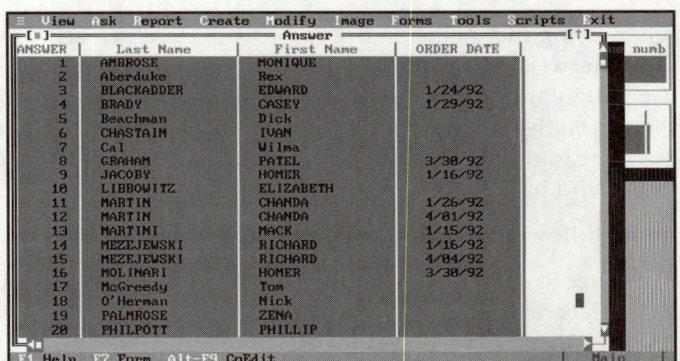

You now see the Answer table with the results of the query.

Notice that the customers who have not placed orders do not have a date entry in the Order Date field. This is an example of an asymmetrical outer join query. For a quick test of the inclusion operator, remove the inclusion operator from the Cust1 query form, and then perform the query again.

Creating Inclusive Link Queries

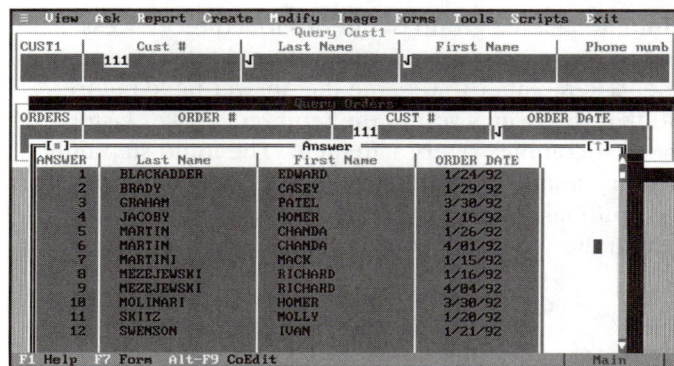

You now see the same query performed without the inclusion operator.

You can see the difference between the inner and outer join queries. When you need to see not only records that meet a specified criteria but also those that do not, try the outer join query.

Multiple Inclusive Links

Using the inclusion operator, you can perform multiple query form outer joins. Multiple inclusive queries also are known as *symmetrical* outer join queries. When you use the multiple form of the inclusion operator, you must keep the following points in mind:

- You must use the inclusion operator in the linking field in the query form that contains the records you want included.
- When using multi-query forms, you must use either an inclusive or an exclusive link for a pair of query lines. You cannot combine them.
- You can combine the use of inclusive and exclusive links as long as they do not involve the same pairs of lines.
- You can use the inclusion operator with any specific example element only once per line and twice per query statement.
- The order in which Paradox processes links is from the most exclusive to the least exclusive: exclusive links, asymmetrical outer join, and then symmetrical outer join.

As you perform more queries with your own data, try the inclusive link queries. You may be surprised what your data can tell you.

Using Advanced Queries

You also may find it helpful to chain a group of queries together. Process a general query, and then further refine your question using the Answer table as part of the query statement. Remember to rename the Answer table before doing this. You may find that this brings you to the required answer faster than trying to create one very complex query statement. The multi-step query, query-Answer-query, is a very simple method of refining a query to extract information from a large multi-table database. Using this method, you can more quickly and easily find the specific data you require.

Summary

In this chapter, you learned to build multi-table query statements. You then learned to perform calculations based on your queries and to summarize data based on groups of records. Finally, you learned to use inclusive links to build a query that results in both matching records and nonmatching records.

Specifically, you learned the following key points about using Paradox 4:

- To build a query statement, open query forms for each table with the Ask option.
- To move from query form to query form, use F3 (Up Image) and F4 (Down Image).
- To place example elements in linking fields, press F5 and enter the element. The element can be any number or alphabetic character.
- To perform calculations on data in fields and then display the results in a new field in the Answer table, use the CALC operator.
- To add records from one table to another when they have incompatible structures, use an INSERT query. Place the INSERT operator in the far left column of the query form for the target table.
- To remove records that meet query criteria from a table or tables, use the DELETE query.
- To make global changes to selected records, use the CHANGETO query.
- To find records that meet specified criteria, use the FIND query.
- To group records based on a criterion, use the AVERAGE, COUNT, MAX, MIN, and SUM operators.
- To perform summary calculations based on group data, use CALC with group operators.

Summary

- To include records that do not meet the query criteria, use the Inclusive operator (!).

In the next chapter, you will learn to create multi-table tabular and free-form reports. You will also learn to use calculated fields and summary calculations within the report.

12

Creating Tabular, Free-Form, and Multi-Table Reports

An overview of the Paradox report

Using the tabular report

Creating reports with linked tables

Using groups

Printing the report

Creating free-form reports

You have already created a simple, single table report. And you have created multi-table forms and queries. Now you are ready to tie these procedures together and create your own reports that draw information from several tables.

The primary purpose of a database is not just to collect data, but to be able to manipulate that data and present it in a meaningful way. This purpose requires creating some type of output from the raw data contained in tables, and will generally result in a report. A report can be many things, including a sales invoice, a list, or a mailing label.

12

Creating Tabular, Free-Form, and Multi-Table Reports

> **Key Terms in This Chapter**
>
> *Master table* — The table used on which to base the report specification. Generally, all of the master table's records will be printed.
>
> *Lookup table* — A table that is linked to the master table. This must be a keyed table, and the key field must exist in the master table.
>
> *Expression* — A group of characters, fields, and operators that represents a value. Used when placing a calculated field.
>
> *PAGEBREAK* — A key word used in the report specification to force Paradox to start a new page at a specified point.

An Overview of the Paradox Report

When you create a report, you first tell Paradox which table to base the report on, and then you choose a tabular or free-form format.

You learned in Chapter 8 the basic details of creating a report specification, saving it, and using it to output the report with live data. You also learned that by grouping records, you can control the format and meaning of your report. The Paradox Report Designer can be used to adjust and fine-tune a report.

In this chapter, you will learn to link tables to create multi-table reports. Later in this chapter, you will also learn to remove blank spaces between fields, and to use field and summary calculations in reports.

Using the Tabular Report

The tabular report is the most common report specification. With the Paradox Report Designer, you can customize a tabular report to appear in almost any format you require. This chapter will show you how to create a sales invoice. Much of what you learned about creating free-form and multi-table forms in Chapter 10 will apply to this chapter.

You will build a multi-table report specification using linked tables. When you created a multi-table form, you built a master form and then linked the detail forms. Now as you design your report, you will create the master report specification and link it to *lookup* tables. The principle is almost the same.

Creating Reports with Linked Tables

Multi-table reports enable you to maintain your database in smaller and more manageable tables. You can also create reports from different parts of the data more easily.

Choosing the Master Table

The first step in creating a multi-table report specification is to determine which table to use as the master table. This step may not be as easy as it seems. Paradox does not build reports in exactly the same manner in which it builds forms.

While the Paradox report uses a master table for the basis of the report design, the table may not be the same table you used when creating a multi-table form. Similar to the multi-table form, Paradox does not support the many-to-many relationship between tables for reports.

The multi-table form, Order Form, uses the Orders table as the master table. The two detail tables, Cust1 and Lineitem, are used for most of the information that is entered through the master form. You are using a one-to-one relationship between Cust1 and Orders, and a one-to-many relationship between Orders to Lineitem.

On the other hand, the multi-table report uses the reverse relationship—the table that contains the most direct detail information for the master table. This is the table from which you want Paradox to print all the records. At the same, each of the *lookup* tables must be directly linked to the master. You cannot link a table through a lookup table to the master table; only a single level of table nesting is supported by Paradox.

Choosing the Lookup Tables

After you have selected your table to serve as the master table, you must then choose the lookup tables. If your purpose in this chapter is to create a sales invoice, then you will need data from the Lineitem, Cust1, and Orders tables.

337

Two rules apply to the selection of a lookup table:

- A lookup table must be keyed. If the key is concatenated, then each of the keyed fields must have a corresponding field in the master table. The corresponding fields must contain the same type of data; the field name does not have to be the same.
- A lookup table can only be linked to the master table, not to another lookup table.

You can use a master table field only once as a link to a lookup table. If your master table has only three fields, you can then link a maximum of three lookup tables.

With your current database structure, you have a problem in constructing this relationship. If you use the Orders table as a master, you will not be able to link the Lineitem table because you do not have a field that corresponds to the key field Item Code. The Cust1 table can only link to Orders, and Lineitem does not have a link to Cust1.

You can use the following two options to work around this dilemma:

- You can create a dummy table with the structure you need and create the report specification for this table. Then use a query to pull the data together into the Answer table. You can then either copy the report specification to the Answer table or add the records to the dummy table.
- You can also restructure the Lineitem table to include a field for Cust # so that you can link the Lineitem table directly to the Cust1 table. If you choose this option, use the validity check **TableLookup Orders A**llCorrespondingFields **H**elpAndFill. The Cust # field will then be automatically filled in for you as you add new records.

You can probably find other options for working around this problem—use your imagination as you work with your tables. For the purposes of this chapter, use the second option. Remember to add the customer information into the new field in Lineitem for the existing records. You will have to do this manually.

Creating Reports with Linked Tables

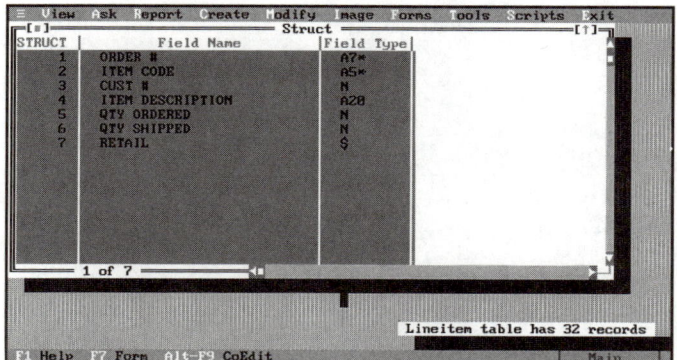

Here, you can see the new table structure for Lineitem.

Now that you have updated the Lineitem table, you can use it as the master table with Cust1 and Orders linked to it.

Establishing the Link

After you have determined which table will be the master and which tables will be used as the lookup tables, you are ready to proceed with the report specification.

To create the table links, do the following:

1. Select **R**eport from the Main menu bar.
2. Choose the **D**esign option, and select the table on which to base the master report specification. Choose the Lineitem table and press ⏎Enter.
3. Select Unused Report, number 1.
4. Enter the report description. For example, type **INVOICE** and press ⏎Enter. Then select the **T**abular option.

339

Creating Tabular, Free-Form, and Multi-Table Reports

12

Here, you see the default report specification for the Lineitem table.

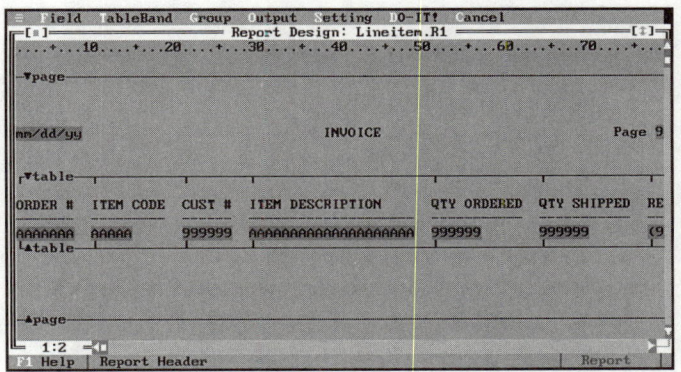

5. Select **F**ield **L**ookup to link a lookup table.

Here, you see the cascading Lookup option menu.

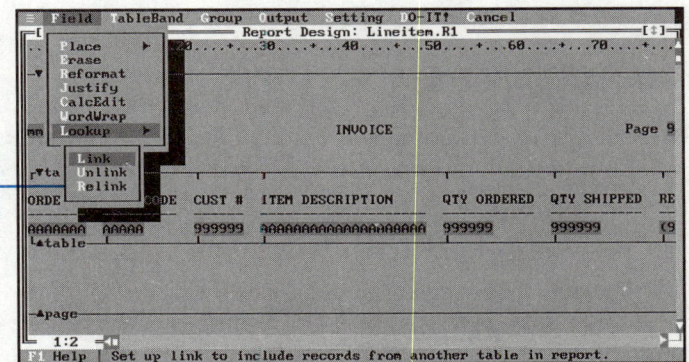

6. Choose the **L**ink option.

   You now see the Table Selection dialog box.

7. Enter the name of the table to use as a lookup table. Type **Cust1** and press ⏎Enter.

Creating Reports with Linked Tables

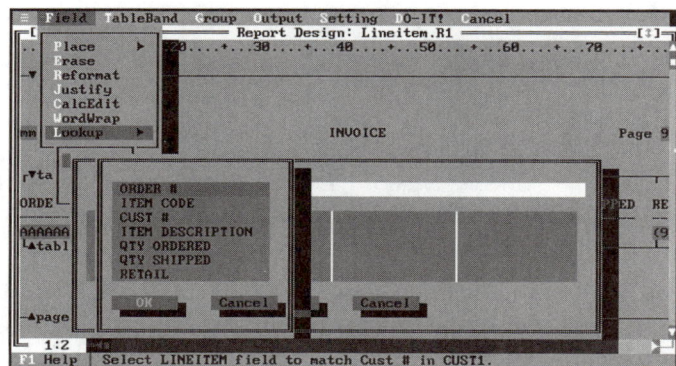

You now see the Field list box.

This Field list box contains field names from the master table. You must choose the appropriate field(s) to link to the lookup table Cust1's key field(s). Remember, if the lookup table uses a multiple field key, you must link each key field to a field in the master table.

Notice this message in the status bar: Select LINEITEM field to match Cust # in CUST1. The message tells you that Lineitem is the master table and that the only key field in Cust1 is Cust #.

8. Choose the appropriate field. Select CUST #. After you make this selection, the Field list disappears.
9. Now link the second lookup table. Select the **F**ield **L**ookup **L**ink option. Choose the table, Orders, and use the Order # field as the linking field.

Unlinking Tables

If you find that a linked table is unnecessary, you can unlink it. However, unlinking a lookup table from a master table can have potentially serious consequences.

When you unlink a lookup table, all the fields that came from the lookup table are deleted from the report specification. Any calculated fields that used one of the deleted fields for the calculation are deleted. Any group bands based on a lookup table field are also removed.

To unlink a lookup table from the master table, do the following:

1. Select **F**ield **L**ookup from the menu bar.
2. Choose the **U**nlink option.

341

Creating Tabular, Free-Form, and Multi-Table Reports

Here, you see the dialog box listing the currently linked lookup tables.

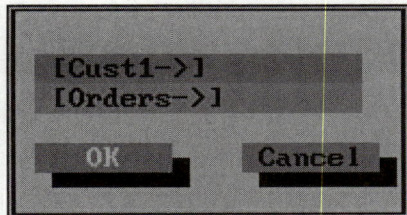

3. Select the table you want to unlink and press [Enter] or select **OK**. Remember, pressing [Enter] now will delete all fields associated with the selected lookup table. If you choose not to unlink the table at this time, press [Esc] or select **Cancel**.

Relinking Tables

If you accidentally choose the wrong field with which to link a lookup table to the master table, you do not have to **U**nlink it and then **L**ink again. You can **R**elink a lookup table.

The **R**elink option enables you to reselect the field the lookup table uses to link to the master table. Using this option will not change any currently placed fields or calculated fields.

Customizing the Report Specification

You have now linked the necessary lookup tables and are ready to use the now available fields in your report specification. Begin your report specification by doing the following:

1. Erase the following fields by placing the cursor on them and selecting **F**ield **E**rase:

    Date field: mm/dd/yy

    Page number: 999

    Also delete the literal Page by either using [Del] or [Backspace].

2. Erase the following table bands by selecting **T**ableBand **E**rase and placing the cursor inside the band and pressing [Enter]:

    ORDER #

    CUST #

3. Delete the second page width by selecting the **S**etting **P**ageLayout **D**elete options and then selecting **OK**.

Creating Reports with Linked Tables

4. Turn on the vertical ruler by pressing Ctrl+V. The vertical ruler will help as you place literals and fields.

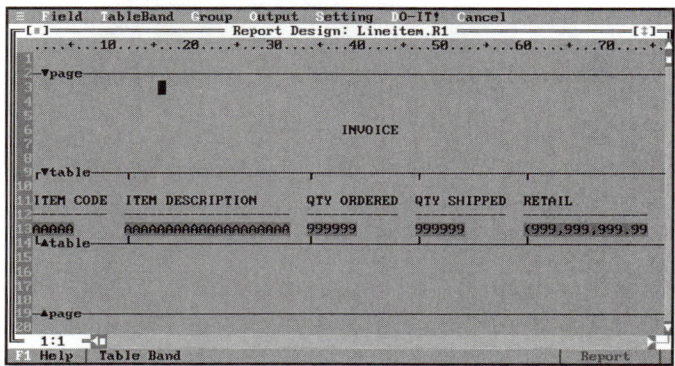

Your report specification should now look like this.

5. You will eventually need to place another field after the Retail field. Start by making the descriptive literals above the table fields into two lines. Move the cursor to line 10 on the vertical ruler, position 1 on the horizontal ruler, and type **ITEM**.

6. Move the cursor to the right 13 spaces and type **ITEM**.

    Move 14 spaces to the right and type **QTY**.

    Move 10 spaces to the right and type **QTY**.

    Move 9 spaces to the right and type **UNIT**.

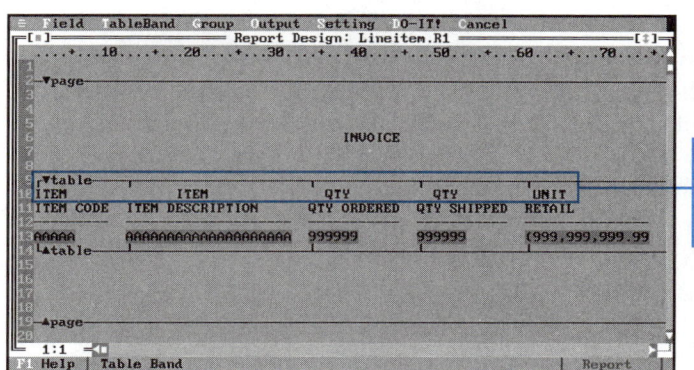

Here, you see the first line of the new descriptions entered.

343

Creating Tabular, Free-Form, and Multi-Table Reports

7. Now place the cursor in row 11, position 1. Press (Del) 5 times. The word CODE will move so that it is now underneath ITEM.
8. Move the cursor to the next word, ITEM, and press (Del) twice and the **space bar** twice. This step allows the word DESCRIPTION to move to the left only 2 spaces.
9. Move the cursor to the word QTY and press (Del) 4 times to delete the word and the space. Repeat this step in the next table band.
10. Move to the word RETAIL, type **PRICE**, and press (Del) once to delete the L.

You should now see a report specification like this.

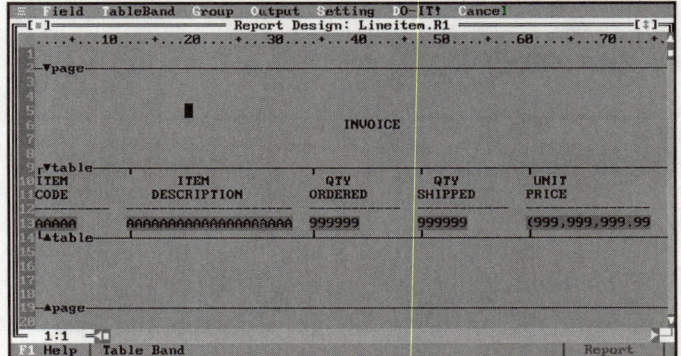

You have adjusted all the field titles, and now need to adjust the width of the table bands.

11. To make it easier to adjust the table band width, move the cursor to row 12, position 1. Now press (Ctrl)-(Y). This step deletes row 12.

   If you do not do this step, you will have to make each of the dashed lines in each table band smaller. Paradox will stop and beep when you come to 1 space between the right-most part of a literal or field and the left side of the next table band.

12. Move the cursor to the first table band, ITEM CODE. Place the cursor in the last position, about row 11 on the horizontal ruler. You can be in any row, so long as you have the cursor located between the table band lines.

   An easy way to place the cursor, is to place it one space to the left of the next field mask. Paradox always left justifies the field masks in their own table band.

344

13. Select **T**ableBand **R**esize and press ⏎Enter (move the cursor to the required location now if you have not already done so). Press ← to move the column in, or make it narrower. Leave 2 spaces between the Item Code field mask and the Item Description field mask.

    Repeat this step for each of the remaining fields.

14. You also will need to reformat the Unit Price field. Place the cursor on the field mask. You see the message in the status bar, RETAIL. Select **F**ield **R**eformat, and then select **D**igits from the dialog box. Use → to decrease the number of digits displayed until only 3 are displayed. Press ⏎Enter to select, and then press ⏎Enter again to accept the default value of 2 decimal places.

15. Adjust the Unit Price table band width if necessary.

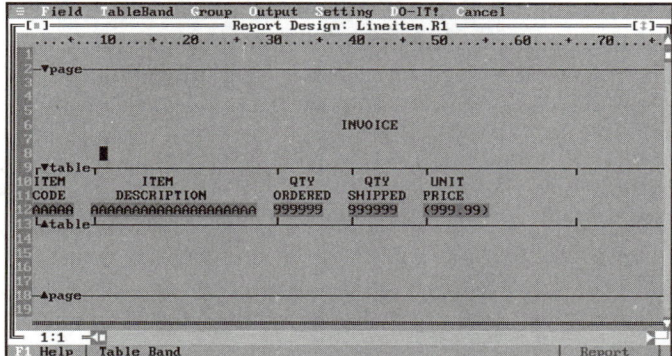

Here, you see the final change to the existing fields in the table band.

By default, Paradox places all the table's fields in the table band. You may have to remove some fields because they are not appropriate for this section of the report, or not needed. You may have to make room for a calculated field. You can also place more than one row of fields in the table band if this would better fit your report layout.

Using Groups

Paradox's capability to group records is one of the most powerful features of the Report Designer. Using the Group command enables you to determine the order in which your data will be organized.

345

Creating Tabular, Free-Form, and Multi-Table Reports

12

You can use Groups to establish the locations of headers and footers in a report. You can use the Paradox Summary Calculation feature to compute various statistics about groups and the overall report. You can also use grouping to arrange your data for clarity and ease of use.

Using the Group Bands

As mentioned in Chapter 8, you can group records in three ways:

By **F**ield Records are grouped together by the same value in a specified field. For example, you can group records by the same invoice number or same last name.

By **R**ange Records are grouped together for a certain range of values in a specified field. For example, you can group records by all last names beginning with the same letter or all orders in the same month.

By **N**umberRecords A specified number of records are grouped together. You can use this method to group records not being sorted in another way. You can also use this method inside of another group band for easier reading.

For the report specification you are building, you will use a group band to sort your report by Order/Invoice number. The number you had assigned as an order number will now be used as an invoice number. To assign a group band, do the following:

1. Select **G**roup **I**nsert **F**ield from the menus.
2. Choose the Order # field from the menu. Now move the cursor to line 7 (any position) and press ⏎Enter.

   You will notice that the group band is placed two lines above and below the table band. This is the default setting that Paradox uses for group bands.

For this example, only a single level of grouping, the invoice number, is needed. Paradox supports up to 16 levels of grouping. Group bands are sorted in order of priority. The first group band, the one closest to the page band, is given the highest priority. The group band closest to the table band is given the lowest priority.

Using Groups

For example, if you were creating a list of employees, you could group them by division, then by department, and then alphabetically by last name, or by seniority.

Adjusting the Group Band

The size of the default group band is often not wide enough to place the information you may need to place. You can easily increase or decrease the width of any of the bands located in the report specification. To make the necessary adjustments, do the following:

1. Move the cursor to row 3, position 1 and press Ctrl-Y. The row is deleted and the entire report specification moves up one row.
2. Now move the cursor to row 10, inside the header of the Order # group. Press Ins. The cursor changes from a large blinking block to a blinking dashed line.
3. Press Enter 6 times. The Order # group header section should now be 8 rows wide. This change does not affect the footer.
4. Move the cursor down to row 21 and press Enter twice.

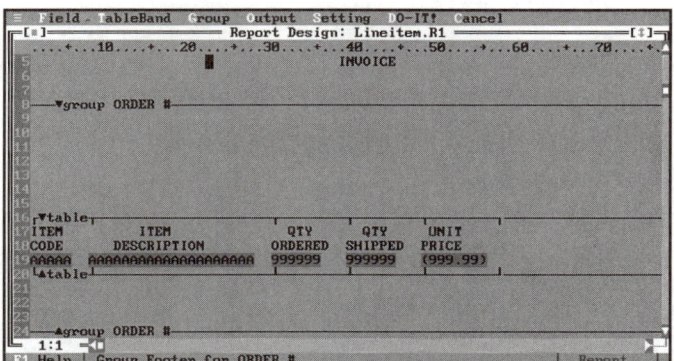

Your report specification will now look like this.

Notice that the entire report specification no longer fits in one screen. Rows 1 through 4 have scrolled up beyond the screen.

Placing Fields in the Group Band

Fields can be placed in a group band just as they are in the table band with one major difference: you do not have to create a table band column for each field. Within the group and page band, you can place fields in any location.

347

Creating Tabular, Free-Form, and Multi-Table Reports

If you try to place a field too close to the right-hand edge, you run the risk of not having adequate space for the field.

To place regular fields inside the group band, do the following:

1. Move the cursor in row 9, position 5. Enter the following literals at the positions indicated. The first number is the row followed by the position. For example row 9, position 1 is shown as 9,1.

Position	Literal Value
9,5	Invoice #:
9,45	Invoice Date:
10,4	Customer #:
10,45	Phone Number:
11,1	Name:
12,1	Street:
13,1	City, ST, Zip
14,1	Country
15,1	Enter a line of dashes (–) across the screen.
21,1	Enter a line of dashes (–) across the screen.
22,40	Invoice Total:

You can now see the Invoice form with all literal values placed.

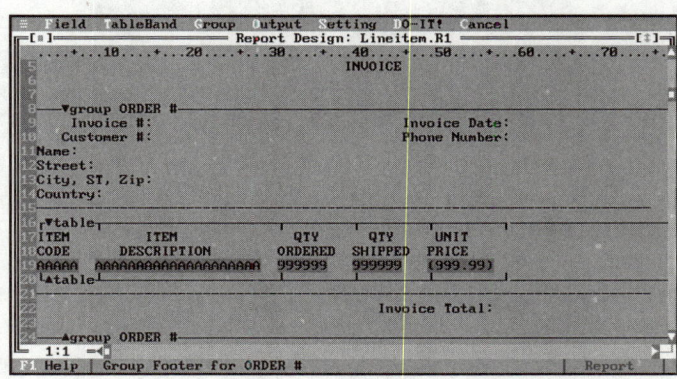

Using Groups

2. Move the cursor beside the literal, Invoice #:. Select the **F**ield **P**lace **R**egular option, select ORDER #, and press ⏎Enter twice.

3. Move the cursor beside Customer #: and place the Cust # field, using the menu selections in step 2. Remember, the Cust # field is a number field. You will have to press ⏎Enter a third time to accept the default of zero decimal places.

4. Move the cursor beside Invoice Date: and select the **F**ield **P**lace **R**egular option. From the Field list box select the [Orders->] option. From the next Field list box, select ORDER DATE, and then select date option **2**.

   The Order Date field is selected from the list of fields available from the lookup table, Orders.

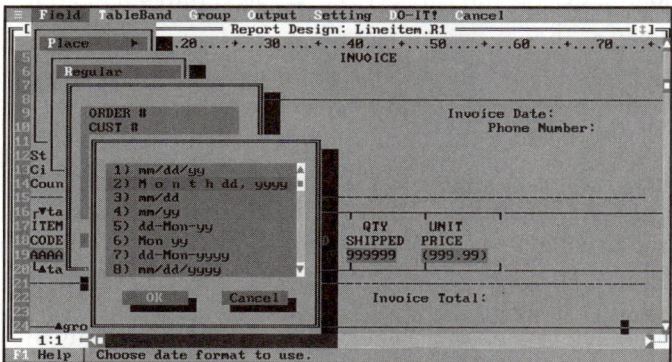

Here, you see the Date Format dialog box. Remember, you can select from 12 different date formats for a report.

5. Move the cursor beside the Phone Number field, select the **F**ield **P**lace **R**egular option, and move the cursor to the end of the Field list. Select [Cust1->]. Now you see the list of fields for the Cust1 lookup table. Select Phone Number and press ⏎Enter to place the field.

6. Move the cursor to Street: and place the Street field from the Cust1 lookup table as you did in step 5.

7. Move the cursor to Country: and place the Country field from the Cust1 lookup table.

349

Creating Tabular, Free-Form, and Multi-Table Reports

12

Here, you can see that all the regular fields have been placed in the report specification.

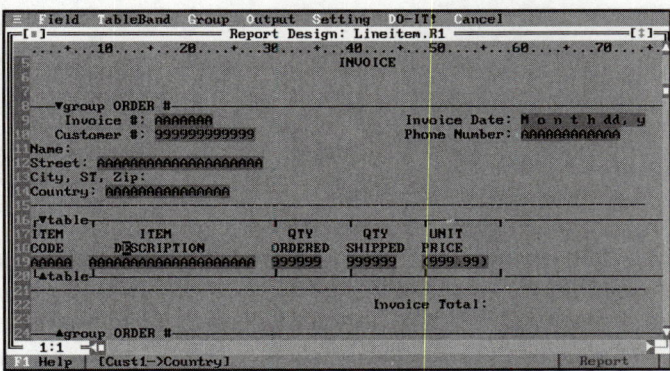

Notice that two of the fields—Name and City, ST, Zip—have not been filled in. You will do this in the next section.

Working with Calculated Fields

As you have already learned, Paradox is able to do a variety of calculations with either numbers or alphanumeric fields. You will remember from earlier chapters that a field name used in a calculation will be referred to as:

   [fieldname]

A field from a lookup table that is used in a calculation must refer not only to the field name but to the table as well. You would use a format like this:

   [tablename–>fieldname]

For the invoice report, you will use three calculated fields with regular fields. Two of these will be alphanumeric fields and the third will be an arithmetic calculation. The reason that you would want to use the alphanumeric fields in a calculation is primarily for aesthetics. You will be combining the fields Last Name and First Name together, and then City, State, and Zip/Postal Code. If an invoice with a customer name placed like the following does not bother you, you may not want to take the time to create the calculated field:

   MACK   MARTINI

Otherwise, do the following:

1. Move the cursor to row 11, position 10. Select **F**ield **P**lace **C**alculated from the menu.

Using Groups

2. Enter the following expression into the text box in the displayed dialog box:

   [CUST1->FIRST NAME]+" "+[CUST1->LAST NAME]

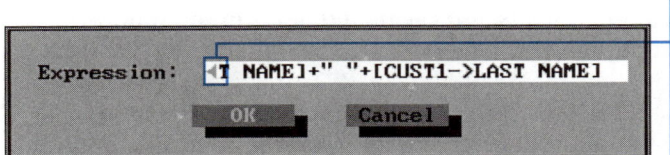

Here, you can see the expression you want to calculate in the dialog box. Notice that only a part of the calculation is shown. The left-facing arrow indicates that there is more.

3. Press ↵Enter three times, to accept the expression, to place the field in the current location, and, finally, to accept the default field size.
4. Move the cursor down two rows and to the left to position 16. Again, select **F**ield **P**lace **C**alculated from the menu.
5. Enter this expression:

   [CUST1->CITY]+", "+[CUST1->STATF]+" "+[CUST1->ZIP/POSTAL CODE]

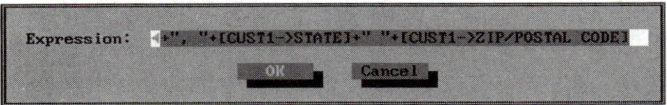

You can see the expression you entered into the dialog box.

Press ↵Enter three times.

6. Now you must add the calculated field that will display an extended cost for each line item. Move the cursor to row 17, at the beginning of the last table band. You must now add this table band to the report. Select **T**ableBand **I**nsert. Press ↵Enter once to place the new table band at the current cursor location.
7. Move the cursor to the right 3 spaces and type **EXTENDED**. Then move down one row and place the cursor under the X and type **PRICE**. Move the cursor down and to the beginning of the table band.

351

8. Select **F**ield **P**lace **C**alculated. Enter the following expression into the dialog box:

   [QTY ORDERED]*[RETAIL]

   Press ⏎Enter. Adjust the field mask display to read (9,999) and press ⏎Enter. Press ⏎Enter one final time to accept the default display of two decimal places.

You have placed all the regular fields and calculated fields in the report specification. Depending upon your own needs, you could change the last calculated field to multiply the QTY SHIPPED by RETAIL if you are charging a customer for items that are actually shipped. The example used in step 8 would generally be the format used for a prepaid order.

Using the Summary Operations

You will often need to place summary information for groups within a report. When using summary calculations with numeric fields, you can use any of the summary operators: sum, maximum, minimum, count, and average. You can use the summary operators maximum, minimum, count, and average with a date field. With alphanumeric fields, you can use the count, minimum, and maximum summary operators.

Generally, the usual place to put a summary field is in the group footer for the group on which the summary is based. Paradox does allow you to place the summary field anywhere in the report specification. A field being summarized does not have to appear in the report specification; it must be in the list of regular fields for the master or a lookup table.

When creating the summary fields, you have a choice of calculated or regular. A summary field based on a regular field is applied to the data contained in that field. For example, if you were creating an employee list which is grouped by department, you could place a regular summary field that counts the number of employees in the department. This is a **P**er Group summary. Using the same field, you could also use an **O**verall summary that would give you a count of all employees.

Using Group Summary Calculations

To create a summary field that displays an invoice total, you must use a calculated summary field.

Using Groups

In this section you will build several summary fields by doing the following:

1. Select **F**ield **P**lace **S**ummary **C**alculated from the menu.
2. Enter the following expression into the dialog box:
   SUM([QTY ORDERED] * [RETAIL], GROUP)

   Then press ⏎Enter. Move the cursor so that it is located to the right of the literal `Invoice Total:`, and press ⏎Enter again. Press ← until the field mask display reads `(99,999)` and press ⏎Enter. Press ⏎Enter a last time to accept the default setting of two decimal places.

   This summary field will total each invoice and display the total amount due.

3. Select **F**ield **P**lace **S**ummary **R**egular from the menu.

   You now see the Field list box displayed.

4. Choose the Qty Shipped field and press ⏎Enter. Choose the **S**um option and then the **P**er Group option from the displayed menu boxes. Move the cursor to row 22, position 23 and press ⏎Enter twice to place the field.

5. Move the cursor to position 1 of this row and type this description for the field: **Total Items Shipped:**.

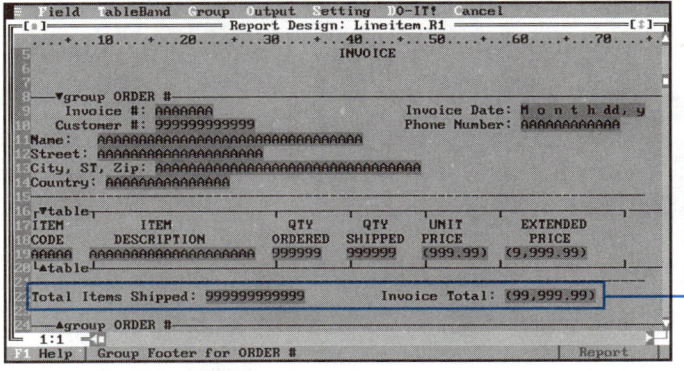

Here, you see the summary fields placed in the report specification.

If your state requires you to collect a sales tax, you can easily make a few minor adjustments to the report specification to include this information. For this example, a 5% tax is charged.

6. Move the cursor to position 1, row 22 and press Ins. Then press ⏎Enter twice. You should now have two blank lines inserted above `Total Items Shipped:`.

353

Creating Tabular, Free-Form, and Multi-Table Reports

7. Move back to row 22, and then right until the cursor is located above the I in `Invoice Total:`. Type **Sales Tax:**.
8. Select **F**ield **P**lace **S**ummary **C**alculated from the menu.
9. Enter the following expression into the dialog box:

   SUM([QTY ORDERED] * [RETAIL], GROUP) * .05

10. Press [Enter] to place the field, adjust the field mask to read (99,999), and press [Enter] twice to accept the field and two decimal places.
11. Move the cursor down one row and to the left until it is underneath the S in `Sales Tax:`. Type a dashed line (–) underneath this field.
12. You now need to edit the Invoice Total calculation because it does not include the amount of the sales tax. Remember, the calculated expression only sums the total of Qty Ordered multiplied by Retail price. The tax calculation needs to be included in the Invoice Total calculation. Select **F**ield **C**alcEdit, place the cursor on the field mask you want to edit, and press [Enter].

You now see the CalcEdit dialog box. The expression selected is displayed in the text box.

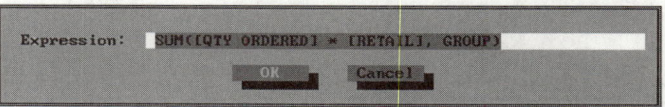

When the expression is first displayed, you will notice that it is highlighted. Pressing some keys, such as the **space bar**, will delete the expression from the text box. If you accidentally delete the expression, press [Esc] and then [Enter]. This step moves you back one step and then forward again with the formula again displayed.

13. Press [←] or [→], or [Ins] to remove the highlight. Then enter the necessary change to the calculation; type ***1.05**.

Here, you can see the completed expression.

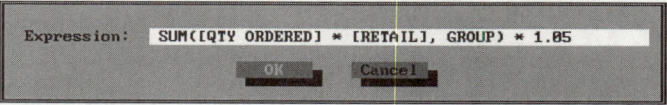

14. Press [Enter]. You see the message `New expression recorded` in the message box.

Using Groups

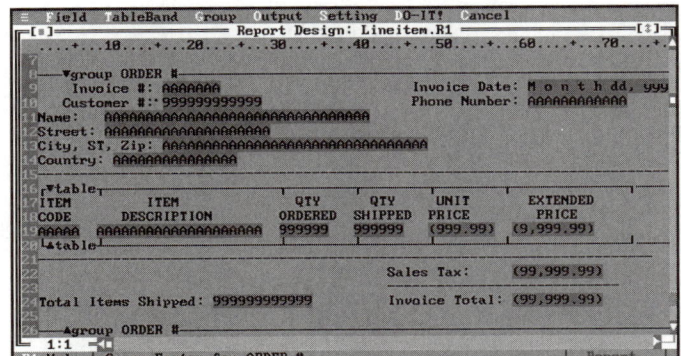

Now you can see the invoice complete with each field.

These summary calculations entered into the report specification are all based on the Order # group.

Using Overall Summary Calculations

You can also create calculations that are based on the entire report. To build an overall summary calculation, do the following:

1. Move the cursor down until it is below the page footer line. This position should be row 32. Press [Ins] and insert 5 blank rows.
2. Now type the following literals, or titles:

Position	Title
32,25	Batch Summary Statistics
33	Dashed line (–) across form
34,1	No. of Invoices:
34,40	Total Sales:
35,1	No. of Items Ordered:
35,40	Total Sales Tax:
36,1	No. of Items Shipped:
36,40	Total Receipts:

355

Creating Tabular, Free-Form, and Multi-Table Reports

12

Your screen should now look like this.

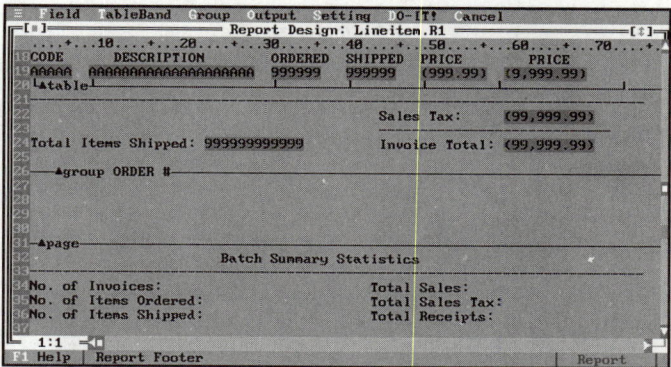

3. Select the **F**ield **P**lace **S**ummary **R**egular option and choose the Order # field. Select **C**ount **O**verall, place the field beside No. of Invoices:, and press ⏎Enter three times.

4. Select the **F**ield **P**lace **S**ummary **R**egular option and choose the Qty Ordered field. Select **S**um **O**verall, place the field beside No. of Items Ordered:, and press ⏎Enter three times.

5. Select the **F**ield **P**lace **S**ummary **R**egular option and choose the Qty Shipped field. Select **S**um **O**verall, place the field beside No. of Items Shipped:, and press ⏎Enter three times.

6. Select the **F**ield **P**lace **S**ummary **C**alculated option and enter the following expression:

   SUM([QTY ORDERED] * [RETAIL])

   Press ⏎Enter once to accept the expression, place the field beside Total Sales:, adjust the field mask to display (999,999), and press ⏎Enter twice.

   You will notice that in a calculated summary expression, you do not specify that the calculation is an overall calculation. Paradox uses **O**verall as the default setting. You must specify if a group summary is to be performed, or else Paradox will base a summary on the overall report.

7. Select the **F**ield **P**lace **S**ummary **C**alculated option and enter the following expression:

   SUM([QTY ORDERED] * [RETAIL]) * .05

   Press ⏎Enter once to accept the expression, place the field beside Total Sales Tax:, adjust the field mask to display (999,999), and press ⏎Enter twice.

Using Groups

8. Select the **F**ield **P**lace **S**ummary **C**alculated option and enter the following expression:

   SUM([QTY ORDERED] * [RETAIL]) * 1.05

   Press ⏎Enter once to accept the expression, place the field beside Total Sales Tax:, adjust the field mask to display (999,999), and press ⏎Enter twice.

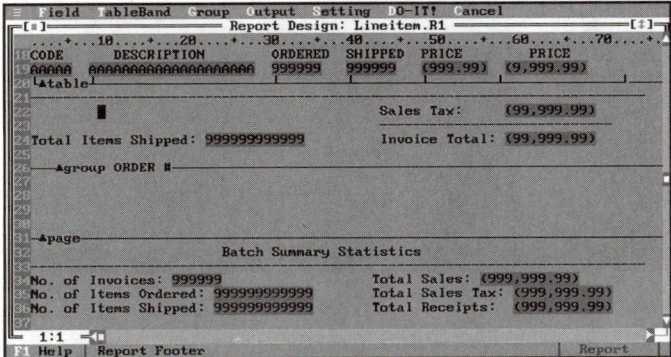

Here, you can see the Batch Summary Statistics completed in the report footer.

Summary statistics enhance the overall picture of your report and are very useful, especially in long reports. The Batch Summary Statistics at the end of a group of invoices can tell you at a glance how many items you sold, the number of invoices shipped, the shipping charges if any, and the total sales.

Augmenting the Report

Paradox offers some final options you may want to use: how to place forced page breaks and where to print group and table band titles.

Using the Report Previewer

At this point, you may want to see how your report looks with real data in place of field masks. When you preview your report, you can see what adjustments you may need to make. To preview your report, do the following:

1. Select **O**utput **S**creen to view the report in the Report Preview window.

Creating Tabular, Free-Form, and Multi-Table Reports

12

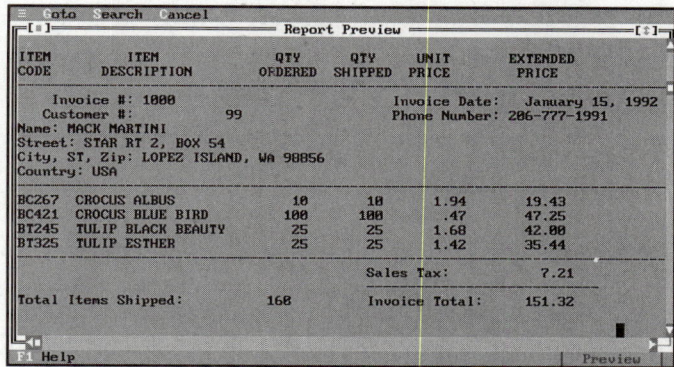

Here, you see how the invoice will look when printed.

2. Use ↓ or PgDn to display the remaining invoices in this report.

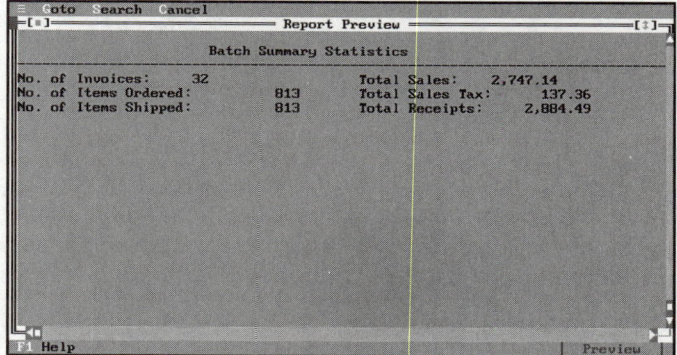

Here, you see the end of the report showing the Batch Statistics.

Adjusting the Report Specification

You may have noticed that several things are still not right with the form. Using the Report Preview window is the best place to catch them. These are the items you need to adjust:

- The page breaks do not fall between invoices. Some invoices run over and are displayed over two pages.
- The table band field titles only display once for each page, and are shown above the customer information.
- The customer information needs better field alignment.
- The Batch Summary needs better field alignment.

Using Groups

To make these final adjustments to the report specification, do the following:

1. Select **C**ancel **Y**es from the Report Previewer menu. You are returned to the Report Designer window.

2. To place a forced page break, move the cursor to the position required. In this case, you want each invoice to appear as a separate page. Move the cursor to line 25, position 1.

3. The page break command *must* be placed in position 1 or else Paradox interprets it as a literal. Type **PAGEBREAK** (one word, not two).

   If you wanted the page to break above the total line, you would place the Pagebreak command at line 21. For this example, you want each group to print on a single page. If you were using multiple groups, you would select an intermediate group to use for the break place or places.

4. Select **S**ettings **F**ormat **G**roupsOfTables. You see the message `Settings changed` displayed.

   As already discussed, this setting forces the table field titles to print above the table fields.

5. To better align the customer field information, you can add space between the literal titles and the field masks so that the field masks are all aligned, or you can add space before the literal titles and push the lines so that the field masks are aligned. The choice is a matter of individual preference.

   Place the cursor just in front of the field mask for name and press [Ins]. Press the **space bar** until the field mask is aligned with the Cust # field above. Now do the same to the Street and Country fields.

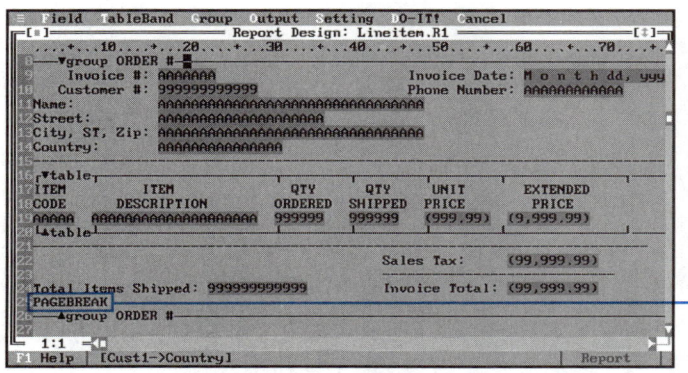

You now see the customer information fields realigned, and the Pagebreak command inserted.

359

Creating Tabular, Free-Form, and Multi-Table Reports

When moving fields in this manner, you must be cautious on lines that have either literals or fields further to the right of the field you are moving. As you move a field, Paradox moves the entire line, not just the field.

6. Move down to the report footer and adjust the field mask for `No. of Invoices:`.

   Notice that the next field and literal on the same line, `Total Sales:`, has moved also.

7. Move the cursor over and use either [Del] or [Backspace] to move the title `Total Sales:` back to its original position. Then move over to the field mask and press the *space bar* until the field mask is aligned with the two others below it.

Your report specification should now look like this.

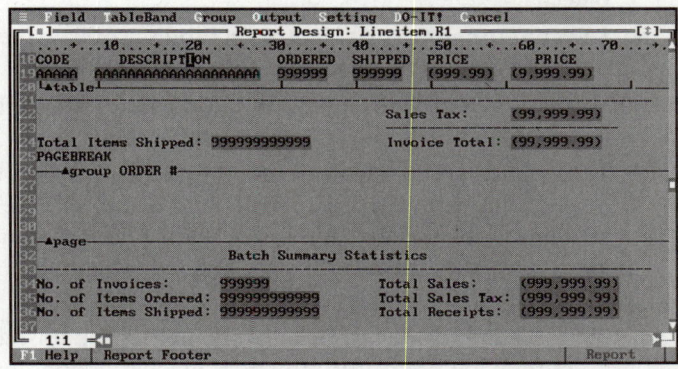

8. Recheck the report specification with the Report Previewer again. Select **O**utput **S**creen.

Here, you see page 1 of the report—invoice #1000 again.

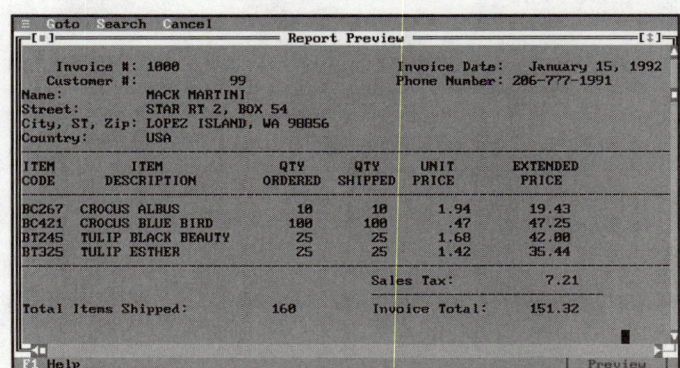

360

Using Groups

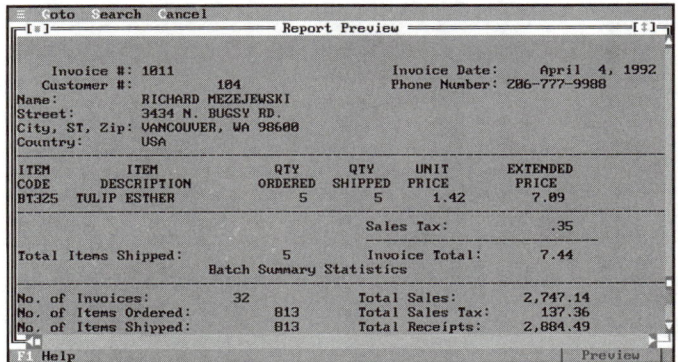

Here, you see the end of the report.

At this point, the only changes you need to make are the following:

- A dashed line between the table band field titles and the fields to separate them.
- Report Footer summaries should appear on their own separate pages.
- The company name and address should appear on the page header.

9. Return to the Report Designer window and move the cursor to row 19, position 1, and press ⏎Enter. A blank line opens up. If not, remember to press Ins and try again.

10. Type a dashed line (–) across the report specification. You will notice that as you move the dashed line across the table band, the line stops and Paradox beeps at you at the beginning of the next table band. You must stop and press → once and then continue. Paradox does not allow you to type a literal across the table band boundary.

11. Move to row 33 and press ⏎Enter to insert a blank row. Type **PAGEBREAK** to create a page break before the Batch Summary Statistics page.

12. Move the cursor to row 7, position 1 and type:

    Marissa's Plantasy, Rt. 1, Box 39

    Phone: 503-555-2999

    Forest Grove, OR 97036

361

Creating Tabular, Free-Form, and Multi-Table Reports

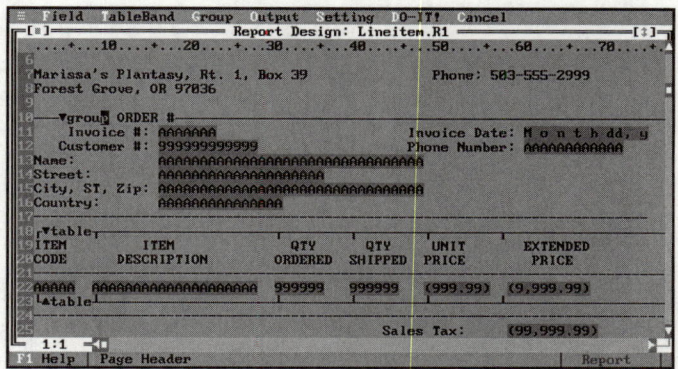

Here, you see the final view of the report specification.

Now that the report specification meets your requirements, you can save the specification and use it.

Printing the Report

As discussed in Chapter 8, you can print the report as needed. To print a copy of this report, select the Report Output Print option, and then select the table and report. To print only a selected group of pages, use the Report RangeOutput option.

If you use this invoice report to print invoices from the same Lineitem table, purge or delete your records periodically. As you add new records, Paradox creates a report that includes all the records, even if you have printed them before.

One easy way around this problem is to create a second table that is identical to the Lineitem table and copy the report specification to it. Use this table as the original entry table, printing the invoices from it, and then use the Tools More Add option to add the printed records into the permanent Lineitem table. When you get to Chapter 14, on using scripts, you will learn to automate this process.

Selecting a Printer

By default, Paradox assumes that your printer is connected to the first parallel printer port, LPT1. If you have your printer connected to a different port, are using a serial port, or have more than one printer, you will then need to use

Printing the Report

the Custom Configuration Program (CCP). To change the printer settings, do the following:

1. Select the **S**etting **S**etup **C**ustom option.

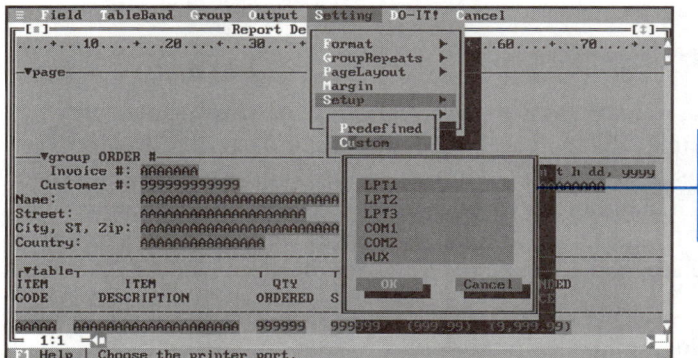

Here, you see the menu box with the printer port options.

2. Select the printer port for this report. This option will be saved with this report specification.

    If you need to change this setting permanently, use the System menu (≡) and the **U**tilities **C**ustom **R**eports **P**rinter Setup option.

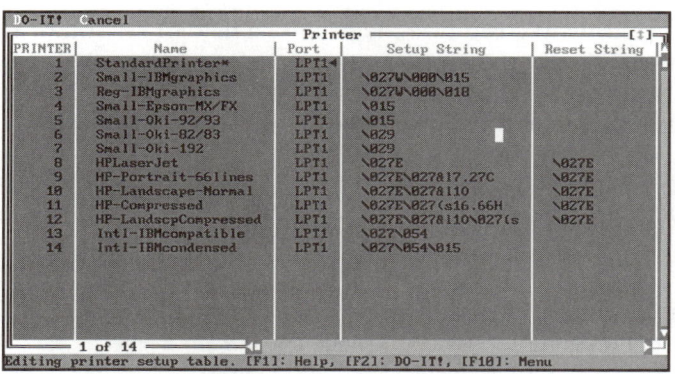

Here, you can see the Printer Customization table.

This table lists the predefined printer selections. When you make this selection, you are in the Edit mode. The default printer has a star, or asterisk (*), displayed beside its name. The printer port is listed in the next column; the default is LPT1. Remember, changes made with the CCP are permanent.

363

Creating Tabular, Free-Form, and Multi-Table Reports

3. If your printer requires a setup string, enter it in the dialog box now displayed. If you do not want to enter a setup string, press [←Enter]. Press [←Enter] a second time or enter the reset string if required for your printer. You now see the message Setup information recorded.

Using Setup Strings

Printer setup strings are used to control the output from your printer. By default, Paradox assumes that you are printing to a standard IBM graphics compatible printer using normal sized letters and print quality. A normal page is 8 1/2 inches by 11 inches, and is 60 lines of type with a form feed control at the end of the page. To use an expanded or compressed font for this report specification, or to change the number of lines per inch, etc., you would do the following:

1. Select the **S**etting **S**etup **C**ustom option.
2. Choose the printer port to which your printer is connected.
3. Enter the setup string for the font or the other change you need. Press [←Enter].
4. Enter the reset string to return the printer settings to normal, and press [←Enter].

Again, settings changed in this manner are saved with the report specification.

You can also use a setup string to customize the print of a field or section of a report. For example, you can have the report header print in a large type, with the remaining part of the report printing in normal type. To do this technique, place the setup and reset strings as a calculated field. Try this by doing the following:

1. Move the cursor to row 5, position 30, select **F**ield **P**lace **C**alculated, and enter the following expression in the dialog box:

    \014 \027E

    This step sets an Epson FX, MX, or RX printer to an expanded font in emphasized mode. Press [←Enter] twice to place the field.

2. Move the cursor until it is beside the E in the title, INVOICE, select **F**ield **P**lace **C**alculated, and enter the following expression in the dialog box:

    \020 \027F

    This step resets the printer to normal text. Press [←Enter] twice to place the field.

Printing the Report

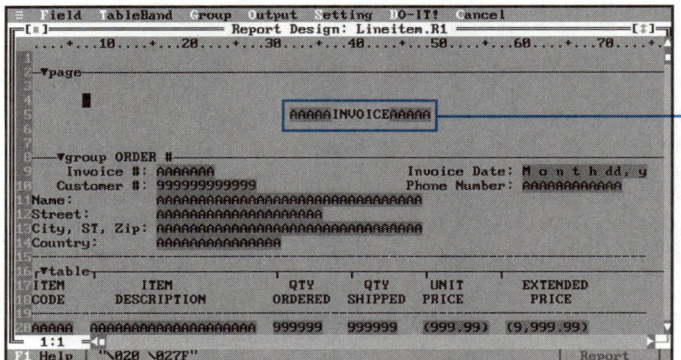

Here, you can see the two field masks for the printer strings on either side of INVOICE.

3. Select **F2** or **D**O-IT! to save the report specification.
4. Select the **R**eport **R**angeOutput **L**ineitem report **1**-INVOICE **P**rinter option. Choose a beginning page of **12** and an ending page of **13**, and press ⏎Enter.

Here, you see the first page of the output of the Invoice report specification.

Here, you see the second page of the output.

365

Temporary Printer Overrides

You can temporarily override the printer setups by using the **R**eport **S**etPrinter **O**verride option from the Main menu. Use this option to make a temporary change, such as sending the report to a printer connected to a different printer port.

You can also use this option to change a setup or reset string. To reverse the changes made by **O**verride, use the option **R**egular. You will see the message `Printer overrides deleted`. If you do not remove a printer override setting, it will be deleted automatically when you exit the program.

Creating Free-Form Reports

The second Paradox report type is the free-form report. While a tabular report specification is more similar to the table format, the free-form report specification is more like the form format. With the free-form format, you are not restricted to a table band and its columns. You can place fields in any position you want.

A free-form report specification is flexible enough to be used for many tasks, such as:

- Preprinted forms, checks, invoices, purchase orders, etc.
- Form letters
- Mailing labels

With the free-form report specification, you can automatically have Paradox delete unnecessary spaces and lines from fields.

Designing a Free-Form Report

When using the free-form Report Designer, you create the report specification in much the same way as the tabular report. In this section, you will design a form letter to your customers about their orders. Do the following:

1. Select the **R**eport **D**esign **ORDERS 1**-Unused Report option. Use the report description **O**rder **L**etter, and select **F**ree-form.

Creating Free-Form Reports

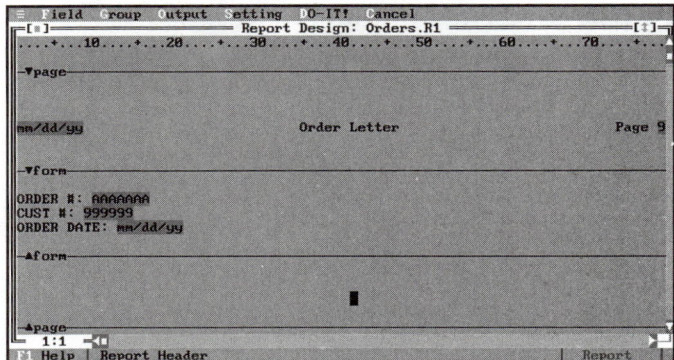

Here, you see the default free-form report specification.

2. Delete all fields and literals from both the Page Header and Form area of the report specification. The fastest way is to use Ctrl-Y. You can insert new lines again as needed.

3. Enter the following in the Page Header area, starting on row 4.

   Marissa's Plantasy

   Route 1, Box 39

   Forest Grove, OR 97036

4. Move the cursor to row 3, position 50, select the **F**ield **P**lace **D**ate option, and select date format **2**. Press Enter.

   You now need to link the Orders table with the Cust1 table.

5. Select the **F**ield **L**ookup **L**ink **Cust1** option and select the Cust# field as the linking field.

6. Move the cursor to the top line in the form band of the report specification, position 1, and type **Dear**.

7. Move the cursor one space to the right of the literal, Dear, select **F**ield **P**lace **R**egular, and select [Cust1->]. Then choose First Name from the next Field list displayed and press Enter twice.

8. Move the cursor to the right one space, select **F**ield **P**lace **R**egular, and select [Cust1->]. Then choose Last Name and again, press Enter twice.

9. Move the cursor down two lines and back to position 1 and type:

   Thank you for your order. It was received and processed on

10. Select **F**ield **P**lace **R**egular, ORDER DATE, and then choose date format **1**.

11. Continue the text of the letter:

367

Creating Tabular, Free-Form, and Multi-Table Reports

. You should expect to receive it within two weeks.

If you have any questions regarding your purchase, please do not hesitate to call. We are happy to answer any of your plant and landscaping questions.

Sincerely,

Marissa

You now have a basic form letter you can use as an acknowledgment of a customer's order. To create any form letter, follow this procedure.

Grouping Records

You can group free-form reports just as you can group tabular report specifications. The process is the same. To group your form letter by customer, do the following:

1. Select **G**roup **I**nsert **F**ield Order #. Move the cursor to row 7, above the form line and press [⏎Enter].

   This step groups the letters by the Order # and makes filing the letters with the invoices easier. It also places a blank line between the company address and the customer address.

2. Now place the cursor on the top line of the form band and add four blank lines.

3. Move the cursor back to row 9, and add the following fields in the positions indicated:

Position	Field
9,1	[Cust1->]First Name
9,17	[Cust1->]Last Name
10,1	[Cust1->]Street
11,1	[Cust1->]City
11,18	[Cust1->]State
11,21	[Cust1->]Zip/Postal Code

Place a comma between the City and State fields.

Creating Free-Form Reports

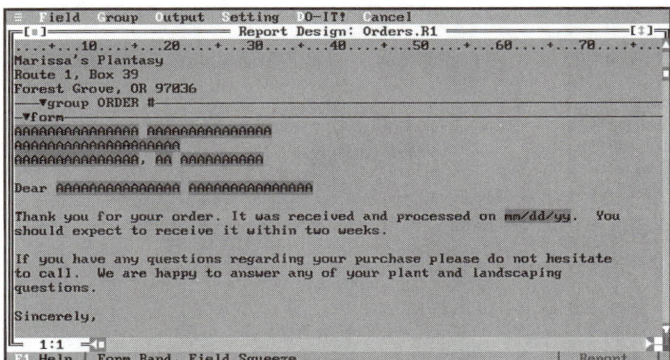

Your report specification should now look like this.

4. Use the **O**utput **S**creen option to preview the report.

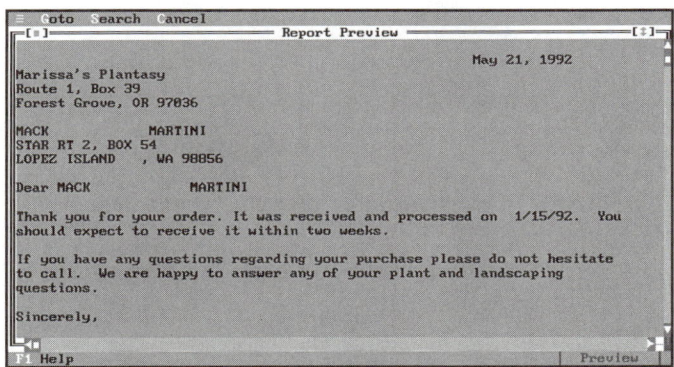

Here, you see the report. While close, the spacing between fields is not quite right.

5. Select the **S**etting **R**emoveBlanks **F**ieldSqueeze **Y**es option.

You now see the message Settings changed. This setting tells Paradox to remove all blank spaces between fields. This setting makes fields such as First Name and Last Name appear in a typed format. Use this option instead of the alphanumeric calculated field like you did in the tabular report specification.

The Squeeze options are available only with fields that are contained within the form band. If you include fields in a group band, they will not be squeezed. You would need to use the alphanumeric calculated field.

Creating Tabular, Free-Form, and Multi-Table Reports

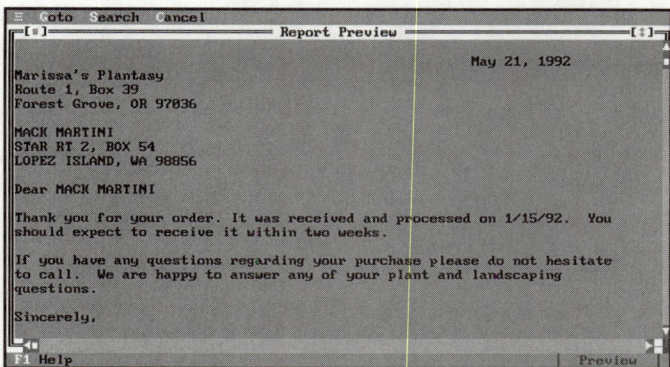

Here, you see the completed letter.

6. Select F2 or **DO-IT!** to save the report specification.

Designing a Mailing Label

You can also use the Paradox free-form report specification to print mailing labels. To create a report specification for continuous mailing labels, do the following:

1. Select **R**eport **D**esign **Cust1 3**-Unused Report. Use the report description **Mailing Labels**, and select **F**ree-form.
2. Delete all fields and literals from both the Page Header and Form area of the report specification. Again, use Ctrl-Y. You can insert new lines again as needed.

    Mailing labels do not require report headers and footers, so delete all the lines contained there.
3. Enter the following in the Form area, starting on row 4. Select **F**ield **P**lace **R**egular and place the following fields on the rows listed. For fields placed on the same row, put a blank space between each one.

Creating Free-Form Reports

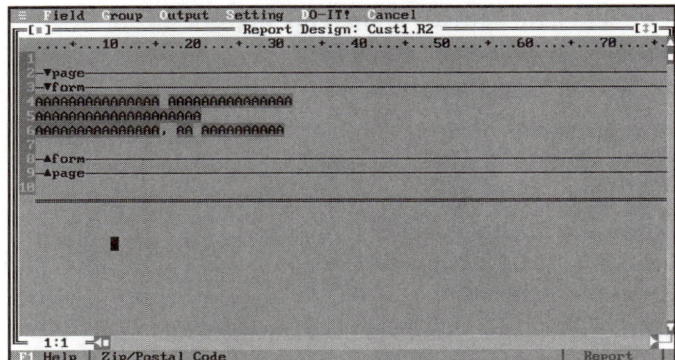

You should now have a report specification that looks like this.

Row	Field
4	First Name
4	Last Name
5	Street
6	City
6	State
6	Zip/Postal Code

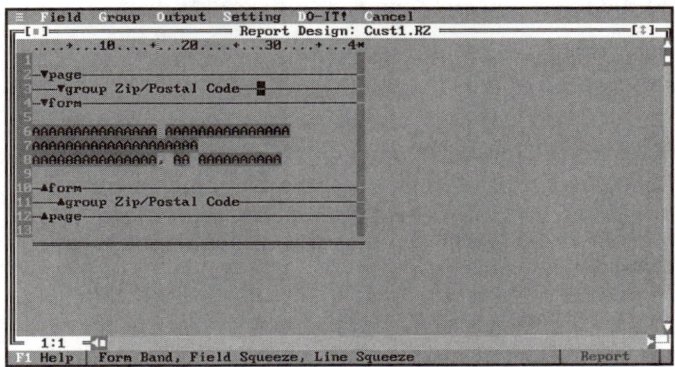

You now see the completed report specification for one-across continuous mailing labels.

371

Creating Tabular, Free-Form, and Multi-Table Reports

4. Select **G**roup **I**nsert **F**ield `Zip/Postal Code`. This step sorts your labels by the Zip/Postal Code for mass mailings.
5. Remove the extra lines the group band inserted.
6. Select **S**ettings **R**emoveBlanks and select both options, **L**inesqueeze **Y**es **V**ariable and **F**ieldsqueeze **Y**es.
7. Depending upon the labels you are using, you may need to adjust your page size. A common mailing label is 15/16 inches by 3 1/2 inches and accommodates 6 lines. Add a blank line inside of the form band: one at the top and one at the bottom.
8. Adjust the page width by selecting **S**ettings **P**ageLayout **W**idth 40.
9. The last setting you must now choose is **S**etting **L**abels **Y**es. This step sets the printer for continuous labels.
10. If you are creating labels you want to print across a sheet, such as laser printer labels, add the appropriate number of page widths to the report specification. Select **S**etting **P**ageLayout **I**nsert until the page indicator in the bottom left of the window indicates the correct number of pagewidths available.

Summary

In this chapter, you learned how to use the Paradox tabular reports to create a multi-table report. You then learned to use calculated fields and summary fields. Then you learned to design a free-form report specification and to create a mailing label.

Specifically, you learned the following key points about Paradox 4:

- To choose the master table used in the report specification, select the table that will have all its records printed, and that you can link to all lookup tables.
- To link a lookup table to the master table, you must have a direct linking field from the lookup table to the master table, and the field must be keyed. Use the **F**ield **L**ookup option and choose the field in the master table to link to the key field in the lookup table.
- To unlink a lookup table, select **F**ield **L**ookup **U**nlink. When you use this option, you will delete any fields from the lookup table.
- To change the linking field in the master table, use the **F**ield **L**ookup **R**elink option.

Summary

- To group records within the final report, use group bands by selecting the **G**roup **I**nsert option. Select **F**ield to group a selected field, **R**ange to group a specified range of records, or **N**umberRecords to group a certain number of records in a group.
- To delete lines from the report specification, place the cursor at the far left-hand side of the report and press `Ctrl`-`Y`. Any literals or fields in the line will be deleted.
- To place a field from either the master or lookup table into the report specification, select **F**ield **P**lace **R**egular, and then choose the field name. Place the field where required and press `↵Enter`.
- To use calculated fields, select **F**ield **P**lace **C**alculated. Enter the expression you want to calculate in the dialog box.
- To use summary calculations, select **F**ield **P**lace **S**ummary. Choose between **R**egular or **C**alculated. Regular summary summarizes data about a regular field. A calculated summary summarizes information about a calculated field.
- To summarize information about a group, you must use the Per Group operator in the expression, such as SUM([QTY ORDERED] * [RETAIL], GROUP).
- To edit a calculated expression, select **F**ield **C**alcEdit, and then choose the calculation you want to edit.
- To insert a page break between groups or at any required point, place the Pagebreak command at the far left side of the report specification. Paradox will then insert a page break at this point.
- To temporarily reset the printer options, use the **R**eport **S**etprinter **O**verride option, and then select the necessary changes.
- To remove blank spaces, select **S**etting **R**emoveBlanks **F**ieldsqueeze. To delete blank lines in the printed report, select **S**etting **R**emoveBlanks **L**inesqueeze. Selecting the **F**ixed option moves all blank lines to the bottom of a page, while the **V**ariable option just removes the lines.
- To print labels, select the **S**etting **L**abels to tell Paradox to print continuous labels.
- To print several labels across a page, add the necessary page widths to the report specification. Remember to adjust the page width to the actual label width.

In the next chapter, you will learn to present your data visually using graphs. You will also learn to use Paradox's powerful capacity to annotate your graphs.

13

Representing Data with Graphs

You have now learned to create tables, enter data, use forms, create a printed report, and query your tables for specific types of information. In this chapter you will learn how to prepare the potentially easiest-to-understand summary of your data, the graph.

Paradox contains a fully integrated set of graphing tools you can use to display your data visually. As you learn to use the Paradox graphing features, you will find them an indispensable and a powerful way to present data. You can create a report with all your information and your summaries, and you can use a graph to emphasize the highlights of your presentation.

An overview of Paradox graphs

Designing graphs

Modifying graphs

Choosing output and saving

13 Representing Data with Graphs

> **Key Terms in This Chapter**
>
> *Series*
> A set of data displayed on a graph. Each series is a separate field of data.
>
> *X- and y-axes*
> The horizontal and vertical sides of a graph. The x-axis is always the horizontal side, while the y-axis is always the vertical side.
>
> *Transformation*
> A group of rules Paradox uses when converting a table into a graph.
>
> *Crosstab*
> A table created by converting, or summarizing, a single column of data in terms of two other fields. Used to extract multiple values in one table for graphing.

An Overview of Paradox Graphs

Using Paradox's graphics capabilities, you can display your data, highlighting different aspects with different graph selections. As with reports and forms, Paradox can create an instant graph from a table when you press Ctrl-F7. Paradox has a wide array of graphing tools you can use to customize a graph to your needs.

Elements of a Graph

You should be familiar with several elements that are applicable to almost all graphs. Knowing these elements and their locations on a graph will enable you to understand this chapter more fully.

An Overview of Paradox Graphs

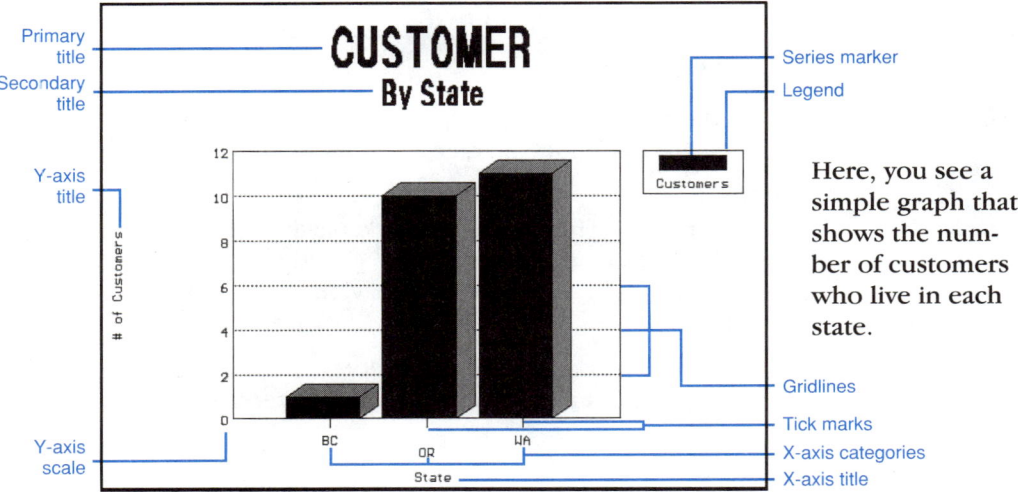

Here, you see a simple graph that shows the number of customers who live in each state.

The following are the basic elements that make up each graph. You can customize and adjust each element to suit the needs of your data.

Table 13.1
Graph Elements

Element	Description
Primary title	Unless you override, Paradox will use the table name as the primary title for a graph.
Secondary title	Title you enter to further designate the graph.
X- and y-title	Titles explaining the meaning of either the x- or y-axis.
X-axis categories	Field names associated with the x-axis. The x-axis can be either numbers or alphanumeric fields, except when using an X-Y graph.
Y-axis scale	Displays the scaling used for the y-axis. This could be $ dollars or 1000's of dollars, or percentages. The y-axis always displays some type of numeric value.
Tick marks	A short line, usually displayed on the x-axis, to help distinguish a graph marker with its title.

continues

377

Representing Data with Graphs

Table 13.1 Continued

Element	Description
Gridlines	A dashed line across the graph on the y-axis to help visually determine marker locations across the graph.
Legend	A box displaying the series markers with their associated names. Used to help you identify the meaning of a marker without having to refer to the data.
Series marker	A special marker—line type, colored, or shading—designating a particular series on the graph.

Paradox Graph Types

Paradox can create ten different basic graph types. You can also use four override types if you want to combine graph types. With this option, you can emphasize a particular point in your data, by using a different graph type for one series of data.

Depending upon the data you are graphing, you will need to choose one of the various graph types.

Bar graphs are the most common graph seen in business presentations. Each series of data is displayed side-by-side. A bar graph can show several series of values compared to the different x values.

An Overview of Paradox Graphs

13

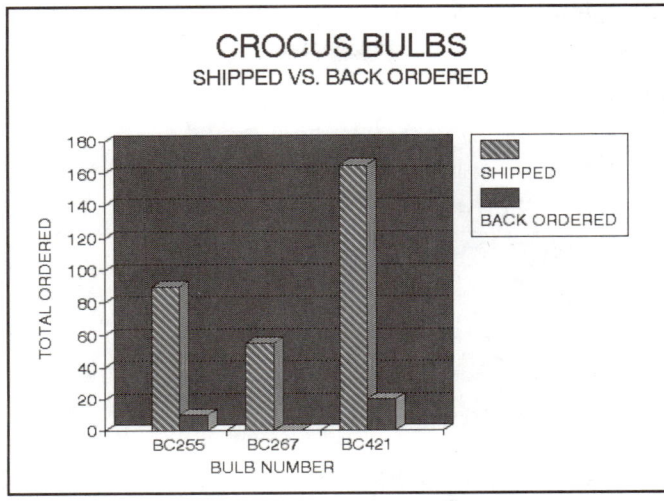

This bar graph displays shipped and back-ordered products.

In 3-D bar graphs, you can display the same information you can display in bar graphs. The 3-D graph adds an illusion of depth to the series bar.

Stacked bar graphs display each series of data, one on top of the other. A bar graph easily displays how one series relates to the whole, compared to an individual x value.

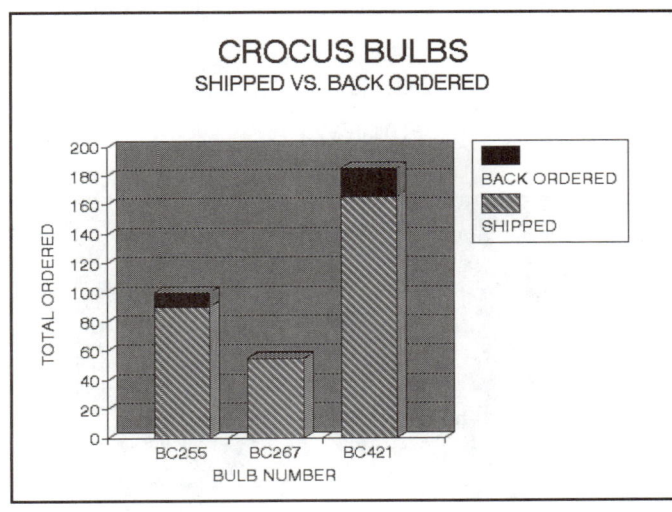

By using a stacked bar graph, you can see the relative proportion of fully and partially shipped orders.

379

Representing Data with Graphs

An alternative to the bar graph is the rotated bar graph. The same information is displayed with the bars going across the graph instead of up.

Here, you see a rotated bar graph showing shipped vs back-ordered product.

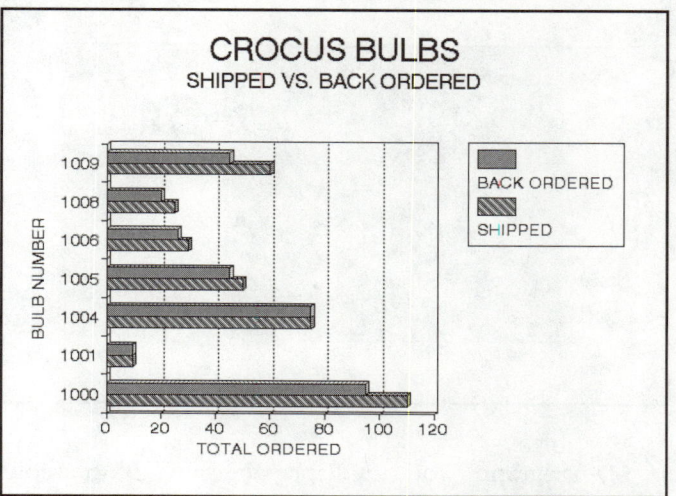

Line graphs are often used to show trends over time. All the points in the series are connected by a single continuous line. You can display up to six different series and lines in a single graph. A line graph is not suited for several series that are not well differentiated. You can end up with a jumbled mass of lines.

Here is a simple line graph.

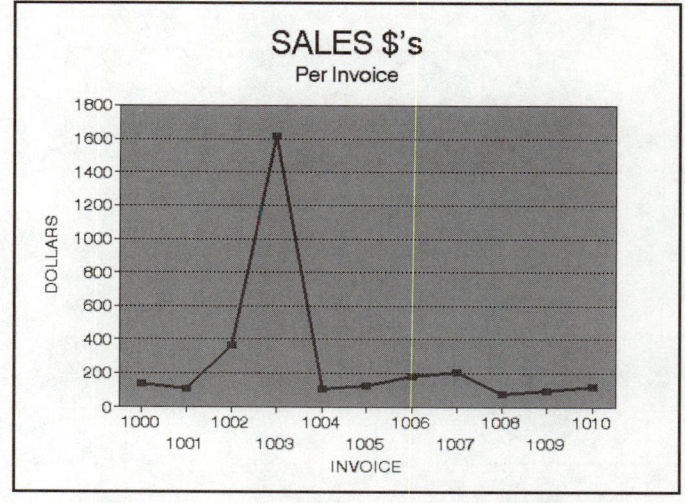

An Overview of Paradox Graphs

Markers only is a variation of the line and marker combination. Only markers are displayed as points on the graph. The combination of line and markers can make a several series line graph much easier to distinguish.

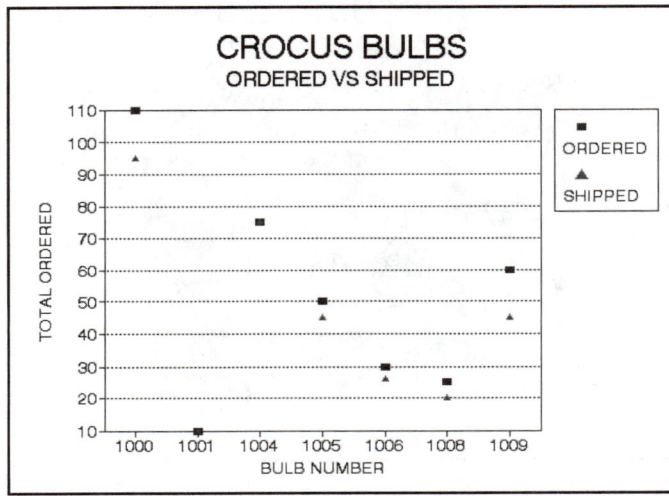

Here, you see a marker graph showing ordered product vs shipped product.

Pie graphs can display up to nine series. Each slice of a pie represents a piece, usually a relative percentage of the whole. You can also selectively cause a slice of a pie to explode outward to emphasize this part.

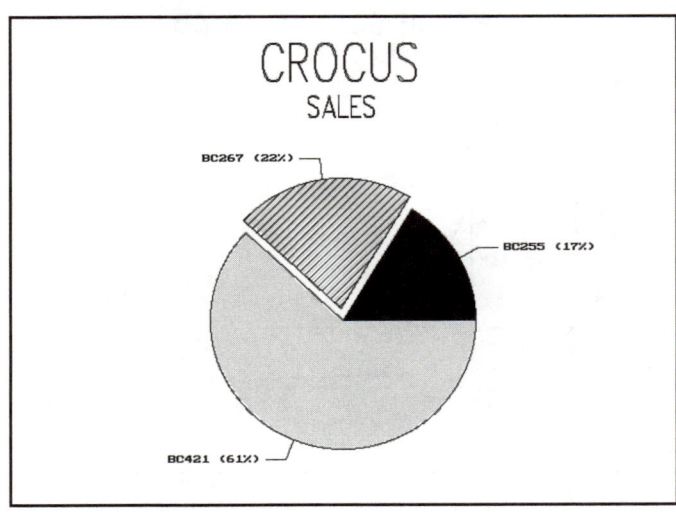

Here, you see a pie graph that shows relative sales of different products. One slice is exploded to highlight the data.

Representing Data with Graphs

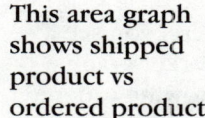

Area graphs, like stacked bar graphs, show cumulative totals and show trends like a line graph.

This area graph shows shipped product vs ordered product.

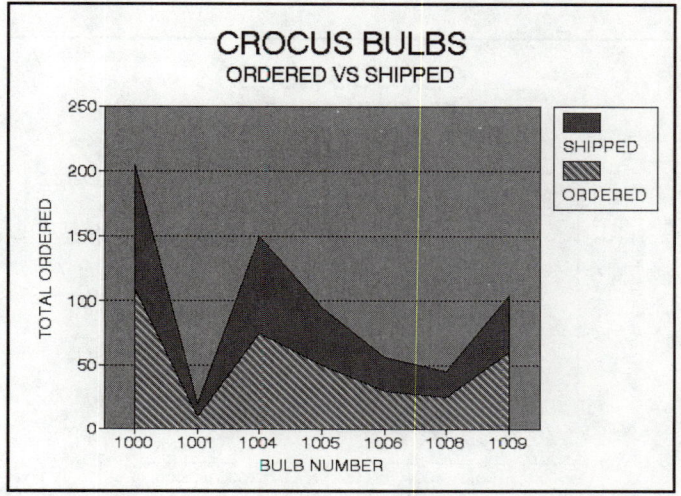

X-Y graphs are often used to display price and quantity. You can use these graphs only to compare one number series with another number series. You can use dates with the X-Y graphs.

This X-Y graph shows how most customers are price sensitive. As the price of the item goes up, fewer items are ordered.

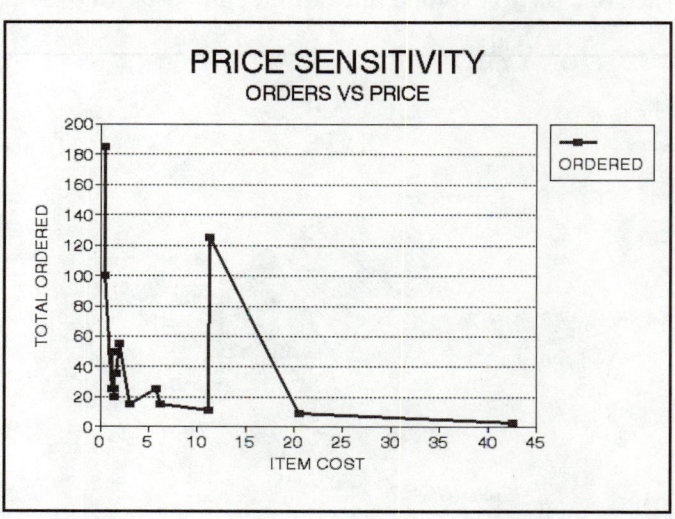

Generally, you will display a single graph type when presenting data. Paradox does enable you to select an override graph type for a selected series. You can use a line or bar graph with markers or combined line markers for an override graph type. Be selective in your use of the combined graph type.

When creating your own graph, experiment with the different graph types to determine the one that presents your data in the most effective way.

Designing Graphs

Paradox builds graphs from tables. Before you can begin to create a graph, you must first understand how Paradox converts tables into graphs.

Generally, you will find that you did not set up your tables with creating a graph in mind. To pull the required data into the necessary order for a graph, you need a good understanding of QBE. Often you can best build a graph from the information gathered into the Answer table. A graph specification is a Paradox object but not a member of a specific table's family. You can use a graph specification with any table, so long as the needed information is contained in the table. The action of converting table data into a graph is called a *transformation*.

Working with Transformations

Before Paradox can create a graph from the information from your table, you must first determine that your data is ready to be transformed. The following are general guidelines regarding transformations:

- All *series* must be a column of numeric data in the table. For pie graphs, the data can be no more than nine rows. For other graphs, you can use a maximum of six columns for series data.
- The x-axis must also be located in a column. The x-axis, used only for labels, can contain either numeric or alphanumeric data, except in the X-Y graph.
- Paradox uses only the current table image for the basis of a graph. Therefore, you must provide all the necessary information in a single table. Because Paradox can display only a maximum of six series of data, a table with a maximum of seven columns—six series and one x-axis—is required.

Representing Data with Graphs

For the x-axis data, Paradox makes the following assumptions:

- With keyed tables, Paradox uses the last, or rightmost, key field for the x-axis values. Because this is the last field used for tie breakers, it should be a good indication of the value contained in the record.
- With unkeyed tables, Paradox uses the first, or leftmost, nonnumeric field for the x-axis values.
- For each of the x-axis values, Paradox displays a tick mark and a label. The series values are grouped for each x-axis value.

Paradox makes the following assumptions about the series values:

- The column that currently contains the cursor becomes the first data series. Every value in that column is used in the graph.
- All series fields must be numeric. Paradox uses the next five numeric columns as additional series.
- Paradox uses the field names of each series as the legend labels to correspond to the series marker.
- By default, Paradox assigns the name `Totals` to the y-axis as the title. Paradox uses the table name as the graph's main title.

Using the Default Graph

Just as Paradox provided you with a standard report and form specification, Paradox also has an instant graph specification. When you press `Ctrl`-`F7`, Paradox creates a graph using the default graph specification and the current table displayed on the desktop.

The graph specification, unlike the report and form specifications, is not a simple format you can view on-screen. The graph specification is a group of many settings that Paradox uses to create the default graph. Modifying these settings is discussed in the section "Modifying the Graph" later in this chapter.

To be able to quickly create a graph, you must keep the number of columns and series to a minimum, and restrict the number of x-axis values to be graphed. Paradox will try to graph all the x-axis values in a table. To create an instant graph, do the following:

1. Build a query using the Invnty table. Checkmark the Item Code and Retail fields by pressing `F6`, and type the expression `>=2` in the Cost field. Press `F2`.

Designing Graphs

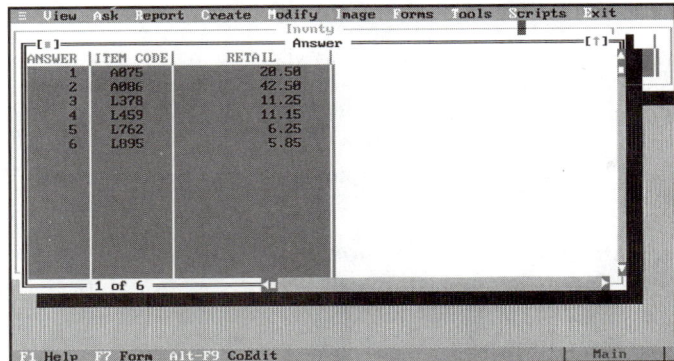

Here, you see the resulting Answer table.

This table contains an Item Code field that can provide the needed x-axis labels and a single column of numeric data Paradox can graph.

2. Place the cursor in the Retail field. This step indicates that the field is to be used as the series. To create the graph, press Ctrl-F7.

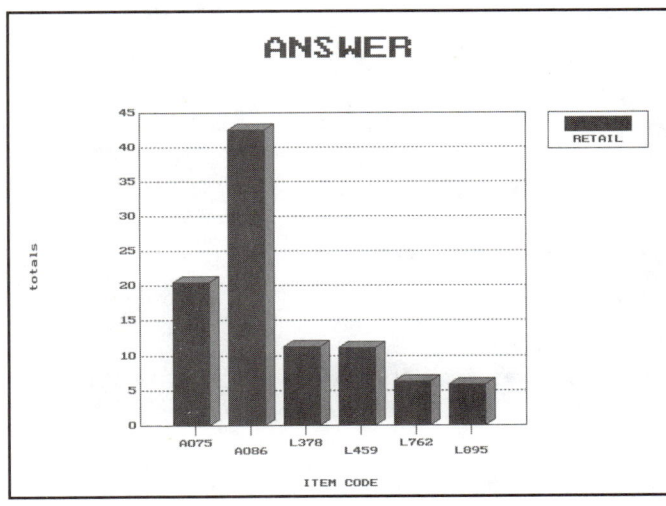

Here, you see the instant graph created from the Invnty table.

As already mentioned, the default instant graph that Paradox uses is a stacked bar graph. You can see in this example that Paradox uses the table name, Answer, as the default graph title.

385

Representing Data with Graphs

Creating a Crosstab

Generally, you will find that you want to compare a series of data. Too often, the data set you want to compare is all contained in the same field. For example, say that you want to find out which customers have ordered at least five of an item, with a retail value greater than two dollars, and what the items were.

To create an instant graph showing this information, you need to break down the quantity of each item ordered by the customer. Currently, your database is not structured to give you this information. You can easily create a query that will give you the information about who ordered what and how many, but the *what*, or item code, is a single column and cannot be divided. Paradox has a solution to this problem, called the *crosstab*. You can use the crosstab feature to break this data into the field types you need. To create a crosstab, do the following:

1. Create a query using the Lineitem table. Place checkmarks in the Item Code, Cust #, and Qty Ordered fields. Type the expression >=5 in the Qty Ordered field. In the Retail field, type >=2. Press F2.

Here, you see both the query form and the resulting Answer table.

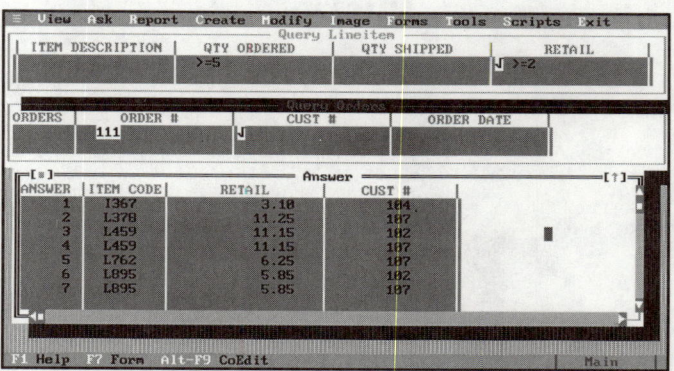

The Answer table is still not in the format that you need for the crosstab. Use the Rotate command, Ctrl-R, to move the columns so that they are in a Cust #, Item Code, and Qty Ordered order.

2. Place the cursor in the Item Code field and press Ctrl-R. The Cust # field is now in the correct place.

3. Place the cursor in the Qty Ordered field and press Ctrl-R again. Now the fields are in the correct order for the crosstab.

386

Designing Graphs

4. To build the crosstab, move the cursor to the series Cust # field, and then press Alt - x.

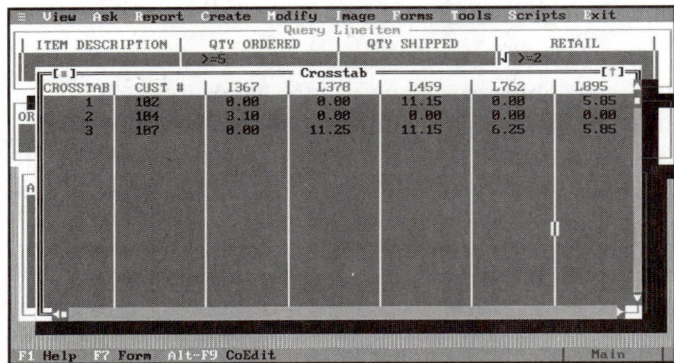

Here, you see the resulting crosstab table.

The columns have been resized, using **I**mage **C**olumnSize so that you can see all the columns.

5. Move the cursor to the first numeric field, I367, and press Ctrl - F7 to create the instant graph.

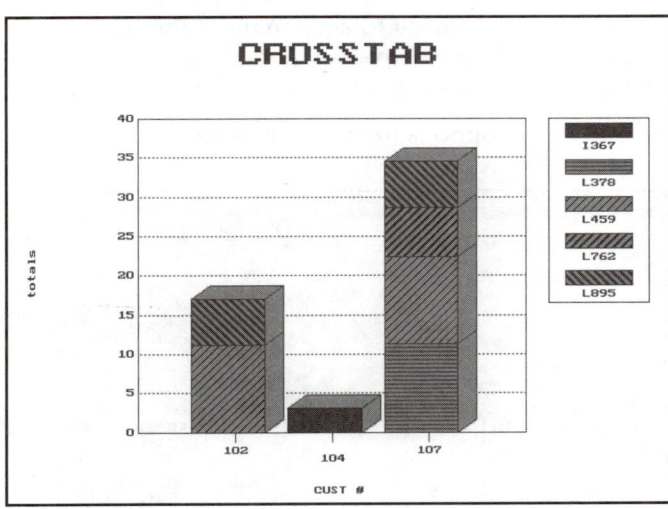

Here, you can see the instant graph, Crosstab.

Representing Data with Graphs

You have now seen how to use a query to extract a selected data set. You then used the Rotate Column command, Ctrl-R, to place the columns in the correct order, and then the Crosstab command, Alt-x, to convert the Answer table to a Crosstab table. You then based the graph on the Crosstab table.

If you want to use the Crosstab table again, then use the **T**ools **R**ename command and rename the table with a permanent name. This is a temporary Paradox table.

Modifying the Graph

You can modify any of the default graph settings by using the available options on the **I**mage **G**raph menu. The Graph Designer is accessed by using the **I**mage **G**raph **M**odify options.

Selecting the Graph Type

As discussed, you will find that some graph types are better able to display certain types of information. Try all the different types of graphs to see for yourself how your data is displayed. You need to keep in mind the type of data you are attempting to graph and to what you are comparing it. To see how your crosstab data looks using another graph type, do the following:

1. Select the **I**mage **G**raph **M**odify options from the Main menu.

Here, you see the opening screen, Customize Graph Type.

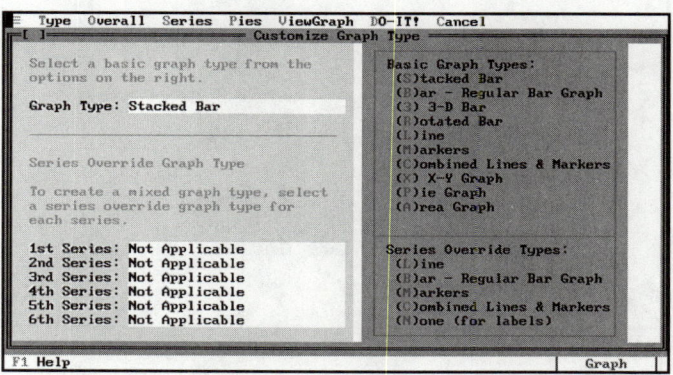

388

Modifying the Graph

As you can see, the default setting `Stacked Bar` is displayed in the Graph Type selection box.

2. The other graph options are displayed in the box to the right, `Basic Graph Types`. To select another graph type, press the letter or number that is highlighted in parentheses in the graph type name. Type L for **L**ine graph.

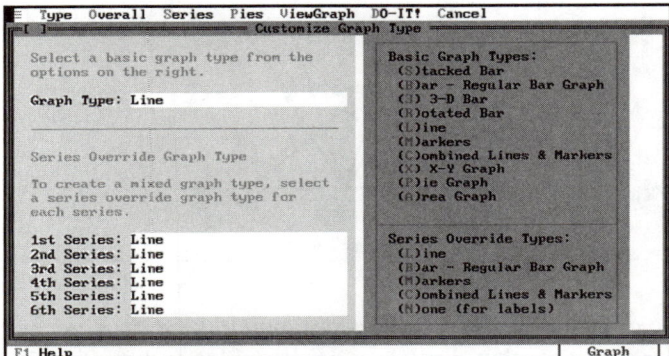

You can see the new graph type, `Line`, now is displayed in the Graph Type box, and in the Series Selection box below.

The override types are available only with certain graph types. When you select a graph type that allows you to select an override type for a series, the Override Graph Type box is filled in with the graph type selected for each of the series as you see in the preceding figure. If the override type cannot be used for a series, you will see the notation `Not applicable` displayed beside each series.

3. To see the selected graph type, Line, choose **V**iewGraph **S**creen from the menu bar.

389

Representing Data with Graphs

13

Here, you see the resulting line graph.

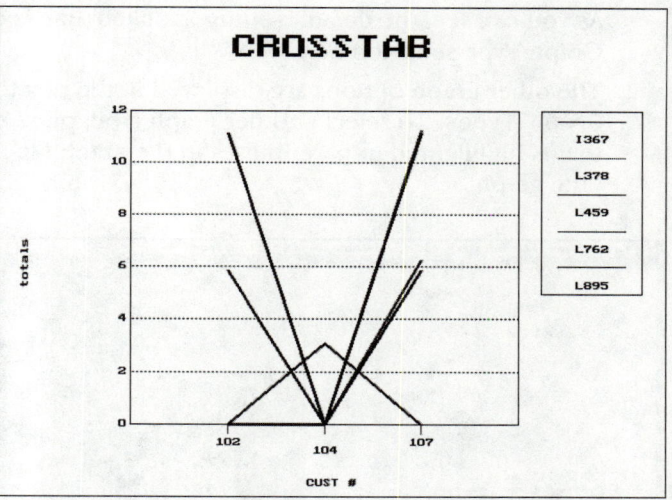

This is an example of a graph type that does not match the data. Line graphs work better with data that displays more variables and fewer zero values.

4. Change the graph type to Bar by pressing 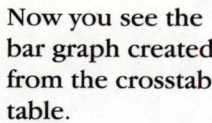, and then view the graph using the **V**iewGraph **S**creen option again.

Now you see the bar graph created from the crosstab table.

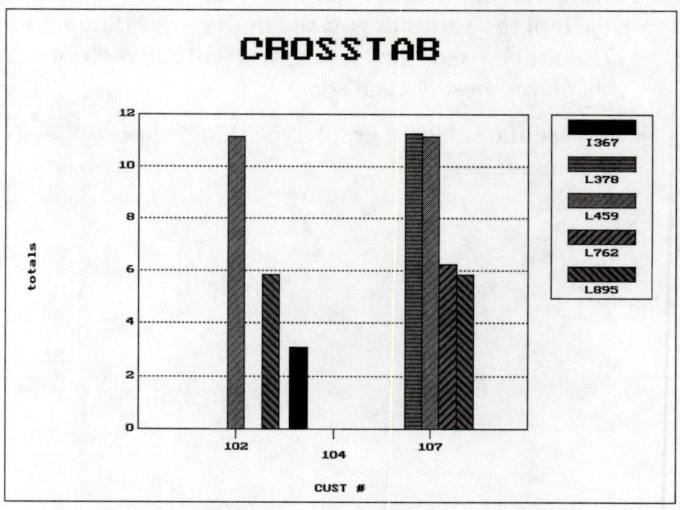

Modifying the Graph

You can easily tell that customer 107 has four bars displayed. It is more difficult to distinguish, however, to whom the bars displayed near customers 102 and 104 belong. If you look closely at your screen, you can see that each customer has five spots available for a bar. The bars always remain in the same relative position for the series. Item I367 is the first item in the series; customer 102 did not order that item, so Paradox leaves a blank space for the bar, indicating zero. Customer 104 only ordered this item, and the bar is located in the first position, which is to the left of the customer label tick mark. Customer 107 also did not order this item and, therefore, has a blank space for the item. If needed, you can adjust the column order by using the Column Rotate command.

Say you wanted to use the Override Graph Type feature. You would press ⬇. The cursor would move to the Override Graph Type box. You would then place the cursor on the series to be overridden and press the letter for the required override type.

The graph override feature is an excellent way to highlight a specific set of data. In the next figure, you can see the sales for four territories, divided by quarter years. The latest quarter, 1992 2nd Quarter, is highlighted by using an override graph type of combined line and marker.

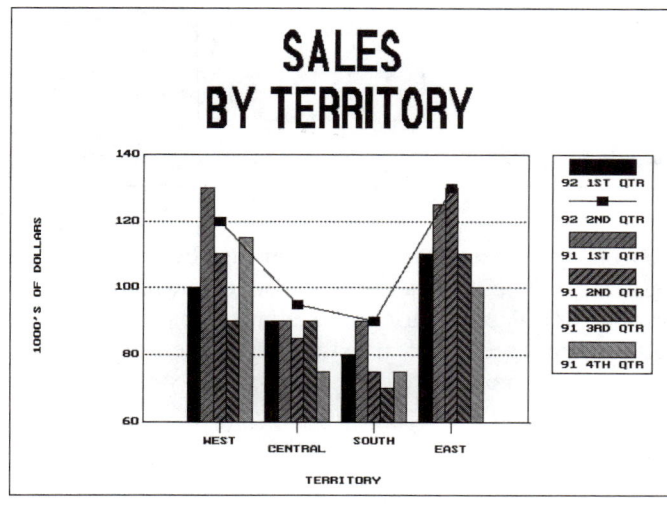

Here, you see a graph displayed with an override graph for a series.

391

Representing Data with Graphs

Using the Overall Settings

Paradox lets you alter many graph settings, enabling you to change the appearance of your graph. You can alter the graph titles, colors, scaling, and labels of the x- and y-axes, as well as the grid and frame colors and patterns, and the page layout for a printed copy of your graph.

Adding Titles

By default, Paradox uses a set of titles for your graph. At times, these titles may be adequate. At other times, you may want to enhance the titles and their display. To add and adjust the titles of your graph, do the following:

1. Be sure that you are at the Customize Graph Type screen. Select **O**verall from the menu bar, and then select **T**itles.

You now see the Customize Graph Titles screen.

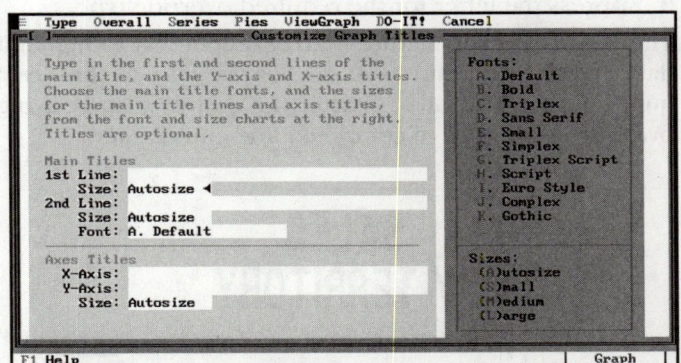

Paradox allows you to use a two-line main title. You can then have a major title and a lesser title. These titles can often be used with a series of similar graphs. All the graphs for a presentation may use a similar major title, and then a secondary title that better identifies the particular graph. You can also add more descriptive x- and y-axes titles. Paradox also gives you a choice of 11 fonts and 4 sizes.

2. With the cursor in the Main Titles section, 1st Line, type **Customer Sales**.
3. Move the cursor to the Size field and press ⌊L⌋ for large size font.
4. Move the cursor to the 2nd Line field and type **High $ Value & More than 5 each Item**.

Modifying the Graph

5. Select **M**edium for font size.
6. Choose **B** for bold font. Use the various fonts so that you have a good idea of what each looks like.
7. For the x-axis, type the title **Customer Number**.
8. For the y-axis, type the title **Total Number of Items Bought**.
9. Select the **L**arge font size.

   The font sizes vary depending upon the text location. The font used in the main titles is much larger than that used for the x- and y-axes.

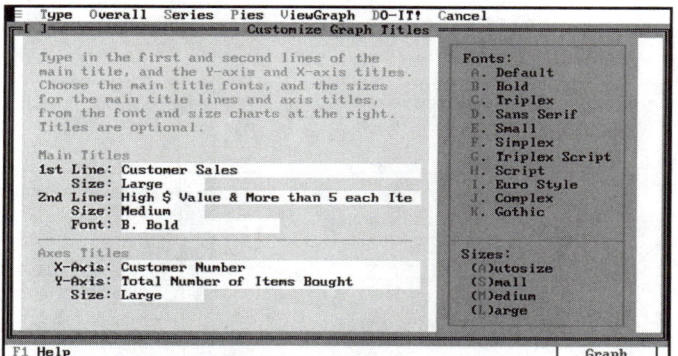

Here, you see the Customize Graph Titles screen completed.

10. Select **V**iewGraph **S**creen to view the graph adjustments.

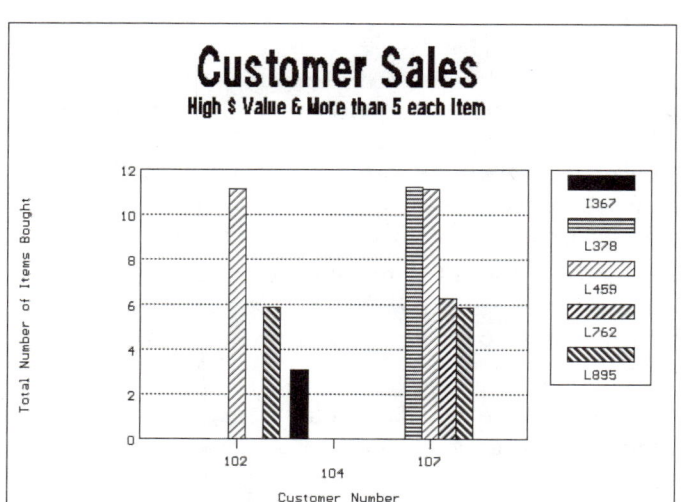

You can now see the new graph titles.

393

Representing Data with Graphs

Altering the Graph Colors

Using the **O**verall **C**olor option, you can adjust the colors Paradox uses to display your graph on the screen or as printed output if you have a printer that supports color. When you select either the **S**creen or the **P**rinter option, Paradox displays the Customize Graph Colors screen. For this discussion, you will adjust only the screen colors. To adjust the overall colors of your screen, you must have a color monitor, then do the following:

1. Select **O**verall **C**olors from the Graph menu bar and pull-down menu.
2. Select the **S**creen option on the menu box to display the Customize Graph Colors screen.

Here, you see the Customize Graph Colors screen.

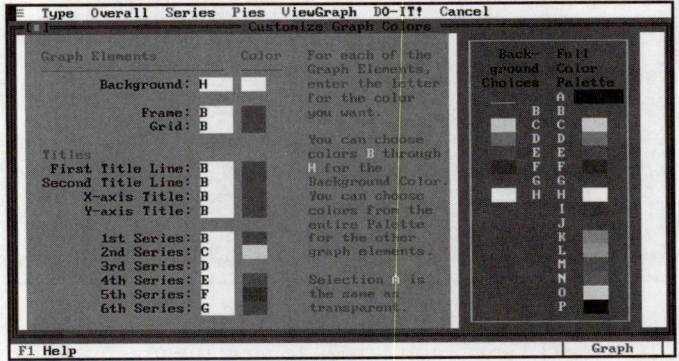

With the options available, you have 7 background colors you can use, and 15 foreground colors. Paradox also gives you the choice, A, which Paradox calls *transparent*. Selecting A for a foreground color is the same as choosing the color option you are using for the background. If you use the same color options for the fore- and background, your selected item becomes invisible or transparent. This option is useful if you want to temporarily remove a title from view or a printed copy.

3. Select an item to change the color of by moving the cursor to select it, and then type the letter of the new color choice. If you have a color screen, move the cursor down to First Title Line and type N.
4. Now select **V**iewGraph **S**creen.

   To change a color setting back to its default setting or color, you must either manually change it as you did in step 3, or select **C**ancel from the menu bar. This step cancels all graph settings you have made.

394

Modifying the Graph

Customizing the Graph Axes

When you create a graph and specify the x- and y-axes, Paradox makes many assumptions about how to display your data. By default, Paradox scales the x- and y-axes by starting from zero and then extending the graph scaling to just beyond the largest number to be graphed. Paradox also sets the increment of the y-axis scaling to a value that will fit with the range.

Paradox displays one tick mark for each x value. For some x-axis values, you may want to suppress some of the labels. Do this only if they are too long to display and if they are a range of consecutive numbers or dates. When using specific labels, such as Cust #, you will not want to suppress any of the labels. Paradox uses the default setting of alternating the tick labels, which prints or displays them on alternating lines.

Using Paradox's capability to manually scale an axis, you can zoom in on a graph to display small variations. For example, if you had a graph that had values of 100, 110, 105, and 107, you could have trouble distinguishing these differences in a graph that used a scale of 0–110. To adjust the scaling of a graph, do the following:

1. Select **O**verall **A**xes from the menu bar and pull-down menu.
2. Move the cursor to the y-axis column. Select **M**anual. Move the cursor down to the Low field and type **2**. Move down to the High field and type **7**. Move down to the Increment field and type **1**.

   Generally, you will only adjust the scaling on the y-axis. The only exception is the use of an X-Y graph. This is because the x-axis usually only contains labels that do not have a scaling to be adjusted.

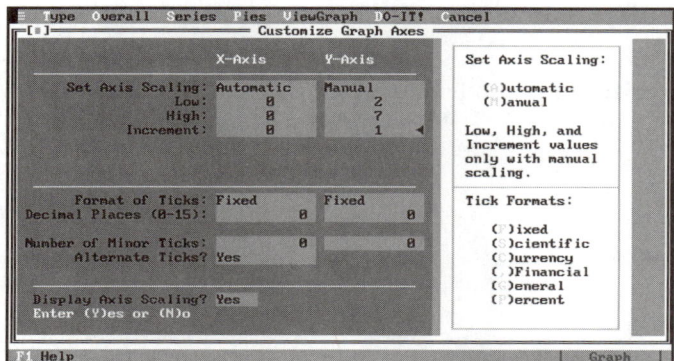

Here, you see the Customize Graph Layout for Printing screen.

395

Representing Data with Graphs

3. Now select **V**iewGraph **S**creen to display the adjustments.

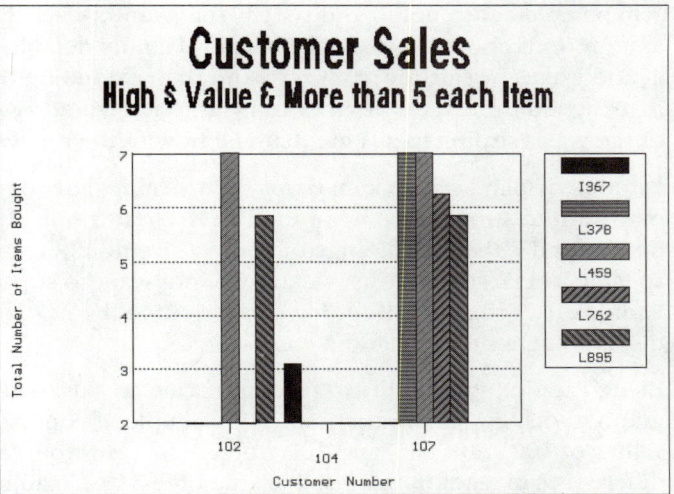

You can see the adjustments made to the y-axis scaling.

4. Reverse the changes you made. Set the y-axis scaling to **A**utomatic and the Low and High values to **0**.

Changing Grids and Frames

You have the option to change the gridlines Paradox places across the graph to help you display the relative scaling of bars and lines. You also can decide to display or not to display the frame around the graph. To adjust these settings, do the following:

1. Select **O**verall **G**rids.

   You see the Customize Grids and Frames screen.

Modifying the Graph

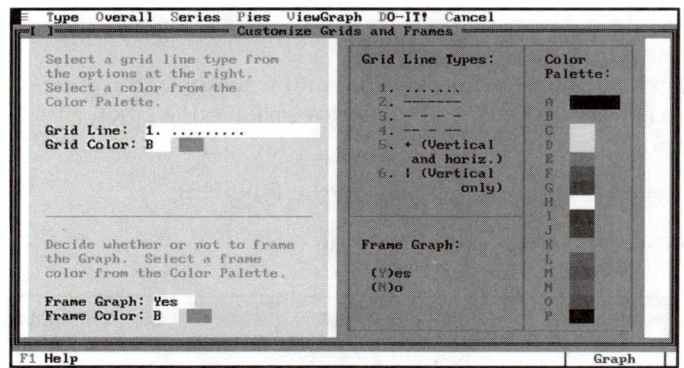

From here, you can change the type and color of the line Paradox uses as the gridline across your graph and the frame color.

2. You have six different options of gridlines from which to select. Paradox chooses the default option of 1. This gridline, composed of dots or periods, is usually a good choice. The gridline helps viewers to see the y-axis scaling without distracting them from the data. To select another gridline, type the number of the choice you would like. Type **3**.

3. Now select **V**iewGraph **S**creen to see the results of your choice.

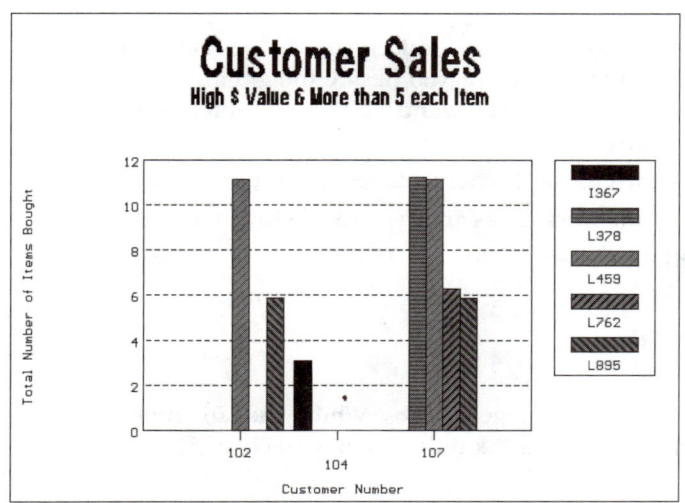

Here, you can see the gridline changed from dots to dashes.

397

Representing Data with Graphs

Altering the Series Settings

You can also use the **S**eries option to change some of the settings for a series of data, such as the legend labels or a specific interior series value label, and change marker types and fill patterns.

To change the default legends and series labels, do the following:

1. Select **S**eries **L**egendsAndLabels from the menu.

Here, you see the Customize Series Legends and Labels screen.

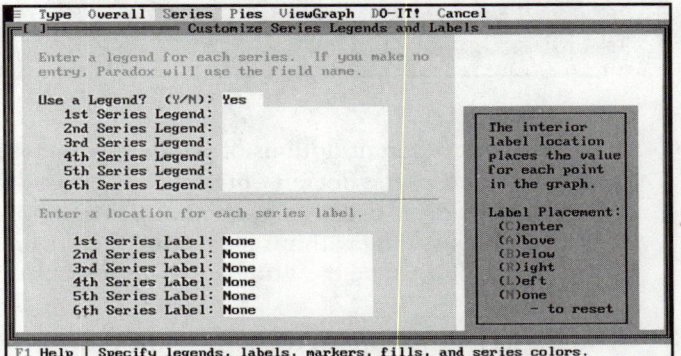

A series legend is the text you place underneath the marker inside the legend box; the legend box is displayed beside the graph. By default, Paradox uses the field name for a legend. In this example, the current legend text is the Item Code.

2. Move the cursor down to the 1st Series Legend and type **G. Robinet**.

3. Move the cursor to the next series and type the following:

   2nd   **L. C Blanc**
   3rd   **L. BlushPk**
   4th   **L. StarStk**
   5th   **L. Rosario**

You may need to adjust your legend titles. While you can enter up to 19 characters in the field, Paradox only displays 10 characters in the legend box.

The series label will display the exact value for each series. You choose the location of the display. Use this option to highlight a specific series and not display all series. You can easily end up with an unreadable graph.

Modifying the Graph

4. Move the cursor down and make the following choice:

   1st   Above

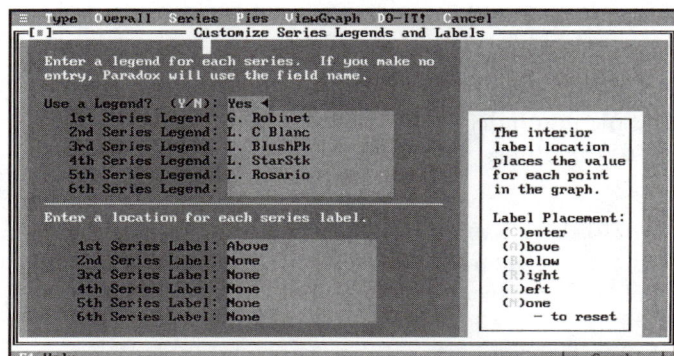

Here, you see the Customize Series Legends and Labels screen completed.

5. Select **V**iewGraph **S**creen to display the new graph.

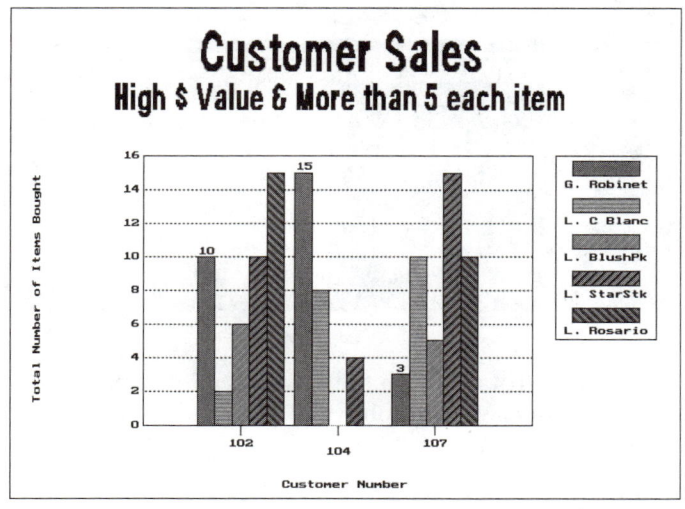

You now see the new adjustments to the graph.

Notice that the locations for the series labels vary in their locations. Some are above the top of the bar, others are below, and so on.

6. Reset the series labels to **N**one.

399

Representing Data with Graphs

Selecting Pie Graph Settings

Pie graphs have their own Settings window. Using the **P**ies option on the Graph menu bar, you can select fill patterns, screen and print colors, whether to explode a pie section, and label formats.

In many ways, the pie graph is easier to use because you can work with only two columns of data. The pie graph displays each value in the series in terms of its relative proportion to the others. To create a pie graph, do the following:

1. Open the query form for Lineitem and type **1000** in the Order # field. Paradox will draw the data only from order # 1000. Place a checkmark in the Item Code field and the example element **1** in the Qty Ordered field. In the Retail field, type the example element **2** and the formula **,calc 1*2 as Total**. Remember to press F5 to enter the example elements 1 and 2 in both the fields indicated and in the formula.

Here, you see the Answer table from the above query.

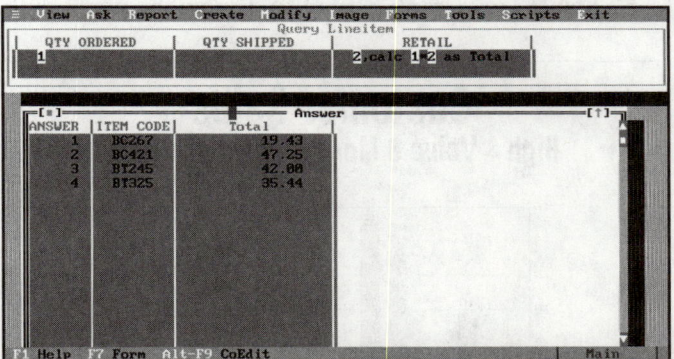

2. Now move the cursor to the Total field in the Answer table. Select **I**mage **G**raph **M**odify and choose the graph type **P**ie.
3. Change the **O**verall **T**itles to read:

   Main: **Customer Orders**

   2nd Line: **By Order Number**
4. Select **V**iew Graph **S**creen.

   You now have a pie graph for which you can alter the specifications.

Modifying the Graph

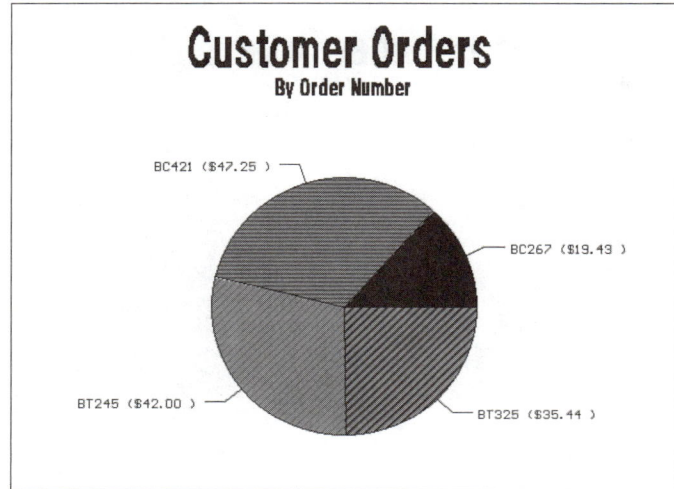

Here, you see the default pie graph.

5. To select the **P**ies options, press P.

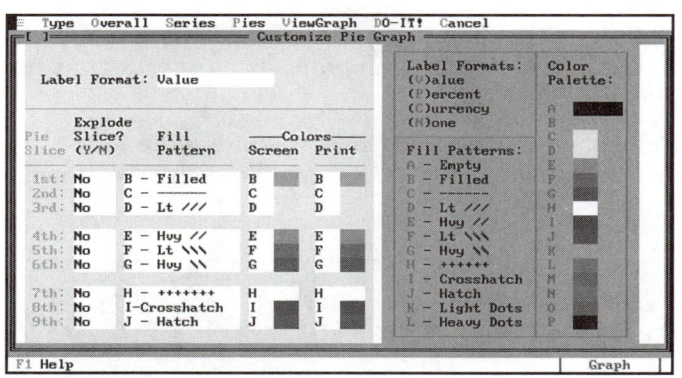

Here, you can see the Customize Pie Graph screen.

6. Change the Label Format from **V**alue to **P**ercent.
7. Move the cursor to 1st field in the Pie Slice section, and type a **Y** in the Explode Slice field. Press ↵Enter twice and change the screen color to P by pressing P.
8. Press ↵Enter three times to move to the 2nd slice field for the fill pattern. Press I for Crosshatch.
9. Move to the 3rd slice field and change the filled pattern to **H**.
10. Now select **V**iewGraph **S**creen.

401

Representing Data with Graphs

13

Here, you see the pie graph created by your new graph specification.

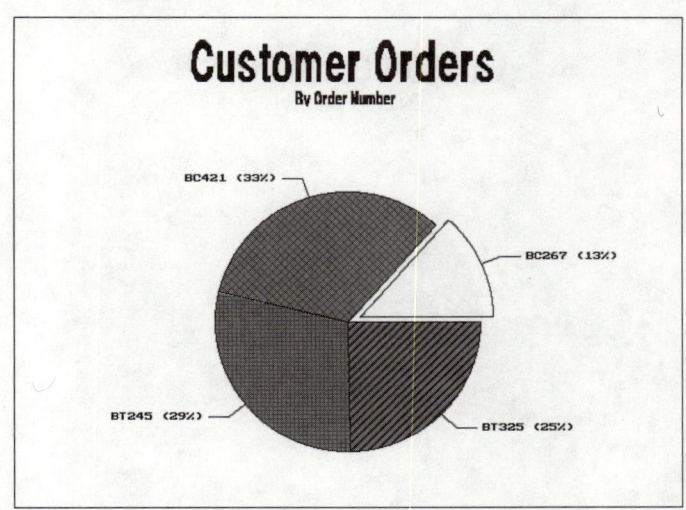

Choosing the Output and Saving

Just like the report specification you have already created, you can output the graph to more than just the screen. You also can print a copy of your graph to a graphics capable printer, a plotter, and a file.

Before you can print a graph, you must tell Paradox what printer or plotter you will use, and where it is. You must do this by using the **U**tilities **C**ustom **G**raph **P**rinter options on the System menu (≡).

Here, you can see the Graph Printer Settings window.

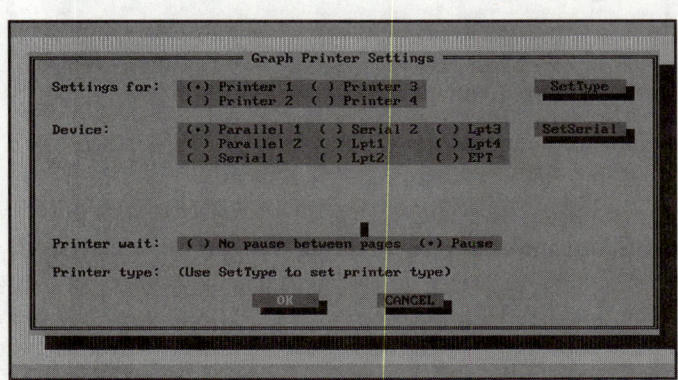

402

Choosing the Output and Saving

To select a graphics printer and give printer specifications, follow these steps:

1. Select the printer you are using.
2. Choose the printer port where the printer is located.
3. Choose the printer manufacturer for your printer, and then select the printer model from the supplied lists, and finally the printer mode, or quality.

   Use the default Printer Wait option for continuous feed paper unless you are manually feeding the printer.
4. Select OK.

Paradox will now save the printer specifications for the graphics printer you have selected.

Setting the Page Layout and Printing

To make adjustments to the standard Paradox page layout, you must use the Customize Graph Layout for Printing window. To adjust the page specification, do the following:

1. From the Graph menu, select Overall PrinterLayout.

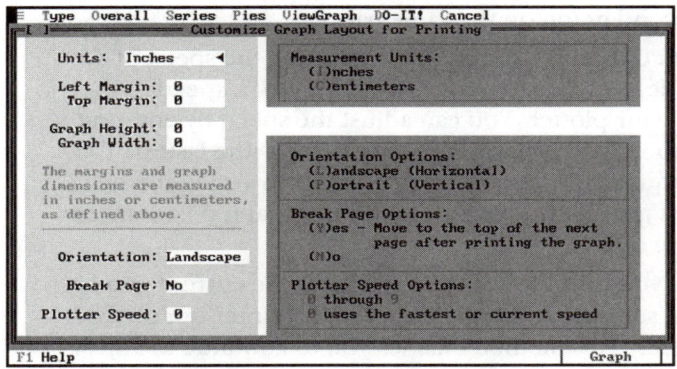

Here, you see the Customize Graph Layout for Printing screen.

2. Make the required changes for your graph. The default settings are described in the text that follows.

   Units are measured in inches. You can change the unit to centimeters by placing the cursor on the field and pressing C.

403

Representing Data with Graphs

Left Margin tells Paradox where to start printing from the page's edge. This option uses the selected units.

Top Margin tells Paradox where to start printing at the top of your paper from the edge. This option uses the selected units.

Graph Height tells Paradox how tall the graph can be. The default setting of zero says that Paradox can use the entire page.

Graph Width tells Paradox how wide the graph can be. The default setting of zero says that Paradox can use the entire page.

The right margin is determined by the left margin and graph width. The bottom margin is determined by the top margin and the graph height.

Orientation tells Paradox in what direction to print the graph. The default, Landscape, prints the graph down the entire page. In other words, the left side of the graph begins printing at the top of the page. The alternative is Portrait mode. Selecting Portrait tells Paradox to print the graph with the top of the graph starting at the top of the page. Portrait mode is a good method for printing two graphs on a single page. Adjust the Graph Width to 8 inches and the Graph Height to 5 1/2 inches.

Leave the Break Page default, No, selected. Paradox will not send a formfeed to the printer when the first graph is completed, enabling you to print a second graph on the same page.

The Plotter Speed option is used only for adjusting the speed of a plotter's pens. The default setting of zero sets the pen speed to the fastest speed for your plotter. You can adjust the speed by entering a number from 1 to 9, with 1 being the slowest and 9 the fastest. You can improve the quality of your plotter's work by lowering the pen speed as the pens get older. If you are plotting a graph on a transparency, use a setting of 2.

To print a graph, you have two options. To print the current graph using the current settings, select the ViewGraph Printer option from the Graph Designer. This method enables you to continue to adjust graph settings if the output is not what you need. You can also use the Image Graph ViewGraph Printer options to print the current graph from the currently saved graph specification.

Choosing the Output and Saving

Saving the Graph as a File

You can also save a graph as a file. Paradox can save a graph file in three formats. Your choice will depend on your future needs and output devices for this graph. You must choose the graph file type from the Graph Designer menu, by selecting **O**verall **D**evice **F**ile.

The following are the three formats in which you can save a graph file:

CurrentPrinter   This is the Paradox format that is created for the printer you specified as the Graph Printer.

EPS   Encapsulated PostScript file formats can be used by many graphics and desktop publishing programs and can be printed on a PostScript compatible printer.

PIC   A standard format that many spreadsheet programs use for graph settings.

After you have selected the file format, you can use the **V**iewGraph **F**ile command from the Graph Designer or the Main menu.

Saving the Graph Specification

A graph specification is saved temporarily for use in the current Paradox session when you press [F2] or select **D**O-IT! from the Graph Designer menu. To permanently save the graph specification so that it can be used again, do the following:

1. Select **I**mage **G**raph **S**ave from the Main menu bar.
2. Enter a name for the graph specification. Again, make the name descriptive enough so that you will know what the graph does. You are only allowed eight spaces because Paradox will save the specification as a separate DOS file. Type **CORDPIE** for Customer ORDrder PIE. Press [↵Enter].

405

Representing Data with Graphs

Retrieving the Graph Specification

To retrieve a graph specification for use again, do the following:

1. Select **I**mage **G**raph **L**oad from the Main menu bar.
2. Enter the name of the graph specification or press `Enter` to display the list of available graph specifications in the list box.
3. Select the required graph, and press `Enter`.

The selected graph specification is loaded. Use it as needed. Any modifications you make will not become a permanent part of the saved specification unless you use the **I**mage **G**raph **S**ave and copy the new specification over the old one's name.

Summary

In this chapter, you learned to graph data using the Paradox default graph specification. You learned how to change the default graph specifications, use other graphs, and change titles. Finally, you learned to print a graph and save the new specification.

Specifically, you learned the following key points about Paradox 4:

- Paradox builds a graph, using the current table on the desktop.
- To build a graph, place the cursor in the column that contains the first series of graph points. These must be numerical values.
- To view the Paradox instant graph, press `Ctrl`-`F7`.
- To use a query and build a graph, use an Answer table.
- To adjust the columns in a table, use the Rotate command, `Ctrl`-`R`.
- To compare a series of data from the same field, use the **P**aradox crosstab, `Alt`-`x`. Place the cursor in the field you want to use as the x-axis value and press `Alt`-`x`. Paradox will build the crosstab table.
- To change the default graph settings, select **I**mage **G**raph **M**odify. Select the required changes from the different options available in the Graph Designer.
- To change the graph type, select **T**ype from the Graph Designer menu, and select the graph type required.
- To change the default graph title settings, select **O**verall **T**itles. Enter the title required, adjust font sizes, and style from this menu also.

Summary

- To alter screen or printed colors for a graph, select **O**verall **C**olors, and then choose either **S**creen or **P**rinter. Make the adjustments you require for the graph settings.

- To adjust the x- or y-axes settings, select **O**verall **A**xes. You can adjust the scaling, the high and low settings, and tick formats.

- To set your graph for a specific paper size and orientation, select the **O**verall **P**rinterLayout option.

- To specify the output device, select **O**verall **D**evice, and then choose to send the graph to a printer, plotter, or file.

- To add interior labels and adjust legend labels, select **S**eries **L**egendsAndLabels. Type the required legend labels for the required series. To place an interior label for a series, specify the location of the label. Paradox then places the exact value of the graph series in the location you specified.

- To change a series marker or fill pattern, use the **S**eries **M**arkersAndFills option. Select the required changes from the screen.

- To make adjustments to pie graphs, select **P**ies from the menu. You can then select colors for screen or printing, fill patterns, and select slices to explode from the graph.

- To view the changes you have made to your graph settings, use the **V**iewGraph option. You can choose to **P**rint or **S**creen your current graph.

- To save a graph specification as a file, select **D**O-IT! from the Graph Designer menu. Then use the **I**mage **G**raph **S**ave option from the Main menu. To load a previously saved graph specification, use the **I**mage **G**raph **L**oad command.

In the next chapter, you will learn to create and use Paradox scripts. You will learn to use an instant script, and then to record and play back your own script. You will also learn to make a script that will be executed automatically when you load Paradox.

Using Paradox Scripts

Two of the things the computer supposedly does best is save time and effort. Paradox can help you save time and effort by doing repetitive tasks as a *script*, or keyboard macro. The Paradox script is a series of recorded keystrokes you can play back at anytime.

This chapter will introduce you to the use of a script and show you how to create, save, and reuse your own script. With the use of scripts, you can make many of the everyday database functions usable for almost anyone.

An Overview of the Paradox Script

The Paradox script has much in common with what many programs call *macros*. Using the Paradox script functions, you can automate almost any task you can do yourself— especially tasks that are very repetitive in nature.

Paradox has the capability to record your keystrokes and play them back on command. If you find yourself performing the same function over and over, record these tasks as a script. Then tell Paradox to do the function for you. This feature can save you both time and frustration over the occasionally missed keystroke.

14

An overview of the Paradox script

Creating an instant script

Creating a new script

Playing a script

Editing a script

Working with special script codes

Recording a query script

Using the INIT script

Using Paradox Scripts

14

> **Key Terms in This Chapter**
>
> *Script* A saved record of keystrokes and menu selections that can be played back at any time to produce certain results.
>
> *Editor* A simple text editor that can be used to edit a script. It can also be used with PAL programs.
>
> *Script codes* The Paradox script equivalent of a keystroke or menu selection.

Macro capabilities are just one aspect of the Paradox script. You can also create your own turnkey database system, complete with its own tables, menus, forms, reports, and queries by using the *Paradox Applications Workshop* and the *Paradox Application Language (PAL)*. The use of the Paradox Personal Programmer and PAL, however, are not covered in this book.

Creating a Paradox script can be very easy. When you build a new script, Paradox saves it as an object. A script, like the graph specification, is not a member of a table's family. Any script is available for use with any table.

One word of caution: if you create a script for a specific table and then you later restructure that table, Paradox does not adjust the script to the new table. You must do that yourself using the Script Editor.

You can create scripts in one of four ways:

- An instant script is created when you press Alt-F3.
- A regular script is created when you select **S**cript, **B**eginRecord.
- A script is created when you select **S**cript, **Q**uerySave.
- When you become more familiar with scripts, you can write your own with the Paradox Editor. Select **S**cripts **E**ditor **N**ew.

Each of these methods are discussed in the next sections of this chapter.

410

Creating an Instant Script

Creating a new script can be as easy as pressing Alt-F3 and typing away. A script created in this manner is called an *instant script*.

An instant script can be used any number of times during the current Paradox session only. Paradox creates a temporary file called *Instant.SC*. When you exit Paradox, or change working directories, this script is deleted.

For example, if you plan to edit several different tables during a single Paradox session, you can create an instant script that clears the desktop and opens the file selection window ready for the next table to be edited. To create an instant script, do the following:

1. Press Alt-F3.

    The message Beginning recording of Instant... is displayed in the message box, and then an R is displayed in the bottom right-hand corner of the desktop.

2. Perform the following commands to record them as the instant script:

    Press Alt-F8 to clear the desktop, and then press F10 to select the Main menu. Select **M**odify **E**dit.

3. Press Alt-F3 to stop recording.

    You will see the message Ending recording of Instant....

You now have an instant script recorded for your use. To use the instant script, clear the desktop by pressing Alt-F8, and then press Alt-F4.

Almost instantly, you see the Table list box displayed on the screen. You now only have to select the next file you want to edit. If you had created a longer script with more keystrokes, the script would take longer to complete. Your screen would not be updated until Paradox completed the instant script, and then your screen would refresh.

To start an instant script, you must be in the same mode as when you recorded the script. The instant script recorded above was recorded in the Main mode. If, however, you are now in a different mode, such as the Edit mode, and you press Alt-F4, you would see this error message: Script error—select Cancel or Debug from menu.

411

Using Paradox Scripts

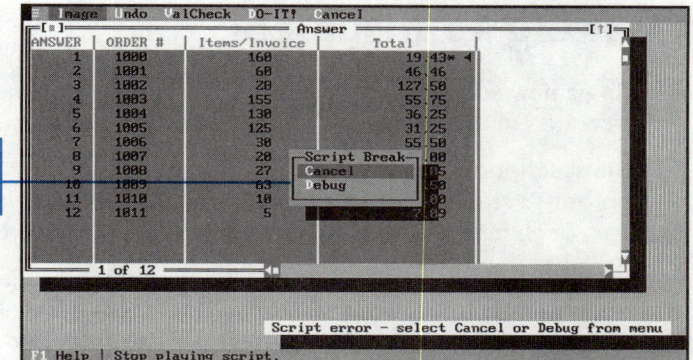

The Script Break dialog box is also displayed.

You have two options: you can Cancel the script or you can select Debug. Canceling is generally the easiest and most-recommended option. Selecting Debug shows you the reason that the script did not work with the message Not a possible menu choice and displays the problem line of the script at the bottom of the screen.

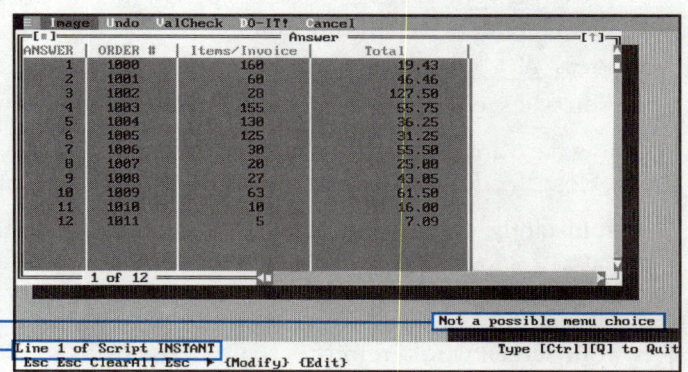

Here, you can see the problem script line displayed and the reason for the problem.

Creating a New Script

When you want to record a script to use from session to session, you will use the regular Paradox script recording method. A script recorded with the Scripts BeginRecord command can be saved as a permanent file.

As with many of the other Paradox functions you have learned, write down what you want to do with a script, where you need to go, and what files and fields are involved. Writing down these items can save you a lot of editing time later.

Creating an Instant Script

Recording the Script

In this section, you will create a script that opens the Cust1 table, finds the next available empty record line, and then opens the Add new Customer form. This type of script can be very helpful for a data entry clerk who can add customers and other data well, but who may not be familiar with the tables and other Paradox commands.

When you select **S**cripts **B**eginRecord, Paradox will ask you to name the new script. You are limited to an eight character name. To record a new script, do the following:

1. Select **S**cripts **B**eginRecord and enter the script name **New_Cust**. The underscore (_) is used between New and Cust because you cannot leave a space in a file name.

   You will see the message Beginning recording of New_Cust... displayed in the message box. Now all keystrokes will be recorded until you select **S**cripts **E**ndRecord.

2. To begin the script, press [Alt]-[F8] to clear the desktop. Then select **M**odify **E**dit, type **Cust1**, and press [↵Enter].

3. You now have the Cust1 table displayed on the desktop. Press [End]. The cursor is now located on the last record in the table.

4. Press [F10]. Select **I**mage **P**ickFormCreating an Instant Script and **3**. Press [↵Enter], and then press [PgDn].

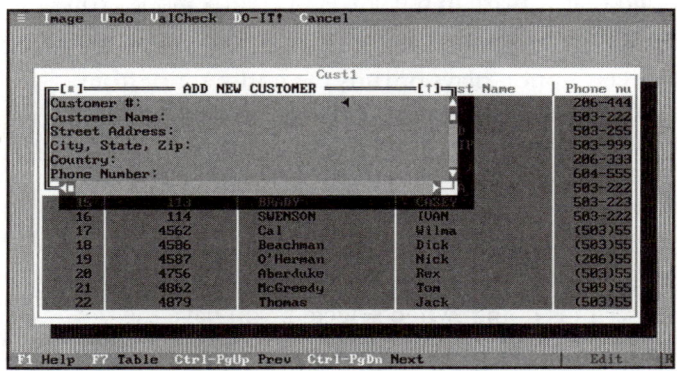

You now can see the blank customer add form displayed.

You have now completed the script as you wanted. You now have to exit from the Paradox Edit mode and end the script.

413

Using Paradox Scripts

5. Because your Cust1 table has been created so that the Cust # field is a required field, you cannot exit this field without either entering a value and creating the record, or pressing `Del` and deleting the record. Press `Del`.
6. Select **C**ancel, **Y**es from the menu.

Ending the Recording of the New Script

You must now end the recording of the new script. Until you tell Paradox that the script is complete and not to record anything further, any keystroke, command, or data you enter will be recorded. To end the recording of this script, do the following:

1. Select **S**cripts on the Main menu.

   You will notice that the **S**cripts menu box has a new series of selections.

2. Select **E**nd-Record. You see the message `Ending recording of New_Cust....`

Playing a Script

After you have created a script using **S**cript **B**eginRecord, you can use the script at any time, provided that you are in the correct Paradox mode. You have three options for playing a script:

Play   The Play option plays or runs the entire script from start to finish. The screen remains constant until Paradox has completed the script. When the script is complete, the screen is refreshed with the current image.

ShowPlay   The ShowPlay option is extremely useful when debugging a script or showing another person what the script is doing. When selected, you have the option of a Fast or Slow speed.

Playing a Script

RepeatPlay   The RepeatPlay option is used to play a script a specified number of times. Paradox runs the script and the screen remains the same until the script is complete. When the script is complete, the screen is refreshed with the current image. To stop the script at any point, press `Ctrl`-`Break`. This key combination stops the script and displays the message `Interrupting script....` You will also see the Script Break menu box. Choose Cancel to cancel the script. Choose Debug to see the script at the stopping point.

Using Play for a Script

When you want to play a script, you will usually use the Play option. This option plays, or runs through, the script from start to finish at Paradox's fastest speed. You will not see any changes in the screen until Paradox completes the script, and then the current image is displayed. To use the Play option, do the following:

1. Select Scripts from the Main menu.
2. Choose the Play option. Select the script you want to play from the list box, or type the name of the script in the text box.
3. When you have selected the script name and press `Enter` or double-click the name from the list box with the mouse pointer, Paradox immediately executes the script.

Using ShowPlay for a Script

When playing a script, the ShowPlay option can be of great help when you are first using and/or debugging the script. When this option is selected and you have chosen the script to play, Paradox gives you the option of two speeds: Fast or Slow.

The Fast option runs the script slow enough that you can see what is happening, but you may not be able to catch every detail of the screen.

The Slow option is useful in teaching situations. Paradox executes the script slowly enough so that all the screen details can be seen before the next step is executed.

415

Using Paradox Scripts

To use the **S**howPlay option to execute the script you just created, do the following:

1. Select **S**cripts **S**howPlay. You see a list box displayed. Press ⏎Enter to see the list of scripts or type **New_cust** and press ⏎Enter.

Here, you see the menu options leading to the start of the script.

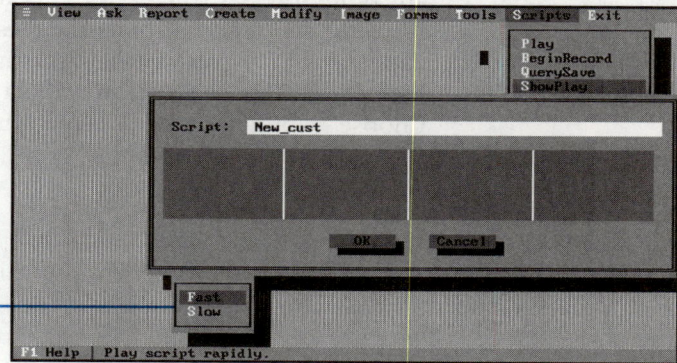

2. Choose the **S**low option for the first run through. When you press ⏎Enter, Paradox starts the script and plays it to the end.

Using RepeatPlay for a Script

The RepeatPlay option enables you to play a script a specified number of times. Use this option for making a change to all records in a table, or when you want a graph or query to be continuously updated when other users may be CoEditing a table. To use the RepeatPlay option, do the following:

1. Select **S**cripts **R**epeatPlay. Choose the script you want to use.

Here, you see the dialog box in which you enter the number of times to repeat a script. Entering **C** in the box will continuously replay the script.

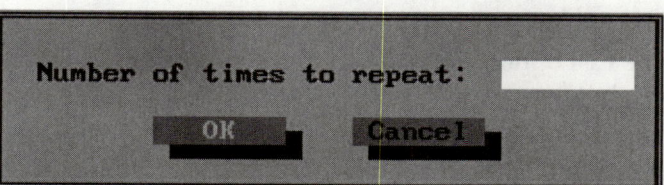

416

Editing a Script

2. Enter either a number for the number of times to replay the script or enter **C** to continuously replay.

   If you use the C option, you will have to use Ctrl-Break to stop the script.

Editing a Script

At times you will need to change or edit a script—especially when you create a new script or when you change a table structure a script uses. The Paradox Editor is a simple text editor that creates an ASCII or DOS text file.

You have probably already noticed that the New_cust script does not stop at the new record. It goes on to close Edit mode and returns to the Main menu. This is because when you were creating the script, you had to exit from Edit mode and then tell Paradox to stop recording. You now need to edit the script and remove the parts of the script that are not needed. To edit the script, do the following:

1. Select **S**cripts **E**ditor **O**pen, and select the script from the list box or type its name. Type **New_cust** and press Enter.

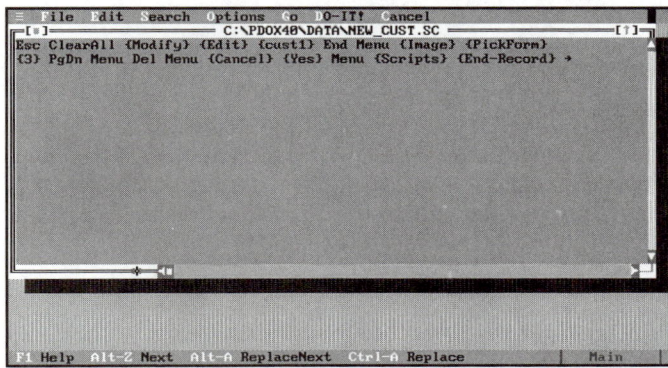

Here, you see the Paradox Editor window with the New_cust script displayed in the window.

You must be able to read the text of the script before you can edit it. All text that is within braces ({ }) are menu options. Generally, the remaining text are Paradox code words for the keys you pressed. The text of the script now reads:

Esc ClearAll {Modify} {Edit} {cust1} End Menu {Image} {PickForm} {3} PgDn Menu Del Menu {Cancel} {Yes} Menu {Scripts} {End-Record} →

Using Paradox Scripts

The translation is as follows: Esc ClearAll is the Paradox interpretation of Alt-F8 to clear the desktop, {Modify} the menu selection Modify, {Edit} the menu selection Edit, {cust1} the Cust1 table, End pressing End to move the cursor to the last record in the table, Menu selecting the menu by pressing F10, {Image} the menu option Image, {PickForm} the menu option PickForm, {3} selecting form 3, PgDn pressing PgDn to open the next blank record.

This is as far as you want the script to go. You should be left at the blank form for the next customer. The rest of the script says: Menu tried to select the menu, but remember this is a required field and Paradox would not let you make a menu selection, Del pressed Del to delete the blank form, Menu selected menu by pressing F10, {Cancel} selected the Cancel option, {Yes} selected the Yes option, Menu selected the Main menu, {Scripts} selected Scripts, and {End-Record} finally selected End-Record to stop the script from recording. "→" this is the Paradox end of file marker.

2. To edit the script, move the cursor to the second line at the end of the word PgDn. Press Del to delete the unwanted part of the script.

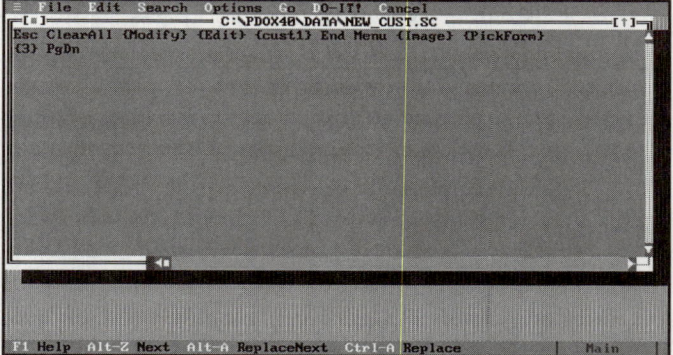

Here, you see the edited script.

3. Press F2 or select DO-IT! from the menu.
4. Now to test the script again, select Script ShowPlay, New_cust, Fast.

Working with Special Script Codes

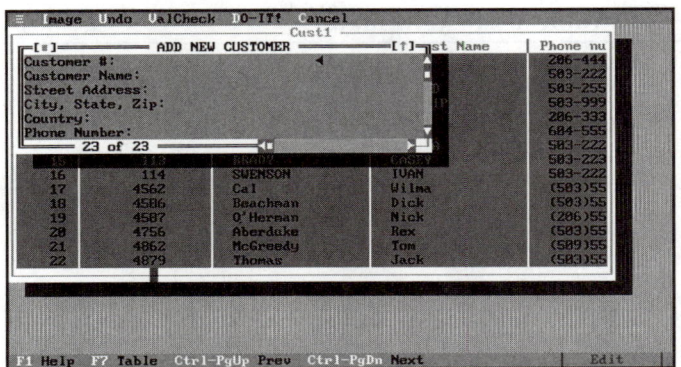

The script has finished with the form displayed and in Edit mode.

While editing a script with the Paradox Editor is a simple process, you should be careful with any additions and deletions you make. Be sure to completely test your script after you make a change.

From the Script Editor window, selecting the **G**o option on the menu will save the script and then run the script. The main advantage to using F2 and then **S**cript **S**howPlay is that you can watch the playback to see the changes that you have made.

Working with Special Script Codes

When editing the New_cust script, you saw the use of some of Paradox's special script codes. All menu commands are enclosed in braces ({ }), while other keys are represented by special code words. As much as possible, Paradox uses words that are similar to their function. Table 14.1 gives you a list of the code words and their meanings.

Table 14.1
Special Code Words in Scripts

Code Word	Meaning
Home	Home
End	End
PageUp	PgUp
PageDown	PgDn

continues

Using Paradox Scripts

Table 14.1 Continued

Code Word	Meaning
LeftArrow	←
RightArrow	→
UpArrow	↑
DownArrow	↓
Insert	Ins
Delete	Del
Backspace	←Backspace
Escape	End
Enter	↵Enter
Tab	Tab
Shift-Tab	Reverse Tab
Ctrl-Break	Ctrl-Break
Ctrl-Home	Ctrl-Home
Ctrl-End	Ctrl-End
Ctrl-LeftArrow	Ctrl-←
Ctrl-RightArrow	Ctrl-→
Ctrl-Backspace	Ctrl-←Backspace
Ctrl-PageUp	Ctrl-PgUp
Ctrl-PageDown	Ctrl-PgDn
Alt-X	CrossTab
Ctrl-D	Ditto
Ctrl-F	FieldView
Ctrl-R	Rotate
Ctrl-Y	DeleteLine
Ctrl-U	Undo
Ctrl-Z	Zoom

Working with Special Script Codes

Code Word	Meaning
Alt-Z	ZoomNext
F1	Help
F2	Do_It!
F3	UpImage
F4	DownImage
F5	Example
F6	Check
F7	FormKey
F8	ClearImage
F9	EditKey
F10	Menu
Alt-F3	InstantRecord
Alt-F4	InstantPlay
Alt-F5	FieldView
Alt-F6	CheckPlus
Alt-F7	InstantReport
Alt-F8	ClearAll
Alt-F9	CoeditKey
Ctrl-F6	CheckDescending
Ctrl-F7	GraphKey
Shift-F6	GroupBy

While you will probably not memorize this list of special code words, having a basic idea of what a word means and where to find the list can help when translating a script.

Using Paradox Scripts

Recording a Query Script

You may find that you perform the same or a very similar query again and again. Some query forms can become quite complex, and the need to rebuild one can be a daunting task.

Paradox can speed up this task by enabling you to save a query statement as a query script. After you have created your query statement and have tested it to ensure that it performs as you need, do the following:

1. With the query statement displayed on the screen, select **S**cripts **Q**uerySave.

Here, you see the dialog box for the Query Script name.

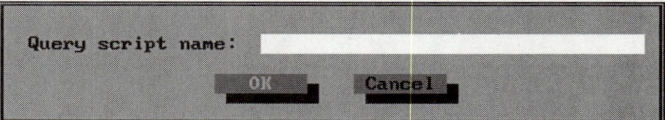

2. Just as with regular scripts, you cannot use a name longer than eight characters. Type **Customer** and press ⏎Enter.

   The query statement is saved as a script. The next time you need to use this query, select **S**cript **P**lay, Customer, and the query statement will be rebuilt.

Here, you see the Customer query script in the Paradox Script Editor window.

In this script, you can see the table name listed; the query statement fields are shown inside of (|) lines. Example elements are preceded by an (_) underscore line. The script begins with the special code Query and ends with Endquery.

422

Using an Automatic Script

Again, when creating a complex query statement, save it using the **S**cript **Q**uerySave feature. This can sometimes save you literally hours of effort.

Using an Automatic Script

For some applications, you may want a script to run every time Paradox is loaded—for example, the script created earlier in this chapter that loaded the Cust1 table, and then opened the next empty record in Form view.

If you have a data entry clerk who uses this table and form and nothing else, you can tell Paradox to run this script each time. Each time you start the Paradox program, it looks for a script called INIT. If this script is found, then it will run immediately. To create the INIT script, you can build a new script and name it INIT, or you can rename the script New_cust. To rename the script, do the following:

1. Select **T**ools **R**ename **S**cript.
2. Choose the script you want to rename, type **New_cust**, and press ↵Enter.
3. Enter the new script name. Type **INIT** and press ↵Enter.

To test the script, exit Paradox, and then restart the program.

When you do this procedure, you will see that Paradox now also plays the INIT script, opening the Cust1 table and selecting the Add New Customer form with a blank record.

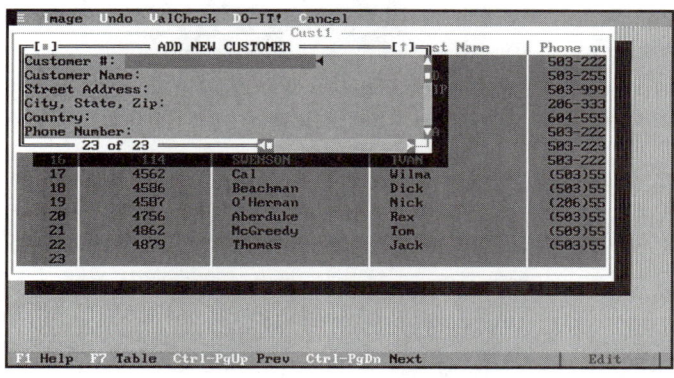

Here, you see the results of using an INIT script.

Using Paradox Scripts

As you can see, scripts can help you in many ways. You can use a script to start an application for you, or to reduce the effort and possible errors by playing a repetitive series of keystrokes for you.

As you use scripts, you will find more uses for them. You can also use one script that runs several smaller scripts. This is often the easiest way to create a complex script. For more information on this subject, see the Paradox *PAL Reference* guide.

Summary

In this chapter, you learned to create and plan a Paradox script. You then learned to record and play back a script, and to edit the script using the Paradox Script Editor. Finally, you learned to create the Paradox INIT script to automatically play a script every time you load Paradox.

Specifically, you learned the following key points about using scripts in Paradox:

- To record an instant script, press Alt-F3. When you have completed the keystrokes and operations, press Alt-F3 to stop recording.
- To replay the instant script, press Alt-F4. To save an instant script, use the **T**ools **R**ename option before you exit from the program.
- To record a regular script, select **S**cripts **B**eginRecord and enter the name for the script. Then enter the script needed, and select **S**cripts **E**nd-Record when you have completed the script.
- To watch a script in action, use the **S**cripts **S**howplay option. Select either **F**ast or **S**low running speed.
- To play a script in a normal Paradox mode, select **S**cripts **P**lay. Paradox then runs the script and refreshes your display when the script is complete.
- To play a script several times, use the **S**cripts **R**epeatPlay option. Enter the number of times you want the script to be repeated, or enter **C** to have the script play continuously.
- To edit a script, use the Paradox script editor. Choose **S**cript **E**ditor **O**pen. Make the required changes and select **D**O-IT!.
- To create a Query script, build the query statement on the screen. Make sure that it operates as needed, and then select **S**cripts **Q**uerySave. Enter a name for the query and press Enter.
- To have Paradox execute a script each time you start the program, create an INIT script.

Installing Paradox 4.0

This appendix covers the installation procedures for a stand-alone or single-user system. Network installation is not covered here. Network administrators should see the *Network Administrator's Guide* included with the Paradox program for help.

Paradox 4.0 comes on either 5 1/4-inch 360K disks or 3 1/2-inch 720K disks. Use the version that fits with your system, if you have both sizes of disk drives, the 3 1/2-inch disks require fewer disk changes.

Starting the Installation

Start the installation procedure at the DOS prompt. Use the current hard disk drive on which you want to install Paradox—usually drive C. Your DOS prompt should read C>. Many systems display the prompt in other ways, such as: C:\> or with the date and time.

To start the installation, follow these steps:

1. With the DOS prompt displayed, place the disk marked "Disk 1 - Installation" into the appropriate floppy disk drive. For this appendix, the floppy drive is A:.

Installing Paradox 4.0

2. Type **a:install** and press [⏎Enter]. The initial installation screen is displayed. Read the information displayed.
3. To continue with the installation, press [⏎Enter]. To cancel at this time, press [Esc].
4. The next screen asks you to specify the location of the source drive. The default is A:. If the Installation disk is in drive A, press [⏎Enter]. If you are installing Paradox from another drive, enter the correct drive name and press [⏎Enter].

    The next screen asks whether you are conducting a stand-alone installation, a network installation, or an optional software installation. The last option assumes that you have already successfully installed Paradox.

5. Select the first option and press [F2].

    The Signature screen is displayed.

Completing the Signature Screen

You must complete all the information on the Signature screen or Paradox will not continue the installation procedure. Complete the screen by doing the following:

1. Press [⏎Enter]. A box is displayed. Type your name, and then press [⏎Enter] again.
2. Use [↓] to select the next option, Company name. Again, press [⏎Enter], type your company name—or your name if you bought this copy for your own use—and press [⏎Enter].
3. Again, use [↓] to select the next option, Serial number. Your program serial number is located on the 5 1/4-inch Installation disk. Type the serial number into the box, and press [⏎Enter].
4. The next two options, Country Group and Sort Order, are already filled in with a default setting of United States and ASCII. Unless you either live in another country or have some special sorting needs, accept the default settings. Press [F2].

Editing the Configuration File

Paradox now looks at the CONFIG.SYS file located in the root directory of your hard disk. Paradox checks to see whether you have specified an adequate number of files and buffers. As you can see from the message displayed, Paradox does not find the correct number of files or buffers located in the CONFIG.SYS file.

If you are comfortable with making the changes to your CONFIG.SYS file, then you can select the Leave CONFIG.SYS Alone option. Otherwise, select the default, Modify CONFIG.SYS. Paradox will then make the adjustment for you.

Completing the Installation Screen

On the next screen, you can customize the location of the Paradox program and the installation of the optional programs.

You can install each of the optional softwares at a later time by selecting the Optional Software Installation option on the second install screen. The optional software is not covered in this book and takes a considerable amount of additional disk space. If you decide at a later time that you do want to try your hand at using the Application Workshop, you can install the program then.

To complete the Installation screen, do the following:

1. Move the highlighted bar down to the Install Application Workshop option and press `Enter`. Then select **N**o from the pop-up menu box. Do the same with the next option, Install PAW Sample App.
2. If you are planning on trying the tutorial that comes with Paradox, you will want to install the sample tables and sample application. Otherwise change these options to **N**o also.
3. Press `F2` when you have completed the Installation screen.

Completing the Installation

As the installation continues, you see a series of files displayed on the bottom half of your screen. As needed, Paradox displays a pop-up box, asking you to insert the next disk. Paradox tells you which disk to insert.

Installing Paradox 4.0

Always be sure to read the message in the pop-up box. Depending upon the answers you gave during the installation questionnaire, you may not always use all the disks.

When Paradox has completed reading all the disks that it needs, it will compile the program.

Next, you see the final message box that tells you that you have successfully installed the program. Press any key now to continue. Any keystroke returns you to the DOS prompt.

To start Paradox, type **CD\PDOX40** and press **Enter**. At the next C> prompt, type **PARADOX**. The program quickly loads into memory, and you see the Paradox desktop displayed on your screen.

Shortcut Keys

This appendix lists the various shortcut keys and key combinations you can use with Paradox. While many of these shortcut keys are discussed in the text of this book, you can use this appendix to find a particular shortcut quickly.

The Function Keys and Other Main Keyboard Keys

The function keys are used extensively throughout Paradox. Each of the function keys and its combinations along with other main keyboard keys are listed in table B.1.

Shortcut Keys

Table B.1
Function Keys and Other Main Keyboard Keys

Shortcut Key(s)	Description
F1	Help
F2	**D**O_IT!
F3	Previous image, or up image
Alt-F3	Instant script record
F4	Next image, or down image
Alt-F4	Instant script play
F5	Example element in query
Shift-F5	Maximize/Restore active window
Alt-F5	Field view, or calls Editor if in a memo field, and then toggles back to table
Ctrl-F5	Move/Size active window
F6	Checkmark in query
Shift-F6	Group By in query
Alt-F6	Check Plus in query
Ctrl-F6	Check Descending in query
F7	Form toggle
Alt-F7	Instant report
Ctrl-F7	Instant graph
F8	Close active window
Alt-F8	Clear desktop
Ctrl-F8	Close active window
F9	Edit mode
Alt-F9	CoEdit
F10	Menu
Tab	Next field

Menu Keys

Shortcut Key(s)	Description
Shift-Tab	Previous field
Backspace	Erase character to left of cursor
Ctrl-Backspace	Erase current field or text box
Enter	Select command; move to next field; insert line
Esc	Move back one command
Ctrl-Break	Cancel current task; use with caution during sort or query

Menu Keys

Within menus, you can move between menu commands in several ways. Table B.2 lists the alternatives.

Table B.2
Menu Keys

Shortcut Key	Description
↑	Moves up one command on a pull-down or cascading menu
↓	Moves down one command on a pull-down or cascading menu
→	Moves right one command on a menu bar
←	Moves left one command on a menu bar
End	Moves to the last command on either a menu bar of a pull-down or cascading menu
Home	Moves to the first command on either a menu bar of a pull-down or cascading menu
First letter of menu item	Selects the command immediately

431

Shortcut Keys

Table View Keys

Within Table view, many keys have different uses than they do in other modes. Table B.3 lists the keys' functions in Table view.

Table B.3
Table View Keys

Shortcut Key(s)	Description
↑	Up one record
↓	Down one record
→	Next field
←	Previous field
Home	First record same field
End	Last record same field
Ctrl-Home	First field same record
Ctrl-End	Last field same record
Ctrl-←	Left one screen
Ctrl-→	Right one screen
PgDn	Down one screen
PgUp	Up one screen

Form View Keys

Within Form view, many keys have different uses than they do in other modes. Table B.4 lists the keys' functions in Form view.

Field View Keys

Table B.4
Form View Keys

Shortcut Key(s)	Description
[↑]	Previous field up or left
[↓]	Next field down or right
[→]	Next field up or right
[←]	Previous field down or left
[Home]	First record same field
[End]	Last record same field
[Ctrl]-[Home]	First field same record
[Ctrl]-[End]	Last field same record
[PgUp]	Next page or record
[PgDn]	Previous page or record
[Ctrl]-[PgDn]	Next record same field
[Ctrl]-[PgUp]	Previous record same field

Field View Keys

Within Field view, many keys have different uses than they do in other modes. Table B.5 lists the keys' functions in Field view.

Table B.5
Field View Keys

Shortcut Key(s)	Description
[↑]	Up one line in a wrapped field in forms
[↓]	Down one line in a wrapped field in forms
[→]	One character right
[←]	One character left

continues

433

Shortcut Keys

Table B.5 Continued

Shortcut Key(s)	Description
Home	First character of field
End	Last character of field
Ctrl-→	One word right
Ctrl-←	One word left
Ins	Insert/Overwrite mode toggle
Del	Delete character at cursor

Edit and CoEdit Mode Keys

Within Edit and CoEdit modes, some keys have different uses than they do in other modes. The key functions in table B.3 work in Edit and CoEdit mode also. Table B.6 shows the additional keys.

**Table B.6
Edit and CoEdit Keys**

Shortcut Key(s)	Description
Ins	Inserts a new record
Del	Deletes the current record
Ctrl-Backspace	Deletes entire field entry

Form Designer Keys

Within the Form Designer, many keys have different uses than they do in other modes. Table B.7 lists keys' different functions.

Report Designer Keys

Table B.7
Form Designer Keys

Shortcut Key(s)	Description
[↑]	Up one line
[↓]	Down one line
[→]	One character right
[←]	One character left
[Home]	First line
[End]	Last line
[Ctrl]-[Home]	Beginning of line
[Ctrl]-[End]	End of line
[Ins]	Insert/Overwrite mode toggle
[Del]	Delete character at cursor
[PgUp]	Move up one page, multiple page forms only
[PgDn]	Move down one page, multiple page forms only
[Alt]-[C]	Toggle color palette on or off, only after area or border has been selected

Report Designer Keys

Within the Report Designer, many keys have different uses than they do in other modes. Table B.8 lists the keys' different functions.

Table B.8
Report Designer Keys

Shortcut Key(s)	Description
[↑]	Up one line
[↓]	Down one line
[→]	One character right

continues

Shortcut Keys

Table B.8 Continued

Shortcut Key(s)	Description
←	One character left
Home	First line
End	Last line
Ctrl-Home	Beginning of line
Ctrl-End	End of line
Ins	Insert/Overwrite mode toggle
Del	Delete character at cursor
PgUp	Move up one screen
PgDn	Move down one screen
Ctrl-←	Left one window screen
Ctrl-→	Right one window screen
↵Enter	Insert new line, only in Insert mode
Ctrl-Y	Delete from cursor to end of line; if cursor at beginning of line, line will be deleted
Ctrl-V	Toggle vertical ruler

Report Previewer Keys

Within the Report Previewer, many keys have different uses than they do in other modes. Table B.9 lists the keys' different functions.

Table B.9
Report Previewer Keys

Shortcut Key(s)	Description
↑	Scroll up one line
↓	Scroll down one line
→	Scroll right one character

Other Special Key Combinations

Shortcut Key(s)	Description
←	Scroll left one character
Home	Scroll left one window screen
En	Scroll right one window screen
Ctrl-PgUp	Beginning of report
Ctrl-PgDn	End of report

Other Special Key Combinations

Other key combinations not yet discussed are listed in table B.10.

Table B.10
Miscellaneous Combination Keys

Shortcut Keys	Description
Ctrl-D	Ditto, copy contents of above field
Ctrl-E	Editor, starts the Paradox Editor
Ctrl-F	Field view, alternative to Alt-F5
Alt-K	View conflicting Key Violation records in CoEdit mode
Alt-L	Lock toggle, locks or unlocks a record, or confirms selected record when key violation occurs in CoEdit mode
Ctrl-R	Rotate columns
Ctrl-U	Undo change
Alt-X	Create CrossTab
Alt-Z	Zoom Next
Ctrl-Z	Zoom

B

437

Index

Symbols

! (exclamation point) inclusion operator, 329-332
#record field type, 216
* (asterisk), 70
.. (double period) wild card, 97, 177
< (less than) comparison operator, 191, 312
<= (less than or equal to) comparison operator, 191, 312
= (equal to) comparison operator, 191, 311-312
>= (greater than or equal to) comparison operator, 191, 312
> (greater than) comparison operator, 191, 311-312
@ (at sign) wild card, 97, 177
π (display subsequent pages), 136
π (move between records), 140
≡ (System menu), 24
√ (check mark), 171
3-D bar graphs, 379

A

active
  query forms, 175
  window, 31
adding records
  between tables, 318-322
  CoEdit mode, 116-118
  DataEntry mode, 100-104
  Edit mode, 86-89, 130
  Standard form, 141-143
Adding records from Tempord to Orders message, 254
AllCorrespondingFields option, 266
alphanumeric fields, 66
  combining, 316-317
  HighValue validity check, 258
  LowValue validity check, 258
  shortening, 244-245
Answer table, 168, 174, 193-195
  editing, 194
  fields, selecting, 196, 307-308
  saving, 194-195
  sorting, 193
area graphs, 382
arrow buttons, scroll bars, 36
AS special operator, 181-182

Paradox 4 QuickStart

ascending sort order, 154, 163-164
ASCII (American Standard Code for Information Interchange), 154
Ask command, 26, 170, 176, 196
asterisk (*), 70
at sign (@) wild card, 97, 177
Auto validity check, 268-271
autoconfirm function, 270-271
AVERAGE operator, 326-328
axes, graph, customizing, 395-396

B

backing out (canceling)
   of dialog boxes, 42
   of menus, 42
bands, 200
   decreasing size, 232
   group, 207, 221, 346-347
     editing, 347, 359-362
     placing fields within, 347-350
   headers, 206
   increasing size, 232
   literals, 206
   page, 206
   report, 206
   table, 207, 221-223
   triangles, 205
bar graphs, 378-379
Binary data type, 66
binary field, 69
Binary Large Objects (BLOBs), 69
blank lines, report specification, 223
BLANK special operator, 184-186
Blink screen attribute, 300
BLOBs (Binary Large Objects), 69
Border option, 296-298
Borrow command, 72
borrowing structures, 60, 71-73, 82
boxes, drawing in forms, 296-298
browsing, 41

C

CALC operator, 313-317, 327-328
CalcEdit dialog box, 354
calculated fields, 216, 285-287, 350-352
calculations
   alphanumeric values, 316-317
   arithmetic values, 313-315
   fields, 67
Cancel command, 42
canceling
   changes
     DataEntry mode, 113
     Edit mode, 99
   dialog boxes (backing out), 42
   functions, 42
   menus (backing out), 42
   with mouse, 42
case sensitivity, 97
Change option, 204
CHANGETO query, 324-325
characters, Picture field, 261
check marks, 167, 171
child window, 134
Close box, 40
Close command, 40
closing
   forms, 150-152
   tables, 152
   windows, 40
CoEdit mode, 13, 84
   adding records, 116-118
   deleting records, 120
   editing records, 116-118
   inserting records, 120
   saving changes, 123
   searching for records, 120-122
   shortcut keys, 434
   validity checks, 255-256
colors
   forms, adding, 299
   graph, adjusting, 394

440

Index

Column Rotate command, 131
columns, 10
   deleting, 213-214, 232
   inserting, 214-215, 232
   labels, 215
   moving, 127-131
   rotating, 128-131
   width, 124-125, 131
Comma format, 126
commands
   Ask, 170, 176, 196
   Borrow, 72
   Cancel, 42
   Close, 40
   Column Rotate, 131
   Create, 46, 63
   Delete, 80
   Ditto, 94-95, 105-106, 120
   DO-IT!, 98-99, 113, 156
   Field CalcEdit, 218
   Field Place, 217
   Field Place Regular, 221
   Field Reformat, 218
   FileFormat, 77-78, 82
   Group Insert Field, 220
   Image, 106
   Image ColumnSize, 125, 131
   Image Format, 126-127
   Image Format Date, 66
   Image KeepSet, 129
   Image Move, 127-131
   Image TableSize, 124, 131
   Image Zoom, 107, 145
   Image Zoom Field, 148, 152
   Image Zoom Record, 152
   Image Zoom Value, 152
   KeepEntry, 113
   Maximize/Restore, 36
   Modify, 85
   Modify CoEdit, 41
   Modify DataEntry, 41, 48, 100
   Modify Edit, 41, 141
   Modify MultiEntry, 41
   Modify Sort, 153-155
   Next, 38-40
   Report Change, 202
   Report Design, 202, 207
   Report Output, 203, 227-228
   Report RangeOutput, 203
   Rotate Column, 128-129
   Scripts BeginRecord, 412-414
   Setting PageLayout Delete, 212
   Settings Format GroupsOfTables, 225
   TableBand Erase, 213
   TableBand Insert, 214
   Tools Delete, 82
   Tools Rename Table, 193-194
   Undo, 91-94, 104-105, 118-120
   View, 78-79, 170
   Window, 38-40
   Zoom, 95, 106, 145
   Zoom Next, 95, 106, 145
comparison operators
   < (less than), 191, 312
   <= (less than or equal to), 191, 312
   = (equal to), 191, 311-312
   >= (greater than or equal to), 191, 312
   > (greater than), 191, 311-312
Compatible format, 60, 77
compressed fonts, 212
concatenated keys, 245-247
CONFIG.SYS file, editing, 427
copying records (contents), 130
COUNT operator, 326
Create command, 26, 46, 63
creating
   databases, 46-48, 60-63
   directories, 21
   queries, 170-171
   Query forms, 26
   query statements, 171-175

Paradox 4 QuickStart

report specification, 204, 232
reports, 203-204
    Instant Reports, 200
    Standard Report, 200
scripts, 411-414
tables, 26
crosstabs, creating, 386-388
Currency field, 68, 82, 126
CurrentPrinter format, 405
cursor
    moving, 211
    Report Previewer, 203
Customize Graph Colors screen, 394
Customize Pie Graph screen, 401
Customize Series Legends and Labels screen, 399

D

data integrity, 65
data types, 81
    Binary, 66
    Short number, 66
    Unknown, 66
databases
    adding information, 48
    creating, 60-63
    designing, 45
    families, 9-11
    flat-file, 6-7
    objects, 6, 9-11
    querying, *see* queries
    relational, 6-7, 40
    structure, creating, 46-48
DataEntry mode, 13, 84, 99, 104-106, 113-115
    adding records, 100-104
    canceling changes, 113
    deleting records, 112
    inserting records, 111-112

    saving changes, 113
    searching for records, 106-111
    validity checks, 255-256
date field, 69, 216, 258-259
date formats, 219
dates, 69, 216, 260
default
    dates, 260
    graph specification, 384-385
    sort order, 154
    values, 259-260
Default validity check, 259-260
defining
    sort order, 162-164
    tables, 71
Delete command, 80, 247
DELETE query, 322-323
deleting
    columns, 213-214, 232
    fields, 77, 82, 232
    lines, report specifications, 222
    objects, 82
    page widths, 211-213, 232
    pages, 213
    records, 130, 322-323
        CoEdit mode, 120
        DataEntry mode, 112
        Edit mode, 94
    tables, 79-82
descending sort order, 154, 163-165, 193
Design option, 204
Designer mode, *see* Report Designer
designing
    free-form forms, 275-276
    free-form reports, 366-368
    graphs, 383-388
    mailing labels, 370-372
    multiple record forms, 288-290
    report specifications, 207-210
    tables, 63-64

442

Index

desktop, 14, 19-27
dialog boxes, 20
    backing out (canceling), 42
    CalcEdit, 354
    Form Description, 278
    Picture, 262-263
    Script Break, 412
    Tools More Directory, 22
directories
    creating, 21
    subdirectories, 22
    working, 21-22
displaying
    fields, justification, 136
    forms, windows, 14
    graphs, 396-397
    Standard Form, 134-138
    tables
        format, 126-127
        windows, 14
    titles, fields, 224-225
    values, duplicate, 176-177
Ditto command, 94-95, 105-106, 120
DO-IT!, 78, 82, 98-99, 113, 156
DOS Protected Mode Interface (DPM), 15
double period (..) wild-card operator, 97, 177
DPM (DOS Protected Mode Interface), 15
duplicate values
    queries, 177
    tables, 157-159
duplication, 115

E

Edit mode, 13, 84
    adding records, 86-89, 130
    canceling changes, 99

    Field View, 90-91
    inserting records, 98
    saving changes, 99
    searching for records, 95-97
    shortcut keys, 434
    validity checks, 255-256
editing
    canceling changes
        DataEntry mode, 113
        Edit mode, 99
    CONFIG.SYS file, 427
    fields, 130, 218-220, 243-245
        Field view, 143-144
        Form view, 152
        types, 73-74
    forms, 301
    group bands, 347, 359-362
    literals, 215
    options, viewing reports, 224
    records
        CHANGETO query, 324-325
        CoEdit mode, 116-118
    report specification, 358-362
    saving changes
        CoEdit mode, 123
        DataEntry mode, 113
        Edit mode, 99
    screen attributes, 300-301
    scripts, 417-419
    table bands, 359-362
    tables, Answer table, 194
    transaction log, 84, 91-94
EPS format, 405
equal to (=) comparison operator, 191, 311-312
erasing fields, 242-243
example elements, linking query forms, 309-310
exclamation point (!) inclusion operator, 329-332
extensions (files) Rxx, 202

443

F

families, 6, 9-11, 202
Field CalcEdit command, 218
Field Place command, 217
Field Place Regular command, 221
Field Reformat command, 218
field types, 216
Field View, 84, 130
   Edit mode, 90-91
   shortcut keys, 433-434
fields, 7, 10, 60, 63
   adding, 239-241
   alphanumeric, 66
      combining, 316-317
      HighValue Validity check, 258
      LowValue Validity check, 258
      shortening, 244-245
   binary, 69
   calculated, 285-287, 350-352
   calculations, 67
   changing type, 247-248
   character limit, 41
   currency, 68
   date, 69, 258-260
   deleting, 77, 82, 232
   displaying, justification, 136
   editing, 130, 218-220, 243-245
      Field view, 84, 143-144
      Form view, 152
   erasing, 242-243
   fixed length, 67
   formats, 131
   formatting/reformatting, 218-220
   inserting, 75-76, 82, 216-217, 232
   masks, 210
   memo, 67, 77
   moving, 216, 241-242
   moving between, 139-140
   multiple line, wrapping, 298
   names
      editing, 74-75
      entering in free-form forms, 279-281
   naming, 64-65, 82
   numbers, 67
   placing in group bands, 347-350
   placing within forms, 281-285
   queries, 171-175
   records, 60
   reformatting, 218
   replacing, 216
   required, entering, 263-264
   selecting
      Answer table, 196
      for query statements, 307-308
   short number, 69
   size, 65-70, 287-288
   sort indexes, 164
   sorting
      by many fields, 159-162
      by single field, 157-159
      descending order, 193
   summary, 352-355
   titles, displaying, 224-225
   type, 65-74, 82
   unknown, 69
   see also key fields
FileFormat command, 77-78, 82
files
   CONFIG.SYS, editing, 427
   extensions, Rxx, 202
   Instant.SC, 411
   linking, key fields, 7
   maintenance, 27
   text, saving reports, 230-231
Filled option, 269
FillNoHelp option, 266
FIND query, 325
Fixed format, 126
fixed length fields, 67

Index

flat-file databases, 6-7
folders, 59
fonts, compressed, 212
Form Description dialog box, 278
Form Designer, 275
    editing forms, 301
    opening, 277-279
    shortcut keys, 434-435
    status bar, 279
Form menus, 137-138
Form view, 103, 130, 134-138
    editing fields, 143-144, 152
    searching for records, 144-150
    shortcut keys, 432-433
Form window, 135-137
formats
    Comma, 126
    Compatible (table structure), 77
    CurrentPrinter, 405
    dates, 219
    display, tables, 126-127
    EPS, 405
    fields, 131
    Fixed, 126
    General, 126
    logical AND, 186
    logical OR, 186
    PIC, 405
    queries, 168-169
    Scientific, 126
    Standard (table structure), 77
    tables
        Compatible, 60
        Standard, 60
formatting fields
    Currency, 126
    Number, 126
    reformatting, 218-220
forms, 10, 13, 134, 274
    accessing, 275
    boxes, drawing, 296-298
    calculated fields, 285-287
    changing, 27
    closing, 150-152
    color, adding, 299
    designing, 27, 275-276
    displaying, windows, 14
    editing, 301
    fields
        labels, 279-281
        placing within, 281-285
        sizing, 287-288
        wrapping, 298
    lines, drawing, 296-298
    multi-table, 290-291
        linking tables, 294-295
        master form, creating, 292-294
        referential integrity, 291-292
        unlinking tables, 295-296
    multiple record, 288-290
    opening, 151
    prompts, placing, 300
    query, 26, 175
        CALC expressions,
            constructing, 313-317
        creating statements, 171-175
        linking, 309-310
        saving, 195-196
    screen attributes, editing,
      300-301
    Standard, 139-150
    tables, viewing, 139
Forms Designer, 13
Forms option, 27
frames, graph, 396-397
free-form forms
    designing, 275-276
    field labels, 279-281
    fields, placing within, 281-285
free-form reports, 366
    designing, 366-368
    grouping, 368-370
    mailing labels, designing,
      370-372

445

free-form standard specification, 202
function keys, 41, 429-431
functions, canceling, 42

G

General format, 126
Graphical User Interface (GUI), 14
graphics, 19
graphs, 12-14
   3-D bar, 379
   area, 382
   axes, customizing, 395-396
   bar, 378-379
   colors, adjusting, 394
   converting from tables, 383-384
   crosstabs, creating, 386-388
   default specification, 384-385
   designing, 383-388
   elements, 376-378
   frames, adjusting, 396-397
   grid lines, editing, 396-397
   legend labels, adjusting, 398-399
   line, 380
   page specification, setting, 403-404
   pie, 381, 400-402
   printing, 403-404
   rotated bar, 380
   saving, 405
   scaling, 395-396
   series, 398-399
   specification, 405-406
   stacked bar, 379
   titles, adding, 392-393
   types, 378, 382-383, 388-391
   X-Y, 382
greater than (>) comparison operator, 191, 311-312
greater than or equal to (>=) comparison operator, 191, 312
grid lines, editing, 396-397

group bands, 207, 221
   adjusting, 347
   assigning, 346-347
   editing, 347, 359-362
   placing fields within, 347-350
Group Insert Field command, 220
groups, records, 220-221, 325-326
   calculated fields, creating, 350-352
   field titles, 225
   queries, 326-327
   sort order, 220
   sorting by, 232
   summary calculations, 327-328
   summary fields, creating, 352-357
GUI (Graphical User Interface), 14

H

hard disk, CONFIG.SYS file, editing, 427
hardware requirements, 16
headers, 206
Help, 42, 45
HelpAndFill option, 266-267
High value recorded message, 258
HighValue validity check, 256-259

I

Image command, 27, 106
Image ColumnSize command, 125, 131
Image Format command, 126-127
Image Format Date command, 66
Image KeepSet command, 129
Image Move command, 127-131
Image Move option, 307
Image TableSize command, 124, 131
Image Zoom command, 107, 145
Image Zoom Field command, 148, 152

Index

Image Zoom Record command, 152
Image Zoom Value command, 152
images, 123-129
inactive windows, 32
inclusion (!) operator, 329-332
inclusive link queries, creating, 329-332
indexes
   primary, 159
   secondary, 159, 164
   sorting, 164
INIT script, creating, 423-424
inner join queries, 329-331
INSERT query, 318-322
inserting
   blank lines, 223
   columns, 214-215, 232
   fields, 75-76, 82, 216-217, 232
   literals, 232
   records, 130
      CoEdit mode, 120
      DataEntry mode, 111-112
      Edit mode, 98
installing Paradox, 425-428
Instant Reports, 200, 231
instant scripts, creating, 411-412
Instant.SC file, 411
Intense screen attribute, 301
Intense-Reverse screen attribute, 301
introduction screen, 21

J-K

JustCurrentField option, 266
justification, fields, 136

KeepEntry command, 113
key fields, 7, 60, 63, 70-71, 82, 95, 99, 113-115, 245-248
key violations, 99, 113-115, 122-123, 130
keyboard
   CoEdit mode keys, 434
   Edit mode keys, 434
   Field view keys, 433-434
   Form Designer keys, 434-435
   Form view keys, 432-433
   function keys, 41, 429-431
   menu keys, 431
   miscellaneous keys, 437
   Report Designer keys, 435-436
   Report Previewer keys, 436-437
   Table view keys, 432
keyed tables, 154, 164
keys
   concatenated, 245-247
   movement, 140-141
   tables, 70-71
keystrokes, recording, 195
Keyviol table, 249-254

L

labels, 215
less than (<) comparison operator, 191, 312
less than or equal to (<=) comparison operator, 191, 312
LIKE special operator, 182-183
line graphs, 380
lines
   deleting, report specifications, 222
   drawing in forms, 296-298
linking
   field, 63
   files, key fields, 7
   query forms, 309-310
   tables, 10, 41, 294-295, 339-341
literals, 210, 216
   bands, 206
   editing, 215
   inserting, 232
      field titles as, 279-281

logical AND format, 186
logical OR format, 186
Lookup option, 269
lookup tables, 264-265
   relinking, 342
   selecting, 337-339
   unlinking, 341-342
LowValue validity check, 256-259

M

mailing labels, 370-372
Main menu, menu bar options, 26-27
masks (fields), 210
master table, selecting, 337
matching in searches, 95
matching values (queries), 177
MAX operator, 326-328
Maximize icon, 34
Maximize/Restore command, 36, 209
maximizing windows, 34-36, 209-210
memo field, 67, 77
menu bar, 20, 23, 26-27
menu keys, 431
menus
   backing out (canceling), 42
   desktop, 25-27
   Form, 137-138
   pull-down, 20
   Report, options, 203-204
   selecting items, 24
   Sort, 156-157
   System (≡), 24
message window, 29
messages
   Adding records from Tempord to Orders..., 254
   High value recorded, 258

Non-consecutive key found for CUST #, 246
   Settings changed, 369
   Value between .25 and 30.00 is expected, 258
MIN operator, 326-328
mode indicator, 25-29, 85
modes
   CoEdit, 13, 84, 115-123
      shortcut keys, 434
      validity checks, 255-256
   DataEntry, 13, 84, 99, 104-106, 113-115
      validity checks, 255-256
   Designer, *see* Report Designer
   Edit, 13, 84-98, 130
      shortcut keys, 434
      validity checks, 255-256
   Previewer, *see* Report Previewer
Modify command, 85
Modify CoEdit command, 41
Modify DataEntry command, 41, 48, 100
Modify Edit command, 41, 141
Modify MultiEntry command, 41
Modify option, 26, 41
Modify Sort command, 153-155
mouse, 15, 19, 30-31
   canceling operations, 42
   moving between windows, 38
   pointer, 15, 20
movement keys, 140-141
moving
   between fields, 139-140, 151
   between records, 140-141, 151-152
   between windows, 38
   columns, 127-131
   cursor, next page width, 211
   fields, 216, 241-242
   windows, 34
multi-table forms

Index

boxes, drawing, 296-298
color, adding, 299
designing, 290-292
editing, 301
lines, drawing, 296-298
linking tables, 294-295
master form, creating, 292-294
prompts, placing, 300
screen attributes, editing, 300-301
unlinking tables, 295-296
multi-table reports, 201
multi-user systems, *see* networks
multiple query statement conditions, 186-187, 190

N

naming
  fields, 64-65, 74-75, 82
  tables, 62-63, 82
networks, 16-17, 115
NewEntries option, 253
Next command, 38-40
No-Trimming option, 245
Non-Blink screen attribute, 301
Non-consecutive key found for CUST # message, 246
Normal screen attribute, 300
NOT special operator, 183-184
Number field, formatting, 67, 82, 126

O

object windows, 31-40
objects, 6-8, 11, 14
  deleting, 82
  families, 6, 9-11
  forms, 10
  graphs, 12
  records, 10
  reports, 11
  scripts, 12-13
  tables, 9-10, 60
Oops! option, 245-247
opening
  Form Designer, 277-279
  forms, 151
operators, 168
  AVERAGE, 326-328
  CALC, 313-317, 327-328
  comparison
    < (less than), 191, 312
    <= (less than or equal to), 191, 312
    = (equal to), 191, 311-312
    >= (greater than or equal to), 191, 312
    > (greater than), 191, 311-312
  COUNT, 326
  inclusion (!), 329-332
  MAX, 326-328
  MIN, 326-328
  OR, 187, 311-312
  special, 180-191
  SUM, 326
  summary, grouping records, 326-327
  wild-card, 178-180
    .. (double period), 177
    @ (at sign), 177
Optional Software Installation option, 427
options
  AllCorrespondingFields, 266
  Ask, 26
  Border, 296-298
  Change, 204
  Create, 26
  Delete, 247
  Design, 204
  DO-IT!, 78
  editing, viewing reports, 224
  Filled, 269

449

Paradox 4 QuickStart

FillNoHelp, 266
Forms, 27
HelpAndFill, 266-267
Image, 27
Image Move, 307
JustCurrentField, 266
Lookup, 269
Main menu, menu bar, 26-27
Maximize/Restore, 209
menus, previewing reports, 229-230
Modify, 26, 41
NewEntries, 253
No-Trimming, 245
Oops!, 245-247
Optional Software Installation, 427
Output, 204
Output Screen, 223
Overall Color, 394
Picture, 269
Play, 414-415
PrivateLookup, 266
Range Output, 204
Relink, 342
RepeatPlay, 415-417
Report, 26
Report menu, 203-204
Report Output Print, 362
Report RangeOutput, 362
Report SetPrinter Override, 366
Scripts, 27
Series, 398-399
SetPrinter, 204
ShowPlay, 414-416
Sort, 98
Style FieldNames Show, 283
Tools, 27
Trimming, 245
Update, 253
View, 26, 41, 82, 135
OR operator, 187, 311-312

Orders table, 238, 253-254
outer join queries, 329-332
Output option, 204
Output Screen option, 223
Overall Color option, 394
Override Graph Type feature, 391
overwriting records, 99

P

page
  bands, 200, 206
  breaks, reports, 359
  field type, 216
  numbers, 216
  widths, 211-213, 232
page specification, graphs, 403-404
pages, deleting, 213
Paradox
  hardware requirements, 16
  installing, 425-428
  software requirements, 16
  starting, 20, 22
parent window, 134
patterns (queries), 168
period, double (..), 97
PIC format, 405
Picture dialog box, 262-263
Picture option, 269
Picture validity check, 260-263
pie graphs, 381, 400-402
Play option, 414-415
playing scripts, 414-417
pointer mouse, 15, 20
PostScript printers, 15
Previewer mode, *see* Report Previewer
previewing reports, 223-230, 357-358
primary indexes, 159
printer specification, 403
printers

Index

fonts, compressed, 212
postscript, 15
selecting, 362-364
setup strings, 364-365
temporary overrides, 366
printing
   Instant Reports, 200
   literals, 215
   reports, 26, 200, 227-231, 362-366
   setup strings, 200
PrivateLookup option, 266
Problems table, 254-255
prompts, placing in forms, 300
pull-down menu, 20

Q

QBE (Query By Example), 13, 168-171, 174-180
queries, 196
   CHANGETO, 324-325
   check marks, 167, 171
   comparison operators, 191-193, 311-312
   constructing, 170
   creating, 170-171
   DELETE, 322-323
   duplicate values, 176-177
   fields, 171-175
   FIND, 325
   format, 168-169
   forms, 171-175
   group records, 326-327
   inclusive link, creating, 329-332
   inner join, 329-331
   INSERT, 318-322
   logical AND format, 186
   logical OR format, 186
   matching values, 177
   operators, 168
   outer join, 329-332
   patterns, 168
   similar values, 177-180
   special operators
      AS, 181
      BLANK, 185-186
      LIKE, 182
      NOT, 183
   tables
      adding records, 318-322
      deleting records, 322-323
      editing records, 324-325
      example elements, creating, 309-310
      finding records, 325
      multiple, 306-312
      selecting, 170
   wild-card operators, 177-180
   see also QBE
Query By Example, *see* QBE
query form
   CALC expressions, constructing, 313-317
   creating, 26
   linking, 309-310
   saving, 195-196
query statements, 168, 196
   creating, 171-175, 307
   multi-table, 306-308
   multiple conditions, 186-190
   refining, 311
   saving as query script, 422-423

R

Range Output option, 204
#record field type, 216
recording
   scripts, 413-414
   keystrokes, 195
records, 7, 10, 59, 60

451

adding, 88-89
    between tables, 318-322
    CoEdit mode, 116-118
    DataEntry mode, 100-104
    Edit mode, 86-89, 130
    from Tempord table to Orders table, 253-254
    Standard form, 141-143
character limit, 41
copying contents, 130
deleting, 130, 322-323
    CoEdit mode, 120
    DataEntry mode, 112
    Edit mode, 94
editing
    CHANGETO query, 324-325
    CoEdit mode, 116-118
fields, 60
groups, 220-221, 325-326
    queries, 326-327
    sort order, 220
    summary calculations, 327-328
inserting, 130
    CoEdit mode, 120
    DataEntry mode, 111-112
    Edit mode, 98
moving between, 140-141, 151-152
overwriting, 99
queries, 329-332
rows, 60
searching for, 130, 196
    CHANGETO query, 325
    CoEdit mode, 120-122
    DataEntry mode, 106-111
    Edit mode, 95-97
    Form view, 144-150
sorting, 111, 122-123
viewing, 103
reformatting fields, 218-220, 232
regular field type, 216
relational databases, 6-7, 40

Relink option, 342
RepeatPlay option, 415-417
replacing fields, 216
Report Change command, 202
Report Design command, 202, 207
Report Designer, 202-223, 226, 435-436
Report menu, options, 203-204
Report option, 26
Report Output command, 203, 227-228
Report Output Print option, 362
Report Previewer, 202-204, 223, 436-437
Report Previewer window, 357-362
Report RangeOutput command, 203
Report RangeOutput option, 362
Report SetPrinter Override option, 366
report specification, 201-204
    bands, 200, 232
    blank lines, 223
    columns, 214-215
    creating, 204, 232
    customizing, 342-345
    designing, 207-210
    editing, 358-362
    families, 202
    fields, 216-217
    free-form standard, 202
    literals, 215-216
    mailing labels, creating, 370-372
    removing lines, 222
    saving, 203, 226
    tabular, 202
reports, 11-13, 199-205, 336
    bands, 200, 205
        group, 207
        page band, 206
        table, 207, 221-223
    creating, 203-204
        customizing specification, 342-345

Index

Instant Reports, 200
linking tables, 339-341
lookup tables, selecting, 337-339
master tables, selecting, 337
relinking tables, 342
Standard Reports, 200
unlinking tables, 341-342
date fields, 216
date formats, 219
format, *see also* report specification
free-form
designing, 366-368
grouping, 368-370
mailing labels, designing, 370-372
group bands, 346-350
grouping, 346-350
multi-table, 201
page field, 216
previewing, 223-230, 357-358
printing, 26, 200, 227-231, 362-366
saving, 230-231
settings, changing, 225-226
sorting by groups, 232
Standard, 203
summary calculations, 352-357
tabular, 200, 205, 336-337
time fields, 216
viewing
editing, 224
previewing, 223
see also Report Designer; Report Previewer
Reports Designer, 13
Required validity check, 263-264
Resize corner, 32
resizing windows, 32-34
resorting automatically, 99
Restore icon, 35

restoring windows, 34-36
Reverse screen attribute, 301
Rotate Column command, 128-129
rotated bar graph, 380
rotating columns, 128-131
rows, records, 60
Rxx file extension, 202

S

saving
changes
CoEdit mode, 123
DataEntry mode, 113
Edit mode, 99
graphs, 405
image settings, 129
query form, 195-196
report specifications, 203, 226
reports as text file, 230-231
structures, tables, 78
tables, 194-195
Scientific format, 126
screens
attributes, editing, 300-301
Customize Graph Colors, 394
Customize Pie Graph, 401
Customize Series Legends and Labels, 399
Help, 42-45
introduction, 21
opening display, 23
Signature, 426
Script Break dialog box, 412
Script Editor, 417-419
scripts, 12-13, 27, 195, 409-410
code words, 419-421
creating, 411-414
editing, 417-419
INIT, creating, 423-424
playing, 414-417
recording, 413-414

453

Paradox 4 QuickStart

renaming, 423
repeating, 416-417
running automatically, 423-424
Scripts BeginRecord command, 412-414
Scripts option, 27
scroll bars, 20, 36-38
searching, 152, 196
   case sensitivity, 97
   CoEdit mode, 120-122
   comparison operators, 191-193
   DataEntry mode, 106-111
   Edit mode, 95-97
   for records, 130, 325
   Form view, 144-150
   key field, 95
   matches, 95
   special operators, 180
      AS, 181-182
      BLANK, 184-186
      LIKE, 182-183
      NOT, 183-184
   wild-card operators, 97, 177-180
      .. (double period), 177
      @ (at sign), 177
secondary indexes, 159, 164
Series option, 398-399
servers, networks, 16-17
SetPrinter option, 204
Setting PageLayout Delete command, 212
settings
   images, saving, 129
   pie graphs, selecting, 400-402
   reports, changing, 225-226
Settings changed message, 369
Settings Format GroupsOfTables command, 225
setup strings, 200
Short number data type, 66
short number fields, 69
ShowPlay option, 414-416

Signature screen, 426
similar values (queries), 177-180
single key tables, 70-71
sizing
   fields, 218, 287-288
   tables, 131
software requirements, 16
Sort menu, 156-157
Sort option, 98
sort order, 162-164
Sort Questionnaire, 155-156, 164
Sort To table, 155-156
sorting, 154-164
   Answer table, 193
   ascending order, 154, 163
   by groups, 232
   by many fields, 159, 162
   by single field, 157-159
   descending order, 154, 163-164
   fields, descending order, 193
   indexes, 159, 164
   order, 157
      ascending, 154, 163
      default, 154
      defining, 162-164
      descending, 154, 163-164
      groups, 220
   primary indexes, 159
   records, 111, 122-123
   secondary indexes, 159
   standard order, 154
   tables
      key field, 60
      re-sorting, 155
      re-sorting automatically, 99
   tie breaking, 162-164
special operators, 180-191
   AS, 181-182
   BLANK, 184-186
   LIKE, 182-183
   NOT, 183-184
specifications

454

Index

graphs, 405-406
printer, 403
reports, 200-202
stacked bar graph, 379
Standard form, 139-150
adding records, 141-143
displaying, 134-138
Standard format, 60, 77
Standard Reports
creating, 200
redirecting to screen or file, 203
standard sort order, 154
starting Paradox, 20-22
statements, query, 168
creating, 171-175
fields, selecting, 307-308
refining, 311
saving as query script, 422-423
selecting tables, 306-307
stations, networks, 16
status bar, 23-25
Form Designer, 279
Table view, 137-138
structures table, 61-62, 81
borrowing, 60, 71-73, 82
changing, 26
saving, 78
Style FieldNames Show option, 283
subdirectories, working directory, 22
SUM operator, 326
summary field, 216, 352-355
summary operators, 326-327
symmetrical outer join queries, 331-332
System menu (≡), 24

T

Table view, 89
shortcut keys, 432
status bar, 137-138
TableBand Erase command, 213
TableBand Insert command, 214
TableLookup validity check, 264-268
TableOfGroups, 224
tables, 9-10, 13, 41, 46, 59-60
adding information, 48
Answer, selecting fields, 307-308
bands, 207
adjusting, 221-223
editing, 359-362
child windows, 137
closing, 152
columns, width, 124-125
converting into graphs, 383-384
creating, 26
default values, 259-260
definition, 71
deleting, 79-82
designing, 63-64
displaying
format, 126-127
windows, 14
duplicate values, 157-159
editing, 194
families, report specifications, 202
fields
adding, 239-241
changing type, 247-248
concatenated key, 245-247
editing, 243-245
erasing, 242-243
key, 245-248
moving, 241-242
required, entering, 263-264
formats, 60
forms, 27
image, 27, 123-129
key field, 60-63, 82
keyed
re-sorting, 155
sorting, 154, 164
Keyviol, 249-254

455

linking, 10, 41, 294-295, 339-341
lookup, 264-265, 337-339
master, selecting, 337
naming, 62-63, 82
objects, 60
Orders, 238, 253-254
Problems, 254-255
queries
   example elements, creating, 309-310
   fields, selecting, 307-308
   multiple, 306-312
   selecting tables, 306-307
relinking, 342
restructuring, 236-271
saving, 194-195
selecting for query, 170
single key, 70-71
size, 124, 131
Sort To, 155-156
sorting, 154-164
   by many fields, 159, 162
   by single field, 157-159
   resorting automatically, 99
structures, 46, 61-62, 81
   borrowing, 60, 82, 71-73
   changing, 26
   formats, 77
   saving, 78
target, 100
temporary, 62, 99
   Answer, 168, 174
   Answer table, 193-195
unlinking, 295-296, 341-342
validity checks, 255-256
   Auto, 268-271
   Default, 259-260
   HighValue, 256-258
   LowValue, 256-258
   Picture, 260-263
   Required, 263-264
   TableLookup, 264-268

viewing, 78-82, 139
   see also databases; sorting
tabular report specification, 202
tabular reports, 200, 205, 336, 337
target table, 100
temporary tables, 62, 99, 168, 174, 193-195
text, 215
   see also literals
text files, reports, saving as, 230-231
tie breaking (sorting), 162-164
time field type, 216
title bar, 20
titles
   fields
      displaying, 224-225
      entering, 279-281
      graph, adding, 392-393
Tools Delete command, 82
Tools More Directory dialog box, 22
Tools option, 27
Tools Rename Table command, 193-194
transaction log, 84, 91-94, 130
transformations, 383-384
triangles, *see* bands
Trimming option, 245

U

Undo, 93, 130
Undo command, 91-94, 104-105, 118-120
Unknown data types, 66
unknown fields, 69
unlinking tables, 295-296, 341-342
Update option, 253

V

validity checks, 255-256
   Auto, 268-271
   Default, 259-260

Index

HighValue, 256-259
LowValue, 256-259
Picture, 260-263
Required, 263-264
TableLookup, 264-268
Value between .25 and 30.00 is expected message, 258
values
   default, 259-260
   duplicate, 176
   matching, 177
   similar, 177-180
   specifying for date fields, 258-259
View command, 26, 41, 78-79, 82, 135, 170
viewing
   pages, subsequent, 136
   records, 103
   reports
      editing, 224
      pre-printing, 203
      previewing, 223
   table, 78-79, 82
      forms, 139
   see also browsing

W

wild cards, 97, 177-180
   .. (double period), 97, 177
   @ (at sign), 97, 177
Window command, 38-40
windows, 20
   active, 31
   child, 134
   Close box, 40
   closing, 40
   Form, 135-136
   form, 14, 137
   inactive, 32
   maximizing, 34-36, 209-210
   message, 29
   mode indicator, 85
   moving, 34
   moving between, with mouse, 38
   object, 31-40
   parent, 134
   Report Previewer, 357-362
   resizing, 32-34
   restoring, 34-36
   scroll bars, 36-38
   tables, 14
working directory, 21-22

X-Y

X-Y graphs, 382

Zoom command, 95, 106, 145, 152
Zoom Next command, 95, 106, 145, 152

Computer Books from Que Mean PC Performance!

Spreadsheets

1-2-3 Beyond the Basics	$24.95
1-2-3 for DOS Release 2.3 Quick Reference	$ 9.95
1-2-3 for DOS Release 2.3 QuickStart	$19.95
1-2-3 for DOS Release 3.1+ Quick Reference	$ 9.95
1-2-3 for DOS Release 3.1+ QuickStart	$19.95
1-2-3 for Windows Quick Reference	$ 9.95
1-2-3 for Windows QuickStart	$19.95
1-2-3 Personal Money Manager	$29.95
1-2-3 Power Macros	$39.95
1-2-3 Release 2.2 QueCards	$19.95
Easy 1-2-3	$19.95
Easy Excel	$19.95
Easy Quattro Pro	$19.95
Excel 3 for Windows QuickStart	$19.95
Excel for Windows Quick Reference	$ 9.95
Look Your Best with 1-2-3	$24.95
Quattro Pro 3 QuickStart	$19.95
Quattro Pro Quick Reference	$ 9.95
Using 1-2-3 for DOS Release 2.3, Special Edition	$29.95
Using 1-2-3 for Windows	$29.95
Using 1-2-3 for DOS Release 3.1+, Special Edition	$29.95
Using Excel 4 for Windows, Special Edition	$29.95
Using Quattro Pro 4, Special Edition	$27.95
Using Quattro Pro for Windows	$24.95
Using SuperCalc5, 2nd Edition	$29.95

Databases

dBASE III Plus Handbook, 2nd Edition	$24.95
dBASE IV 1.1 Quick Reference	$ 9.95
dBASE IV 1.1 QuickStart	$19.95
Introduction to Databases	$19.95
Paradox 3.5 Quick Reference	$ 9.95
Paradox Quick Reference, 2nd Edition	$ 9.95
Using AlphaFOUR	$24.95
Using Clipper, 3rd Edition	$29.95
Using DataEase	$24.95
Using dBASE IV	$29.95
Using FoxPro 2	$24.95
Using ORACLE	$29.95
Using Paradox 3.5, Special Edition	$29.95
Using Paradox for Windows	$26.95
Using Paradox, Special Edition	$29.95
Using PC-File	$24.95
Using R:BASE	$29.95

Business Applications

CheckFree Quick Reference	$ 9.95
Easy Quicken	$19.95
Microsoft Works Quick Reference	$ 9.95
Norton Utilities 6 Quick Reference	$ 9.95
PC Tools 7 Quick Reference	$ 9.95
Q&A 4 Database Techniques	$29.95
Q&A 4 Quick Reference	$ 9.95
Q&A 4 QuickStart	$19.95
Q&A 4 Que Cards	$19.95
Que's Computer User's Dictionary, 2nd Edition	$10.95
Que's Using Enable	$29.95
Quicken 5 Quick Reference	$ 9.95
SmartWare Tips, Tricks, and Traps, 2nd Edition	$26.95
Using DacEasy, 2nd Edition	$24.95
Using Microsoft Money	$19.95
Using Microsoft Works: IBM Version	$22.95
Using Microsoft Works for Windows, Special Edition	$24.95
Using MoneyCounts	$19.95
Using Pacioli 2000	$19.95
Using Norton Utilities 6	$24.95
Using PC Tools Deluxe 7	$24.95
Using PFS: First Choice	$22.95
Using PFS: WindowWorks	$24.95
Using Q&A 4	$27.95
Using Quicken 5	$19.95
Using Quicken for Windows	$19.95
Using Smart	$29.95
Using TimeLine	$24.95
Using TurboTax: 1992 Edition	$19.95

CAD

AutoCAD Quick Reference, 2nd Edition	$ 8.95
Using AutoCAD, 3rd Edition	$29.95

Word Processing

Easy WordPerfect	$19.95
Easy WordPerfect for Windows	$19.95
Look Your Best with WordPerfect 5.1	$24.95
Look Your Best with WordPerfect for Windows	$24.95
Microsoft Word Quick Reference	$ 9.95
Using Ami Pro	$24.95
Using LetterPerfect	$22.95
Using Microsoft Word 5.5: IBM Version, 2nd Edition	$24.95
Using MultiMate	$24.95
Using PC-Write	$22.95
Using Professional Write	$22.95
Using Professional Write Plus for Windows	$24.95
Using Word for Windows 2, Special Edition	$27.95
Using WordPerfect 5	$27.95
Using WordPerfect 5.1, Special Edition	$27.95
Using WordPerfect for Windows, Special Edition	$29.95
Using WordStar 7	$19.95
Using WordStar, 3rd Edition	$27.95
WordPerfect 5.1 Power Macros	$39.95
WordPerfect 5.1 QueCards	$19.95
WordPerfect 5.1 Quick Reference	$ 9.95
WordPerfect 5.1 QuickStart	$19.95
WordPerfect 5.1 Tips, Tricks, and Traps	$24.95
WordPerfect for Windows Power Pack	$39.95
WordPerfect for Windows Quick Reference	$ 9.95
WordPerfect for Windows Quick Start	$19.95
WordPerfect Power Pack	$39.95
WordPerfect Quick Reference	$ 9.95

Hardware/Systems

Batch File and Macros Quick Reference	$ 9.95
Computerizing Your Small Business	$19.95
DR DOS 6 Quick Reference	$ 9.95
Easy DOS	$19.95
Easy Windows	$19.95
Fastback Quick Reference	$ 8.95
Hard Disk Quick Reference	$ 8.95
Hard Disk Quick Reference, 1992 Edition	$ 9.95
Introduction to Hard Disk Management	$24.95
Introduction to Networking	$24.95
Introduction to PC Communications	$24.95
Introduction to Personal Computers, 2nd Edition	$19.95
Introduction to UNIX	$24.95
Laplink Quick Reference	$ 9.95
MS-DOS 5 Que Cards	$19.95
MS-DOS 5 Quick Reference	$ 9.95
MS-DOS 5 QuickStart	$19.95
MS-DOS Quick Reference	$ 8.95
MS-DOS QuickStart, 2nd Edition	$19.95
Networking Personal Computers, 3rd Edition	$24.95
Que's Computer Buyer's Guide, 1992 Edition	$14.95
Que's Guide to CompuServe	$12.95
Que's Guide to DataRecovery	$29.95
Que's Guide to XTree	$12.95
Que's MS-DOS User's Guide, Special Edition	$29.95
Que's PS/1 Book	$22.95
TurboCharging MS-DOS	$24.95
Upgrading and Repairing PCs	$29.95
Upgrading and Repairing PCs, 2nd Edition	$29.95
Upgrading to MS-DOS 5	$14.95
Using GeoWorks Pro	$24.95
Using Microsoft Windows 3, 2nd Edition	$24.95
Using MS-DOS 5	$24.95
Using Novell NetWare, 2nd Edition	$29.95
Using OS/2 2.0	$24.95
Using PC DOS, 3rd Edition	$27.95
Using Prodigy	$19.95
Using UNIX	$29.95
Using Windows 3.1	$26.95
Using Your Hard Disk	$29.95
Windows 3 Quick Reference	$ 8.95
Windows 3 QuickStart	$19.95
Windows 3.1 Quick Reference	$ 9.95
Windows 3.1 QuickStart	$19.95

Desktop Publishing/Graphics

CorelDRAW! Quick Reference	$ 8.95
Harvard Graphics 3 Quick Reference	$ 9.95
Harvard Graphics Quick Reference	$ 9.95
Que's Using Ventura Publisher	$29.95
Using DrawPerfect	$24.95
Using Freelance Plus	$24.95
Using Harvard Graphics 3	$29.95
Using Harvard Graphics for Windows	$24.95
Using Harvard Graphics, 2nd Edition	$24.95
Using Microsoft Publisher	$22.95
Using PageMaker 4 for Windows	$29.95
Using PFS: First Publisher, 2nd Edition	$24.95
Using PowerPoint	$24.95
Using Publish It!	$24.95

Macintosh/Apple II

Easy Macintosh	$19.95
HyperCard 2 QuickStart	$19.95
PageMaker 4 for the Mac Quick Reference	$ 9.95
The Big Mac Book, 2nd Edition	$29.95
The Little Mac Book	$12.95
QuarkXPress 3.1 Quick Reference	$ 9.95
Que's Big Mac Book, 3rd Edition	$29.95
Que's Little Mac Book, 2nd Edition	$12.95
Que's Mac Classic Book	$24.95
Que's Macintosh Multimedia Handbook	$24.95
System 7 Quick Reference	$ 9.95
Using 1-2-3 for the Mac	$24.95
Using AppleWorks, 3rd Edition	$24.95
Using Excel 3 for the Macintosh	$24.95
Using FileMaker Pro	$24.95
Using MacDraw Pro	$24.95
Using MacroMind Director	$29.95
Using MacWrite Pro	$24.95
Using Microsoft Word 5 for the Mac	$27.95
Using Microsoft Works: Macintosh Version, 2nd Edition	$24.95
Using Microsoft Works for the Mac	$24.95
Using PageMaker 4 for the Macintosh	$24.95
Using Quicken 3 for the Mac	$19.95
Using the Macintosh with System 7	$24.95
Using Word for the Mac, Special Edition	$24.95
Using WordPerfect 2 for the Mac	$24.95
Word for the Mac Quick Reference	$ 9.95

Programming/Technical

Borland C++ 3 By Example	$21.95
Borland C++ Programmer's Reference	$29.95
C By Example	$21.95
C Programmer's Toolkit, 2nd Edition	$39.95
Clipper Programmer's Reference	$29.95
DOS Programmer's Reference, 3rd Edition	$29.95
FoxPro Programmer's Reference	$29.95
Network Programming in C	$49.95
Paradox Programmer's Reference	$29.95
Programming in Windows 3.1	$39.95
QBasic By Example	$21.95
Turbo Pascal 6 By Example	$21.95
Turbo Pascal 6 Programmer's Reference	$29.95
UNIX Programmer's Reference	$29.95
UNIX Shell Commands Quick Reference	$ 8.95
Using Assembly Language, 2nd Edition	$29.95
Using Assembly Language, 3rd Edition	$29.95
Using BASIC	$24.95
Using Borland C++	$29.95
Using Borland C++ 3, 2nd Edition	$29.95
Using C	$29.95
Using Microsoft C	$29.95
Using QBasic	$24.95
Using QuickBASIC 4	$24.95
Using QuickC for Windows	$29.95
Using Turbo Pascal 6, 2nd Edition	$29.95
Using Turbo Pascal for Windows	$29.95
Using Visual Basic	$29.95
Visual Basic by Example	$21.95
Visual Basic Programmer's Reference	$29.95
Windows 3.1 Programmer's Reference	$39.95

For More Information,
Call Toll Free!
1-800-428-5331

*All prices and titles subject to change without notice.
Non-U.S. prices may be higher. Printed in the U.S.A.*

Teach Yourself with QuickStarts from Que!

The ideal tutorials for beginners, Que's QuickStart Books use graphic illustrations and step-by-step instructions to get you up and running fast. Packed with examples, QuickStarts are the perfect beginner's guides to your favorite software applications.

MS-DOS 5 QuickStart
Que Development Group

This is the easy-to-use graphic approach to learning MS-DOS 5. The combination of step-by-step instruction, examples, and graphics make this book ideal for all DOS beginners.
DOS 5
$19.95 USA
0-88022-681-1, 420 pp., $7^3/_8$ x $9^1/_4$

Windows 3.1 QuickStart
Ron Person & Karen Rose

This graphics-based text teaches Windows beginners how to use the feature-packed Windows environment. Emphasizes such software applications as Excel, Word, and PageMaker, and shows how to master Windows' mouse, menus, and screen elements.
Through Version 3.1
$21.95 USA
0-88022-730-3, 500 pp., $7^3/_8$ x $9^1/_4$

1-2-3 for DOS Release 2.3 QuickStart
Release 2.3
$19.95
0-88022-716-8, 500 pp., $7^3/_8$ x $9^1/_4$

1-2-3 for DOS Release 3.1+ QuickStart, Special Edition
Releases 3, 3.1, & 3.1+
$29.95 USA
0-88022-843-1, 975 pp., $7^3/_8$ x $9^1/_4$

1-2-3 for Windows QuickStart
1-2-3 for Windows
$19.95 USA
0-88022-723-0, 500 pp., $7^3/_8$ x $9^1/_4$

dBASE IV 1.1 QuickStart
Through Version 11
$19.95 USA
0-88022-614-5, 400 pp., $7^3/_8$ x $9^1/_4$

Excel 3 for Windows QuickStart
Version 3 for Windows
$19.95 USA
0-88022-762-1, 500 pp., $7^3/_8$ x $9^1/_4$

MS-DOS QuickStart, 2nd Edition
Version 3.X & 4.X
$19.95 USA
0-88022-611-0, 420 pp., $7^3/_8$ x $9^1/_4$

Q&A 4 QuickStart
Versions 3 & 4
$19.95 USA
0-88022-653-6, 450 pp., $7^3/_8$ x $9^1/_4$

Quattro Pro 3 QuickStart
Through Version 3.0
$19.95 USA
0-88022-693-5, 450 pp., $7^3/_8$ x $9^1/_4$

Windows 3 QuickStart
Version 3
$19.95 USA
0-88022-610-2, 440 pp., $7^3/_8$ x $9^1/_4$

WordPerfect 5.1 QuickStart
WordPerfect 5.1
$19.95 USA
0-88022-558-0, 427 pp., $7^3/_8$ x $9^1/_4$

WordPerfect for Windows QuickStart
WordPerfect 5.1 for Windows
$19.95 USA
0-88022-712-5, 400 pp., $7^3/_8$ x $9^1/_4$

To Order, Call:
(800) 428-5331
OR
(317) 573-2500

Personal computing is easy when you're using Que!

Using 1-2-3 for DOS Release 2.3, Special Edition
$29.95 USA
0-88022-727-8, 584 pp., $7^3/_8$ x $9^1/_4$

Using 1-2-3 for DOS Release 3.1+, Special Edition
$29.95 USA
0-88022-843-1, 584 pp., $7^3/_8$ x $9^1/_4$

Using 1-2-3 for Windows
$29.95 USA
0-88022-724-9, 584 pp., $7^3/_8$ x $9^1/_4$

Using 1-2-3/G
$29.95 USA
0-88022-549-7, 584 pp., $7^3/_8$ x $9^1/_4$

Using AlphaFOUR
$24.95 USA
0-88022-890-3, 500 pp., $7^3/_8$ x $9^1/_4$

Using AmiPro
$24.95 USA
0-88022-738-9, 584 pp., $7^3/_8$ x $9^1/_4$

Using Assembly Language, 3rd Edition
$29.95 USA
0-88022-884-9, 900 pp., $7^3/_8$ x $9^1/_4$

Using BASIC
$24.95 USA
0-88022-537-8, 584 pp., $7^3/_8$ x $9^1/_4$

Using Borland C++, 2nd Edition
$29.95 USA
0-88022-901-2, 1,300 pp., $7^3/_8$ x $9^1/_4$

Using C
$29.95 USA
0-88022-571-8, 950 pp., $7^3/_8$ x $9^1/_4$

Using Clipper, 3rd Edition
$29.95 USA
0-88022-885-7, 750 pp., $7^3/_8$ x $9^1/_4$

Using DacEasy, 2nd Edition
$24.95 USA
0-88022-510-6, 584 pp., $7^3/_8$ x $9^1/_4$

Using DataEase
$24.95 USA
0-88022-465-7, 584 pp., $7^3/_8$ x $9^1/_4$

Using dBASE IV
$24.95 USA
0-88022-551-3, 584 pp., $7^3/_8$ x $9^1/_4$

Using Excel 3 for Windows, Special Edition
$24.95 USA
0-88022-685-4, 584 pp., $7^3/_8$ x $9^1/_4$

Using FoxPro 2
$24.95 USA
0-88022-703-6, 584 pp., $7^3/_8$ x $9^1/_4$

Using Freelance Plus
$24.95 USA
0-88022-528-9, 584 pp., $7^3/_8$ x $9^1/_4$

Using GeoWorks Ensemble
$24.95 USA
0-88022-748-6, 584 pp., $7^3/_8$ x $9^1/_4$

Using Harvard Graphics 3
$24.95 USA
0-88022-735-4, 584 pp., $7^3/_8$ x $9^1/_4$

Using Harvard Graphics for Windows
$24.95 USA
0-88022-755-9, 700 pp., $7^3/_8$ x $9^1/_4$

Using LetterPoerfect
$24.95 USA
0-88022-667-6, 584 pp., $7^3/_8$ x $9^1/_4$

Using Microsoft C
$24.95 USA
0-88022-809-1, 584 pp., $7^3/_8$ x $9^1/_4$

Using Microsoft Money
$19.95 USA
0-88022-914-4, 400 pp., $7^3/_8$ x $9^1/_4$

Using Microsoft Publisher
$22.95 USA
0-88022-915-2, 450 pp., $7^3/_8$ x $9^1/_4$

Using Microsoft Windows 3, 2nd Edition
$24.95 USA
0-88022-509-2, 584 pp., $7^3/_8$ x $9^1/_4$

Using Microsoft Word 5.5: IBM Version, 2nd Edition
$24.95 USA
0-88022-642-0, 584 pp., $7^3/_8$ x $9^1/_4$

Using Microsoft Works for Windows, Special Edition
$24.95 USA
0-88022-757-5, 584 pp., $7^3/_8$ x $9^1/_4$

Using Microsoft Works: IBM Version
$24.95 USA
0-88022-467-3, 584 pp., $7^3/_8$ x $9^1/_4$

Using MoneyCounts
$24.95 USA
0-88022-696-X, 584 pp., $7^3/_8$ x $9^1/_4$

Using MS-DOS 5
$24.95 USA
0-88022-668-4, 584 pp., $7^3/_8$ x $9^1/_4$

Using Norton Utilities 6
$24.95 USA
0-88022-861-X, 584 pp., $7^3/_8$ x $9^1/_4$

Using Novell NetWare, 2nd Edition
$24.95 USA
0-88022-756-7, 584 pp., $7^3/_8$ x $9^1/_4$

Using ORACLE
$24.95 USA
0-88022-506-8, 584 pp., $7^3/_8$ x $9^1/_4$

Using OS/2 2.0
$24.95 USA
0-88022-863-6, 584 pp., $7^3/_8$ x $9^1/_4$

Using Pacioli 2000
$24.95 USA
0-88022-780-X, 584 pp., $7^3/_8$ x $9^1/_4$

Using PageMaker 4 for Windows
$24.95 USA
0-88022-607-2, 584 pp., $7^3/_8$ x $9^1/_4$

Using Paradox 4, Special Edition
$29.95 USA
0-88022-822-9, 900 pp., $7^3/_8$ x $9^1/_4$

Using Paradox for Windows, Special Edition
$29.95 USA
0-88022-823-7, 750 pp., $7^3/_8$ x $9^1/_4$

Using PC DOS, 3rd Edition
$24.95 USA
0-88022-409-3, 584 pp., $7^3/_8$ x $9^1/_4$

Using PC Tools 7
$24.95 USA
0-88022-733-8, 584 pp., $7^3/_8$ x $9^1/_4$

Using PC-File
$24.95 USA
0-88022-695-1, 584 pp., $7^3/_8$ x $9^1/_4$

Using PC-Write
$24.95 USA
0-88022-654-4, 584 pp., $7^3/_8$ x $9^1/_4$

Using PFS: First Choice
$24.95 USA
0-88022-454-1, 584 pp., $7^3/_8$ x $9^1/_4$

Using PFS: First Publisher, 2nd Edition
$24.95 USA
0-88022-591-2, 584 pp., $7^3/_8$ x $9^1/_4$

Using PFS: WindowWorks
$24.95 USA
0-88022-751-6, 584 pp., $7^3/_8$ x $9^1/_4$

Using PowerPoint
$24.95 USA
0-88022-698-6, 584 pp., $7^3/_8$ x $9^1/_4$

Using Prodigy
$24.95 USA
0-88022-658-7, 584 pp., $7^3/_8$ x $9^1/_4$

Using Professional Write
$24.95 USA
0-88022-490-8, 584 pp., $7^3/_8$ x $9^1/_4$

Using Professional Write Plus for Windows
$24.95 USA
0-88022-754-0, 584 pp., $7^3/_8$ x $9^1/_4$

Using Publish It!
$24.95 USA
0-88022-660-9, 584 pp., $7^3/_8$ x $9^1/_4$

Using Q&A 4
$24.95 USA
0-88022-643-9, 584 pp., $7^3/_8$ x $9^1/_4$

Using QBasic
$24.95 USA
0-88022-713-3, 584 pp., $7^3/_8$ x $9^1/_4$

Using Quattro Pro 3, Special Edition
$24.95 USA
0-88022-721-4, 584 pp., $7^3/_8$ x $9^1/_4$

Using Quattro Pro for Windows, Special Edition
$27.95 USA
0-88022-889-X, 900 pp., $7^3/_8$ x $9^1/_4$

Using Quick BASIC 4
$24.95 USA
0-88022-378-2, 713 pp., $7^3/_8$ x $9^1/_4$

Using QuickC for Windows
$29.95 USA
0-88022-810-5, 584 pp., $7^3/_8$ x $9^1/_4$

Using Quicken 5
$19.95 USA
0-88022-888-1, 550 pp., $7^3/_8$ x $9^1/_4$

Using Quicken for Windows
$19.95 USA
0-88022-907-1, 550 pp., $7^3/_8$ x $9^1/_4$

Using R:BASE
$24.95 USA
0-88022-603-X, 584 pp., $7^3/_8$ x $9^1/_4$

Using Smart
$24.95 USA
0-88022-229-8, 584 pp., $7^3/_8$ x $9^1/_4$

Using SuperCalc5, 2nd Edition
$24.95 USA
0-88022-404-5, 584 pp., $7^3/_8$ x $9^1/_4$

Using TimeLine
$24.95 USA
0-88022-602-1, 584 pp., $7^3/_8$ x $9^1/_4$

Using Turbo Pascal 6, 2nd Edition
$29.95 USA
0-88022-700-1, 800 pp., $7^3/_8$ x $9^1/_4$

Using Turbo Pascal for Windows
$29.95 USA
0-88022-806-7, 584 pp., $7^3/_8$ x $9^1/_4$

Using Turbo Tax: 1992 Edition Tax Advice & Planning
$24.95 USA
0-88022-839-3, 584 pp., $7^3/_8$ x $9^1/_4$

Using UNIX
$29.95 USA
0-88022-519-X, 584 pp., $7^3/_8$ x $9^1/_4$

Using Visual Basic
$29.95 USA
0-88022-763-X, 584 pp., $7^3/_8$ x $9^1/_4$

Using Windows 3.1
$27.95 USA
0-88022-731-1, 584 pp., $7^3/_8$ x $9^1/_4$

Using Word for Windows 2, Special Edition
$27.95 USA
0-88022-832-6, 584 pp., $7^3/_8$ x $9^1/_4$

Using WordPerfect 5
$27.95 USA
0-88022-351-0, 584 pp., $7^3/_8$ x $9^1/_4$

Using WordPerfect 5.1, Special Edition
$27.95 USA
0-88022-554-8, 584 pp., $7^3/_8$ x $9^1/_4$

Using WordStar 7
$19.95 USA
0-88022-909-8, 550 pp., $7^3/_8$ x $9^1/_4$

Using Your Hard Disk
$29.95 USA
0-88022-583-1, 584 pp., $7^3/_8$ x $9^1/_4$

Find It Fast with Que's Quick References!

Que's Quick References are the compact, easy-to-use guides to essential application information. Written for all users, Quick References include vital command information under easy-to-find alphabetical listings. Quick References are a must for anyone who needs command information fast!

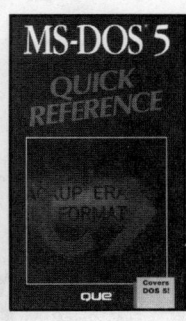

1-2-3 for DOS Release 2.3 Quick Reference
Release 2.3
$9.95 USA
0-88022-725-7, 160 pp., 4¾ x 8

1-2-3 for DOS Release 3.1+ Quick Reference
Releases 3, 3.1, & 3.1+
$9.95 USA
0-88022-845-8, 160 pp., 4¾ x 8

1-2-3 for Windows Quick Reference
1-2-3 for Windows
$9.95 USA
0-88022-783-4, 160 pp., 4¾ x 8

AutoCAD Quick Reference, 2nd Edition
Releases 10 & 11
$8.95 USA
0-88022-622-6, 160 pp., 4¾ x 8

Batch File and Macros Quick Reference
Through DOS 5
$9.95 USA
0-88022-699-4, 160 pp., 4¾ x 8

CorelDRAW! Quick Reference
Through Version 2
$8.95 USA
0-88022-597-1, 160 pp., 4¾ x 8

dBASE IV 1.1 Quick Reference
Through Version 1.1
$9.95 USA
0-88022-905-5, 160 pp., 4¾ x 8

DR DOS 6 Quick Reference
Version 6
$9.95 USA
0-88022-827-X, 160 pp., 4¾ x 8

Excel for Windows Quick Reference
Excel 3 for Windows
$9.95 USA
0-88022-722-2, 160 pp., 4¾ x 8

Fastback Quick Reference
Version 2.1
$8.95 USA
0-88022-650-1, 160 pp., 4¾ x 8

Hard Disk Quick Reference, 1992 Edition
Major hard disks & MS-DOS 5
$9.95 USA
0-88022-826-1, 160 pp., 4¾ x 8

Harvard Graphics 3 Quick Reference
Version 3
$9.95 USA
0-88022-887-3, 160 pp., 4¾ x 8

Harvard Graphics Quick Reference
Version 2.3
$8.95 USA
0-88022-538-6, 160 pp., 4¾ x 8

Laplink III Quick Reference
Laplink III
$9.95 USA
0-88022-702-8, 160 pp., 4¾ x 8

Microsoft Word Quick Reference
Through Version 5.5
$9.95 USA
0-88022-720-6, 160 pp., 4¾ x 8

Microsoft Works Quick Reference
Through IBM Version 2.0
$9.95 USA
0-88022-694-3, 160 pp., 4¾ x 8

Paradox 3.5 Quick Reference
Version 3.5
$9.95 USA
0-88022-824-5, 160 pp., 4¾ x 8

MS-DOS Quick Reference
Through Version 3.3
$8.95 USA
0-88022-369-3, 160 pp., 4¾ x 8

Norton Utilites 6 Quick Reference
Version 6
$9.95 USA
0-88022-858-X, 160 pp., 4¾ x 8

PC Tools 7 Quick Reference
Through Version 7
$9.95 USA
0-88022-829-6, 160 pp., 4¾ x 8

Q&A 4 Quick Reference
Versions 2, 3, & 4
$9.95 USA
0-88022-828-8, 160 pp., 4¾ x 8

Quattro Pro Quick Reference
Through Version 3
$8.95 USA
0-88022-692-7, 160 pp., 4¾ x 8

Quicken 5 Quick Reference
Versions 4 & 5.0
$9.95 USA
0-88022-900-4, 160 pp., 4¾ x 8

Windows 3 Quick Reference
Version 3
$8.95 USA
0-88022-631-5, 160 pp., 4¾ x 8

Windows 3.1 Quick Reference
Through Version 3.1
$9.95 USA
0-88022-740-0, 160 pp., 4¾ x 8

WordPerfect 5.1 Quick Reference
WordPerfect 5.1
$9.95 USA
0-88022-576-9, 160 pp., 4¾ x 8

WordPerfect Quick Reference
WordPerfect 5
$8.95 USA
0-88022-370-7, 160 pp., 4¾ x 8

WordPerfect for Windows Quick Reference
WordPerfect 5.1 for Windows
$9.95 USA
0-88022-785-0, 160 pp., 4¾ x 8

To Order, Call: (800) 428-5331
OR (317) 573-2500

Free Catalog!

Mail us this registration form today, and we'll send you a free catalog featuring Que's complete line of best-selling books.

Name of Book _____

Name _____

Title _____

Phone ( ) _____

Company _____

Address _____

City _____

State _____ ZIP _____

Please check the appropriate answers:

1. Where did you buy your Que book?
   - ☐ Bookstore (name: _____)
   - ☐ Computer store (name: _____)
   - ☐ Catalog (name: _____)
   - ☐ Direct from Que
   - ☐ Other: _____

2. How many computer books do you buy a year?
   - ☐ 1 or less
   - ☐ 2-5
   - ☐ 6-10
   - ☐ More than 10

3. How many Que books do you own?
   - ☐ 1
   - ☐ 2-5
   - ☐ 6-10
   - ☐ More than 10

4. How long have you been using this software?
   - ☐ Less than 6 months
   - ☐ 6 months to 1 year
   - ☐ 1-3 years
   - ☐ More than 3 years

5. What influenced your purchase of this Que book?
   - ☐ Personal recommendation
   - ☐ Advertisement
   - ☐ In-store display
   - ☐ Price
   - ☐ Que catalog
   - ☐ Que mailing
   - ☐ Que's reputation
   - ☐ Other: _____

6. How would you rate the overall content of the book?
   - ☐ Very good
   - ☐ Good
   - ☐ Satisfactory
   - ☐ Poor

7. What do you like *best* about this Que book?
   _____
   _____

8. What do you like *least* about this Que book?
   _____
   _____

9. Did you buy this book with your personal funds?
   - ☐ Yes   ☐ No

10. Please feel free to list any other comments you may have about this Que book.
    _____
    _____
    _____

— Que —

Order Your Que Books Today!

Name _____

Title _____

Company _____

City _____

State _____ ZIP _____

Phone No. ( ) _____

Method of Payment:

Check ☐ (Please enclose in envelope.)

Charge My: VISA ☐   MasterCard ☐

American Express ☐

Charge # _____

Expiration Date _____

Order No.	Title	Qty.	Price	Total

You can **FAX** your order to 1-317-573-2583. Or call 1-800-428-5331, ext. **ORDR** to order direct.
Please add $2.50 per title for shipping and handling.

Subtotal _____

Shipping & Handling _____

Total _____

— Que —

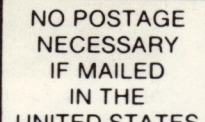

BUSINESS REPLY MAIL
First Class Permit No. 9918   Indianapolis, IN

Postage will be paid by addressee

11711 N. College
Carmel, IN 46032

BUSINESS REPLY MAIL
First Class Permit No. 9918   Indianapolis, IN

Postage will be paid by addressee

11711 N. College
Carmel, IN 46032